Southern Biography Series

SOUTHERN BIOGRAPHY SERIES

EDITED BY FRED C. COLE AND WENDELL H. STEPHENSON

EDITED BY T. HARRY WILLIAMS

DAVID FRENCH BOYD

DAVID FRENCH BOYD, 1885

DAVID FRENCH BOYD

Founder of Louisiana State University

Germaine M. Reed

LOUISIANA STATE UNIVERSITY PRESS

Baton Rouge and London

Designer: Dwight Agner
Type face: VIP Primer
Typesetter: Graphic World, Inc., St. Louis, Missouri
Printer and binder: Kingsport Press, Inc., Kingsport, Tennessee

Publication of this book was assisted by the American Council of
Learned Societies under a grant from the Andrew W. Mellon
Foundation.

LIBRARY OF CONGRESS CATALOGING IN PUBLICATION DATA

Reed, Germaine, 1929–
    David French Boyd, founder of Louisiana State University.

    (Southern biography series)
    A revision of the author's thesis, Louisiana State University.
    Bibliography: p.
    Includes index.
    1. Boyd, David French, 1834–1899. 2. Educators—Louisiana
—Biography. 3. Louisiana—Biography. 4. Louisiana State Uni-
versity and Agricultural and Mechanical College—History. I.
Title. II. Series.
LA2317.B567R43 1977   370'.92'4 [B]   77–446
ISBN 0–8071–0266–0

To my parents, Joseph and Germania Memelo

Contents

Illustrations

Preface

IN 1857, armed with the best liberal education his parents and his native state could provide, David French Boyd left Wytheville, Virginia, to seek his fortune on the frontier. He hoped to find work as a schoolmaster or as a civil engineer on a railroad project in East Texas, but the panic of 1857 and the advice of some newly made friends ended those ambitions. Instead, he took a job in Homer, Louisiana, as professor of mathematics in the struggling Homer College. The position proved temporary but the vocation was permanent. For the next forty years David Boyd dedicated himself to furthering the cause of higher education in Louisiana. What follows is a record of the hardships and heartaches he endured in that cause.

When David Boyd came to Louisiana, plans to establish a "State Seminary of Learning" for the higher education of Louisiana youth were already well advanced. By January, 1860, the school was operating under the able leadership of Superintendent William T. Sherman, a West Point graduate and a former major in the United States Army. David, one of the original faculty, taught Latin and English under Sherman until the Civil War caused both men to leave the school for military service in opposing armies. By that time, however, David's attachment to Louisiana and the seminary was so strong that he planned to resume his career as soon as possible. When influential politicians managed to secure his release from the service, he left northern Virginia in mid-1863 in order to reopen the seminary. But federal activity in Louisiana caused him to rejoin the Confederate Army where he remained until the Trans-Mississippi Department surrendered in

May, 1865. Not until the following October did the school reopen under its new superintendent, David French Boyd.

For the next fifteen years David struggled heroically to keep the seminary, renamed the Louisiana State University in 1870, from closing its doors. Despite a costly fire, Radical Reconstruction, overwhelming poverty, and growing hostility to his administrative policies, he succeeded until an unfriendly Board of Supervisors managed to remove him in 1880. He was recalled four years later but the homecoming proved a failure. Old antagonists were still active, and the school no longer needed him to ensure its existence. In 1888 he resigned to start a second exile which lasted almost a decade. Finally, after years of poverty, humiliation, and defeat, he returned to the university as professor of moral philosophy. Two years later he was dead, a sad and bitter man whose last days were plagued by overwork and the sense that no one appreciated his strenuous efforts in behalf of the school.

Although David Boyd's effective contribution to Louisiana State University ended some twenty years before his death, his life was not a failure. He saved the school from physical and political destruction; he secured a small but regular income for it to guarantee its continued operation; but most important, the charter he composed for it in 1877 provided later administrators with a broad and liberal framework within which they could construct a modern university.

Acknowledgments

I AM greatly indebted to many people and institutions for their assistance and cooperation in the preparation of this biography. The staff of the Louisiana State University Department of Archives, past and present, was especially helpful. Virginia Ott and Margaret Fisher deserve particular mention. So too does Carolyn Dixon, formerly associated with the Archives Department of Auburn University. All illustrations are reproduced herein by courtesy of the Louisiana State University Archives. Mrs. Annie Boyd Grayson of Baton Rouge, a niece of David Boyd, shared her memories with me in an interview and several letters. The extensive criticism of William I. Hair was invaluable, as was the prompt and careful editing provided by Martha Lacy Hall of the Louisiana State University Press. Others whose support should be mentioned are Patrick Kelly, head of the Social Sciences Department, Georgia Institute of Technology, and the directors of the Georgia Tech Foundation, Incorporated. Above all, however, thanks are owed to T. Harry Williams and Merl Reed. Williams proposed this study, directed it as a dissertation, and encouraged me to revise it for publication. Merl Reed typed the first draft, took over most of my household responsibilities, and gently bullied me into completing what I often tried to quit.

DAVID FRENCH BOYD

Chapter I

Marking Time

IN 1857 David French Boyd was an unhappy young man. He was twenty-three years old, well educated, and healthy, but he was also unemployed, disillusioned, and disappointed in love. His father's business was moving toward bankruptcy; his own attempt to run a private day school had ended in failure; and to complete his misery, the woman he loved had broken their engagement. Under the circumstances, the young man had few regrets about leaving his birthplace, Wytheville, Virginia, for a new life somewhere along the southwestern frontier.

The home David Boyd left had been established by his father, Thomas Jefferson Boyd, about 1830. Born in Charlottesville, Virginia, and named after a prominent citizen of that place, Thomas Jefferson Boyd was a self-made man. At thirteen, he left home to work for a local storekeeper who later provided him with free room and board while he attended a local day school. A year spent reading law in Richmond and two more as a student in the newly established University of Virginia completed his formal education. Admitted to the state bar about 1828, Thomas Jefferson Boyd moved shortly thereafter to Wytheville in southwestern Virginia where in 1833 he married Minerva Ann French, his law partner's sister-in-law.[1]

1 Thomas M. Owen, *History of Alabama and Dictionary of Alabama Biography* (Chicago, 1921), III, 187–88; Thomas Jefferson Boyd to [?], 1890, copy, in Genealogical Scrapbook, LeRoy Boyd Papers, Department of Archives, Louisiana State University; Marcus Wilkerson, *Thomas Duckett Boyd: The Story of a Southern Educator* (Baton Rouge, 1935), 10–12.

For the next twenty-five years, while Thomas Jefferson Boyd practiced law, promoted Wytheville, and participated in politics, Minerva
produced children. The first child, David French Boyd, born October
5, 1834, was followed by two sons who died in infancy. Next came
William Henderson, Charles Rufus, Mary French, Cynthia McComas,
and Ella Minerva. Another son, Thomas Duckett, and a fourth girl,
Elizabeth Bright, completed the Boyd family.[2]

To support his large household Thomas Jefferson Boyd supplemented his earnings as an attorney by speculating in land, promoting
mining, street paving and railroad ventures, operating a hotel, and
holding public office. In 1839 he won a seat on the Wytheville town
council which he held until his death in 1893. Then, between 1848
and 1853, he represented Wytheville in the Virginia House of Delegates, after which he served an additional six years on the Virginia
Board of Public Works.[3]

Railroad promotion and politics kept Thomas Jefferson Boyd so
busy in Richmond and elsewhere that his family rarely saw him or
heard from him. Not unnaturally, Minerva felt neglected. In a penciled
note added to a letter her husband's business agent sent his employer
in 1849, Minerva remarked, "I was sorry you did not write to me. I am
getting a little jealous of Mr. Trucks [the agent] who seems to get all
the letters." Another letter the Boyd children sent their absent father
bore a similar postscript. Written in 1852, it pleaded with "Papa" to
come home soon, but Minerva doubted that the younger Boyds even
knew who "Papa" was. David Boyd, then away at boarding school,
fared little better. Of the few letters he received from his busy father
during the fall of 1850, every one began with an apology for not
writing.[4]

David received his earliest education in private schools run by
Wytheville young people who did not plan to make teaching a career—
probably because of the low pay they received. For one four-month
term David's tuition bill came to just eight dollars. By the time he was
eleven or twelve, his teachers were usually struggling young lawyers

---

2   Owen, *History of Alabama*, III, 187; List of Thomas J. Boyd's children in Genealogical
    Scrapbook, LeRoy Boyd Papers.
3   Thomas Jefferson Boyd to [?], 1890, copy in Genealogical Scrapbook, LeRoy Boyd Papers.
4   James Trucks to T. J. Boyd, June 4, 1849, Minerva Boyd and children to T. J. Boyd, May 9,
    1852, T. J. Boyd to David F. Boyd, October 27, November 17, December 12, 25, 1850, all in
    David Boyd Papers, Department of Archives, Louisiana State University.

trying to earn a bare living while they built a practice. Years later David remembered them as stern disciplinarians, "wielders of the rod of correction and enlightenment." One had switched him soundly for throwing gravel in a schoolmate's face. The face, incidentally, belonged to J. E. B. Stuart.[5]

In the fall of 1850 David enrolled in a classical boarding school in Staunton, Virginia. Highly regarded as a preparatory institution, the school sent many of its pupils to the University of Virginia, which David planned to attend. He thought one year of study at Staunton would be sufficient, but he stayed for two. They were not particularly happy years. In one of his first letters home David complained of his roommate's "bad habits" whereupon his father suggested that he ask the principal for permission to move. But, Thomas Boyd warned, he would have to be discreet or the other boys would accuse him of carrying tales.[6]

New roommates did not ease David's problems of adjustment. Only two weeks after securing other quarters he wrote his family about a fistfight with another student. The other boy "insulted" him, David explained, but Thomas Boyd wanted more details. Urging his son never to start a fight but to defend himself bravely if attacked, he cautioned David against overhasty defense of his honor. A fuller account confirmed his misgivings. David had been holding something in his hand which the other boy knocked to the ground. David told him he was "no gentleman," whereupon the fists began flying. To call someone "no gentleman" was pretty strong language, Thomas Boyd remarked. It should be based upon something just as strong to be justified. "Master your temper," he chided, at the same time urging his thin-skinned son to continue working at his Greek and not to become discouraged.[7]

Sparse as it was, Thomas Boyd's correspondence with David reveals many things about both individuals. The father, obviously a strong person, was a "booster," a man who worked hard in the interests of his part of the state, as he understood those interests. For him, the achievement of "progress" for Wytheville (*i.e.*, railroads, land surveys,

5 Receipt of Jane Childs, February 1, 1840; bill to Thomas J. Boyd for tuition, November, 1845, in David F. Boyd Family Papers, Thomas J. Boyd Papers, Department of Archives, Louisiana State University; Flora Stuart to David F. Boyd, April 28, 1896; David F. Boyd, "Boyhood of J. E. B. Stuart" (MS in David Boyd Papers).
6 Minerva Boyd to David F. Boyd, September 28, 1850, Thomas J. Boyd to D. F. Boyd, September 5, 1850, in David Boyd Papers.
7 Thomas J. Boyd to David F. Boyd, September 22, 28, October 10, 1850, *ibid.*

street paving) came before party and at times before family. But for David, away from home for the first time, the older man's preoccupation with business seemed more like neglect. He must have said as much because letters from Thomas Boyd usually began with excuses for failing to write or visit the lonely scholar. Unfortunately, what the father described as unavoidable, the son interpreted as indifference.[8]

Thomas Boyd was not indifferent; he was simply not very warm or demonstrative. Actually, the letters he did send reflect the usual parental concerns. David must avoid partisan politics, master his temper, persevere in his studies, and cultivate female companionship in order to develop refinement and overcome his bashfulness. The trouble, from David's point of view, was that all of these injunctions were delivered like so many lectures. They were edifying but somehow impersonal; uplifting but detached. In short, they might just as well have been expressed by the boarding school chaplain.

Not even David's outstanding scholastic record managed to elicit much paternal response. The boarding school sent home report cards every month, along with a list of demerits for misconduct. Yet, over a two-year period, Thomas Boyd's letters referred only three times to David's grades (they ranged from superior to perfect in every course except Bible) and twice to his conduct (in one quarter he amassed two demerits out of an allowable seventy-five). At least somebody in the family was impressed, however. In the spring of 1852 William Boyd wrote his absent father that he was anxious for "Brother Dave" to return from school. "I wish I was as good and studious as he is," he added.[9]

David entered the University of Virginia in September, 1852. Eighteen and optimistic, he thought two years at Charlottesville would be enough to complete the undergraduate program, after which he planned to pursue the master's degree. Impressed by his ambition, one of his aunts worried about his stamina. He was, she thought, "not very

8 As time passed, the relationship between Thomas Jefferson Boyd and David Boyd grew more strained whereas between Minerva and her son it remained very close. Thomas Boyd was even more alienated from his second son, William, whom he thought beyond redemption, but Minerva wrote David that "Willie has been treated cruelly." Thomas J. Boyd to David Boyd, October 27, November 17, December 12, 1850, Minerva Boyd to David Boyd, September 7, November 23, [1858,] ibid.

9 Thomas J. Boyd to David F. Boyd, September 22, 28, October 10, 1850, January 7, 12, September 29, October 15, 1851, March [?], 1852, [William H. Boyd] to Thomas J. Boyd, May 9, 1852, ibid.

strong in constitution." In fact, the Boyd family was remarkably healthy and long-lived, considering the level of medical knowledge and the quality of treatment available in the middle of the nineteenth century. The aunt's concern probably arose because of her nephew's slight stature and sedentary habits. An entry David made in a diary on his wedding day in 1865 records his height as only five feet, six inches, and his weight at one hundred and thirty pounds. As for his favorite pursuits, he clearly preferred books to hunting, fishing, and physical activity, even as a child. One brother remembered him during his school days as so ambitious to succeed in his studies that he temporarily impaired his eyesight.[10]

The University of Virginia proved to be considerably more demanding than David's preparatory school. In 1852 it was composed of three departments: law, medicine and "academic." David enrolled in the last named, which offered work in three "literary" and three "scientific schools." To qualify for a bachelor's degree, a student had to graduate in two literary schools (ancient languages, modern languages, or moral philosophy) and in two scientific schools (mathematics, natural philosophy, or chemistry). He must also earn at least a "distinction" or 75 percent, in the remaining two schools. Finally, he had to present an acceptable essay to the faculty on some appropriate literary or scientific topic. Even more demanding, the master's degree required graduation in all six academic schools, a comprehensive examination by the entire faculty, and a formal thesis on an assigned topic.[11]

During his first year, David studied ancient languages, modern languages, and mathematics, but inadequate preparation led him to drop Greek well before the session ended. As for his other courses, the only one in which he received even a "distinction" was mathematics. Heartily discouraged, he took the following oath: "Having failed to graduate on any of my tickets this session of 1852–1853, I do now solemnly swear, that if I return next session, I will graduate on the tickets of

10   C. M. McComas to D. F. Boyd, January 2, 1853, *ibid.*; William H. Boyd to LeRoy Stafford Boyd, March 1, 1903, in Genealogical Scrapbook, LeRoy Boyd Papers; David Boyd, Memorandum Book, MS volumes in David Boyd Papers.

11   *Catalog* of the University of Virginia, 1853–54, pp. 28–29, in Printed Materials, David Boyd Papers; John Hammond Moore (ed.), "The Old Dominion Through Student Eyes, 1852–55: The Reminiscences of Thomas Hill Malone," *Virginia Magazine of History and Biography*, LXXI (July, 1963), 302. "Distinctions" were certificates awarded to students who earned at least 75 percent in a final examination of a particular "school," far less than was required for graduation.

Latin, French, Mathematics and Natural Philosophy, [or] the equal thereto. So help me God. David F. Boyd." [12]

Unfortunately, perseverence and hard work were not enough and David was still far short of his goal when the next year ended. He managed to graduate in two schools but received only a "proficiency" in two others. Shattered by the experience, he refused even those diplomas to which he was entitled and left abruptly for home. Later Thomas Jefferson Boyd tried to rectify his son's hasty action by contacting the chairman of the faculty, Dr. Gessner Harrison. Harrison sympathized with David's "mortification" and thought the faculty would probably grant the spurned diplomas, if only because of the young man's excellent character and faultless deportment. But, he added, it would have been "more reasonable" of David to accept his academic limitations. "A man has no more right to be discontented with the peculiar character of his mind than with the height of his body. His business is to make good use of his . . . faculties." [13]

When he finally left Charlottesville in June, 1856, David had been graduated in four schools: ancient and modern languages (Latin and French), mathematics, and moral philosophy. In addition he had earned a "distinction" in natural philosophy. Some time during his four years he also studied German, Greek, chemistry, and civil engineering. But he did not complete all the requirements for graduation from the university. This point is of some significance because most of David's friends, his colleagues, and even his family thought he held not only the bachelor's but also a master's degree from the University of Virginia. Leroy Stafford Boyd, David's son, was certainly of that opinion when in 1902 he began compiling material for a family history and wrote the University of Virginia seeking all available information about his father's student career. The university reply included a list of all the courses studied by David but said nothing about degrees or graduation. Still compiling in 1913, Leroy Boyd again contacted the university. This time an official replied that although David Boyd was a graduate in four schools of the university, he could "not properly be called a

---

12 *Catalog* of the University of Virginia, 1853–54, Printed Materials; Report of the University of Virginia to parents of D. F. Boyd, June 29, 1853; Pledge of David Boyd, June 25, 1853, all in David Boyd Papers.

13 S. A. Steger to LeRoy Boyd, January 6, 1913, in Selected Letters, LeRoy Boyd Papers; Gessner Harrison to T. J. Boyd, August 9, 1854, in David F. Boyd Family Papers, Thomas J. Boyd Papers.

graduate of the University of Virginia." Leroy wrote back at once, apparently asking if his father were not recorded as a Master of Arts graduate. Again the answer was negative. Faculty records, admittedly brief, did not list David F. Boyd as an M.A. graduate either.[14]

David's plans for employment when he arrived in Wytheville were somewhat unsettled. Before leaving Charlottesville he and a friend had talked about establishing a preparatory school. But the friend decided to study law, and David, lacking other prospects, resorted to answering and inserting advertisements for schoolteaching positions in several Virginia newspapers. The response was encouraging. During August he received several offers, one from as far away as Quincy, Florida. By that time, however, he had decided to set up for himself. In a prospectus dated August 30, 1856, David announced plans to open "An English, Classical and Mathematical School" in Wytheville on September 15.[15]

The school began as advertised, but it did not prosper, and David accepted a tutoring position at Gordonsville, Virginia, beginning in February, 1857. His employer, James Newman, offered what David regarded as generous terms: free board and $650 for a ten-month school year. He also encouraged David to bring some of his Wytheville students with him, a suggestion that seems to have disturbed both David and his father. If Newman was soliciting pupils from Wytheville, they reasoned, his school project must be in trouble. Newman tried to reassure the Boyds, but Thomas Boyd was not convinced, asking instead that Newman cancel David's commitment. But the Gordonsville man replied that his plans were too far advanced to consider such a request. Besides, he explained, his son had known David at the university and recommended him highly. Then, in a separate letter to David, Mr. Newman repeated his reasons for not terminating the agreement, commenting that Thomas Boyd's request to end it did not seem to be

14 Alexandria (La.) *Democrat*, August 3, 1859; James M. Garnett, "Reminiscences of the Louisiana State Seminary in 1867," Louisiana State University *Alumnus*, V (1909–10), 20; Walter L. Fleming, *Louisiana State University, 1860–1896* (Baton Rouge, 1936), 32; John Patton to L. S. Boyd, October 28, 1902, in Scrapbook, David Boyd Papers; S. A. Steger to LeRoy S. Boyd, January 6, 26, 1913, in Selected Letters, LeRoy Boyd Papers. The author confirmed Leroy's findings on a visit to the University of Virginia in August, 1963.
15 C. M. Blackford to D. F. Boyd, July 14, 1856, Caleb Hollowell to D. F. Boyd, August [?], 1856, C. H. DuFonte to David Boyd, August 18, 1856, James Newman to David Boyd, August 19, 1856, all in David Boyd Papers; *Prospectus* for school, Wytheville, Va., August 30, 1856, in Printed Materials, *ibid.*

based on sound argument. He ended by leaving it all up to David's "candid consideration."[16]

Apparently David sent Mr. Newman a scorching response around February 1, 1857, in which he accused him of insulting his and his father's "honor." Newman returned an icy but correct reply on February 5, denying any intent to affront the Boyds, senior or junior, and expressing amazement that any remarks of his could be so construed. He concluded by releasing David formally from the job. Finally, David wrote Newman on February 10 claiming that his (David's) letter accusing Newman of insulting him and his father was "based on a contingency, which has [since] been removed by yourself." That is, David *inferred* that Newman's letter to his father was meant to be insulting. On that basis he wrote an insulting reply. If, however, as now seemed clear, no insult were intended, then Newman should disregard David's letter of February 1. This somewhat tortuous defense of his intemperate letter received no answer.[17]

The Boyd-Newman correspondence is interesting because it highlights several aspects of David's personality. He was sensitive, easily offended, and quick tempered, and he had a tendency to overreact, particularly if he thought his honor had been impugned. Coupled with his amazing capacity to compose outraged prose, these traits sometimes led him to fire off long and extravagant letters to his supposed antagonists. However, David usually thought better of his outbursts later and tried to repair the damage. The result was generally the despatch of another letter, designed partly to mollify the injured party, but mostly to justify his own intemperate action.[18]

The real reason David wanted to cancel his agreement with Mr. Newman may well have been romantic. Early in 1857 he became engaged to Miss Ella Spiller, an attractive local belle. If he left Wytheville for the Newman job he would be solvent but lonesome. On the other

16   James Newman to David F. Boyd, August 19, September 4, 6, October 13, November 3, December 23, 1856, January 1, 12, February 5, 1857, in David Boyd Papers; James Newman to Thomas J. Boyd, January 3, 12, 1857, in David F. Boyd Family Papers, Thomas J. Boyd Papers.
17   James Newman to David F. Boyd, February 5, 1857, David F. Boyd to James Newman, February 10, 1857, in David Boyd Papers.
18   See for example the voluminous correspondence concerning David's Egyptian venture in Letterbooks, David Boyd Papers (cited hereinafter as David Boyd Letterbooks), and his exchanges with Samuel Lewis in 1870, in David F. Boyd Letters and Papers, Walter L. Fleming Collection, Department of Archives, Louisiana State University, hereinafter cited as Boyd Letters, Fleming Collection.

hand, if he stayed in town he could court Miss Spiller at leisure, but hardly expect to marry her in the forseeable future. The problem was soon resolved but not very happily from David's point of veiw. By late May, 1857, his private school was foundering badly, his father's business affairs were more desperate than ever, and Ella Spiller had decided to break the engagement. Whether David's financial prospects or another man caused her to reconsider is not clear, but the effect on David certainly was. With little reason to remain in Wytheville, he again resorted to the classified section of various newspapers, and two weeks later a firm offer of a schoolteaching position arrived from Lamar County, Texas. It took three months for him to settle his affairs, but finally, in October, 1857, David left Virginia for what he imagined were greater opportunities along the southwestern frontier.[19]

The journey southward gave David plenty of time to reconsider his plans. So did chance acquaintance with two fellow travelers. One, W. R. Johnson of Virginia, was also Texas bound and also looking for employment. Via New Orleans and Shreveport he and David ultimately reached Marshall, Texas, where Johnson took a job with a railroad company. David considered the same course, but another new friend, Judge W. B. Egan, persuaded him to apply instead for a teaching position at Homer College in Homer, Claiborne Parish, Louisiana.[20]

The Egan family, Judge W. B. Egan, his brother Dr. J. C. Egan, and their father, Dr. Bartholomew W. Egan, migrated to North Louisiana from Virginia sometime during the 1840s. All three men actively supported higher education in their adopted state, and all three would be instrumental in securing teaching positions for David or in promoting educational institutions of which he later became a part. But in 1857, when David first met Judge W. B. Egan, the latter's interests were centered on Homer College. Begun in one room around 1850 and incorporated five years later under the auspices of the North Louisiana Methodist Conference, the school had just announced plans to offer bachelor's and master's programs in the arts and sciences. Land do-

---

19 William H. Boyd to LeRoy Boyd, March 19, 1903, in Genealogical Scrapbook, LeRoy Boyd Papers; L. A. Auman to David Boyd, January 14, April 8, 1859, William Auman to David Boyd, December 30, 1860, Minerva Boyd to David Boyd, May 1, 1861, P. A. N. Starkes to D. F. Boyd, June 7, 1857, all in David Boyd Papers.

20 Morton B. Howell to Alfred T. Howell, October 27, 1857, W. C. Johnson to David Boyd, March 15, 1858, in David Boyd Papers; A. A. Gunby, "Life and Services of David French Boyd," Louisiana State *University Bulletin* (June, 1904), 2–5; Dr. J. C. Egan, Appendix to "Life and Services of David French Boyd," *ibid.*, 29.

nated in 1856 enabled the Board of Trustees to begin construction of a
new building, and the following year the first college level students
appeared for registration.[21]

Named professor of mathematics in the newly opened school,
David initially seemed pleased with his job. Louisiana and Louisianians, however, were another story. A description of his new home
sent to his brother Charlie was so unfavorable that Charlie doubted he
could ever live there, and a Texas friend, after receiving a similar account, expressed regret that David had to live among such "rough
people." He thought David was surrounded by Parisians. Still another
letter must have been critical of Louisiana in general and Louisiana
belles in particular. The recipient advised David to quit the state if his
job or the climate proved too demanding. As for the girls, he remarked,
"I would like very much to happen in Homer on some Sunday & find
you walking with one, with her 'ancient' bonnet on. I certainly would
believe that the heat had operated on your brain. But . . . should you
fall upon [one] worth some $200,000, take her with all the appurte-
nances."[22]

Not every visitor to Homer and North Louisiana found the place so
unattractive. J. W. Dorr took a horse and buggy tour through the area
in the spring and summer of 1860. He was employed by the editorial
department of the New Orleans *Crescent*, and between April and July,
1860, twenty-seven of his descriptive letters appeared in the paper's
columns. Homer, which Dorr visited in mid-July, was characterized as
one of the "most picturesque and pleasant places I have yet seen in
Louisiana." The town boasted seven or eight hundred residents, two
newspapers, numerous businesses, a Methodist and Baptist Church,
and attractive homes. Construction of the new courthouse and the
well-attended Female College convinced Dorr of the town's prosperity.

21 The Egans were prominent in Louisiana political and educational circles for years. Dr. J. C.
    Egan served as state senator 1868–72; Judge W. B. Egan was a justice of the state supreme
    court at his death; Bartholomew Egan helped to found Mt. Lebanon, a Baptist college, and
    Judge W. B. Egan helped to organize both Homer College and Louisiana State University. All
    three Egans served on the board of the last named institution. New Orleans *Daily Picayune*,
    November 19, 1902; Gunby, "Life and Services of David French Boyd," 2–5, 12–13; J. C.
    Egan, Appendix *ibid.*, 31; J. W. Mobley, "The Academy Movement in Louisiana," *Louisiana
    Historical Quarterly*, XXX (July, 1947), 77; J. Fair Hardin, "The Early History of the Louisi-
    ana State University," *Louisiana Historical Quarterly*, XI (January, 1928), 13; J. W. Nichol-
    son, *Stories of Dixie* (New York, 1915), 125–27.
22 Charles R. Boyd to D. F. Boyd, January 15, 1858, W. R. Johnson to D. F. Boyd, March 15,
    1858, J. F. Gleaves, Jr., to David F. Boyd, February 14, 1858, all in David Boyd Papers.

The only drawback, he thought, was the difficulty in getting there. The town's landing place was twenty miles away, and visitors had to hire a horse or horse and buggy at Minden, Louisiana, to travel the hilly, crooked road.[23]

Whatever its charms for Dorr in 1860, Homer failed to attract David in 1858. By March his interest in Texas had rekindled, and he was thinking of quitting his teaching job to seek employment as a civil engineer on the Texas and Pacific Railroad. But a friend advised him to stay where he was. The railroad, he wrote, was as "uncertain as Texas weather." Minerva Boyd was also troubled by her son's proposal to leave Homer College. She accused him of his father's failing: inability to stick by anything long enough to prosper from it. If he had to leave teaching, she suggested, why not study law? "I am afraid of your P.R.R. (Pacific RR)—you will get over among the Rocky Mountains before you know what you are about & the first thing I hear, your scalp will be dangling from a horrid Indian's wampum [belt?]. I can't bear the idea of your going in that road. Please don't think of it."[24]

But David continued to "think of it," although he considered other courses as well. There was a good chance that he might be offered another teaching job at Rocky Mount in Bossier Parish, Louisiana. In the meantime, he planned an extensive trip on horseback through southwest Arkansas, the Indian territory, and across Texas as a summer vacation. He intended to leave about mid-July, and, if a suitable job with the railroad did not develop before September, he could always return to Homer. It is not clear how much of Texas he actually visited, but David must have been greatly impressed with the town of Paris in Lamar County. He wrote his family a long, favorable description of the place and even applied for a job in the only school. Paris was too small to support two teachers at the time, but David's correspondent promised to keep him in mind.[25]

23 Walter Pritchard (ed.), "A Tourist's Description of Louisiana in 1860," *Louisiana Historical Quarterly*, XXI (October, 1938), 76–77.
24 Minerva French Boyd to D. F. Boyd, April 12, 1858, W. R. Johnson to D. F. Boyd, March 15, 1858, in David Boyd Papers.
25 Minerva French Boyd to D. F. Boyd, April 12, September 7, 1858, C. R. Boyd to D. F. Boyd, June 15, 1858, E. Langly to D. F. Boyd, September 9, 1858, T. G. Wright to D. F. Boyd, October 27, 1858, all *ibid*. David kept a brief diary of his trip during the summer of 1858. An edited version appears in Germaine M. Reed (ed.), "Journey Through Southwest Arkansas, 1858," *Arkansas Historical Quarterly*, XXX (Summer, 1971), 161–69.

Back in Louisiana, Homer College was facing a crisis. Unable to hire a suitable president, the trustees decided to suspend operations until they could secure a full staff and complete the building. Consequently, David decided to fill Homer's educational void. In a printed folder he announced the opening of an "English, Classical and Mathematical School." But before the project could be realized, David accepted the principalship of the Homer College high school division which did function during the academic year 1858–1859. Years later, Professor J. W. Nicholson of Louisiana State University remembered the high school as "very modern" and well run. The principals, he recalled, were able men like David F. Boyd and Edwin H. Fay (later state superintendent of public education), "graduates" of the best colleges in the country.[26]

That Claiborne and the surrounding country were desperately in need of *any* sort of school is attested to by the following letter which a prospective patron addressed to David in September, 1858: "Mr. Boyd, when I saw you last Saterday in homer I was not serten whether I wod bring my sons to your colleg or not So I did not find no plas to board them I have com to the concluson to bring them on of them is sick at present So please looke round and if you can get eny plas fer them to board write to me and I will bring them direct your leter . . . [?] Jackson parish. David Colvin."[27]

After one full year in Louisiana, David was still unhappy in Homer. At least one cause must have been the concern he felt for his family's financial plight. Only a few days after he left Virginia they gave up their home and moved into the Depot Hotel, an investment property which Thomas Boyd had purchased some years before. In his letters to David, Thomas Boyd usually appeared quite optimistic about his chances of staving off complete financial ruin. Hoping to sell his huge landholdings in order to cancel his other indebtedness, he thought income from the hotel would certainly support his large family when the weather improved and the new railroad brought tourists to the town. Meanwhile, David must not think of giving up his chances in Louisiana. His offers to return to Virginia were appreciated, but only the sale

---

26   W. B. Egan to Dr. J. S. Saunders, July 15, 1859, in David Boyd Papers; *Prospectus* for an "English, Classical and Mathematical School," September, 1858, in Printed Materials, *ibid.*; Nicholson, *Stories of Dixie*, 106.

27   David Colvin to D. F. Boyd, September 22, 1858, in David Boyd Papers.

of his land could rid Thomas Jefferson Boyd of what he delicately referred to as "my embarrassment."[28]

Other letters from home were more disheartening. An aunt wrote that "your Pa's affairs *are in a desperate state*" and asked David to help save his mother's slaves from the auction block. Minerva Boyd's letters confirmed the grim news. She had had to sign away her interest in all property, even her favorite "servants," and she doubted whether the sale of her husband's land would cover all the debts. Thomas Boyd's affairs, wrote Minerva, were in worse shape than he would admit. She did not wish to burden David, but, "If your Pa's insane desire to speculate will be shunned by his sons 'tis all I ask of them." Finally, at David's request, an uncle went to Wytheville in December, 1858, to determine just how serious the situation was. He reported that Thomas Boyd owed about $170,000 and stood little chance of ever paying it off. David's father, the uncle concluded, "didn't know how to use money; if he were out of this mess he'd be in another." In any event David might as well stay in Louisiana. He could do no good in Virginia.[29]

David was not convinced. A friend wrote him that the only newspaper around Wytheville was up for sale. If David were back in Virginia, the friend suggested, he could make a living with the paper and study law in his spare time, something his Louisiana friend Judge W. B. Egan had been urging him to consider. But David's father opposed the newspaper scheme because "they [the townspeople] neglected you when you were here." Probably reflecting his own disenchantment with the citizenry of Wytheville, Thomas Boyd realized all too clearly by 1859 that thirty years of public service to the community was no substitute for solvency. One of his sons wanted to leave Wytheville because the people were so unfriendly, and even the maid was mortified when other slaves chided her about her master's straitened circumstances. Her prestige must have slipped another notch in May, 1859, when Thomas Boyd lost his bid for reelection to the State Board of Public Works.[30]

28   T. J. Boyd to D. F. Boyd, December 2, 1857, January 24, 1858, *ibid.*
29   C. M. McComas to D. F. Boyd, December 15, 1857, Minerva Boyd to David Boyd, undated [1858], March 22, 1858, H. French (uncle) to D. F. Boyd, January 23, 1859, *ibid.*
30   J. T. Gleaves to David Boyd, January 21, 1859, in Alphabetical File, Fleming Collection; Cynthia Boyd (sister) to D. F. Boyd, November 1, 1858, Thomas J. Boyd to David Boyd, February 4, June 28, 1859, Minerva Boyd to David Boyd, April 18, 1859, all in David Boyd Papers.

Financial ruin was not the only dreary subject of the letters David received from home. William Henderson Boyd, five years younger than David, was everything his older brother was not. He drank, smoked, gambled, and caroused with "vile women." Finally, Thomas Boyd ordered him out of the house, and he sought refuge among his mother's numerous relatives. Distressed to the point of illness by the conflict in her family, Minerva begged David to write his brother and urge him to reform. Other relatives were more direct. They wanted David to assume responsibility for his black-sheep brother, and even William thought it was a good idea. There was nothing much doing at his relatives' home, and they doubted his ability to learn law. Consequently, when David offered to pay William's fare to Louisiana, everyone was relieved.[31]

There was another explanation for David's apparent unhappiness in Homer during 1858 and 1859. Ella Spiller, the young woman with whom he had been in love before he left Wytheville, had married someone else. As long as she was single, Ella Spiller formed the principal topic of the many letters David exchanged with a Virginia friend, L. A. Auman. But following her marriage in December, 1858, to Alex Brown, a young attorney, Auman wrote David, "I cannot even conjecture how the news will effect [sic] you."[32]

As the summer of 1859 approached, David was more undecided about his future than ever. Homer still did not attract him in spite of the salary increase he would receive if he stayed on as principal of the high school. Wytheville needed a teacher in May, but by July the position had been filled, and Thomas Boyd advised him to stay where he was. Minerva, on the other hand, wanted him to come home at any cost; he could be a smith if worse came to worse.[33]

Minerva Boyd's letters begging David to abandon Louisiana reflect the special relationship which existed between them. In September, 1858, she confided that she had "so many things to tell you that I can't write, so many things I can speak of to none but you. I never thought I

31 Minerva Boyd to David French Boyd, November 23, [1858], April 29, 1859, T. J. Boyd to David Boyd, March 21, 1858, April 30, 1859, H. French to D. F. Boyd, January 23, 1859, C. F. McComas (aunt) to David Boyd, September 20, November 20, 1859, William Boyd to David Boyd, May 21, November 12, [1859], all in David Boyd Papers.
32 Leopold A. Auman to David Boyd, February 28, June 5, 1858, January 14, 1859, ibid.
33 L. A. Auman to D. F. Boyd, May 2, 1859, T. J. Boyd to D. F. Boyd, April 30, June 28, 1859, Minerva Boyd to David Boyd, undated, ibid.

should miss you so much." Her other sons, who preferred their friends to her, were no comfort and her husband just buried himself in the newspaper whenever she wanted to converse. It must have come as a bitter blow, therefore, when Daivd announced in July, 1859, that he would not be coming home after all. He was leaving Homer, however, having made arrangements to fill another teaching position at Rocky Mount in Bossier Parish, Louisiana.[34]

The job at Rocky Mount was to begin in September, but even before he left Homer, David learned of his appointment as professor of ancient languages in the newly organized Louisiana State Seminary of Learning at Pineville. The seminary Board of Supervisors advertised for professors in several New York, Washington, and New Orleans newspapers during the spring and summer of 1859, and by August over eighty candidates had applied. An even forty sought the post to which David was finally named, but in the opinion of a local editor a better choice could not have been made. "Mr. Boyd is a talented, worthy, energetic, industrious and deserving young man," he informed his readers. "He has been teaching for the last two years . . . in our town and has exhibited such proficiency and thorough scholarship . . . as to give entire satisfaction."[35]

Throughout the fall of 1859 David marked time in Bossier Parish which he found no more appealing than Homer. But at least his stay there would be brief. In January he would begin a new job in a new institution. "I hope to hear better accounts from that new place you are going to," wrote his brother encouragingly. Neither one of them could know then that David's affiliation with "that new place" would last until his death forty years later.[36]

---

34 Minerva French Boyd to David French Boyd, September 7, 1858, W. B. Egan to J. S. Saunders, July 15, 1859, Charles R. Boyd to David F. Boyd, July 25, 1859, *ibid.*
35 Fleming, *Louisiana State University*, 30–32; (Homer, La.) *Claiborne Advocate*, August [?], 1859, quoted in Virginia newspaper, unidentified, undated, in David Boyd Papers.
36 Charles R. Boyd to David Boyd, September 6, 1859, in David Boyd Papers.

Chapter II

Apprenticeship

THE "NEW PLACE" to which David Boyd went very late in 1859 was Rapides Parish, Louisiana. Alexandria, a town of some sixteen hundred people, was the parish seat. Some three hundred miles from New Orleans via the Mississippi and Red rivers, it was close to the geographical center of the state. Just above the town there were rapids which, in low water, seriously hampered travel upstream. Even below Alexandria the Red River's depth varied radically, causing residents and merchants much inconvenience. At times one could wade the stream; at other times it was thirty feet deep. But low water and floods did not impede Alexandria's growth. By 1860 it had several brick buildings, a new courthouse, and two hotels. A third hotel, the Ice House, was nearing completion. Soon travelers on their way to Texas by water or stage could enjoy the uncommon luxuries of steam heat, gas, and water in every room. There was a theater in the new hotel, and for those who sought other diversions, the town provided restaurants, barrooms, billiard parlors, two newspapers, and three churches.

Opposite Alexandria on the north bank of the Red River, almost hidden in the pinewoods, was the village of Pineville. A steam ferry connected it with Alexandria, and a wagon road, 3½ miles long, ran into the forest to the site of the Louisiana State Seminary of Learning.[1]

---

1 Prichard (ed.), "A Tourist's Description of Louisiana," 47–52.

The Louisiana legislature's decision to locate the seminary far from any metropolitan center was in keeping with prevailing educational theories and agrarian prejudices. After considerable wrangling, the solons settled upon Rapides Parish because it was centrally located, easily reached by water, and considered relatively free from disease. Perhaps the most compelling reason for their choice was the fact that Rapides was the home of General G. Mason Graham, the most ardent and dedicated supporter of the seminary project.[2]

Graham, whose formal association with the school lasted until 1885, was born in Fairfax County, Virginia, in 1807. He attended West Point for three years and the University of Virginia for one. In 1828 he migrated to Rapides Parish and ultimately became a planter of considerable means. His educational background, his brief service as a captain of a Louisiana brigade in the Mexican War, and Louisiana's repeated failure to establish an enduring "classical" college convinced General Graham of the superiority of schools organized like West Point and Virginia Military Institute. As a leading member of the Board of Supervisors, therefore, he did his utmost to shape the Louisiana State Seminary in their image.[3]

Begun in 1856 and ready for occupancy late in 1859, the seminary building must have presented an incongruous as well as impressive sight to anyone who saw it for the first time. Walter Fleming, the historian of Louisiana State University, described it as "three lofty stories high, with five four-story towers. It extended around three sides of a quadrangle one hundred seventy feet front by one hundred seventeen feet deep. There were seventy-two large rooms, and to each floor was a wide gallery; the heavy walls were crenellated, and the whole building finished in white. Located on a high hill in an opening in the pine woods, surrounded by the open pine forest of trees sixty to eighty feet to the first branches, the Seminary building was an imposing spectacle."[4]

The first course of study at the seminary also reflected the dominant influence of General Graham. In the stern words of a Board of Supervisors' report, a thorough knowledge of English would be incul-

2 Fleming, *Louisiana State University*, 22–24.
3 G. M. Stafford, "Autobiography of Geo. Mason Graham," *Louisiana Historical Quarterly*, XX (January, 1937), 2–17. For a more complete discussion of the school's organization, see Fleming, *Louisiana State University*, 27–38.
4 Fleming, *Louisiana State University*, 26.

cated and "incidental thereto, a knowledge of the construction of the Ancient Classic Languages." French or Spanish would also be taught. "However, as the *Physical Sciences* have so rapidly advanced of late years, and no practical education is complete without considerable knowledge of the *Exact* Sciences, the Board have selected Professors qualified to teach Mathematics thoroughly, with Natural Philosophy embracing Mechanics and the laws which govern all Machinery and Physical forces; also Chemistry and its application to agriculture and the Arts." All this plus instruction in surveying, drawing, engineering, and architecture claimed the Board, would make "this Seminary the equal of any in the U.S."[5]

Besides David, the seminary's first faculty or Academic Board included William Tecumseh Sherman, superintendent and professor of engineering; Anthony Vallas, professor of mathematics and natural philosophy; E. Berté St. Ange, professor of modern languages, and Francis W. Smith, professor of chemistry, minerology, geology, and instructor of infantry tactics. Sherman was a West Point graduate and a retired army major. Before his appointment as superintendent of the seminary he had engaged in banking and law, but neither provided an adequate income. In June of 1859, he wrote an old friend, Major Don Carlos Buell, then assistant adjutant general to the secretary of war, inquiring about vacancies in the War Department. Buell sent him a circular advertising for a superintendent of a military college about to be opened in Louisiana. He advised Sherman to apply, noting that G. Mason Graham, one of the supervisors of the new school, was a half brother of Sherman's former commanding officer, General R. B. Mason.[6]

Anthony Vallas and E. Berté St. Ange were Hungarian and French respectively. Vallas left his homeland for political reasons in 1850. At the time of his appointment to the seminary, he had lived in New Orleans about eight years. Academically his credentials surpassed those of all his colleagues. He held a Ph.D. and was a minister of the Episcopal Church. St. Ange was a former officer in the French navy. He too

---

5 *Report* of the Board of Supervisors of Louisiana Seminary of Learning, November 17, 1859, in Printed Materials, David Boyd Papers.

6 A surgeon, Dr. John Sevier of Kentucky, was also employed by the board. *Report of the Board of Supervisors of the State Seminary of Learning to the Legislature of the State of Louisiana, January, 1860* (Baton Rouge, 1860), 4–5, 9; W. T. Sherman, *Memoirs of General William T. Sherman by Himself* (Bloomington, Ind., 1957), 142–43.

lived and taught in New Orleans, but when elected to the seminary faculty was teaching private students in Rapides Parish. The fifth member of the Academic Board was Francis W. Smith, professor of chemistry and commandant of cadets. At twenty-two he was the youngest professor on the staff. A graduate of the Virginia Military Institute and the University of Virginia, Smith was sojourning in Europe when appointed to his professorship in August of 1859. Superintendent Sherman, in a letter to his wife, described him as "one of the real Virginia F.F.V.'s, a very handsome young man of twenty-two who will doubtless be good company."[7]

"Good company" was about all that Sherman and his staff could count on to relieve an otherwise isolated and somewhat spartan existence. Both Sherman and Vallas were married, but only Vallas, the head of a large family, managed to secure housing near the seminary. Sherman chose to leave his family in Ohio and live with the single professors in the school building until suitable quarters could be built. When he first saw it in November, 1859, Sherman thought the seminary was "gorgeous" and "too good for the purpose." It was completely unfurnished but he moved in nevertheless. After engaging local carpenters to build benches, tables, and blackboards, he traveled to New Orleans to buy books and additional furniture so that the school might open as advertised on January 1, 1860. Meanwhile, Sherman urged his faculty to come to the seminary as soon as possible. He warned David to bring with him everything he might need, including furniture for his room. As for books, they would have to be ordered from New York. Even New Orleans was not well supplied.[8]

In spite of the advice, David did not reach the seminary until January 1, 1860, the day before classes were to begin. He reported at once to Sherman's office and from that meeting forward there developed a special relationship between the two men which neither time nor circumstances ever managed to erode. Sherman's son, Philemon T. Sherman, noted years later that "David Boyd . . . was his [W. T. Sherman's] closest friend; their intimacy—in spite of the widest divergence in po-

7   Fleming, *Louisiana State University*, 31–33, 39; W. T. Sherman to his wife, December 16, 1859, in M. A. DeWolfe Howe (ed.), *Home Letters of General Sherman* (New York, 1909), 169.
8   W. T. Sherman to his wife, November 12, December 12, 1859, in Howe (ed.), *Home Letters of General Sherman*, 166–67; Fleming, *Louisiana State University*, 38–41; W. T. Sherman to David Boyd, November 27, December 15, 1859, in William T. Sherman Letters as College President, David F. Boyd Papers.

litical opinions—continued unimpaired by war and separation up to my father's death."[9] Sherman's own estimate of David was certainly favorable. After their first meeting he wrote his wife that "Professor Boyd is a young man . . . a very clever gentleman," and, in another letter written a few years later, he described David as "my favorite among the officers (Professors) of the academy at Alexandria." The feeling was reciprocated. For David, Sherman's departure from the seminary in 1861 was like "parting with a father and a dear, loving friend both in one person. I never lost this feeling for him a jot or tittle."[10]

David soon learned that Sherman had not exaggerated when he described the seminary's isolation. Furniture for his room had to be shipped from New Orleans, and sufficient textbooks to supply his Latin classes were simply unavailable. Until they could be obtained from New York he had to conduct his classes orally.[11]

This presented no particular problem for David, who was extremely articulate and excelled at formal composition. After a brief welcoming statement and an explanation of how he came to be in Louisiana, he expounded at length on the virtues of the seminary's liberal curriculum. Its military feature would build gentlemanliness, morality, and strong bodies, while courses in English, literature, Latin, and Greek would broaden the students' horizons, giving them some respite from more precise studies like mathematics. "To have a solely military and scientific school," he advised his young listeners, "is to cramp the intellect."[12]

Audience reaction was not recorded, but David's rhetorical skills soon won so much renown that students who had to deliver speeches began seeking him out as a ghost-writer. He even tailored his material to suit the occasion. One speech, prepared for delivery at the seminary's first Public Day, July 4, 1860, urged harmony and support for the Union: "Let us then meet today as Americans, as members of one

---

9   Response to a toast by Philemon Sherman (son) at Alumni Society meeting, Baton Rouge, January, 1910, in Louisiana State University *Alumnus*, V (1909–10), 88–90.

10 W. T. Sherman to his wife, quoted in Walter L. Fleming, "General W. T. Sherman as a College President," Louisiana State *University Bulletin*, III (1912), 7; David F. Boyd, "General W. T. Sherman as a College President," *ibid.*, I (1910), 7. Boyd's remarks were probably originally delivered before veterans' groups in Ohio and Kentucky in 1896.

11 Bill of sale for furniture from C. Flint and [?] Jones, Royal Street, New Orleans, to David Boyd, January 12, 1860, in David Boyd Papers; Fleming, *Louisiana State University*, 48.

12 David Boyd, speech, [January, 1860], in Louisiana State University Official Papers, Fleming Collection, hereinafter cited as Official Papers, Fleming Collection.

great family. . . . This day let us cease our strife . . . [and] from Maine to California resolve that henceforth, there shall be no North—no South."[13] Only two months later another cadet asked David to write a speech for delivery at a John C. Breckinridge barbecue. The famed southern "fire-eater," William Yancey, would be there, and the cadet was sure David could compose a suitable address.[14]

Ghostwriting was extracurricular. Inside the classroom David was a serious and dedicated instructor. Reminiscing in 1896, one of his first students at the seminary described him as "a man of commanding scholarship and a most thoroughgoing and energetic teacher, exacting yet kind. Like Nelson and England, he expected every man to do his duty."[15] Those who did not had their shortcomings recorded. In a small rollbook kept during the first session David noted the following cadet offenses: improper language, loitering, playing chess, throwing dice, chewing tobacco in class, and spitting on the floor. More serious matters were reported to the superintendent. Two student compositions went to Colonel Sherman because their authors signed them "I received and gave help" rather than "I neither gave nor received help." This "wilful disregard" of orders rather than one composition's attack on Latin as a "useless study" prompted Latin professor Boyd to report the two cadets.[16]

In addition to his duties as a professor, David had to assume various family and financial responsibilities during his first session at the seminary. To save some of his father's land in Wytheville, he pledged himself to pay five thousand dollars in five yearly installments. He also accepted full physical and financial responsibility for his scapegrace brother William. Early in January, 1860, Thomas Boyd sent Willie to Louisiana to get him away from his "evil companions, male and female," in Virginia. He promised to reimburse David at some later date, trusting meanwhile that Willie would be a "good boy & a good stu-

13   Speech for Cadet H. B. Taliaferro, master of ceremonies at Public Day, July 4, 1860, *ibid.* Taliaferro was the only cadet at the seminary who joined the Union forces. Fleming, *Louisiana State University*, 121.
14   L. Delahoussaye to D. F. Boyd, September 17, 1860, in David Boyd Papers.
15   W. L. Bringhurst, a student at the seminary in 1860–61, later became a professor at Texas Agricultural and Mechanical College. His "Recollections of the Old Seminary," published first in the Dallas *Morning News*, August 3, 1896, were reprinted in the Louisiana State University *Alumnus*, V (1909–10), 16.
16   Roll Book, January, 1860, MS volumes, Compositions by Cadets H. N. Phillips and T. P. Hyams, undated, in David Boyd Papers.

dent." But the rehabilitation program was a failure. By April, Willie had left the seminary on the grounds of ill health, leading a skeptical Thomas Jefferson Boyd to remark when the prodigal reached Wytheville, "He appears perfectly well, and I incline to think he is more lazy than sick and cares nothing for education."[17]

In spite of the seminary's isolation and the demands his job and family made upon him, David did have many forms of recreation and diversion available if he chose to pursue them. Hunting, fishing, and hiking, none of which particularly appealed to him, were the most common pastimes of the cadets. Visitors to the seminary were always welcome, and Sherman entertained frequently because he considered dances and parties healthy and civilizing for the cadets. The guests, principally planters and their families from the surrounding area, reciprocated by inviting the professors and some of the older cadets to their homes. Most accepted eagerly but David was shy and usually shunned all social occasions, especially if eligible young women were likely to be present. This tendency to withdraw disturbed his mother who felt that nothing would give David more confidence and "ease of manner" than the company of refined young ladies. "You will see the time yet," Minerva Boyd admonished, "when you will regret not having gone more into society. The next time you are invited, go for my sake."[18]

What Minerva did not at first appreciate was that David was still very much in love with Ella Spiller Brown, the young woman to whom he had once been engaged. Alex Brown, for whom she had rejected him, died a few months after their marriage, and David's hopes revived, especially after he learned from William Auman, an old Wytheville friend, that Ella Brown had ended her mourning and was again being courted. David must have answered Auman immediately because within days Auman wrote again, this time declaring that he had no idea his casual reference to Mrs. Brown would touch such a responsive chord. It was like "pouring oil into a hidden flame," Auman remarked, adding that he regretted having brought up a subject upon which David's "entire happiness" and even his "very existence" seemed to depend. "I knew that you had loved Mrs. B. once and that

17   T. J. Boyd to David F. Boyd, January 12, April 22, 1860, Minerva and T. J. Boyd to David Boyd, January 23, 1860, L. A. Auman to David Boyd, April 13, 1860, all in *ibid*.
18   Fleming, *Louisiana State University*, 42–43, 79–81; Prichard (ed.), "A Tourist's Description of Louisiana in 1860," 53–54; Minerva and T. J. Boyd to David Boyd, January 23, 1860, Minerva Boyd to David F. Boyd, August 29, October 9, 1860, in David Boyd Papers.

you had even been engaged to her, but thought that absence and time had long ago effaced that love."[19] Auman advised David not to visit Mrs. Brown unless she encouraged him in some way, but James Gleaves, another friend, urged him to come home at once before Mrs. Brown found someone else. "If she ever loved you, she will again," Gleaves reasoned. "Mrs. B is a widow, she well knows that her chances for marrying are not so good now as they were before she married B. . . . You know very well how a lady in her situation feels & if you want to marry her now is the time for you to strike."[20]

Meanwhile, David did not write his family at all. Minerva Boyd thought he must be ill because his last letter sounded so "hopeless & sad." She begged David to confide in her, promising to keep private anything he sent to her through a third party rather than to the family home. Ultimately she found out what was troubling her son. From someone in Wytheville she learned that David had never loved anyone but Mrs. Brown and that he was probably writing to the young widow. If so, she was sorry because she thought it a hopeless case. "She [Mrs. Brown] is now rich and ambitious," Minerva reported to David, "& of course would like to marry for wealth, family and position. . . . I should be truly sorry if you should be again disappointed."[21]

In time David did begin a private correspondence with his mother, admitting that he still loved Ella Brown and asking for advice. Minerva answered that she did not know Ella's feelings but that she very much feared he would be hurt again. "If she writes you 'no,' dear child, do forget her," Minerva urged. "Go into the society of other ladies; I assure you there are many quite as pretty & good—I am afraid if she were your wife, I never could love her for all the pain she has given you. What do you want to marry a widow [sic] for? Remember David she rejected you for another & call up some French pride. The Boyds have courage but not pride."[22]

Ten months later, in the spring of 1862, David was still hopelessly in love with Mrs. Brown. By that time he was serving with the Confederate Army in northern Virginia and managed to see her at least once while she was visiting in Richmond. Later he wrote his brother, then

19 L. A. Auman to David Boyd, January 14, April 8, 1859, in David Boyd Papers; William Auman
    to David Boyd, December 11, 30, 1860, in Alphabetical File, Fleming Collection.
20 Jas. T. Gleaves to D. F. Boyd, January 11, 1861, in David Boyd Papers.
21 Minerva Boyd to David F. Boyd, March 31, 1861, *ibid*.
22 *Ibid*., May 1, 1861.

on leave in Wytheville, inquiring about her. But Charlie obviously did
not share David's high regard for Mrs. Brown. "Don't misunderstand
me as trying to prejudice you against the lady of your choice," Charlie
responded, "but I do say that a more scheming, ambitious woman
never lived . . . . I say this, convinced of its truth, from personal obser-
vation. . . . Having as much self-esteem as I have thought you had, I
have wondered that you could persist in your love for one who I know
cares not for any man *unless* he be a man of wealth and fame." [23]

David finally gave up. Whether family appeals to his pride or out-
right rejection by Mrs. Brown was responsible is not clear. But in any
case, he was still melancholy as late as March of 1863. A Louisiana
friend tried to cheer him up:

> I had hoped the war would get that crank out of your brain, & that you would
> find out you are *not* the most miserable man in the world. No. No. No. When
> the war is over you will resume your Chair [at the seminary]. . . . You will &
> *shall* get a wife, you will have a house & then such cart loads of '*truck*' will go
> over the ferry from Mrs. C. [Clarke] to Mrs. B. [Boyd] with lots of stewed candy
> from the little *C's* to the little *B's*. I wish paper was not so scarce. I would like to
> give you another ½ sheet on this theme. [24]

In spite of his introverted nature, his conscientious attention to his
duties, and his many personal problems, David was not blind to the
many crises that threatened his country's unity in the 1850s. Always
politically conscious, he followed regional and national developments
avidly through the columns of newspapers printed in Richmond and
Washington. His family and friends also kept him informed while he
was at school and after he moved to Louisiana. The Boyd correspondence is full of political commentary, and on David's part at least it reveals a strong and unwavering committment to the Democratic party.
Indeed, the somewhat Whiggish Thomas Jefferson Boyd thought his
son was too committed. Such "blind devotion to party," he once
warned, could cloud a man's judgement and cause him to overlook the
"great interests and good of the country." [25]

By 1860 Thomas Boyd had reassessed his political position and re-

23   C. R. Boyd to D. F. Boyd, March 7, 1862, *ibid.*
24   Powhatan Clarke to D. F. Boyd, March 22, 1863, *ibid.*
25   Thos. J. Boyd to David Boyd, September 5, 1850, October 20, 1851, *ibid.* T. J. Boyd was a
      member of the Virginia legislature, and during his service on the Virginia Board of Public
      Works consistently supported state aid for railroads and highways.

joined the Democratic party. But whether he or David could support the national ticket in the upcoming presidential election remained to be seen. A series of events which occurred during the preceding half decade explains why. In 1854 Congress destroyed the uneasy sectional truce established by the Compromise of 1850 when it passed the Kansas-Nebraska Act. Among other things, the new law repealed the Missouri Compromise (which barred slavery north of the 36'30" parallel except for Missouri) thereby reopening a bitter national debate concerning the status of slavery in the territories. That is, it gave territorial residents, not Congress, the power to allow or outlaw slavery. Predictably, Kansas became a battlefield as proslavery and antislavery forces sought to outdo each other in the settlement and organization of the territory.

On the national scene passage of the Kansas-Nebraska Act and the subsequent violence it engendered contributed to a profound realignment of political parties. The Democrats managed to retain the presidency in 1856, but, like the practically defunct Whigs and the short-lived American or Know-Nothing party, they lost sizable numbers of their northern constituents to the Republicans, an organization only two years old and frankly pledged to prevent the expansion of slavery.

Meanwhile, Congress reflected the country's rapid polarization. Bitter debates and physical assaults occurred in the national legislature with increasing frequency, most notably in 1856, when Representative Preston Brooks of South Carolina beat Massachusetts' Senator Charles Sumner senseless for having insulted his South Carolina kinsman in a vitriolic speech concerning events in Kansas.

Even the Supreme Court could not escape the mounting controversy. In 1857 it declared in *Dred Scott* v. *Sanford* that Congress could not constitutionally bar slavery from the territories. Such laws violated the fifth amendment which prohibits Congress from taking property without due process of law. Slaves were property, reasoned the Court; therefore the Missouri Compromise, passed in 1821 and repealed by implication with the passage of the Kansas-Nebraska Act in 1854, had always been null and void. The effect was electric. Southerners cheered the decision while antislavery forces vowed to repeal it by reconstituting the Court as soon as they won control of the national government.

What David thought of the Kansas struggle and the Dred Scott decision when they occurred is not recorded in his correspondence.

However, two events in 1859 that alarmed and outraged the South did receive his attention and that of his colleagues. John Brown, already notorious for his role in Kansas, raided the arsenal at Harpers Ferry, Virginia, in order to foment a slave rebellion, and several Republican congressmen endorsed an abridged version of Hinton Rowan Helper's book, *The Impending Crisis of the South*, for use as a campaign document. David's aunt in Virginia spoke for many when she commented following the Brown attack, "I hope Governor Wise [of Virginia] *won't* pardon one of them. We are now to sleep with our *eyes open*. You may depend we can't *trust* the people of the North." [26] As for the Helper volume, banned in the South for its violent denunciation of southern economic policy, southern leaders, and the institution of slavery, its endorsement by the Republican party affected David and the little isolated community at the seminary because one of the signers was Congressman John Sherman of Ohio, a younger brother of seminary superintendent William Sherman. Sherman wrote his wife that "Bro. John's signing of Helper's paper" might hurt him [William] in Louisiana. The Board of Supervisors would understand, he thought, but the board depended upon the legislature for funds. [27]

Sherman need not have worried. Although many legislators distrusted his "Black Republican" brother, the superintendent's straightforward and careful explanations of his own conservative views on slavery and abolition finally reassured them. When in the spring of 1860 he considered leaving the seminary for a more lucrative position in England, a host of prominent citizens, including Governor Thomas O. Moore, Braxton Bragg, and P. G. T. Beauregard, urged him not to leave Louisiana. [28]

Nevertheless the crisis building in the nation ultimately forced Sherman to depart. In the late spring of 1860 a bitterly divided Democratic party finally broke up because its northern and southern wings could not agree on a candidate or a statement defining the party's position on slavery in the territories. The southern delegation chose John C. Breckinridge of Kentucky to represent its interests, and northerners endorsed Stephen A. Douglas of Illinois, author of the Kansas-Nebraska

26 C. F. McComas to David F. Boyd, November 20, 1859, *ibid.*
27 William T. Sherman to his wife, December 12, 16, 1859, in Howe (ed.), *Home Letters of General Sherman*, 168, 170. John Sherman's endorsement of Helper hurt him too. Because of it he lost his bid for the House speakership in December 1859.
28 Fleming, *Louisiana State University*, 57–62.

Act and exponent of the principle of popular sovereignty. Those who found neither man acceptable rallied behind John Bell of Tennessee and the Constitutional Union party. Composed of old Whigs and American party men as well as disaffected Democrats, the Constitutional Unionists hoped, somehow, to hold the states together. Meanwhile, the Republicans found their leader in Abraham Lincoln, who, compared to William Seward with his "irrepressible conflict" approach to the nation's problems, represented the more conciliatory wing of a frankly sectional party.

Throughout the summer and fall of 1860 Sherman and David corresponded extensively, reflecting in microcosm the anguish undergone by thinking Americans everywhere during that fateful period. Planning to visit his family in Ohio before traveling to Washington and New York on business, Sherman arranged to leave David in complete charge of the seminary when school closed on July 31. He hoped his young friend would not be too miserable in his isolation and promised to remember his "sacrifice" which enabled the others to enjoy a vacation. Later Sherman sent the lonely David a brief résumé of campaign activity in his home state. Lincoln would certainly carry Ohio, he predicted, if only because of the divided opposition. As for John Sherman, he was busily politicking in northern Ohio where his speeches, like antislavery sentiment, were especially strong. Sherman expected to see his brother soon but despaired of influencing him. With resignation he concluded, "Political majority has passed to the North and they are determined to have it. Let us hope they will not abuse it."[29]

In mid-August Sherman reported from Washington that no one in the capital really expected secession if Lincoln were elected. He saw some chance that Bell or even Douglas might win if fusion efforts by their partisans succeeded in New York. That would give the nation four years of peace and allow time for "ugly feeling" to subside. By mid-September however, Sherman was convinced that the Republicans would win. He personally preferred Bell, but even if Lincoln became president he did not expect violence. What did disturb him was his brother John's unwillingness to challenge William Seward's "irrepressible conflict" theory publicly. John only laughed when William predicted that "extremists" would take control of the Republican party,

---

29 William Sherman to David Boyd, August 5, 13, 1860, William T. Sherman Letters as College President, David F. Boyd Papers.

insisting that Republicans were merely old Whigs, "revived solely by the *unwise* repeal of the Mo. Compromise."[30]

From his lonely post at the seminary David tried to describe southern political sentiment for the absent superintendent. He thought Bell would carry every southern state but South Carolina; even Douglas was running well in certain districts. Decrying the breakup of the Democratic party at Charleston in April and at Baltimore in June, David was sorry the question of slavery in the territories had ever been introduced. But since it was "thrust upon us," and since he thought Breckinridge's position was right, he intended to vote for him. To do otherwise, he believed, would constitute a denial of the South's right to equal enjoyment of all property everywhere in the Union. Unlike Sherman, David *did* fear what might happen if Lincoln were elected. He doubted that any state would actually secede, but there were other ways to disrupt the Union:

In many places in the South, whoever accepts or holds office under Lincoln will be lynched. He (Lincoln) will attempt to enforce the laws; that attempt will be resisted; and once the strife is begun, God only knows where it will stop. What is the use of that Republican Party? As you say, slavery will always go where it pays in spite of Yanceism [*sic*]! Let the law of nature say you shall not take your slave here or there, but let not a clause of the constitution, or an enactment of the Congress say it. It then becomes a threat hurled by one section at the other; and threats ill become the people of a Union.[31]

Sherman thought that David was unduly concerned. Despite his preference for Bell, he considered Lincoln to be a man of "nerve and moderation." Besides, he pointed out, the Republican nominee was connected by marriage to the slaveholding Prestons of Kentucky and Virginia. To a practical man like Sherman all the "clamor" about rights in the territories was foolish because no one with any sense would try to settle places like Utah, Arizona, and New Mexico. That left only Texas where slavery might be extended profitably, and it was all slave territory by treaty. "If we go to civil war for a mere theory," Sherman wrote David in September, "we deserve a monarch, and that would be the final result." But, as David said, because a principle was involved, men would fight over it. The superintendent was sick of the prejudice

---

30   William Sherman to David Boyd, August 19, September 16, 1860, *ibid*.
31   David Boyd to Wm. Sherman, August 30, 1860, in Boyd Letters, Fleming Collection.

on both sides. In Ohio everyone thought planters had nothing to do but hang abolitionists and hold "lynch courts," while southerners thought everyone up North did nothing but aid and abet runaway slaves. If both sides would mind their own business, Sherman concluded, the country would be better off.[32]

From Virginia, David received additional evidence of the political divisiveness threatening the country. One uncle, William H. French of Mercer County, was solidly for Breckinridge but feared the Bell party would carry the state. Unionist sentiment was so strong, he wrote David, that half the slaveholders would sacrifice their property to avoid secession. David's father, Thomas Jefferson Boyd, also supported Breckinridge, but his wife urged David to win him over to Bell. "I don't care who is president," Minerva declared. "I like Abe Lincoln as well as any. Will [David's brother] says he is for Abe—it is a nice time for us for the Nigs to be free Will thinks." [33]

By election day William Sherman was back in Louisiana, but in spite of his eligibility, he did not vote. Rapides Parish went for Breckinridge and so did the state by a small margin. Noting that sentiment for secession was growing in the parish, Sherman wrote his wife that he would leave Louisiana if it seceded. Meanwhile, discipline at the seminary suffered immensely. Cadets broke crockery, fired off pistols in mess hall, and generally ignored the rules, all, the superintendent believed, because of the country's uncertain future.[34]

Secession was soon a reality. South Carolina withdrew from the Union on December 20, 1860, and by the following February, Mississippi, Florida, Alabama, Georgia, Louisiana, and Texas had followed her example. Sherman did not wait for Louisiana to act. On January 10, 1861, Governor Thomas O. Moore ordered the seizure of Federal property in the state, and Sherman, because he had to receive some of it for safekeeping, immediately submitted his resignation. He could not condone such defiance of the Federal government, he wrote his wife, and Washington's failure to coerce South Carolina at Fort Sumter

32 Wm. Sherman to David Boyd, September 16, 30, 1860, in William T. Sherman Letters as College President, David F. Boyd Papers.
33 William H. French to D. F. Boyd, October 19, 1860, Minerva Boyd to David Boyd, October 9, [1860], in David Boyd Papers. David's brother probably meant that emancipation could take little away from an already ruined estate.
34 William Sherman to his wife, November 10, 23, 29, 1860, in Howe (ed.), *Home Letters of General Sherman*, 180–85.

"disgusted" him. Such temporizing would only encourage efforts to prevent Lincoln's inauguration.[35]

On February 4, 1861, the seven seceded states of the lower South met at Montgomery, Alabama, and formed the Confederate States of America. A month later Abraham Lincoln announced at his inauguration that he had no plans to interfere with slavery in any of the states. But, he warned, secession was unlawful and would not be tolerated. Weeks passed, and tension mounted until an embattled Union garrison finally surrendered to Confederate forces at Fort Sumter. Now Washington's "temporizing" was over. President Lincoln called for seventy-five thousand troops to put down the "insurrection," and the nation was at war. Virginia reacted immediately. On April 17, 1861, it left the Union, taking with it some of the best talent of the United States Army. When Robert E. Lee and Joseph E. Johnston "went with their state," they set an example followed by thousands of lesser men. Among them was David Boyd, already pledged to defend Virginia against invasion.[36]

The breakup of the seminary began in February, 1861, when Sherman, his resignation accepted with regret, left Louisiana for the North. Just before his departure, he noted with some bitterness that those who "were most pro-Union last July are now loudest for secession." But if the public utterances of the politicians disillusioned him, they did not chill the warmth of his personal feelings for his Louisiana friends. On his way home Sherman took time to write to David. "If present politicians break up our Country, let us resolve to reestablish it, for the ties 'inter-partes' ought not to be severed. Goodbye." Again, after Sherman joined the United States Army in May of 1861, he wrote David that they were now enemies, but he could not believe it. "No matter what happens," he promised, "I will ever consider you my personal friend, and you shall ever be welcome to my roof."[37]

Other members of the academic staff at the seminary soon followed Sherman's example. Francis Smith and Powhatan Clarke resigned on

---

35 Fleming, *Louisiana State University*, 98–100; William Sherman to his wife, January 5, 8, 13, 1861, in Howe (ed.), *Home Letters of General Sherman*, 189–91.
36 Jas. T. Gleaves to D. F. Boyd, January 11, 1861, in David Boyd Papers.
37 William Sherman to his wife, January 27, 1861, in Howe (ed.), *Home Letters of General Sherman*, 193; William Sherman to David Boyd, February 23, 1861, in Typescript of Sherman-Boyd Correspondence in possession of Annie Boyd Grayson, Baton Rouge; William Sherman to David Boyd, May 13, 1861, in William T. Sherman Letters as College President, David F. Boyd Papers.

May 14, 1861, and left immediately for Virginia. David resigned the same day, but the Board of Supervisors prevailed upon him to reconsider in order that the school might finish the term (July 31). He then requested a leave of absence to be effective June 1. By then, he thought, there would be so few cadets on hand that Professors Vallas and St. Ange could carry on alone. Facing something of a personal dilemma, David wished to do his duty, but he was not sure where it lay. On the one hand he promised the supervisors to remain until they could find a replacement for him. On the other, he wanted to join a company then preparing to leave Rapides to "repel the invasion of his country." Letters from his family only complicated the problem. "Country first with all true hearts in existing emergencies," wrote Thomas Jefferson Boyd in mid-April. But three weeks later he told his son that he would be more useful to Louisiana by remaining at the seminary. David's mother agreed. Both William and Charles, David's younger brothers, were already in service. So were all of his uncles and a "dozen cousins." And, since they would all be in the first battle, no one could possibly accuse the family of cowardice. As for David, she insisted, his duty was to the seminary, at least till the end of the term. He could serve his country better as a professor than as a private.[38]

While David was trying to make up his mind, the somewhat fragile relationship between him and his father suffered another blow. Minerva Boyd, always much closer to her son, inadvertently contributed to the difficulty early in 1861 when she urged David to confide in her and send anything "private" through a third person. Some time later Thomas Boyd discovered this correspondence and was terribly hurt. To make matters worse, some of David's letters were harshly critical of his father. On May 1, 1861, Minerva rather belatedly scolded David. She conceded that Thomas Boyd was not very successful in business, but he was a hard worker and honorable in his dealings. As for his manner, which David thought stern and lacking in affection, Minerva assured her son that Thomas Boyd was proud of him and loved him very much. Two weeks later she wrote again, urging David to send his father a "kind letter." David had returned one of Thomas Boyd's letters unread and Minerva begged him to apologize. He seems to have gone half way.

38 Fleming, *Louisiana State University*, 104; David F. Boyd to the Board of Supervisors, undated, in Boyd Letters, Fleming Collection; Thos. J. Boyd to D. F. Boyd, April 20, May 10, 1861, Minerva F. Boyd to D. F. Boyd, May 16, 1861, in David Boyd Papers.

In time Thomas Boyd wrote, "It seems by your letter to your mother, that you will wait to receive a letter from me, to enable you to decide whether you will be a welcome visitor to your father & mother's roof. Now do pray discard all such notions & come along. Be assured that the foolishness that has been passing in our correspondence is no indication on my part of want of the utmost affection & good feeling in every way for you."[39]

By the time David had settled his family problems, many of his students and colleagues were already in uniform. Dr. Powhatan Clarke was a lieutenant in the Provisional Army of Virginia, and Francis Smith, the former professor of chemistry, had become a military secretary for General Robert E. Lee. "I have the advantage of being thrown quite intimately with all the bugs [important persons], Davis, Genl Cooper," Smith wrote David. Both Clarke and Smith advised David to go to Virginia and enlist there rather than to join a Louisiana outfit. As for the cadets, some were already in Virginia while others waited in Louisiana camps until their units could be filled. "There are very few *military* men on the ground from Brigadier Tracy down to the privates," one of the latter reported to David. "I believe that as far as regards tactics I am as well posted as any of them." The same youth was appalled at the people he met in camp. He told his former professor that men up to the rank of captain who had never drunk or played cards were doing both. But his own company and officers, he was happy to say, had not "fallen to this vice." A cadet writing from Virginia found other aspects of camp life distasteful. Soldiers, he discovered, had to wash their own clothes and cook their own food.[40]

In the end, David did not take Clarke's and Smith's advice. On June 11, 1861, he offered his services by mail to former governor Henry Wise of Virginia, then forming a brigade in that state. But he did not wait for a reply. Instead, he enrolled as a private in Captain L. A. Stafford's volunteer company, then training at Camp Moore, near Amite, Louisiana. General G. Mason Graham expressed great regret when he learned of David's enlistment. Referring to it as "patriotic folly," Mason chastized David for throwing away his life. "In the ranks,

---

39 Minerva Boyd to D. F. Boyd, May 1, 16, 1861, T. J. Boyd to David Boyd, May 24, 1861, in David Boyd Papers.
40 Powhatan Clarke to David Boyd, June 7, 1861, Francis W. Smith to David Boyd, June 4, 1861, R. S. Jackson to David Boyd, June 7, 1861, F. H. Perkins to David Boyd, June 8, 1861, *ibid.*

your mind, your talent, your capacities, of so much value to our state in your present position will be of no more avail than that of the lousiest ragamuffin that may be alongside you, while his greater ability to endure fatigue and exposure, and to handle a musket will make him really more valuable than you. Once 'mustered in' for the war, as you must necessarily be, there is no power to release you, except on a surgeon's certificate of disability."[41]

David spent July 4, 1861 at Tyrone Plantation with General Graham. A few days later he went to New Orleans to join his unit, the Stafford Guards, and by mid-July he was on his way to Virginia. The "event of war," remarked Minerva Boyd, had accomplished what none of her letters could; her favorite son was coming home.[42]

41 David Boyd to H. A. Wise, June 11, 1861, G. Mason Graham to David Boyd, June 26, 1861, in
    G. Mason Graham Letters, Fleming Collection.
42 G. Mason Graham to David Boyd, July 5, 1861, ibid.; G. M. G. Stafford, General Leroy Augus-
    tus Stafford: His Forbears and Descendants (New Orleans, 1943), 34–35; Minerva Boyd to
    D. F. Boyd, June 17, 1861, in David Boyd Papers.

Chapter III

The War Years

WHEN HE arrived at Camp Moore on July 10, 1861, David learned that Lieutenant Colonel E. G. Randolph had appointed him quartermaster sergeant for the Ninth Louisiana Regiment, Provisional Army of the Confederate States of America. He had no particular qualifications for the post; neither would he have much time to learn his duties before his regiment left for Virginia. Colonel Richard Taylor of St. Charles Parish commanded the Ninth Louisiana, of which David's original outfit, the Stafford Guards, made up Company B. A son of President Zachary Taylor and a brother-in-law of Jefferson Davis, Taylor was in Florida when informed of his appointment. He hurried to Camp Moore, hastily inspected his command, and dispatched it at once to Richmond. Then, after a quick trip to New Orleans to settle family affairs and to procure ammunition, Taylor followed his men northward. Richmond was alive with rumors about an impending battle at Manassas some six hours by train from the capital, and Taylor, eager to participate, went immediately to the War Office to arrange transportation for his men. But a delay in departure and repeated mechanical failures enroute kept the Louisianians from reaching Manassas Junction until the fighting was over. The men went into camp, and for the rest of the year the Confederate government attempted to bring some order out of the confusion following the first major engagement of the war.[1]

The lull following Manassas gave civilian and military authorities in the East an opportunity to organize more efficiently. David's regiment, the Ninth Louisiana, together with the Sixth, Seventh, and Eighth from the same state, became the Eighth Brigade and a part of General P. G. T. Beauregard's command. Richard Taylor, in spite of his junior status, was promoted to brigadier general and given command of the Eighth Brigade, and David's rank also rose. On September 2, 1861, he became captain and assistant commissary of the Ninth Louisiana, a promotion he greeted with mixed emotions.[2]

Well before he accepted his commission David had misgivings about the commissary service. Certainly there was nothing glamorous about it compared to, say, the cavalry or the artillery. The corps of engineers, in which his brother Charlie was a second lieutenant, commanded more respect. David asked Charlie about transferring to that branch and the latter urged him to make the change. The commissary service, Charlie thought, was "servile employment" and David's captaincy in it made him little more than a "boss in the business." Letters from David's parents were equally discouraging, if somewhat ambivalent. At various times they advised him to give up "that miserable place" for a more "honorable position" or to retain it because it was safer than any other. Minerva Boyd declared that she would rather get David home safe than have him risk his life in pursuit of "high honor." The only consolation, and that was slight, came from David's friend and former colleague, Francis W. Smith. He thought David, then considering resignation of his "beef captaincy," should hold on a little longer. "Inasmuch as a Beef Captain can fight, while a Captain of men

---

1 Stafford, *General Leroy Augustus Stafford*, 33–36; Richard Taylor, *Destruction and Reconstruction* (London, 1879), 6–12; John D. Winters, *The Civil War in Louisiana* (Baton Rouge, 1963), 22; Andrew B. Booth (comp.), *Records of Louisiana Confederate Soldiers and Louisiana Confederate Commands* (New Orleans, 1920), II, 73; Order of Lt. Col. E. G. Randolph, Ninth Louisiana, July 10, 1861, in David Boyd Papers.

2 Taylor, *Destruction and Reconstruction*, 17, 19; *The War of the Rebellion: A Compilation of the Official Records of the Union and Confederate Armies* (Washington, 1880–1901), Ser. I, Vol. V, 1029–30. Unless otherwise stated, all citations of the *Official Records* refer to Series I. L. R. Walker (Secretary of War) to Captain D. F. Boyd, September 2, 1861, David Boyd Papers.

... [may] not feed," Smith saw nothing dishonorable in the former title.[3]

Another factor contributed to David's desire to resign his commission in the commissary service almost as soon as he assumed it. The second session of the Louisiana State Seminary ended on June 30, 1861, and whether the school would reopen in the fall was left to the Board of Supervisors among whom there was some disagreement. The majority opposed lowering academic standards and the age of admittance simply to attract enough professors and cadets. It also doubted whether the people and the legislature would support an educational institution while the state was at war. By late October, 1861, the board decided not to act without specific legislative approval. Therefore David, who left the seminary for the army on a leave of absence, had no certain job to which he might return. Unless the board changed its position or he could get a transfer to some other service, he was doomed to remain a "beef captain."[4]

Circumstances seemed to offer David a way out late in 1861 when the Louisiana legislature instructed the Board of Supervisors to reopen the seminary. At a December meeting the board set April 1, 1862, as opening day. It also asked David and Francis Smith to return as professors. Now David would have to choose. He hated his humiliating position in the supply service, but worried about the propriety of leaving the army while the war continued. Asked for advice, Francis Smith counseled David to do nothing, at least for a while. The recent Mason-

3   Charles R. Boyd to David F. Boyd, September 13, 1861, T. J. Boyd to David Boyd, December 1, 1861, May 26, 1862, Minerva Boyd to David Boyd, [May], August 18, October 13, 1862, F. W. Smith to David Boyd, December 18, 1861, all in David Boyd Papers. Historians have contributed to the rather unfortunate public attitude concerning the supply services. In *Rebel Brass*, Frank Vandiver notes that most military histories and biographies practically ignore the important subject of supply. "There simply is no comparison, from the standpoint of interest, between the battles of Jackson's campaign in the Shenandoah Valley and the problems encountered by his Chief Quartermaster during the same campaign. But a strong case may be made for asserting that the activities of Jackson's quartermaster were a key to the general's success." Frank Vandiver, *Rebel Brass* (Baton Rouge, 1956), 83. On the other hand, the low opinion David's family had of the supply services was not completely undeserved. John Winters notes that the quality of goods obtained by the Quartermaster's Department was often shocking and that the contractors who supplied it were notoriously corrupt. "Even more disgraceful," he adds, "was the unprincipled conduct of some of the commissary officers. . . . It has been estimated that corrupt commissary officers appropriated nearly one third of every ration requisition, sold it, and pocketed the proceeds. Few men who served as commissary officers for a regiment remained completely free of this organized graft." Winters, *Civil War in Louisiana*, 25.
4   A. Vallas to David F. Boyd, July 26, August 19, September 19, 28, November 11, 1861, in David Boyd Papers; Fleming, *Louisiana State University*, 108–11.

Slidell affair, Smith explained, might bring war between the United States and Great Britain. If that happened, pressure on the South would decrease markedly, and some men might "honorably" leave the army. But until he could be certain that his services were not needed, Smith would not consider accepting the supervisors' offer. In any case, he thought they would hold David's job open.[5]

Apparently David took Smith's advice. The school opened April 1, 1862, as planned, with William Seay in David's old chair as professor of ancient languages *"pro-tem."* Seay, a lawyer, had been editor of the New Orleans *Delta* until General Benjamin Butler suppressed the paper when Federal troops occupied the Crescent City. By June of 1862 he wanted permanent appointment to the chair of ancient languages and the board's executive committee appeared ready to grant his request. David was informed that he must return for the fourth session, beginning November 1, 1862, or forfeit his job. He had until mid-October to make up his mind. It is not clear whether Richmond's refusal to release him or his own sense of duty to the Confederacy determined his course, but some time before the deadline, David submitted his resignation to the seminary's Board of Supervisors.[6]

During his service in Virginia, David's regiment, the Ninth Louisiana, saw action in eastern Virginia and the Shenandoah Valley. As part of Richard Taylor's Eighth Brigade, the Ninth was ordered in the spring of 1862 to join General Thomas J. Jackson, then operating in the valley. There it took part in Jackson's spectacular feats at Front Royal, Winchester, Cross Keys, and Port Republic. Fighting around Winchester was particularly heavy, and while the battle was in progress circumstances contrived to promote David once more. As explained in General Taylor's official report, the brigade's commissary officer, Major Aaron Davis, "carried away by his ardour . . . gathered a score of mounted orderlies and couriers and pursued [a Federal regiment from Maryland] until a volley from the enemy's rear guard laid him low . . . shot through the head."[7] David assumed Major Davis' du-

---

5 T. J. Boyd to David Boyd, January 7, May 26, 1862, Minerva Boyd to David Boyd, [May], 1862, F. W. Smith to David Boyd, December 18, 1861, in David Boyd Papers; Fleming, *Louisiana State University*, 112.

6 A. Vallas to David Boyd, August 21, November 29, 1862, in David Boyd Papers; G. Mason Graham to David Boyd, September 3, 1862, in G. Mason Graham Letters, Fleming Collection.

7 *Official Records*, XII, Pt. 1, p. 800; Taylor, *Destruction and Reconstruction*, 48–95. The latter includes a detailed account of the Eighth Brigade's activity in the first half of 1862.

ties at once and a month later received formal notice of his promotion
to major. By that time, Jackson's corps was supporting Lee in the
Seven Days' battles around Richmond. Ill before the fighting began,
General Taylor was partially paralyzed when it was over. Early in July,
1862, he received promotion to major general and shortly thereafter
left his brigade in Virginia for service in Louisiana. He was replaced by
Brigadier General Harry T. Hays, a New Orleans lawyer, who commanded the brigade until the last months of the war.[8]

David was also sick when the Seven Days' battles ended. Citing
"acute diarrhoea," a regimental physician endorsed his request for a
two-week furlough on July 11, 1862. The next day David left his unit,
then camped near Richmond, to recuperate at his parents' home in
Wytheville. This would be his first furlough and his first visit home
since September, 1861. On that trip, his first to Wytheville since his
departure for Louisiana four years earlier, David had been very disappointed. For one thing, Mrs. Nannie Stuart, a woman he considered
his confidante and "particular friend," was out of town. Later, when
Minerva Boyd told her of David's disappointment at not seeing her and
his general condemnation of Virginians as cold and unfeeling, the em-
pathetic Mrs. Stuart guessed why David was so bitter. "I believe," she
wrote him on New Year's Day, 1862, "that you long ago formed an attachment for one and cherished hopes that were never realized—that
those hopes may have since revived and again [been] disappointed—
and finding that one unworthy of your affection you are too much inclined to class your other friends with her and condemn them all alike."
Mrs. Stuart thought David ought "to quit grieving over spilt milk" and
find someone else before he became a "crusty old bachelor."[9]

The lack of rapport between David and his father was another reason for David's disappointment when he visited Wytheville in September, 1861. He felt more welcome in his "new home 'way down in
Dixie,'" he told Mrs. Stuart, than he did in Wytheville. David also complained to his brother Charlie of Thomas Boyd's seeming lack of affection. Charlie thought David was too sensitive. He admitted that he, too,
used to think "Pa had the same affection for his children that the viper
had for its young," but he knew better now. David ought to allow for

8 *Official Records*, XII, Pt. 1, pp. 800, 917–18; Geo. W. Randolph (Secretary of War) to David
   Boyd, June 25, 1862, in David Boyd Papers; Taylor, *Destruction and Reconstruction*, 76, 93.
9 Nannie Stuart to David F. Boyd, January 1, 1862; application for sick leave, July 11, 1862;
   furlough permit for D. F. Boyd, July 12, 1862, in David Boyd Papers.

the harsh way in which their father had been raised; thrown out at fifteen, friendless and penniless, he had been compelled to make his own way in a "heartless world." David should discard any notions he might have about their father's indifference, thought Charlie, and come home at Christmas to see for himself.[10]

But David did not go home for Christmas in 1861, thereby disappointing the whole family. Minerva Boyd was particularly unhappy. It was March before she could even write her son a note, and by that time David's unit was so busily engaged that her letters often went unanswered. When she finally heard from him late in April, 1862, she urged him to ask his officers for a leave. "I can't see the justice of keeping you always on duty," Minerva complained. "May I not write to Col. [General] Taylor & beg a furlough?"[11]

The truth seems to be that the hypersensitive David, estranged from his father and twice rejected by Mrs. Brown, found little to attract him when he visited Wytheville in September, 1861. Only a debilitating illness made him return there in mid-July of the next year, and then his stay was relatively brief. When he rejoined his unit about August 1, 1862, Jackson was preparing to take part in a series of major engagements at Cedar Mountain, Second Manassas, and Sharpsburg, all of which kept the Army of Northern Virginia busy until mid-September. His troops, formally organized by that time as the Second Corps of that army, then rested around Winchester until late November when they moved southeastward to Fredericksburg, along the Rappahannock. Following the bloody battle that took place there in December, 1862, Jackson settled down in winter quarters for the next several months.[12]

General Jackson enjoyed very pleasant accommodations during the winter of 1862–1863. By that time his fame was so great that wherever he appeared he was deluged with gifts, delicacies, and invitations to enjoy the best the country could offer. It clearly embarrassed him to be the object of so much special consideration, particularly when his troops lacked clothing and even shelter. Some units at Fred-

10 Nannie Stuart to David F. Boyd, January 1, 1862, C. R. Boyd to D. F. Boyd, December 11, 1861, *ibid*.
11 C. R. Boyd to D. F. Boyd, March 7, 1862, Minerva Boyd to D. F. Boyd, March 7, 1862, Minerva Boyd to D. F. Boyd, undated, *ibid*. Minerva's undated letter refers to one written by David dated March 25, 1862, which she did not receive until the end of April.
12 Frank L. Vandiver, *Mighty Stonewall* (New York, 1957), Chaps. 14–18; *Official Records*, XXI, 674–75, contains Brigadier General Harry Hays's account of the Battle of Fredericksburg.

ricksburg suffered more than others. In January, 1863, Brigadier General Harry Hays's adjutant general wrote Louisiana representative John Perkins about the pitiful conditions in camp. Almost no one had shoes or underclothing, he reported, and an overcoat was "an object of curiosity." Many slept in the open for lack of tents, and rations were described as "petty." "Troops of *other* states [are] supplied . . . by . . . contributions from their homes. We from La. have gotten nothing since N.O. fell . . . with the exception . . . of a company in the 9th Regt."[13] Even before the Battle of Fredricksburg, troops were on substitutes and short rations. In November, 1862, David's superiors ordered him to purchase ten pounds of wheat for every hundred men as a substitute for coffee, and pork rather than beef as the meat ration *"one day in every seven."* David must have described the bad conditions in a letter to his family, because early in December Thomas Boyd demanded, "What is the Quartermaster General doing that he don't furnish your soldiers with shoes? I am told that every Jew's shop in Richmond is filled with them to overflowing."[14]

The miserable winter of 1862–1863 at Fredricksburg was the last David would spend in Virginia for almost twenty years. His ceaseless struggle to escape from the commissary service finally succeeded in the spring of 1863, thanks largely to pressure brought on the Confederate War Office by Louisiana politicians. Planning to reorganize the seminary during the summer of 1863, the Board of Supervisors wanted to secure David's release from the army so that he could resume his old chair and serve as acting superintendent. They had tried to get Major Francis Smith for the latter post but he refused to leave the army until the war ended. Aware of the board's intentions, David tried vainly to get his resignation accepted in Richmond. Finally, Judge Thomas Manning, a member of the Board of Supervisors as well as an aide to Louisiana's governor, Thomas O. Moore, appealed to the state's representatives in the capital. They in turn approached the secretary of war, and within six weeks David was a civilian.[15]

13 *Official Records*, XXI, 1097–98; Vandiver, *Mighty Stonewall*, 436–37.
14 Orders, undated and unsigned to Major David Boyd; T. J. Boyd to David Boyd, December 6, 1862, in David Boyd Papers.
15 Fleming, *Louisiana State University*, 115–16; C. S. deElgee to David Boyd, March 30, 1863, Th. C. Manning, Governor Thom. O. Moore, and C. S. deElgee to Henry Marshall, March 31, 1863, H. Marshall to David Boyd, April 29, 1863, Special Order No. 120, Adjutant and Inspector General's Office, Richmond, May 20, 1863, all in David Boyd Papers. David's resignation became effective May 11, 1863.

Even before his release was official David was busy making plans for the seminary. He tried to hire René T. Beauregard, a son of General Beauregard and a former cadet at the school, to serve as commandant and professor of French. But Beauregard declined due to the "uncertainty of holding an office in a state where . . . every inch of soil is within the enemy's grasp." David also corresponded with Major Smith, whose duties as superintendent he would be performing until the latter was available. Happy to cooperate, Smith sent David a detailed plan for reorganization of the seminary's curriculum, fees, personnel, and management.

On May 21, 1863, his resignation finally approved, "Citizen D. F. Boyd" went to see Major Smith at Drewry's Bluff, Virginia, to complete the planning begun by mail. Together they projected a strictly military institution with five professorships: (1) mathematics and natural philosophy; (2) chemistry, minerology, and geology; (3) engineering and applied mechanics; (4) ancient languages and ancient history, and (5) English literature, belles-lettres, and modern history. The first half of the four-year program would be required for all students. But third and fourth-year cadets might specialize in literary or scientific studies. In 1910 a historical account of the seminary's early days noted that the Boyd-Smith proposal drafted in 1863 was "essentially that now generally accepted as the proper organization of college work." [16]

After his meeting with Major Smith, David went to Wytheville where he spent a week resting and concluding his affairs in Virginia. On June 1, 1863, he began a long and circuitous trip to Louisiana. His route, planned by a friend in the Ninth Louisiana Regiment, took him from Wytheville, Virginia, through Bristol and Knoxville, Tennessee, to Stevenson, Alabama. There he left the East Tennessee Railroad and traveled eastward to Dalton, Georgia. At Dalton he boarded the Western and Atlantic Railroad to Kingston and Rome, Georgia, after which he had to go by stage to Jacksonville, Alabama. There David joined the Alabama and Tennessee Railroad to Selma, Alabama, where he switched to a newly constructed line which conveyed him through Meridian, Mississippi, to the capital at Jackson. After a two-day stop-

16 René T. Beauregard to David Boyd, April 28, 1863, pass to Richmond for Citizen D. F. Boyd, May 16, 1863, in David Boyd Papers; F. W. Smith to David Boyd, undated, F. W. Smith to David Boyd, May 13, 1863, in Alphabetical File, Fleming Collection; Proposed reorganization of La. State Seminary and Military Academy by F. W. Smith, copy, May [21], 1863, in Official Papers, *ibid.*; Fleming, *Louisiana State University*, 116.

over he rode southward on the New Orleans, Jackson and Great Northern as far as Brookhaven. Natchez lay directly west of Brookhaven, but in 1863 no rail line connected the two towns. How David covered the intervening distance is not clear, but it proved to be the most expensive part of the trip. From Natchez a ferry carried him across the Mississippi to Vidalia, Louisiana, and another stage took him through Trinity on the Black River and finally to Alexandria. The whole journey from Fredricksburg, Virginia, to Alexandria, Louisiana, consumed twenty-six days and about $275. But considering that both Vicksburg and Port Hudson were under siege, that Federal gunboats commanded the Mississippi, and that Union forces captured Jackson, Mississippi, in May of 1863, David's progress was surprisingly rapid.[17]

Whether his job would still be available when he arrived in Louisiana was doubtful even before David left the army. The Louisiana congressman who secured his release pointed out on April 29, 1863, that Federal troops were then threatening Alexandria. As part of a coordinated action, these troops, under the command of General Nathaniel P. Banks, were supposed to move northward along the Mississippi River from Baton Rouge, capture Port Hudson, and join General Grant in his assault on Vicksburg. But Banks thought he should prepare for the larger action on the Mississippi by first clearing away Confederate forces along the Red River between Alexandria and Shreveport. That explains his presence around the seminary during the latter part of April, 1863. Meanwhile, the school itself ceased to operate on April 23 when the acting superintendent dismissed the cadets to fight the enemy. Federal forces occupied the building briefly but even after their withdrawal the institution did not reopen during the war. On June 23, shortly after David reached Alexandria, the Board of Supervisors formally closed the seminary, vacated the existing professorships, and named the steward custodian of the building.[18]

As July, 1863, began, David found himself out of a job and in need of funds. Fortunately, he had friends in the vicinity. Dr. Powhatan

17 David's route, expenses, and mode of travel between May 19 and June 23, 1863, appear in a
    small manuscript volume in the David Boyd Papers.
18 H. Marshall to David Boyd, April 29, 1863, in David Boyd Papers; Fleming, *Louisiana State
    University*, 114–15; Bruce Catton, *This Hallowed Ground* (New York, 1956), 212, 229, 233;
    Resolution of Board of Supervisors, June 23, 1863, in Official Papers, Fleming Collection. A
    detailed account of Banks's campaign in 1863 appears in Winters, *Civil War in Louisiana*.

Clarke, a former colleague at the seminary, was stationed in Shreveport as a captain of artillery. Married to the former Louise Boyce, daughter of the wealthy Judge Henry Boyce of Rapides, Clarke was a frequent visitor to Alexandria. He arranged to lend David four hundred dollars which the latter planned to use for the trip back to Virginia, but before David could leave the state, a chance arose to rejoin the army on the staff of Major General Richard Taylor, his first commander. Taylor, whose command included all of Louisiana west of the Mississippi, made his headquarters at Alexandria. Early in August, David went to see him, and by mid-September he held a captain's commission as chief of engineers on Taylor's staff.[19]

In his new post David's principal assignment involved refitting Fort De Russy on the Red River. Located about thirty miles below Alexandria, Fort De Russy was still uncompleted when Federal gunboats under David D. Porter, acting in support of General Bank's Teche expedition, appeared before it in early May, 1863. The Confederates managed to save their guns and supplies, but Porter leveled the fort's earthworks and destroyed a log-and-chain raft in the river before withdrawing to the Mississippi to participate in the final action around Vicksburg.[20]

After Vicksburg and Port Hudson fell early in July, General Richard Taylor was sure the enemy would make another attempt to ascend the Red River and subdue all Confederate forces west of the Mississippi. Therefore, rebuilding the ruined Fort De Russy was given high priority. For Chief Engineer David Boyd, the task involved mounting guns, digging earthworks, constructing a powder magazine, and, perhaps most important, driving huge pilings into the riverbed behind which an impassable raft of logs might accumulate.

Begun late in 1863, the work did not go smoothly. In addition to shortages of labor and material, the project suffered from strained relations between Major General Taylor's District Headquarters at Alexandria and Department Headquarters under Lieutenant General Edmund Kirby Smith at Shreveport. When Taylor asked Kirby Smith to

19 Powhatan Clarke to D. F. Boyd, July 9, 10, 1863, M. D. Berengier to D. F. Boyd, August 3, 1863, General Order No. 54 Hdqr. Dist., Western La., September 16, 1863, introducing Capt. D. F. Boyd to the district as Chief of Engineers on General Taylor's staff, in David Boyd Papers.
20 Winters, *Civil War in Louisiana*, 196–97, 204–205.

send the "best engineering officer available" to assist his own crew at De Russy, he did not expect that the engineer, Major H. T. "Fred" Douglas, would be reporting directly to Shreveport. Worse still, Taylor and Douglas disagreed on a basic point: the kind of fort De Russy ought to be. Taylor thought "mere water batteries" were enough to combat enemy gunboats; forts like De Russy should not attempt to withstand "serious land attacks." But Shreveport, inclined to a more permanent defense works, including iron casemates and heavy guns, decided to construct what Taylor later sneered at as a "Red River Gibralter."[21]

When Major General J. G. Walker, after a visit of inspection on Taylor's behalf condemned De Russy as "inadequate for the defense of the river," Taylor must have felt somewhat vindicated. Specifically, Walker's report criticized the placement of guns inside the fort some two or three hundred yards from the river. "Where they now are not more than one shot out of ten would be accurately aimed," he remarked, even if the gunners could *see* the vessels. Boats could not be seen from the fort until the water rose twelve to fifteen feet. But they could sail past with only a three- to four-foot rise. The only thing Walker had any faith in was the log raft being built below the fort to obstruct the passage of the boats. Even that, he reported, was in the wrong place. Because it lay beyond the reach of Fort De Russy's guns, enemy working parties might dismantle it in safety. However, if the piling proved strong enough to sustain the weight of accumulating timber, and if Captain Boyd could obtain four or five hundred Negro laborers and forty or fifty ox teams to throw trees into the river, thus filling the entire space from the piling to Fort De Russy, the river might be made impassable to any boats and the raft impossible to dislodge.

Less than two months later, Taylor and Walker's worst fears were realized. On March 14, 1864, a Yankee land force under Brigadier General J. A. Mower took Fort De Russy from the rear. The Federals lost three killed and thirty-five wounded. They captured ten guns, took 260 prisoners, and killed 5 Confederates. Stalled for two hours by the

---

21 *Official Records*, XXXIV, Pt. 2, pp. 890–92; Taylor, *Destruction and Reconstruction*, 118–19, 136, 153, 155. Taylor had other difficulties with Kirby Smith because of the latter's penchant for organizing bureaus and maintaining an extensive staff. Kirby Smith's staff, commented Taylor, would have done credit to Von Moltke in the Franco-Prussian War.

"impassable" raft in the river, the Federal gunboats arrived too late to fire a shot.[22]

Captain David Boyd managed to escape capture at Fort De Russy only because he was already a prisoner of the Yankees. On February 3, 1864, about four in the afternoon, a band of Louisiana Jayhawkers waylaid him some five miles from Alexandria. Jayhawkers were draft dodgers, deserters, and brigands who took to the swamps or backcountry to escape both civil and military authority. They emerged from time to time to rob and terrorize the helpless and unwary. For seven days after David's capture, General Taylor did not know whether his chief engineer was alive or dead, but on February 8 he learned that David and possibly two other officers had been taken to Natchez, Mississippi, and "sold" to the Federals.

Jayhawkers had become a serious problem in many parts of Louisiana by 1864. After David's capture General Taylor decided to act. He advised General Walker, then headquartered at Marksville near Fort De Russy, that "no officer should be permitted to travel north of the [Red] river from here [Alexandria] to Marksville until we root out this band. At present they number only 15, but the whole population . . . sympathize with them." Taylor did not let popular sentiment stand in his way. He instructed Major R. E. Wyche to drive the outlaws into the swamps, take their horses, and starve them out. Any armed man of draft age who could not account for himself was to be shot on the spot.[23]

When captured, David was carrying five thousand dollars in Confederate currency destined for soldiers at Fort De Russy. Years later David's eulogist, Judge A. A. Gunby, claimed it escaped confiscation because David concealed it in his boot. But in 1904 David's wife corrected the Gunby version. As she remembered the story, David and the

---

22   J. G. Walker to E. Surget, January 17, 1864, in *Official Records*, XXXIV, Pt. 2, pp. 893–94; Robert U. Johnson and Clarence O. Buell (eds.), *Battles and Leaders of the Civil War* (New York, 1887), IV, 349, 362, 369; R. H. Williams, "General Banks's Red River Campaign" (M.A. thesis, Louisiana State University, 1934), 12–14; Winters, *Civil War in Louisiana*, 328–29. In a postmortem, Walker reported to Taylor that despite the Federals' superior numbers, De Russy might have been held for some days without outside relief "but for the vicious system of engineering adopted and the wretched judgement displayed in the selection of the position." *Official Records*, XXXIV, Pt. 1, p. 601.

23   Statement of David Boyd after his release, June 15, 1864, in David Boyd Papers; *Official Records*, XXXIV, Pt. 2, pp. 944, 950–51.

Jayhawkers had to cross the Black River enroute to Natchez. The boat capsized, and during the confusion David supposedly destroyed the money by stamping it into the mud. Either way, the Jayhawkers did not get it. But when they reached Natchez the Yankees paid them one hundred dollars for their prisoner, presumably in Federal currency, thereby making their trip worthwhile.[24]

Considering his plight, David could not have reached Natchez at a more propitious time. It was February 7, 1864, and General William T. Sherman, commander of the Union Army of the Tennessee, would soon be only a few miles away at Vicksburg. Upon discovering this, David wrote his old friend from seminary days, informing him of his circumstances and requesting that he be transferred from Sherman's command to that of General Banks, Department of the Gulf. In Banks's department, David explained, his chances for an early release were much better because Banks and Taylor had an agreement regarding the exchange of prisoners captured west of the Mississippi. Sherman, enroute to New Orleans for a conference with Banks about the upcoming Red River campaign, was delighted to oblige. Late in February he left Vicksburg aboard the steamer *Diana*, stopping at Natchez just long enough to confer with authorities, inspect the town, and pick up prisoner of war Boyd. David was dirty but in good health, Sherman noted, and very happy to see his old friend for the first time in three years. Several hours later, the *Diana* reached the Crescent City, and David was delivered to Federal authorities at 21 Rampart Street. "I never saw a man evince more gratitude," Sherman commented in a letter to his wife. "He clung to me till I came away."

Before Sherman departed New Orleans, David sent him a forlorn note. He wanted to see his old friend once more but doubted that it was possible. "I feel that I shall never meet you again," David wrote, "[so] good bye, and altho' we are *public* enemies, we must always be *private* friends. May God protect you and carry you safe thro' this wicked war. . . . Your *Rebel* friend, D. F. Boyd." Sherman answered the next day. He could not visit David before leaving for Vicksburg, but he assured him of his warm personal regard in a hastily written note. If David ever

24 *Official Records*, XXXIV, Pt. 2, p. 977; Gunby, "Life and Services of David French Boyd," 7–8; annotation of Mrs. David Boyd on unidentified newspaper clipping, quoting Gunby's address, in Scrapbook, David Boyd Papers; Fleming, *Louisiana State University*, 123.

needed a friend in New Orleans, wrote Sherman, he should show the note to General C. P. Stone or General J. J. Reynolds.[25]

Prison life did not suit David. When confined at 21 Rampart Street on March 1, 1864, he did not even have a place to sleep. His request to have a mattress, blankets, and a pillow sent in was immediately honored. But a petition on April 17, complaining about the noise, crowding, and lack of privacy in the prison, and asking for the freedom of the city upon signature of a parole seems not to have been successful. Three weeks later David sent an individual appeal to Colonel D. W. Killborn, commandant of prisons. He was suffering greatly from diarrhea and, although he hesitated to ask for privileges not enjoyed by all prisoners, he hoped to recover his health by spending a few hours outside the prison every day. Reminding the colonel that he had been transferred to the Department of the Gulf at his own request and through the good offices of General William T. Sherman, he also pointed out that in Natchez he had been allowed the "privilege of the [city], day and night, simply on my word of honor." Colonel Killborn returned his request with a note that permission to leave the prison had been denied by the "*Comdg.* Genl." If David needed special treatment, he could go to the hospital.[26]

By the end of May, David's health was worse and so were his relations with the Federal commandant of prisons. Now Killborn agreed to allow his prisoners some freedoms if they signed what David labeled the "*humbug* parole of No. 21 Rampart Street." When David refused to sign, Killborn responded by denying him the right to have visitors. David protested bitterly. "Your *unmanly* and *unofficerlike* treatment of myself and two others have caused us to attempt to escape," he charged. "We shall probably fail. . . . If so, we know what awaits us, but let our fate be all that cowardice, malice and revenge can command, we will meet it as becomes men and Confederate officers." David closed by promising to return good for evil as an object lesson, should Killborn

25 D. F. Boyd, signed account of capture and delivery to Natchez, Mississippi, June 15, 1864, in David Boyd Papers; David Boyd to William T. Sherman, February 13, March 2, 1864, W. T. Sherman to David F. Boyd, March 3, 1864, in Boyd Letters, Fleming Collection; W. T. Sherman to his wife, March 10, 1864, in Howe (ed.), *Home Letters of General Sherman*, 285; Sherman, *Memoirs*, 395–96.
26 D. F. Boyd to [?] Tisdale, provost sheriff, March 2, 1864, petition to C. W. Killborn, Commissary of Prisons, April 17, 1864, David Boyd to C. W. Killborn, May 8, 1864, in David Boyd Papers.

ever become his prisoner. Whether Killborn was impressed is not clear. In any case, he was about to lose a colorful correspondent. Following the Federal withdrawal from the Red River in late May of 1864, Generals Banks and Taylor proceded to carry out their agreement to exchange prisoners. By June 1, Captain David Boyd and two other officers on Taylor's staff were back in Alexandria on parole. Their exchange was considered official on July 25, 1864, when Confederate authorities at the same place turned over three officers of comparable rank to a Federal commissioner.[27]

Because he was in Federal custody between February 7 and June 1, it might be assumed that David missed one of the most significant actions of the Civil War in Louisiana, General Banks's Red River campaign of 1864. As an active participant, he did. But as an observer, David could not have been better placed. On April 14, 1864, he was aboard a Federal transport, the *Polar Star*, at Grand Ecore, Louisiana. The *Polar Star*, being used as a prison ship, had accompanied Admiral Porter's fleet from Grand Ecore toward Shreveport on April 7. As Porter worked his way slowly upstream on April 8, 9, and 10 to a point above Grand Bayou, General Richard Taylor managed to stop Banks's forces at Mansfield (April 8) and Pleasant Hill (April 9). Banks returned to Grand Ecore to regroup, and Porter, finding the water dangerously low, joined him there by April 14. David, in the midst of Porter's fleet and Banks's army, saw a chance to be of service to General Taylor. In the margins of a newspaper, he penciled a detailed account of the location and numbers of Federal gunboats, troops, and guns he had heard about or observed while aboard the *Polar Star*. A Confederate surgeon, allowed aboard the ship to treat sick prisoners, promised to deliver the paper personally to General Taylor, but he broke his promise, and Taylor did not receive the message until the night of April 19. The Confederate cause did not suffer because of the surgeon's broken faith; Taylor had been keeping abreast of Admiral Porter's movements through a specially detailed staff officer assigned to watch the river. Nevertheless, when he finally received David's communication, he ordered a copy sent to General Kirby Smith, then on his way to Arkansas.[28]

27 David Boyd to C. W. Killborn, May 27, 1864, *ibid.*; *Official Records*, Ser. II, Vol. VII, 192–93.
28 David Boyd to General R. Taylor, copy, September 14, 1875, of original dated April 14, 1864, in David Boyd Papers; Taylor, *Destruction and Reconstruction*, 176–77.

David was captured near Alexandria, Louisiana, on February 3, 1864; turned over to the Federals at Natchez, Mississippi, on February 7; delivered to New Orleans by General Sherman as of March 1, and was a prisoner on a Yankee transport at Grand Ecore by April 14. He was back in New Orleans addressing petitions and defiant letters to the Federal commandant of prisons during May, paroled and returned to Alexandria by June 1, and formally exchanged there on July 25. To locate David between February and June, 1864, is not difficult. But to explain his boat trip between April 4 and April 17 involves speculation. It is possible that the Federals, in accordance with Sherman's wishes, were trying to exchange him at the "first opportunity." What could be more convenient than to deliver him personally to his superior, General Taylor, as they carried out their invasion of northwest Louisiana? But low water and Taylor's stubborn resistance apparently altered their plans, just as they affected the course of the entire Red River campaign. Whatever the explanation, David's experience as a Federal prisoner was relatively brief and comparatively interesting. Few captives on either side managed to escape the monotony of prison life by taking a riverboat excursion; fewer still found friends and champions like William Tecumseh Sherman to look after their interests in the middle of a war.[29]

Soon after David was paroled at Alexandria, General Edmund Kirby Smith named Major General John G. Walker to replace Richard Taylor as commander of the District of West Louisiana. The change reflected formal recognition of the long-standing bitterness between Taylor and Kirby Smith. Ultimately, Taylor received orders to cross the Mississippi and assume command of the Department of Mississippi and East Louisiana. Originally he was to take as many men east with him as the Trans-Mississippi could spare. But continued bickering between Taylor and Shreveport and wholesale desertion on the part of the affected troops nullified the plan. Kirby Smith's refusal to allow Taylor to choose the staff officers who would accompany him made matters

29 W. T. Sherman to his wife, March 10, 1864, in Howe (ed.), *Home Letters of General Sherman*, 285. That David was back in New Orleans by mid-April may be deduced from two separate petitions addressed to Colonel Killborn dated May 8 and May 27, 1864. The second states that the first was written after "being here three weeks." This would indicate that David was back in New Orleans by April 17 or 18. David Boyd to C. W. Killborn, May 27, 1864, in David Boyd Papers.

even worse. Finally, Taylor crossed the river alone in the latter part of August, 1864.[30]

Disturbed by Taylor's removal, David corresponded with a friend at Department Headquarters in Shreveport about it. The friend, T. R. Heard, was clearly on Kirby Smith's side. Taylor, he thought, was "insubordinate" and "insolent" and the tool of various politicians who sought to have Kirby Smith removed so that Taylor could take his place. David was not convinced. Early in August he applied to Lieutenant Colonel H. T. Douglas, chief of engineers in the Trans-Mississippi Department, for permission to follow Taylor. This would involve resigning his commission in the engineers but, as David explained to Colonel Douglas, "He [Taylor] was my first & is now the best friend I have in the army." Although Douglas respected David's feelings, he refused to release him until a suitable replacement could be found. David tried again on August 31. This time the request was denied until the replacement, Captain C. M. Randolph, could take over David's duties as chief engineer for the District of West Louisiana. By October 1, 1864, Randolph was ready to take charge, and David was free to join Taylor if Taylor had a post for him and if Richmond approved his resignation.[31]

October passed and no word came from Taylor or Richmond. Meanwhile, Colonel Joseph L. Brent, formerly chief of ordnance and artillery on Taylor's staff, made David a tempting offer. Brent was about to be promoted and named commander of the First Louisiana Cavalry Brigade, District of West Louisiana. He would need an able assistant adjutant general and Captain David Boyd was his choice for the post. David was in something of a dilemma, but Brent offered a simple, practical solution in a note dated November 6, 1864. David should write Taylor, who would have the pending resignation disallowed in Richmond. Meanwhile, David could transfer locally to Brent's staff. If Taylor objected, Brent would acquiesce, and David could join his old commander.[32]

---

30 Winters, *Civil War in Louisiana*, 380–82; Taylor, *Destruction and Reconstruction*, 188–90, 196–97.
31 T. R. Heard to D. F. Boyd, July 7, 1864, D. F. Boyd to H. T. Douglas, August [?], 1864, H. T. Douglas to D. F. Boyd, August 9, 1864, D. F. Boyd to I. N. Galliher, August 31, 1864, C. M. Randolph to D. F. Boyd, October 1, 1864, all in David Boyd Papers.
32 H. T. Douglas to J. L. Brent, October 22, 1864, H. T. Douglas to D. F. Boyd, October 24, 27, 1864, J. L. Brent to D. F. Boyd, November 6, 1864, all *ibid*.; *Official Records*, XLI, Pt. 4, pp. 1017, 1019, 1140.

For most men, Brent's proposal would have been perfectly satisfactory. But David had reservations. In a letter of reply, he thanked General Brent for offering him such a high office, but "thinking and *feeling* it to be my duty to go to Genl Taylor I [am] determined to await his pleasure even if I sh^d sacrifice myself by such course." Sure that Taylor would be calling him soon, David offered to join Brent's staff informally, without a commission of any sort. When he received no reply he assumed that his proposal had been accepted and that Brent was still looking for a permanent appointee.

Unfortunately, Brent never received David's letter, which probably explains why David sensed a certain "misunderstanding" following an interview with the general on November 28. Characteristically, he attempted to clarify the mixup by writing another letter, this one devoted largely to a review of previous correspondence. He still thought it would be better not to join Brent's staff "formally." But to make amends for all the confusion and delay, he was prepared to follow the general's initial proposal, *i.e.*, to become Brent's assistant adjutant formally, subject to Taylor's call.

It must have been a relief to all concerned when a few weeks later General Taylor released David from any obligation. Taylor wrote that he had no openings on his staff, that there were more officers than men in his command, and that he did not expect to remain there long himself.[33]

After the Red River campaign of 1864, military operations in the Trans-Mississippi Department were confined largely to small expeditions, raids, and guerrilla activities. Desertions increased tremendously, and Jayhawkers became a serious threat as the war dragged on. In December of 1864 General Joseph Brent attempted to deal with conditions around Ville Platte and Opelousas. He and many of his staff moved to St. Landry Parish from their base at Camp LeRoy Stafford on the seminary grounds near Pineville. But little was accomplished, and by mid-January, 1865, General Brent and most of his men were back at Camp Stafford.[34]

If things were bad in Louisiana, they were even more discouraging

33 J. L. Brent to D. F. Boyd, November 6, 1864, David Boyd to J. L. Brent, November 29, 1864, Richard Taylor to D. F. Boyd, December 16, 1864, all in David Boyd Papers.
34 J. L. Brent to C. H. Mouton, December 2, 1864, F. Seip to David Boyd, January 18, 1865, *ibid.*

in other theaters of operation. From Virginia, Minerva Boyd wrote of
Yankee raids on saltworks, lead mines, and railroad bridges in and
near Wytheville. Georgia, she had heard, was "subjugated." "If Richmond falls I think the Confederacy is gone. Your father would smite
me if he thought I had expressed such an opinion even to you." Minerva
Boyd was not exaggerating. To David's remark that sentiment for reunion was growing in the West, Thomas Boyd retorted, "I would rather
die a thousand deaths myself & see every member of my family destroyed, than to unite with them again. Let us fight as long as we have
a man to die. . . . Let other states do what they may, I trust Virginia
will never again go into Union with the Yankees." Other states were
clearly ready for peace. Colonel H. T. Douglas, chief engineer on General Kirby Smith's staff, returned to Shreveport from Richmond in
March, 1865. In a letter to David he described Alabama, South Carolina,
and Georgia as "rocking and tottering" to ruin, shame, and disgrace.
Only Virginians had any "nobility," wrote Douglas, and they looked to
Louisiana and the southwest to save the Confederacy. The Trans-
Mississippi Department must overcome its "lethargy." It must not wait
till the Yankees appeared; it must press the attack.[35]

By April 19, 1865, word of Lee's surrender reached Louisiana. General Kirby Smith, hoping to continue the fight in his department, delivered a speech to his men on April 21. He urged them to "prove to the
world that your hearts have not failed in the hour of disaster" and to
"sustain the holy cause." Those who heard his appeal listened with
mixed emotions. Others had long since deserted that cause as hopeless. Meanwhile, General John Pope, Federal commander of the Division of the Missouri, offered Kirby Smith the same terms presented to
Lee at Appomattox, but Kirby Smith rejected them as inconsistent
with his sense of duty and honor. He also urged the governors of Louisiana, Texas, Arkansas, and Missouri to meet in order to decide future
policy in the department. After a conference at Marshall, Texas, on
May 13, the governors instructed Kirby Smith to disband his troops
provided the Federal authorities accepted certain conditions designed
to protect Confederate citizens and preserve public order.

While negotiations continued, desertions increased and lawless
acts multiplied. At Shreveport, Mansfield, Nachitoches, and Alexan-

35 Minerva Boyd to David Boyd, December 29, 1864, T. J. Boyd to David Boyd, December 27,
    1864, H. T. Douglas to David Boyd, March 3, 1865, all *ibid*.

dria there was extensive pillage of government stores by soldiers and civilians. Those few troops who remained at their posts were especially apprehensive. Because the country was overrun with armed deserters, they feared for the safety of their families. Learning that Confederate forces in Texas were deserting in large numbers, General Kirby Smith moved his headquarters to Houston, Texas, on May 18, 1865. There he hoped to rally the forces which remained and fight to the Rio Grande if necessary. General Simon Buckner, left in charge in Shreveport, prepared to move all troops from West Louisiana into the Lone Star State. He had already instructed his subordinates, Major General Harry Hays at Nachitoches, and Brigadier General Joseph Brent at Alexandria, to "make a show of resistance" against an expected Yankee attack along the Red River in order to cover his withdrawal.[36]

But neither Hays at Natchitoches nor Brent, on the front lines at Alexandria, had much faith in their men. Replying to Brent's private letter of May 11, Hays wrote, "It is sad to see our cause going to the devil for want of a little spirit on the part of our troops. *If they* would only fight with determination I would still be hopeful. More than hopeful—sanguine. But this I fear they will not do." A few days later Hays advised Brent, should the enemy advance on him in force, to discover what terms of surrender the Federals would accept. He authorized him to make any temporary convention he felt proper. Those officers still present in Brent's command made the same request. On May 18, in order "to save our State from further and unnecessary desolation," they urged General Brent to take immediate steps toward securing "honorable terms of capitulation."[37]

Because he had received no official instructions from General Simon Buckner and Governor Henry Watkins Allen at Shreveport, General Hays was forced to act on his own authority. In a general order he directed General Brent and two others to meet with United States authorities and to arrange terms for the surrender of Confederate troops and public property in the District of West Louisiana. A letter accompaning his formal order urged Brent to treat with the enemy before he had nothing left to surrender. His men, wrote Hays, were a "lawless

---

36 Winters, *Civil War in Louisiana*, 418–19, 421–25; Harry Hays to J. L. Brent, May 8, 11, 1865, S. B. Buckner to Harry Hays, copy, May 10, 1865, H. T. Douglas to J. L. Brent, May 11, 1865, all in David Boyd Papers.
37 Harry Hays to J. L. Brent, May 12, 17, 18, 1865, Officers' Petition to J. L. Brent, May 18, 1865, in David Boyd Papers.

mass." He hated to turn them loose on the roads with guns but he saw no other course.[38]

As assistant adjutant general, David Boyd was privy to all of General Brent's correspondence. He was also a personal friend of General Harry Hays, having served under him in Virginia. When Hays authorized Brent to surrender, David wrote his old commander a personal note of support. He assured him that to continue fighting was hopeless. "In Texas and La. the army and people are opposed to the action of Gen. Smith & Buckner," he confided. "Somehow they have been led to believe (*erroneously* I hope) that these officers are acting more for their own personal considerations than for the good of the soldiers & citizens." Pointing out that Texas did not want Louisiana troops on her soil, David expressed the fear that the Texans might retaliate by a "re-invasion of La." where people were already starving. "Do you know, General, that many families of this section [Alexandria] are forced to live on *herbs* & roots of the Earth?" he asked. "You are now called upon to save us from our misguided friends."[39]

Even the misguided friends soon saw the futility of continuing the struggle. On May 26, 1865, General Simon Buckner, acting for General Kirby Smith, surrendered the Trans-Mississippi Department to General E. R. S. Canby in New Orleans. Smith approved Buckner's act a few days later. Together with several Confederate civilian and military leaders, Buckner and Smith exiled themselves in Mexico. Several of David's acquaintances intended to join them, but he planned to remain in Louisiana. On June 5, at Alexandria, he gave his parole, and on July 19, 1865, he took the oath of allegiance to the government of the United States.[40]

---

38   Harry Hays to J. L. Brent, covering letter and General Order No. 7, May 18, 1865, *ibid.*
39   David Boyd to Harry Hays, May 18, 1865, *ibid.*
40   David Boyd to H. T. Douglas, June 5, 1865; Parole of David Boyd, June 5, 1865; Oath of Allegiance of David Boyd, July 19, 1865, *ibid.* While officially still a captain, Boyd was acting major and assistant adjutant general to General Joseph Brent, First Louisiana Cavalry Brigade at Alexandria. Winters, *Civil War in Louisiana*, 426.

Chapter IV

Taking Command

EVEN BEFORE the war ended officially in Louisiana, David was busy with plans to reopen the seminary. During the last week of June, 1865, he contacted Governor J. Madison Wells in New Orleans. Wells, a native of Rapides Parish and a Unionist, had become governor of occupied Louisiana in March, 1865, and following the Confederate surrender in May, President Andrew Johnson recognized his authority over the entire state. David wanted Governor Wells to reopen the seminary, to make him custodian of the buildings, and to fill the existing vacancies on the Board of Supervisors. He also petitioned the governor for enough money to make the seminary building habitable in time to begin classes in October. Wells responded promptly and positively. By the middle of July, David was acting superintendent and authorized to spend some $1,700 for necessary repairs.[1]

On July 26, 1865 David made his first trip to the seminary as superintendent. Finding the grounds occupied by Yankee troops and the buildings employed as a hospital, he applied to the local commander for immediate possession. But the Federals did not vacate the premises until August 16. Two years of war and occupation had taken a heavy

---

1   The money represented over $4,800 owed the seminary by the state and on deposit in the Bank of Louisiana. When converted into U.S. currency it came to $1,738 or about thirty-six cents on the dollar. David Boyd to Board of Supervisors, September 2, 1865, in Boyd Letters, Fleming Collection; Walter L. Fleming, "The Louisiana State Seminary, 1865–1869," *Louisiana State University Alumnus*, V (1909–1910), 167–68; Alexandria (La.) *Democrat*, July 26, August 23, 1865.

toll. Fences were gone, doors and windows were missing, floors were
rotting, and the roof leaked. Even worse, the library, the furniture, and
the scientific apparatus had been destroyed or carried off. In an effort
to salvage whatever he could, and with the permission of the Federal
commander, David published the following in a local paper: "NOTICE
TO ALL WHOM IT MAY CONCERN! Many persons in this vicinity are
known to have taken from the State Seminary and to have now in their
possession, furniture, books, and other property belonging to the Institution. They are respectfully asked to return the same *At Once*, and
those who have not the means of transportation will report the fact to
me. Failing to do so within ten days, their names will be furnished to
the military authorities, who will cause them to be arrested and tried
for theft. D. F. Boyd, Acting Supt. Approved by Major Gen. J. P. Haw-
kins." Whether the threat produced any results is not recorded, but
David clearly suspected local residents of pillaging the seminary, or at
least receiving stolen property. Years later, his historian son-in-law,
Walter Lynwood Fleming, gave the Yankees sole credit for vandalizing
the seminary. But a more recent account of Civil War activity in the
area attributes extensive pillage and arson to Jayhawkers and even
Confederate troops.[2]

On September 2, 1865, the seminary Board of Supervisors met at
Alexandria, Louisiana. David, whose authority as acting superintendent expired that day, was unanimously elected to fill the position permanently. He was also designated treasurer and professor of English,
ancient languages, and literature. The board created and filled four
additional professorships: Richard M. Venable, engineering, drawing,
and architecture; John A. A. West, mathematics and natural philosophy; Edward Cunningham, chemistry, minerology, and geology; and
J. P. Bellier, modern languages and literature. Classes were scheduled
to begin on October 2. In the meanwhile, based on David's minimum
estimates, the board urged Governor Wells to negotiate a loan to finance essential repairs and to purchase books and equipment.

The board also considered several reforms suggested by David in a
paper entitled "Memoranda of Facts for the Louisiana State Seminary."

2 David Boyd to Board of Supervisors, September 2, 1865, in Boyd Letters, Fleming Collection;
   Alexandria (La.) *Democrat*, August 23, 1865; Fleming, *Louisiana State University*, 117–21;
   Winters, *Civil War in Louisiana*, 328–29, 373–74. Jayhawkers were deserters, draft dodgers
   and freebooters who preyed upon anyone, regardless of political or military affiliation.

Besides proposing the creation of a preparatory department so that standards of admittance to collegiate classes could be raised the following year, David's memorandum advised a thoroughgoing revision of the curriculum, which he dismissed as "bunglingly arranged." Other suggestions concerned the school calendar, the fees and regulations, and possible sources of revenue. But the most striking of David's recommendations called for eliminating the seminary's military feature and converting the institution into the "Collegiate Dept. of the University of La." Located in New Orleans, the University of Louisiana actually consisted of law and medical departments only, but in September of 1865 neither was operating. Because David thought the war had dealt military education a "death blow," and the seminary's regulations would have to be changed as a result, he proposed the reactivation of the professional departments in the Crescent City school and the conversion of the seminary in Rapides Parish into an academic and engineering branch of the New Orleans institution. After careful deliberation, the board accepted most of David's ideas, but it would not abolish the military system or endorse a merger with the University of Louisiana.[3]

When school began on October 2, 1865, only four students and three professors were on hand. A fourth faculty member arrived two weeks later, but the fifth, Edward Cunningham, did not appear until 1870. Meanwhile, students trickled in. By the end of January, fifty-five were enrolled and more were expected. Conditions must have been spartan. An exhaustive inventory of everything on hand on opening day lists only two chamber pots. However, relief was forthcoming. Governor Wells managed to borrow $15,000 in New Orleans from a private bank, using as collateral the accrued interest of $32,000 owed by the state on the seminary's endowment fund for the years 1862–1866. This would enable the school to operate until the legislature could act, but even David's "characteristic energy and zeal" and his "judicious disbursements" could not offset the most pressing needs. In its first postwar *Report* to the General Assembly in January, 1866, the

3 Minutes of the Board of Supervisors, Louisiana State Seminary of Learning and Military Academy, September 2, 4, 1865, in president's office, Louisiana State University, Baton Rouge, Louisiana; *Report of the Board of Supervisors of the Louisiana State Seminary of Learning and Military Academy* (New Orleans, 1866), 4–7; Memoranda of Facts and Ideas for the Louisiana State Seminary, July 1, 1865, in Official Papers, Fleming Collection; Fleming, *Louisiana State University*, 130–31.

board requested $10,000 for "absolutely necessary" repairs and another $10,000 for chemical apparatus, engineering instruments, and volumes for the library. This was over and above the $32,800 interest owed by the state on the endowment fund and already pledged to secure the loan obtained by Governor Wells. The report concluded with an urgent reminder that "the Board beg the members of the General Assembly not to lose sight of the fact that [income] is in a badly depreciated currency and that the whole country is run wild in prices of labor, materials, provisions, freights and everything else."[4]

The future of the seminary, like that of all state supported institutions, was inextricably bound up with political developments as Reconstruction unfolded in Louisiana. The presidential phase was already well advanced when David became superintendent of the seminary in 1865. As early as December, 1863, President Lincoln put forward his "ten per cent" plan for restoring seceded states. It extended federal recognition to any state government set up by one-tenth or more of the number of persons who had voted in the election of 1860. General Nathaniel P. Banks, Federal commander of the Department of the Gulf, ordered an election of state officers in February, 1864, and Michael Hahn, Bavarian-born but long a resident of Louisiana, together with J. Madison Wells, a Unionist from Rapides Parish who had gone behind Federal lines in 1862, became governor and lieutenant governor respectively. A second election in March, 1864, chose delegates to a convention charged with revising the states's constitution, and six months later the altered document was ratified at a third election which also selected representatives to the General Assembly. By October, 1864, Louisiana's first "free-state" legislature began deliberations. Its political character, like that of the convention, was decidedly Unionist.

The political picture changed profoundly by May, 1865, because of the end of the war, the assassination of Abraham Lincoln, and, especially, the proclamation by President Andrew Johnson of a general amnesty for all those taking an oath of allegiance to support the United States. Within months Louisiana's limited and formerly Unionist electorate was greatly expanded by the addition of newly eligible conservative and former Confederate voters. Responding nimbly, Governor J.

4 *Report* of the Board of Supervisors, 1866, pp. 4–30; Fleming, *Louisiana State University*, 132–33, 143.

Madison Wells (who assumed the office following Michael Hahn's election to the United States Senate) ordered a registration for an election of state officials in November, 1865, and to maintain harmony, the dominant faction of Democrats decided to keep him at the head of the ticket. Predictably, the resulting General Assembly was strongly Democratic.

Meanwhile, chaotic labor conditions and certain operations of the Freedmen's Bureau outraged many Louisiana planters who clamored for legislative action to regulate relations between employers and their former slaves. Governor Wells advised caution, but the lawmakers ignored him, moving instead to enact a number of bills which, from their point of view, would restore economic and social stability to the state. To many northern newspapers and congressional critics, however, these measures and others like them in other southern states, represented nothing more than an attempt to reverse the results of the war.[5]

While Louisiana solons worked to restore "stability" during the winter of 1865–1866, President Andrew Johnson and Radicals in Congress engaged in a duel which would soon take the major issue of Reconstruction—control over the emancipated blacks—out of the hands of conservative state officials. In January, 1866, section seven of the second Freedman's Bureau bill extended military authority to all cases involving freedmen whose rights were denied by local law, custom, or prejudice. The president vetoed the bill, and the Radicals, unable to overrule him, responded with the Civil Rights Act, a much more far-reaching measure which conferred citizenship on the freedman, gave United States courts jurisdiction over cases involving violation of any citizen's civil rights, outlawed discriminatory local legislation, and authorized the president to enforce the act with military and naval power. Charging Congress with an unlawful attempt to control matters reserved by the Constitution to the states, President Johnson vetoed the civil rights bill on March 27. With Radical and conservative Republicans now united over the civil rights issue, Congress overrode

5 Germaine Memelo, "The Development of State Laws Concerning the Negro in Louisiana, 1864–1900" (M.A. thesis, Louisiana State University, 1956), 1–6, 15–27. For detailed and somewhat dated (and biased) accounts of Reconstruction in Louisiana, see John Rose Ficklen, *History of Reconstruction in Louisiana Through 1868* (Baltimore, 1910), and Ella Lonn, *Reconstruction in Louisiana After 1868* (New York, 1918). The most recent work to appear is Joe Gray Taylor, *Louisiana Reconstructed* (Baton Rouge, 1974). Chapters 2 and 3 deal in detail with developments in Louisiana politics, economics, and race relations between 1863 and 1867, when military Reconstruction was instituted by Congress.

the veto, and shortly thereafter, on April 30, 1866, it entertained resolutions proposing the Fourteenth Amendment. Section one essentially
restated the Civil Rights Act, and as Thaddeus Stevens candidly
remarked, placed that law beyond the power of a later Congress to
repeal.[6]

The Fourteenth Amendment was submitted to the states in June,
1866. Having already adjourned, Louisiana's legislators would not
consider it until their next regular session in January, 1867. By that
time Governor Wells was thoroughly at odds with the more conservative General Assembly. He labeled the proposed amendment "just and
proper" and advised speedy ratification. But the legislators, many of
whom had been prominent in the Confederate army or government,
voted unanimously against it. Section three would bar them from holding office unless pardoned by a two-thirds vote of each house of Congress. More odious still from their point of view, the amendment appeared to bestow the suffrage on their former slaves.[7]

During the summer of 1866, Louisiana provided congressional
Republicans with one more argument for a sterner Reconstruction
policy: a race riot. In an attempt to give freedmen the vote and to assure themselves of state office, an alliance of Louisiana Unionists and
Radicals tried to reconvene the 1864 constitutional convention in New
Orleans. Federal troops were present in the city but had no orders from
the War Department to intervene in case of trouble; city officials,
known to be hostile to the planned gathering, were expected to maintain order. As a procession of blacks marched toward the convention
site, thereby setting off a series of confrontations with white citizens
and the city police, the shooting started. When it was over thirty-four
black and three white citizens lay dead. One hundred and nineteen
Negroes and seventeen whites suffered wounds, and police losses to-
taled one killed and ten injured.[8]

The New Orleans riot, the election of former Confederates to high
office, the enactment of the Black Codes, and the South's overwhelm-

---

6 Eric L. McKitrick, *Andrew Johnson and Reconstruction* (Chicago, 1960), Chapter 10; Kenneth M. Stampp, *The Era of Reconstruction, 1865–1877* (New York, 1965), Chapter 4.
7 Memelo, "State Laws Concerning the Negro in Louisiana," 33–36.
8 Ficklen, *History of Reconstruction*, 169; J. G. Randall and David Donald, *The Civil War and
   Reconstruction* (Boston, 1961), 587–88. A good recent summary of events contributing and
   subsequent to the riot is included in Taylor, *Louisiana Reconstructed*, 103–13.

ing rejection of the Fourteenth Amendment convinced many moderate and conservative as well as Radical congressmen that blacks were unsafe in the former slave states. Northern voters apparently agreed. Following the hard-fought election campaign of 1866, Republicans controlled more than two-thirds of the seats in each house of Congress. President Johnson's Reconstruction policy was repudiated and Congress proceeded to pass a series of strong measures designed to coerce the South. Collectively, these laws returned the South to military rule. They required the states to frame new constitutions providing for Negro suffrage, but disqualifying former Confederate leaders from voting or holding office; required ratification of the Fourteenth Amendment before a state could be represented in Congress; empowered the military commanders in each district to begin a registration of voters, including blacks, so that suitable constitutions could be adopted without delay; and vested the power of appointment and removal in the military commander of each district whereas before it had been the president's prerogative.[9]

Reduced to five military districts, each under the command of a prominent Union general, the ten former Confederate states still not represented in Congress saw their presidentially recognized civil governments set aside and martial law imposed. Initially, General Philip Sheridan commanded the Fifth District composed of Louisiana and Texas, but his policies concerning voter registration and the removal of civil officials stirred up such an outcry that Washington soon removed him in favor of General Winfield Scott Hancock. In September, 1867, Louisiana voters, black and white, chose delegates to a constitutional convention. Equally divided by race, the members assembled in New Orleans where they labored for three and a half months before producing a document that the voters approved in April, 1868. State officials were elected at the same time. Henry Clay Warmoth and Oscar J. Dunn, a black, became governor and lieutenant governor, and Congress, finally satisfied that Louisiana was sufficiently reconstructed, voted to seat her representatives, subject only to the state's ratification of the Fourteenth Amendment. All the obstacles had been hurdled; now Louisiana voters could go the polls prepared

9   Randall and Donald, *Civil War and Reconstruction*, 589–91, 595–600; Lonn, *Reconstruction in Louisiana*, 4–5.

to make their contribution to the narrow popular vote victory General U. S. Grant managed to secure in the presidential election of 1868.[10]

It was against this background of political, economic, and social upheaval that David Boyd sought to reopen and revitalize the Louisiana State Seminary of Learning. As already indicated in the report submitted by the board to the General Assembly in January, 1866, the seminary's first and most pressing need was money. To secure it, David went to New Orleans immediately after Christmas, 1865, to plead with the lawmakers. There he embarked upon a second career, lobbying, that lasted as long as he was associated with the school. Indeed, lobbying often absorbed more of his time and effort than his official duties as superintendent and professor. Successful in his first venture among the politicians, David proclaimed on his return to the piney woods in March, 1866, that the "existence & complete success of the Seminary sh^d now be considered a final fact."[11]

David was unduly optimistic. By 1867 the political picture was cloudier than ever, and Louisiana's conservative legislators, uncertain as to what lay ahead, made two-year appropriations for all state institutions, thus insuring the seminary some income until 1869. But well before then the Radical press in New Orleans began to attack the school as a hotbed of unregenerate rebels. In August, 1867, the New Orleans *Republican* printed a series of letters signed "Loyalist" which labeled the seminary "an enclave of the Confederacy." Instead of reflecting "the new order of ideas—one common country, and freedom and equality to all," the institution was a "stronghold of rebel spirit and resistance." Secessionists served on the Board; former rebel soldiers or their sons comprised the student body, and four former Confederate majors made up the academic staff. And, "as if the spite was not sting-

---

10 Garnie William McGinty, *History of Louisiana* (New York, 1949), 211–12; Randall and Donald, *Civil War and Reconstruction*, 618–19, 620, 640; E. Merton Coulter, *The South During Reconstruction, 1865–1877* (Baton Rouge, 1947), 132–38. U. S. Grant did not need Louisiana's electoral vote to win the presidency in 1868, so the vote for Seymour in that state, clearly the result of intimidation, was not seriously challenged. As Taylor makes clear, the only way the state vote could possibly go to Seymour was for every possible Democrat to vote and for large numbers of blacks to stay home or be counted Democratic. The popular vote in the presidential race in Louisiana was tallied at 80,225 for Seymour and 33,225 for Grant. *Louisiana Reconstructed*, 161–73.

11 David Boyd to the students and faculty of Louisiana State Seminary, March 15, 1866, in Official Papers, Fleming Collection.

ing enough, the pirate Raphael Semmes was added . . . in derision of all decency, as professor of moral philosophy."[12]

"Loyalist" followed up his first letter with a second on August 11, 1867. This one outlined the history of the seminary, charging that fire-eating politicians, "maddened by the venom of secession," distorted congressional intent and acted treacherously when they established a combination seminary of learning and military academy. "Well might the supervisors place with their left hand the often quoted inscription: 'By the Liberality of the General Government, the Union, *Esto perpetua*' over the portal of the Seminary while their right hand displayed the dagger that was to murder the Union," declared the outraged "Loyalist." He ended by praising former professor Vallas for having been the only obstacle in the path of the rebel elements at the seminary during 1860–1861.[13]

Finally, a third letter from "Loyalist" accused the seminary's founders of establishing the school in Rapides Parish in order to protect their sons from contact with humble mechanics, tradesmen, and abolitionist sentiment. Logically, argued "Loyalist," the funds to set up the school should have been used to create a collegiate department of the University of Louisiana in New Orleans. But the "lords of the soil, the lords of cotton and sugar," preferred to locate it in the "fire-eating regions of the Red River . . . in the parish of Rapides, the chief seat of gambling, drunkeness and chivalrous rowdyism." The site chosen was too close to Alexandria for the "morals of the place." In a closing shot, which implied that the seminary was some sort of pastoral brothel, "Loyalist" declared, "We have heard of caravans of ladies invading the seminary, assisting to the drill, importuning the faculty for frequent hops, and even of their spending nights within the sacred precincts of this temple of science. We have heard officers charging one another with keeping a disorderly house, and female neighbors fighting for the privilege of being regarded as the favorites of the place." If, in fact, the women of Rapides, singly or in caravans, spent many nights within the

---

12 Fleming, *Louisiana State University*, 142–43; Letter to the editor signed "Loyalist," New Orleans *Republican*, August 10, 1867. "Loyalist" sometimes signed himself "Loyalty." The first term is used here throughout. By the time "Loyalist" wrote his letter, Admiral Semmes had been gone for four months. His tenure at the seminary lasted some eight weeks. Early in March, 1867, he resigned to edit a newspaper in Memphis. Alexandria (La.) *Democrat*, March 13, 1867.

13 Letter to the editor signed "Loyalist," New Orleans *Republican*, August 11, 1867.

"sacred precincts" of the seminary, they must have been a hardy lot.
The cadets slept on the floor until 1886.[14]

The attacks of "Loyalist" did not go unchallenged. The Louisiana
Democrat, an Alexandria paper, remembered sarcastically that the
prewar "aiders and abettors of Treason" at the seminary consisted of
men like Generals William T. Sherman and G. Mason Graham, the latter the "most uncompromising Union man in the South till hostilities
had actually begun." As for Dr. Vallas, the *Democrat* recalled that "said
loyal Doctor used to preach secession in his class-room and altogether
blew the loudest 'secesh' horn in these parts till his treachery to and
sudden desertion from the Southern cause in 1861." "Loyalist," the paper concluded, must be counted a "fool or a knave, or perhaps both."
Charges of immoral conduct at the seminary were probably not taken
seriously by even the most ardent Radicals. But "Loyalist's" attacks on
the school and its management because of its frankly Confederate
character were certainly well founded. David's first academic board
was indeed composed of "four rebel majors"—himself, R. M. Venable,
J. A. A. West, and Edward Cunningham. They were soon outranked,
as "Loyalist" noted, when Admiral Raphael Semmes joined the faculty
in January, 1867. What "Loyalist" did not know was that David also
tried unsuccessfully in 1866 to hire General Joseph Wheeler and Mat-
thew Fontaine Maury, the famous ocenographer and Confederate tor-
pedo expert.[15]

Members of the seminary board were just as "unreconstructed" as
the faculty. At least one supervisor, Bartholomew Egan, emphatically
drew the line at what "Loyalist" called "the new order of ideas—one
common country, and freedom and equality to all." Speaking at commencement exercises in June, 1866, Dr. Egan declared that slavery
was dead and he would not restore it if he could. But, he cried, "God
has never designed for them, [the freedmen] and we can never concede to them, political or social equality. Never! Never!" Two years
later, in August, 1868, board member G. Mason Graham was equally
adamant. In his reply to a prospective professor he wrote, "We of the
school are frankly a white man's party, and negrophilists [*sic*], or those

14   *Ibid.*, August 24, 1867; Fleming, *Louisiana State University*, 458–59.
15   Alexandria (La.) *Democrat*, August 21, November 28, 1866; Fleming *Louisiana State Uni-
     versity*, 132; Bartholomew Egan to David Boyd, November 20, 1866, in Alphabetical File,
     Fleming Collection; D. F. Boyd to S. B. Robinson, November 13, 1866, in David Boyd Papers.

in sympathy with them, can find no favor in our eyes." Describing himself as the Negro's friend, Graham wrote that he would uphold the black man in "all civil rights, but never in Political and Social Equality . . . and this . . . is the general feeling of the gentlemen here."[16]

One feature of the seminary that rendered it potentially vulnerable to political pressure was the beneficiary system. "Beneficiaries" were cadets who received a seminary education at state expense. When the school began operation, the state supported only sixteen beneficiary cadets. The rest paid their own tuition and board. But very shortly the legislature increased the number of beneficiaries to fifty-eight. By 1867, just before Congressional Reconstruction began in Louisiana, the lawmakers raised the number to ninety-eight and agreed to appropriate $400 each for their support. Because state-supported cadets comprised so much of the seminary student body (and brought in such a large part of its revenue), and because parish police juries or, in New Orleans, the district school board, designated state cadets, some feared that black youth would be sent to the seminary if Negroes won control of local government. R. M. Lusher, a former state superintendent of education, a member of the seminary board, and, later, a director of the Peabody fund in Louisiana, was convinced that Radical politicians meant to win control of the seminary and integrate its student body. He informed David in August, 1867, of a Radical political meeting at which Anthony Vallas urged the new "mixed" school board of New Orleans to set aside the list of beneficiaries named by their predecessors. "You can readily infer, therefore, to what the 'Prof.' aspires—the Superintendence of Negro Cadets! Cannot your friend Sherman crush him?" Lusher advised David to have his accounts in order in case the "vandals" seized the school.[17]

Lusher's pessimism concerning Radical intentions was shared by many friends and creditors of the seminary. Stationer James A. Gresham of New Orleans wrote David of his fears while the Radical constitutional convention was in session in the Crescent City. But David thought Gresham took the convention's threats too seriously. The dele-

16 Commencement Address by Dr. Bartholomew Egan, Louisiana State Seminary and Military Academy, June 29, 1866, in Printed Materials, David Boyd Papers; G. Mason Graham to F. V. Hopkins, August 4, 1868, in G. Mason Graham Letters, Fleming Collection; New Orleans *Republican*, August 10, 1867.
17 Fleming, *Louisiana State University*, 27–28, 140, 152; R. M. Lusher to David Boyd, August 30, 1867, in Alphabetical File, Fleming Collection.

gates were "merely making bloody laws; what about the carrying out?" In any case, David doubted that the federal government would support extremism in the states. Congress, he predicted, "will show weakness in the knees" and "the Republican Party cannot carry the north at the next Presidential election if it holds to the Military bill for Southern reconstruction."

Another New Orleans firm, Swarbrick and Company, manifested its uneasiness about the future by shutting off the seminary's credit in the fall of 1867. Even worse, it published the fact in various newspapers around the state. Because Swarbrick was the school's oldest and largest supplier, its action must have disturbed David considerably. Nevertheless, he responded calmly by delivering Swarbrick's manager, J. D. Kenton, a mild lecture on the firm's bad business judgment. By denying the school credit and publishing the fact locally, he argued, Swarbrick merely advertised its own financial instability and pessimism about things to come. If the seminary were liquidated, Swarbrick, as the largest creditor, would be the first to get its money. But, David concluded, the longer the school operated, the better chance Swarbrick and everybody else would have to recover the full amount due them. Meanwhile, the school would cheerfully pay cash.[18]

Privately, David was more disturbed about the seminary's future than his letters to Swarbrick and Gresham indicated. Late in November, 1867, he wrote to Major W. A. Freret, a New Orleans engineer and member of the Board of Supervisors, asking for as much information about political developments as the major could supply. David doubted that the school would be interfered with "except by due process of law growing out of the new constitution." Meanwhile, he hoped that General Winfield S. Hancock, administrator of the Fifth Military District, would act "conservatively." The seminary, he told Freret, had "enough trouble getting along without Radical interference."

The "trouble" to which David referred was financial. As already indicated, the bulk of the seminary's income came from state appropriations, state support of the beneficiary cadets, and the annual interest on the school's endowment fund. All were paid in the form of state warrants, not cash. Because political and economic conditions were so unstable in 1867–1868, the warrants almost never brought more than

18 David Boyd to James A. Gresham, November 24, 1867, David Boyd to J. D. Kenton, November 25, 1867, in David Boyd Letterbooks.

two-thirds of their face value when converted to currency. Of $100,000 appropriated for 1867–1868, the seminary realized only $68,179. To secure even that amount required herculean efforts by David in his extracurricular roles as lobbyist and broker. In less than a year he made three trips to New Orleans for the purpose of obtaining and cashing state warrants for the seminary. One trip, made shortly after military authorities suspended civil government in the state, was especially frustrating. David wrote a New Orleans creditor in November, 1867, that he hated to return to the city "to continue my drudgery of last summer: the honoring of the State's warrants." But in December another $8,000 would be due. "Oh, if they cld be cashed in greenbacks, what a happy man I'd be."[19]

The December trip was not entirely "drudgery." In addition to cashing warrants for sixty-five cents on the dollar, David managed to do some personal shopping and to attend the theater. Three months later, in March, 1868, he was back in the Crescent City. This time, with the help of James Gresham, the school's stationer, and a New Orleans board member, W. C. Black, David cashed warrants for seventy cents on the dollar. He also managed to secure the school's annuity for 1867 but did not cash it because he could not get favorable terms. On his return to Alexandria he wrote the board's vice-president, W. L. Sanford, that he thought the school could "hobble along" financially until the end of the term.[20]

Louisiana voters went to the polls to ratify the newly completed Radical state constitution and to select state officers on April 17 and 18, 1868. David was glad to see how hard Rapides citizens were working for the election of non-Radicals. But he doubted that Robert M. Lusher, a seminary board member and a conservative candidate for state superintendent of public education, could defeat his Radical opponent, the Reverend T. W. Conway. "However," he wrote Vice-President Sanford on election day, "I have a presentiment that the Seminary will not be interfered with, if we have anything of fair legislation." Clearly the board did not share David's complacency. On May 16, 1868, they closed a meeting in New Orleans with the following resolution, "As the Board of Supervisors of the Lou[a] State Seminary of Learning

19   David Boyd to W. H. Freret, November 27, 1867, David Boyd to James A. Gresham, November 24, 1867, *ibid.*; Fleming, *Louisiana State University*, 142–45.
20   David Boyd to W. L. Sanford, April 16, 1868, in David Boyd Letterbooks.

and Military Academy . . . is about to adjourn, it may be to meet no more, We the assembled thereof are not willing to do so without having on record some token of our sense of what is due to Colonel D. F. Boyd by this Board, and by the people of the State of Louisiana, for the clear manner in which he has acquitted himself in the discharge of all the various and arduous duties of his different and combined positions of Superintendent, Treasurer and Professor."[21]

The Board of Supervisors despaired too quickly. It was true that carpetbaggers, scalawags, and blacks would soon control the state. It was also true that Louisiana was about to begin a period of political and economic turmoil from which she would not emerge for many years. But for four and one-half of those years, or until 1873, the school did not fare too badly. In many ways, it enjoyed more generous state support and less political interference than it had before the Radicals took over, and certainly more than it would after a more parsimonious and "business oriented" state government resumed control in 1877.

The reasons are many. For one thing, the seminary was too far out of the mainstream—New Orleans—to interest the politicians. David realized this as early as November, 1867, when he informed a New Orleans friend that he thought it wise to stay away from the city in order to avoid attracting Radical attention to the institution. Another reason for the seminary's relative security was the presence of effective defenders in the legislature, even after Radicals won control of state government in 1868. One of them, Dr. J. C. Egan, represented the Twentieth Senatorial District. Egan, who was David's friend and the son of board member Dr. Bartholomew Egan, wrote an account thirty-five years later in which he described the legislative horsetrading by which conservatives, Radicals, and Negroes managed to subvert the intent of the constitution of 1868. The Radical constitution did not mention the seminary by name, but two articles relative to state-supported institutions of learning were certainly applicable. Article 135 outlawed discrimination in any educational facility established by the state and prohibited the creation of any school for the sole use of one race. Article 142 authorized state establishment of a university in New Orleans provided it did not discriminate among its students on any grounds other

21 Memorandum Book, 1867–68, in MS Volumes, David Boyd Papers; David Boyd to W. L. Sanford, April 16, 1868, in David Boyd Letterbook; Minutes of the Board of Supervisors, May 16, 1868.

than ability. The trick was to observe the letter if not the spirit of the constitution. As Dr. Egan recalled it, "all true people" of Louisiana wanted to provide schools for both races "without bringing upon us the untoward consequences which would follow an attempt at mixed schools." Only the most doctrinaire, like state Superintendent of Public Education T. W. Conway, insisted upon integration. In the legislative session of 1868 Conway submitted a bill which would place all state-established and incorporated institutions under state control, require integration in all public schools, and make attendance compulsory. The bill died in committee. A similar Conway-sponsored bill passed the next year, but its administrative features made it unworkable and Governor Warmoth asked the legislature to frame a new law. In March of 1870, a public education bill was finally enacted. Egan described it as a compromise because, he claimed, it had been carefully designed to provide that "one or more public schools shall be taught in each district," with the distinct understanding that one would be set up for whites and one for blacks. Furthermore, the law left the seminary under the control of its own Board of Supervisors by not granting control over it to the superintendent of public education. To complete the deal, according to Egan, another act passed in 1870 appropriated $35,000 to Straight University, which was exclusively black. In his words, "By assisting the colored people in all their enterprises presented for our support, we finally secured their cooperation *in voting on all measures* for our own race without conflict or clash."[22]

Finally, the seminary managed to escape political interference during the first years of Reconstruction precisely because it played politics so well. In the summer of 1868 David made two trips to New Orleans in order to discover what effect the state's Radical administration might have on the seminary. He came away convinced that Governor Warmoth and Superintendent of Education Conway had no plans to interfere with the operation of the school. Governor Warmoth particu-

22 Fleming, *Louisiana State University*, 153–56; David Boyd to James A. Gresham, November 24, 1867, in David Boyd Letterbooks; Constitution of Louisiana, 1868, pp. 26–27; J. C. Egan, Appendix to Gunby, "Life and Services of David French Boyd," 31–33. For a full discussion of race and the public schools in Louisiana during Reconstruction, see William Preston Vaughan, *Schools For All: The Blacks & Public Education in the South, 1865–1877* (Louisville, Ky., 1974), 78–102, 104–104, and Roger A. Fischer, *The Segregation Struggle in Louisiana 1862–77* (Urbana, Ill., 1974), 88–132.

larly impressed him as being very favorably disposed toward it.[23] But David was practical enough to realize that some gesture of political accommodation might provide the seminary with additional insurance against future interference. While in New Orleans he met and talked with Dr. Francis V. Hopkins, a native of New England and a Republican. Hopkins had been teaching for years in the New Orleans high school, but because the legislature was considering Superintendent Conway's "mixed school" bill, he was afraid he would soon be out of a job. Having heard that a vacancy existed at the seminary, he applied for the position by letter, included his credentials, and mentioned several prominent Radical politicians as references. His letter also inquired about the board members in great detail and seemed to suggest that if Governor Warmoth named a new board, he (Hopkins) might be considered for superintendent.

David, to whom Hopkins sent his letter, understood perfectly. He submitted the application to the board for its consideration and, in a covering letter to Vice-President W. L. Sanford, advised that Hopkins be appointed. It might be "prudent," he wrote, to elect Hopkins professor of chemistry as the "cheapest way" to placate the Radicals. Acting for the board, G. Mason Graham wrote Hopkins in the most candid terms. Seminary administrators had always sought to keep politics out of the school. But now their "head is in the lion's mouth." They might have to exercise a little "policy." If the board could secure some "qualified gentleman of conservative and liberal views" on the faculty, or on the board, and if the gentleman were a Republican, it might be the "right thing to do." Hopkins responded that he shared Graham's sentiments, and a few days later his appointment was announced in an Alexandria newspaper.[24]

Throughout his administration Governor Warmoth manifested in numerous ways the good will he had for the state seminary. When

---

23   If Warmoth had no plans to "interfere" with the seminary, Superintendent of Public Education Conway certainly did. He tried repeatedly to bring the institution under his jurisdiction but despite his friendship with the governor, who did not share his equalitarian views, never succeeded. Fischer, *Segregation Struggle in Louisiana*, 105–107.
24   David Boyd to F. V. Hopkins, August 3, 1868, David Boyd to W. L. Sanford, August 6, 1868, in David Boyd Letterbooks; G. Mason Graham to F. V. Hopkins, August 4, 1868, in G. Mason Graham Letters, Fleming Collection; Fleming, *Louisiana State University*, 152; Alexandria (La.) *Democrat*, August 12, 1868. By 1869, it apparently became good "policy" to make another concession. Harry Lott, a black Radical legislator from Rapides was added to the Board of Supervisors as one of the three members eligible to serve from that parish. *Report* of the Board of Supervisors for 1869.

vacancies occurred on the board of supervisors, he filled them with people suggested by seminary officials. When the legislature considered seminary appropriations, he urged that they be generous. When Radicals attempted to send black cadets to the seminary, he dissuaded them lest they break up the school. Finally, when he reported to the legislature on the condition of the seminary, he praised the academic board for its "zeal, energy and fidelity" and the superintendent for his carefully and competently prepared reports. David appreciated the governor's interest. Shortly after their first meeting he made a comment which aptly summarized relations between the Statehouse and the seminary until 1873: "So far as my self-respect would admit, I have been conciliatory and courteous to the Radical leaders which may possibly have something to do with their conciliatory course towards us. A little politeness does not cost much, and often brings a rich return."[25]

The good will of Governor Warmoth and the relatively liberal appropriations by the Radical legislature certainly made David's task as superintendent more pleasant. But the institution's perennial problem, lack of income, continued to be his major concern. In his annual report for 1866, David suggested at least two methods by which the seminary might balance its books. First, the legislature could increase the number of beneficiary cadets and the amount appropriated for their support. Second, the state could apply for the grant provided under the Morrill Act of July, 1862. The Morrill Act made the proceeds from the sale of federally owned public lands available to the states for the purpose of establishing agricultural and mechanical colleges. If the Morrill funds were added to the seminary endowment, and the seminary became the nucleus for the proposed agricultural and mechanical college, the institution would be considerably less dependent on "the uncertainty of annual Legislative aid."[26]

In 1867 most of David's proposals became law, but the legislators adjourned before the bill to confer the agricultural and mechanical funds on the seminary achieved final passage. David was undismayed. In his annual report, he pressed strongly for the fund on the grounds that it would be foolish for the state to duplicate educational facilities.

25 Fleming, *Louisiana State University*, 158–59; *Report* of the Board of Supervisors for 1868, p. 8; Alexandria (La.) *Democrat*, January 13, 1869; David Boyd to S. O. Scruggs, August 23, 1868, in David Boyd Letterbooks.
26 *Report* of the Board of Supervisors for 1866, pp. 4, 14.

The seminary already had buildings, professors, laboratory equipment, and a library. Besides, he pointed out, all the northern and western states with few exceptions, had bestowed the Morrill grant on existing institutions. David's plea made sense to Governor Warmoth too but the legislature was not impressed. Ten years of heartbreaking struggle would pass before the agricultural fund was finally secured by the state university.[27]

Circumstances forced David to cast about for other possible sources of income. In 1867 an American-born English banker, George Peabody, set up a fund of $3 million for the purpose of promoting education in the South. The philanthropist appointed a board of trustees who in turn selected Barnas Sears, president of Brown University, to administer the fund. David made several efforts to obtain Peabody money for the seminary, but Dr. Sears did not think the school was eligible for a grant. David disagreed. Peabody funds were to be used for teacher training or "normal" schools, he pointed out, and the seminary's beneficiary cadets were required by law to teach two years following graduation. Again he appealed to the Peabody trustees, but again his request was denied.

In April, 1868, David tried a new approach. He asked Dr. Sears for a loan from the Peabody fund, offering seminary annuity warrants as collateral. All of their previous correspondence, David wrote Sears, convinced him that the seminary could not hope for a grant. It would do no good to put forward the same arguments, however excellent they might be. But the school needed money at once. Could it not obtain a loan until political conditions settled down and its warrants could be cashed more advantageously? Then, in a characteristic burst of frankness which probably did little to advance his case, David pointed out to Sears that the Peabody fund and the seminary sought the same ends— the education of indigent youth to be teachers:

You have a preference for 'Normal Schools.' We are as much a Normal School in every respect but the name (which I don't like, and hope we will never bear) as you can possibly build up in the South-west. Not *one* young man out of any five, educated at your Normal Schools will teach longer than *three* years in this country; nor can you expect them to remain teachers, when other callings are so much more lucrative. As to 'Normal Methods' of teaching, I beg leave most

27   *Ibid.*, 1867, pp. 6, 12.

respectfully, to say that it is best to leave every educated man of good sense and discretion to adopt his own method. Too many men, in my humble judgement, are allowed to teach school who have no *common sense*; for them only is a 'method' needed in, as well as *out*, of a school room.[28]

David did not expect much from Sears but a month later, in May, 1868, Robert M. Lusher became subagent of the Peabody fund in Louisiana. After contacting Sears, Lusher told David he could award $1,000 to the seminary if the school would create a "Normal Department." David responded bitterly. It took six pages for him to tell Lusher what he thought of "the *useless* & *objectionable* conditions" proposed by Dr. Sears. "What earthly good," demanded David scornfully, "could come of a *lecture* once a week or once a month on the subject of *school teaching?*" He was glad that the seminary did not indulge in such "*superficial* talk." Later David forwarded the Sears proposal to the Board of Supervisors but recommended that it be rejected.[29]

David became superintendent of the seminary in 1865. He would serve, with the exception of four years, until 1886. But by 1869, when fire destroyed the building and forced the school to move to Baton Rouge, the broad outlines of his administrative style were already emerging. First, he was totally immersed in his many-faceted job. At the seminary he was officially professor, treasurer, and superintendent. Less formally he was clerk, chief disciplinary officer, and sometimes even steward. When the legislature met he went to New Orleans. There, besides acting as the seminary's purchasing agent, he also served as its lobbyist and broker for its securities. Not surprisingly, he asked the Board of Supervisors to relieve him of the treasurership and part of his professorial responsibilities very early in his tenure. But two years later, in 1868, he was still "teaching 4 hours a day—such classes as Calculus, Analytical Geometry, Advanced Algebra & Virgil, together with my duties as Sup't *et.c.*" It was, he wrote a friend, "too much."[30]

Another characteristic which appeared early in David's administrative career was his tendency to draft very ambitious programs for the

28   Francis Butler Simkins, *A History of the South* (New York, 1953), 364; Coulter, *The South During Reconstruction*, 327–28; *Report* of the Board of Supervisors for 1867, pp. 12–13; David Boyd to Barnas Sears, April 17, 1868, in David Boyd Letterbooks.
29   Robert M. Lusher to David Boyd, May 7, 1868, in Alphabetical File, Fleming Collection; David Boyd to the Board of Supervisors, April 18, 1868, David Boyd to Robert M. Lusher, June 1, 1868, in David Boyd Letterbooks.
30   *Report* of the Board of Supervisors for 1866, p. 9; David Boyd to Robert M. Lusher, June 1, 1868, in David Boyd Letterbooks.

expansion of the institution. The seminary ended its first postwar session with five professors and 108 cadets. But even before summer recess the board named four additional professors for the coming academic year on David's recommendation. Commenting on the appointments and the seminary's prospects, a local paper boasted, "The Academic Board . . . is not excelled in ability by any other Faculty of the same size on the continent. With such an institution holding forth such inducements, we cannot see why parents should send their children abroad for Education." The same journal reported 150 students present in November, 1866, and more expected. Its editor endorsed the hiring of more faculty and promised the construction of more facilities if that proved necessary.[31]

David certainly shared the newspaper's enthusiasm, if indeed he was not its source. He expected the seminary to become "the University of the Southwest" and with that in mind, persuaded the Board of Supervisors to appoint Admiral Raphael Semmes and General Joseph Wheeler to the academic board. When Semmes accepted, the local editor was ecstatic. "A thrill of satisfaction must naturally follow the announcement of the valuable acquisition to the faculty," he commented. "As Washington College may now boast of its Lee, the pride and admiration of the Confederate Army, so may the Louisiana State Seminary now boast of its Semmes, the subject of eulogy wherever daring deeds and mighty achievements upon ocean's treacherous flood are made the theme of either song or story."[32]

When David composed his annual report to the Board of Supervisors late in 1866, he commented proudly on the seminary's growth during that year, particularly that of its academic board, which he pronounced "the *largest* and among the ablest academic faculties in the South." The student body too, had increased markedly, totaling 164 as of January 1, 1867. Unfortunately, by the time the report went to the printer in March, the situation had begun to deteriorate. Because of two deaths, eleven dismissals and twenty-one resignations, only 130 cadets remained. At the "present rate of maintenance cost per cadet,"

31   Alexandria (La.) *Democrat*, June 20, November 14, 28, 1866.
32   Minutes of the Executive Committee of the Board of Supervisors, October 24, 28, 1866; David Boyd to S. B. Robinson, November 13, 1866, in David Boyd Papers; Alexandria (La.) *Democrat*, December 19, 1866. The optimism and the prose style in the *Democrat's* references to the seminary are so familiar that one suspects David added part-time journalism to all his other duties.

David estimated, the seminary would finish the spring term some $3,500 in the red. The only way it could break even was to increase enrollment to 200 by July, 1867, and that was unlikely. Therefore, unless the legislature acted quickly, David would have to reduce the staff. He left it to the board to decide whether this could be done "without injustice" before the close of the session.[33]

The 1866 *Report*, while illustrating some of David's best qualities as an educational administrator, also points up some of his serious shortcomings. He was ambitious, farseeing, and intent upon securing the best faculty and facilities for the seminary. But he often tried to accomplish too much, too soon, given the state's financial limitations and the public's lack of support for what David called a "college of the first grade." Besides overstaffing in 1866, David probably spent too much on plant and equipment. His report for the year lists over $8,000 disbursed for the library and laboratory and another $4,200 for "contingencies." Certainly the school needed books, specimens, and staff, but whether it needed them immediately, especially at the cost of running a deficit, was questioned by at least one board member. Dr. Bartholomew Egan, describing himself accurately as "a warm friend" of David and the school, wondered if the superintendent, in his "earnest zeal," had forgotten the old Latin maxim, *Festina Lente* or, go ahead slowly. The legislature and the people would support the seminary only up to a certain point, Egan remarked. "It seems to me . . . you have professors enough for three hundred students. . . . My only fear is that in your great zeal you may run too far ahead of public opinion. I have written this reluctantly but from my great regard for you and my entire confidence in the purity of your purpose. I feel that I owe you the counsel of a friend."[34] Egan's counsel, had it been accepted, might have saved David years of failure, bitterness and grief. The older man never lost his regard for David or the "purity of his purpose," even when David's great zeal led him to pursue administrative policies that brought hostile attacks on the school and personal disaster to its chief executive.

Circumstances, such as the uncertainty surrounding the beginnings of Radical Reconstruction, forced the seminary to retrench. As David explained in his report for 1867, the school had experienced a

33 *Report* to the Board of Supervisors for 1866, pp. 6–10.
34 *Ibid.*, Bartholomew Egan to David Boyd, November 20, 1866, in Alphabetical File, Fleming Collection.

"year of trial." Threatened constantly by political turmoil, bankruptcy, and epidemic, its faculty had necessarily been reduced. But it was still "alive," and someday, he predicted, "full of years and usefulness. . . its halls filled with hundreds of students . . . [the Seminary] will be called one of the great schools of America." Meanwhile, the still ambitious superintendent pointed out some "deficiencies" in the course of study. The seminary still did not teach astronomy, minerology, geology, botany, physiology, history, or constitutional law, he reminded the board. A "distinct professorship" of English language and literature should be added "very soon," and, if money permitted, another of music.

Privately, David's ambitions for the school knew even fewer bounds. To his cousin, James Boyd, he confided, "I intend to advance the scientific departments of the Seminary till there is nothing like them in the South, not even at the Va. Mil. Institute which I believe to be much in advance, scientifically, of any school in Va. The University has been very slow, too slow, in increasing her no. of chairs. . . . She is today but little in advance of where Mr. Jefferson left her in 1826."[35] Apparently, Dr. Bartholomew Egan's maxim, *Festina Lente*, was not one of Latin Professor Boyd's favorites.

Finally, very early in his administrative career, David developed such an extreme devotion to the seminary's well-being that he could not understand the lesser interest of other people. G. Mason Graham commented on David's "singleness of purpose" in 1865. Twenty years later he was still urging him to "divest yourself of that . . . diffidence and self-sacrificing disposition which has so long influenced you in your absorbing devotion, for now a quarter of a century, to the maintenance and welfare of this school, to the most serious and ruinous prejudice of the interests of your family and yourself." David also equated support for the seminary with patriotism and loyalty to Louisiana. When wealthy merchants and planters sent their sons to other states to be educated, he chastized them in local newspapers. It was worth five hundred dollars a year just to gaze upon Robert E. Lee at Washington University, he admitted, but that did not absolve citizens of their duty to Louisiana. As for some of his colleagues, David could not understand why they resigned when they were not paid, or went on

35 *Report* to the Board of Supervisors for 1867, pp. 5–10; David Boyd to James Boyd, August 22, 1868, in David Boyd Letterbooks.

vacations when the seminary was not in session. To build support for the school, he argued, everyone should be willing to work as hard in July and August as in February and March. "All that is necessary [to save the school]," he told a board member, "is for the whole staff . . . to work with *promise of pay* if no money is *available*." [36]

The broad outlines of David's educational theories also began to emerge in the years immediately following the Civil War. David himself was a product of private, preparatory schools and an aristocratic university education. Yet in his first postwar *Reports* he championed public, tax-supported education at all levels, and promoted it in particular for "indigent" youth. His own training consisted of "classical" studies like Latin and mathematics, yet he repeatedly expressed the desire to make the seminary the "leading scientific institution of the South." His educational background was completely lacking in military training, yet he became an ardent advocate of the "military system" as the best method for instilling discipline and responsibility in Louisiana youth. David did not renounce the older, traditional programs of university education; rather, he wanted to keep the best of the old and add to it studies which would meet the needs of a more "practical " age. What he really hoped to provide for Louisiana was a state supported institution that would train young men "mentally, morally, and physically," to assume their responsibilities to themselves and their state. By 1868 he thought the Louisiana seminary was performing that task. The school offered bachelor's degrees in both "literary" and "scientific" subjects. It also provided a degree in civil engineering and, for those who chose to enroll for only one year, there was a commercial school which taught bookkeeping, commercial arithmetic, and penmanship. The state supported ninety-eight cadets, and upon graduation, these young men pledged to teach school in Louisiana for two years. This, thought David, was the "handsomest feature of the institution." [37]

36 G. Mason Graham to David Boyd, undated, quoted in Fleming, *Louisiana State University*, 353; Alexandria (La.) *Democrat*, August 14, 1867; David Boyd to G. Mason Graham, May 28, 1867, in Boyd Letters, Fleming Collection.
37 *Report* to the Board of Supervisors for 1866, p. 11; *ibid.*, 1867, p. 10; David Boyd to James Boyd, August 22, 1868, in David Boyd Letterbooks; Fleming, *Louisiana State University*, 349–50; *Prospectus* of the Louisiana State Seminary of Learning and Military Academy, July 1, 1867, in Printed Materials, David Boyd Papers. David's vision of what a university ought to be was aptly expressed in his *Report* for 1869. Quoting the "noble [Ezra] Cornell," he urged, "Let us have an institution where any person can find instruction in any study!" *Report* to the Board of Supervisors for 1869, p. 21.

David also thought a young man's education took place outside as well as inside the schoolroom. To that end he expended relatively large amounts of the seminary's meager income on books, paintings, prints, and zoological and geological exhibits. Even when the treasury was empty, he ordered expensive reference works for the library. In 1869 visiting legislators pronounced the school and its facilities adequate for the number of students enrolled. But David disagreed. Shortly after the lawmakers departed, he asked the state to appropriate at least five thousand dollars for more books and equipment. At the same time, he appealed to the general public for mineral, geological and fossil specimens, solicited gifts for the library, and commissioned portraits of G. Mason Graham and General William T. Sherman. Finally, because he thought the cadets could acquire something from the "company of ladies" not available in books, David scheduled dances at the seminary on appropriate occasions. In his *Prospectus* for 1867 he noted, "The 'Hop' has worked like a charm during the past two sessions in polishing the manners and refining the feelings of the cadets."[38]

In matters of discipline David's ideas were obviously influenced by those of his famous predecessor, W. T. Sherman. Sherman believed firmly in strict adherence to duty, stern rules and regulations, and full authority, subject only to approval of the board, for the superintendent to govern the institution. However, while Sherman was away during the summer of 1860, the board revised the regulations, giving the faculty equal power with the superintendent in determining such matters as expulsion from the seminary. The same rules applied when David became superintendent in 1865. If a cadet earned enough demerits and the academic board recommended it, the superintendent could dismiss him from the institution. As a last resort, the cadet could appeal to the Board of Supervisors. Sherman opposed the procedure on the ground that it made the superintendent a pawn, subject to pressure from both professors and supervisors. He thought it would encourage student disrespect for authority and by 1866, David had come to the same conclusion. Following the dismissal of a rebellious cadet named Stockton, 111 cadets signed a petition demanding that the con-

38 *Report* to the Board of Supervisors for 1866, pp. 7, 13; *ibid.*, 1867, pp. 5, 11; *Report* of the Joint Committee of the Legislature to Investigate Charitable Institutions, January, 1869, in Printed Materials, David Boyd Papers; *Prospectus*, July 1, 1867, *ibid.*; Alexandria (La.) *Democrat*, July 1, August 12, 1868.

duct of the seminary commandant, Major J. A. A. West, be investigated. Instead of presenting the petition to David, they gave it to Stockton to use as he saw fit. Not wishing to injure the school, Major West offered to resign, but David would not hear of it. However, he did relieve West of his duties as commandant. Then David met with the petitioners, explained the illegality of their action (giving Stockton the petition), and asked them to reconsider. Eleven refused, countering with another petition, whereupon David expelled them for mutiny.[39]

Sherman's prediction proved accurate. Pressured to relent from various quarters, David finally agreed to reinstate those cadets who admitted their error and promised to obey in the future. But Commandant West, despite David's unqualified support, was not so lucky. He resigned his professorship, and David, in a formal letter forwarded to the board, made his own feelings clear concerning the entire affair. "I have made this report . . . only because it is made my duty by the regulations," he wrote. Years later, when he drafted the charter for the proposed Louisiana State University and Agricultural and Mechanical College, David carefully included clauses which required the board to delegate to the president "sufficient authority to . . . maintain proper discipline and good order." Furthermore, he stipulated that in all matters pertaining to student conduct and behavior, "the president alone, and not the faculty or any professor, shall decide and act."[40]

David's extraordinary commitment to his public duties as superintendent of the seminary did not rob him completely of a private life. In the late summer of 1865, he informed Dr. Powhatan Clarke, a former colleague and a close friend, that he planned to marry. Clarke labeled the news "astounding" but accepted with pleasure David's invitation to attend the ceremony, promising to bring with him Father Bellier, the Catholic priest at Alexandria, and General G. Mason Graham. Clarke's own carriage was "*smashed*," so they would make the trip in his father-in-law's large coach, "with four spanking horses." "I want Mrs. B. and

39 Fleming, *Louisiana State University*, 92–93; David Boyd to Board of Supervisors, December 21, 1866, in Official Papers, Fleming Collection.
40 W. E. Seay to David Boyd, December 21, 1866, John A. A. West to David Boyd, August 24, 1867, in Alphabetical File, Fleming Collection; General Order to the Superintendent, January 4, 1867, David Boyd to Board of Supervisors, December 21, 1866, in Official Papers, Fleming Collection; J. A. A. West to David Boyd, January 15, 186 [7], in David Boyd Papers; *Acts of Louisiana*, 1877, No. 145, Section 22.

yourself to say that your wedding was attended by a grandee (keeping a grocery at Cotile!) in a coach and four!"[41]

"Mrs. B.," the former Esther Gertrude Wright of Cheneyville, Louisiana, was twenty-one when she married David on October 5, 1865. He celebrated his thirty-first birthday the same day. Esther, or Ettie, was the youngest of the five living children of Dr. Jesse Durastus Wright and Sarah Robert Grimball Wright. Born in Connecticut and educated at Yale, Jesse Wright migrated to Woodville, Mississippi, where he met the Grimball and Robert families, enroute westward from their homes in South Carolina. Wright traveled with them, settling finally near Cheneyville, Louisiana, in 1820. The next year he married Sarah Robert Grimball, then about sixteen. Like many prominent men of the region, Jesse Wright combined medicine with planting and mercantile interests, devoting himself as well to the promotion of education and the Baptist Church. In time the Wrights acquired a large plantation, North Bend, about one mile from Cheneyville, and it was there that Ettie Wright was born in 1844. Six years later Jesse Wright died, and Sarah Wright sold North Bend in order to purchase Greenwood Plantation from a son-in-law, Leroy Augustus Stafford. At the time Stafford was in financial difficulties, and North Bend was sold to his creditor. By 1858 Stafford's affairs were so improved that he was able to buy Edgewood Plantation adjoining his mother-in-law's Greenwood. But his debt to her was still unpaid when in the spring of 1861, he formed a volunteer company, the Stafford Guards, and left for war. Among the enlisted men was David F. Boyd. Stafford served on the Virginia front until his death from wounds suffered at the Battle of the Wilderness in May, 1864. By that time, David had returned to Louisiana and rejoined the army near Alexandria. Because he was considered a "friend of the family," David promised to visit the bereaved Wright and Stafford families near Cheneyville in June, 1864.[42]

Whether David already knew Ettie Wright in 1864 is not clear. As a young child she studied at home with a Connecticut "school marm,"

---

41 Powhatan Clarke to David Boyd, September 8, 1865, in Alphabetical File, Fleming Collection.
42 Stafford, *General Leroy Augustus Stafford*, 30–34, 39–44, 293–308; MCW [Mary Cornelia Wright] to D. F. Boyd, June 22, 1864, D. F. Boyd to M. C. Wright, June 29, 1864, in David Boyd Papers. Mary Cornelia Wright was Ettie Wright's older sister. Another sister, Sarah Catherine Wright, was Leroy Augustus Stafford's widow and the eldest living child of Jesse and Sarah Grimball Wright. Stafford, *General Leroy Augustus Stafford*, 96.

enrolling a few years later in boarding schools near Cheneyville and Mansfield, Louisiana. In 1857 she went to Kentucky with her mother to visit her only brother, who died before they arrived, and Ettie, then about thirteen, was left at a school in Georgetown, Kentucky. But she was so miserable that Mrs. Wright allowed her to come home, sending her the following year to Minden Female College from which she graduated with honors in July, 1861. David left with the Stafford Guards for Virginia at about the same time. Ettie spent the war years at Greenwood where she occupied the time by teaching the younger children of her absent brother-in-law, Leroy Stafford. Therefore, if Ettie Wright and David Boyd knew each other before 1864, they must have met during one of her school holidays or perhaps during a visit she might have paid to the seminary during 1860–1861 where her nephew, Leroy Stafford's son George was enrolled as a cadet. Described as an accomplished musician by someone who met her in 1860, the attractive Ettie Wright stood a trim five feet, three inches tall when she married David five years later.[43]

News of David's impending marriage surprised his family even more than it did his friend Powhatan Clarke. They learned about it from one of David's friends who visited them in Wytheville. After chiding their son for not telling them earlier, they urged David to come home with his wife the next summer. Meanwhile, David's brother Charlie was on his way to Louisiana because there were no business opportunities available for a young man in Wytheville.[44]

The first months of Ettie and David's married life must have been hectic. The school had just reopened, the whole state was poverty-stricken and the seminary, sacked and occupied by opposing armies during the war, was in great need of repair. Not surprisingly Ettie chose to spend Christmas, 1865, with her family at Cheneyville, thirty miles away. But David stayed at the almost abandoned seminary to

43 Recollections of Esther Gertrude Wright Boyd, 1906, in David F. Boyd Family Papers, Jesse D. Wright Papers, Department of Archives, Louisiana State University; Fleming, *Louisiana State University*, 105; Prichard (ed.), "A Tourist's Description of Louisiana"; David Boyd Memorandum Book, MS Volumes in David Boyd Papers.

44 Minerva Boyd to David F. Boyd, October 4, 1865, in David Boyd Papers. Charlie Boyd tried several things to make a living in Louisiana, none with much success. In 1868 he married Sally Stafford, eldest child of the late General Leroy Augustus Stafford and Ettie Boyd's sister Sarah Catherine Wright Stafford. Alexandria (La.) *Democrat*, March 7, 1866; T. J. Boyd to D. F. Boyd, April 29, 1867, Minerva Boyd to David F. Boyd, February 16, 1869, in David Boyd Papers; Stafford, *General Leroy Augustus Stafford*, 96.

oversee fourteen cadets who could not go home for the holidays. "Even my wife has deserted me," he wrote a friend in New Orleans. He thought the cadets were having a "dull Christmas" although he was "feeding and eggnogging them well."[45]

David and Ettie lived in what one of the professors described as "a wooden structure . . . retired in the woods" from the seminary building. But the unmarried faculty members were frequent guests. One of them, recalling the monotony and isolation of seminary life, remarked that the "presence at table of Colonel Boyd's charming wife prevented some of us from losing all sense of the social life." David probably did not notice the dearth of "social life." As a single professor he had avoided it, and now that he was married and superintendent, he had little or no time for it. In a class book kept during 1866 he scrawled the following daily schedule:

5	rise	12	home and dinner
6	breakfast	1	Seminary
7	Seminary	4	home
8–9		5	Seminary
10	home	6	home and supper
11	Seminary	7	Seminary
		10	home[46]

For Ettie, who came from a large and once wealthy family, the seminary's isolation and a professor's limited income must have required considerable adjustment. Very soon after the ceremony the newlyweds were short of money, and David asked his father for a loan. But Thomas Jefferson Boyd was in worse financial condition than his son. Although he had retired over $200,000 of his prewar debt, he still owed $25,000 in 1865. Even the lots David once owned in Wytheville had been sold during the war to support the Virginia Boyds. T. J. Boyd still owned a half interest in some mountain land which might someday attract "Yankee capitalists," but at the moment he had no funds. "As soon as I can," he promised, "I will send you some help." Instead, the assistance came from David, "If your institution needs another instructor . . . could you not interest your Board of Trustees in favor of your cousin,

45   David Boyd to R. M. Venable, December 25, 1865, in David Boyd Letterbooks.
46   Garnett, "Reminiscences of the Louisiana State Seminary of Learning in 1867," 20; Class Book of 1865–66 in MS Volumes, David Boyd Papers.

Jas. M. Boyd [?] You know he is a very thorough and accomplished scholar."[47]

David did secure a professorship for his cousin at the seminary, but James Boyd suffered from "consumption" which Louisiana's climate seemed to aggravate. After only one year of teaching (1866–1867), he had to take a leave of absence. Once back in Virginia, he married Miss Betty Lawson of Lynchburg and some months later the couple went to Baltimore where James underwent extensive medical treatment during the summer of 1868. When the James Boyds returned to Wytheville late in August, Thomas Boyd reported to David that James seemed "more feeble" than ever. Nevertheless, Minerva urged her son not to cancel his cousin's contract. James and his wife planned to return to the seminary in the fall of 1868, and "only the hope of being independent," she believed, was keeping him alive. David acquiesced. He wrote James a cheering note telling him how much he counted on him and his "chair of chemical engineering" to give the school a "good name." It must have been convincing because by mid-November the James Boyds were back in Louisiana. Unfortunately, James was hopelessly ill and by February, 1869, he was dead. Ironically, James Boyd's sister, Mary Boyd Clopton, sent David a letter just two days before her brother's death in which she accused her cousin of personal responsibility for James's condition. David's encouraging notes of the previous summer urging James to come back to Louisiana had made him feel "obligated," she charged, and David, or the board, ought to give James one thousand dollars at once so that he could return to Baltimore for treatment. "Oh, heed my prayer," she begged, "for when my good, pure, talented, accomplished brother . . . dies, neither I nor others, will hold you quite guiltless, nor the Board, of which you are the representative."[48]

Besides paying the debts which the James Boyds left behind them in Louisiana, David also provided for the lion's share of expenses incurred in sending his cousin's remains back to Virginia. Later, Betty Boyd thanked David profusely for his kindness, but apparently she never repaid the debt. Instead, she dunned the seminary for her hus-

47 T. J. Boyd to David F. Boyd, November 25, 1865, March 24, 1866, in David Boyd Papers.
48 *Report* to the Board of Supervisors for 1867, p. 9; T. J. Boyd to David Boyd, July 28, August 18, 1868, Minerva Boyd to David Boyd, September 6, 1868, D. F. Boyd to T. J. Boyd, telegram, February 18, 1869, Mary Boyd Clopton to David F. Boyd, February 13, 1869, in David Boyd Papers; David Boyd to James M. Boyd, August 22, 1868, in David Boyd Letterbooks.

band's salary through June, 1868, although his death occurred in February. David seems to have refused the request.[49]

In the fall of 1868 David assumed responsibility for still another Virginia Boyd, his youngest brother, Thomas Duckett. Tom was only fourteen when David first offered to "educate and maintain" him at the seminary. Described by a brother-in-law as small but "remarkably bright," Tom soon outdistanced fellow cadets academically. But outside the classroom they teased him unmercifully about his puny physique. Ignore the "wild *La.* boys" and "stay moral," counseled Thomas Boyd, Sr., from Virginia. He sent the young scholar a few jars of applesauce to go along with the advice.[50]

David's responsibilities increased again in the spring of 1869 when Ettie gave birth to twin sons. In breaking the news to his mother, David asked what she would give to see the babies. "I have nothing left of all I once possessed but a handsome silver pitcher," Minerva answered. "That I would gladly give." David wanted to name one of the twins after William Sherman but his mother discouraged him. Although she understood David's motives, others might not; in any case, there would be other sons. Why not wait until time "softened the feeling of Southerners toward their enemies?" Meanwhile, the twins were informally dubbed "Reb" and "Jack" causing R. M. Venable, a former professor at the Seminary, to warn Ettie that his great respect for her would certainly "melt into thin air" if she allowed David to call her children "'Reb' and 'Jack,' the whilom names, forsooth, of two 'purps' of low degree."[51]

By the time his sons were born, it was already apparent to David's friends and family that he was too generous and too self-sacrificing for his own good. Venable hoped the addition of "*responsibilities by the pair*" would make David realize that the seminary was not his only care. "There is a person," Venable commented, "whom I never could

49 D. F. Boyd to T. J. Boyd, Telegram, February 18, 1869, Betty L. Boyd to Richard M. Lawson (brother), February 18, 1869, Mary B. Clopton to D. F. Boyd, February 22, 1869, Betty Boyd to D. F. Boyd, March 16, April 13, 1869, T. J. Boyd to D. F. Boyd, May 9, 1869, all in David Boyd Papers.
50 T. J. Boyd to David F. Boyd, January 28, 1868, Charles Motz (brother-in-law) to David F. Boyd, March 14, 1868, *ibid.*; Thomas J. Boyd to [Thomas D.] Boyd, December 14, 1868, in David F. Boyd Family Papers, Thomas J. Boyd Papers.
51 Minerva Boyd to David F. Boyd, May 23, 1869, in David Boyd Papers; R. M. Venable to David F. Boyd, August 2, 1869, in Alphabetical File, Fleming Collection. Ultimately, the twins were named Thomas J. and Edward J. Boyd. Edward J. died in October, 1871, at Baton Rouge. Genealogical Scrapbook, LeRoy Boyd Papers.

induce you sufficiently to admire and labor for—that is self." But such expressions had little effect. Besides opening his home and pocketbook to relatives, David sent money he could hardly afford to an unemployed former colleague in New Orleans. E. Berté St. Ange was without shoes or winter clothing when he appealed to David in 1867. Eight years later, after several loans, St. Ange was still poor and still promising to repay David at the earliest opportunity.[52]

David himself was so poor by 1867 that he could not afford to leave the seminary during summer vacations even if his extreme dedication to "duty" had permitted it. Plans to visit the Boyds in Wytheville were repeatedly set aside, notwithstanding his parents' pleas that he consider himself and his family as well as the public. Thomas Boyd feared for David's health "to say nothing of the pecuniary distress you subject yourself & wife to by postponing your claims for service till . . . everybody else is paid." Minerva agreed. "You have always worked for others. Give that up, I beseech you," she wrote her dedicated son. "I have lived long enough to know that you will get no thanks for your pains."[53]

The year 1869 proved to be one of triumph and tragedy for David and the seminary. It began on a cautious but hopeful note with David reporting to the board that, despite a depreciation rate as high as thirty-two cents on the dollar, the seminary had managed to meet most of its "current expenses" during 1868. Furthermore, its creditors were willing to "continue their trust" in the coming year. Then, almost casually, David suggested that the school do something to guard against fire. The installation of two large tanks, a force pump, and a hose on the roof of the main buildings, might be a good idea, he thought, and the board ought to think seriously about insuring the property.[54]

Important as they were, mundane concerns like depreciated warrants and inadequate fire protection must have seemed relatively unexciting as the seminary prepared to celebrate the first commencement in its brief history. David began making plans at least a year in advance. In mid-1868, he asked General William Sherman to visit the seminary the following June in order to present the school's first diplomas. Sherman accepted "with the greatest of pleasure," but busi-

52   R. M. Venable to David Boyd, August 2, 1869, E. Bertè St. Ange to David Boyd, September 7, October 22, 1867, September 27, 1875, in Alphabetical File, Fleming Collection.

53   T. J. Boyd to D. F. Boyd, March 24, 1866, January 2, April 29, August 29, 1867, Minerva Boyd to David F. Boyd, May 21, 1866, February 16, 1869, in David Boyd Papers.

54   *Report* of the Board of Supervisors for 1868, pp. 10–11, 16.

ness in New Orleans required him to revise his schedule. Early in 1869 he notified David to expect him, his daughter, and a "Colonel Dayton and lady" about February 10. David was overjoyed. He planned an escort for Sherman's party, dispatching his clerk-secretary, S. B. Robinson, to New Orleans with instructions to charge all of the group's expenses to his (David's) account. If Robinson saw General Richard Taylor, "a great friend of Sheman's," and if Robinson thought Taylor "w^d *take it well*," he should invite Taylor to accompany the party to the seminary. "Also Longstreet," David added.[55]

The Sherman visit was a huge sucess in every way but one. In the midst of the festivities, on February 15, David's consumptive cousin, James Boyd died. Already planning to go with Sherman when he returned to New Orleans, David now had another reason to make the trip. He had to help Betty Lawson Boyd arrange her sad journey back to Virginia. In addition, David probably intended to do some lobbying in New Orleans. The Radical legislature was meeting in extra session, and besides the seminary's regular appropriation bill, it was considering a controversial measure to integrate the public schools.[56]

Well before his twin sons arrived in April, 1869, David was back in Alexandria making final preparations for Commencement Day. Wednesday, June 30, 1869, was sultry and dusty, but large numbers of visitors from all over the state gathered on the seminary grounds to hear a former justice of the Louisiana State Supreme Court, the Honorable H. M. Spofford, deliver the principal address. David also spoke to the graduates. Besides reminding them that knowledge was not necessarily wisdom and that learning which conflicted with common sense ought to be tossed out, David warned the nine young men to "avoid politics & politicians as you would the plague. . . . It is a filthy pool in which no gentleman can dabble without getting befouled." The local press was charmed. Labeling David's speech one of the most able, touching and appropriate of its kind, the editor remarked, "If we had

55 David Boyd to William T. Sherman, June 11, 1868, in David Boyd Letterbooks; W. T. Sherman to David Boyd, June 23, 1868, January 27, 1869, in Typescript of Sherman-Boyd Correspondence; David Boyd to S. B. R. [Robinson], undated, in Official Papers, Fleming Collection.
56 W. T. Sherman to David Boyd, February 22, 1869, Typescript of Sherman-Boyd Correspondence; Mary Boyd Clopton to David Boyd, February 22, 1869, David Boyd to T. J. Boyd, telegram, February 18, 1869, in David Boyd Papers; Edwin W. Fay, *History of Education in Louisiana* (Washington, 1898) 83; Memelo, "State Laws Concerning the Negro in Louisiana," 63–64.

not already seen the Colonel do so many other difficult things, in the course of his arduous labors, we should have been astonished at seeing him appear in his new capacity of orator and finished writer."[57]

So much for triumph. Less than four months later the seminary burned to the ground. Early on the morning of October 15, 1869, fire was discovered in the commissary under the kitchen in the main seminary building. At four A.M. a wall collapsed and three hours later little or nothing remained. Because there was no way to fight the conflagration, cadets and professors concentrated on saving the library, scientific equipment, and school furniture. Personal possessions of the cadets, pictures, maps, commissary stores, and dining room furniture were destroyed. Blaming himself for not having insisted more strongly on precautions against fire, David described the seminary's destruction in his annual *Report* for 1869 as a "heartrending spectacle." But, he continued, "that was no time for tears or despondency." The seminary's future had to be provided for and 143 young men had to be fed and sheltered.[58]

The Ice House Hotel in Alexandria housed the cadets until they could go home, and David began immediately to look for a new building. On his way to New Orleans to confer with Governor Warmoth and the seminary board, he stopped at Baton Rouge where he inspected the Louisiana Institution for the Deaf, Dumb and Blind. Sure that the building, known as the deaf and dumb asylum, could house the seminary temporarily, David asked the board of the institution informally for permission to share the facility. They refused but a persuasive letter from Governor Warmoth and a certain amount of pressure from the Baton Rouge citizenry made them reconsider, subject only to legislative approval.[59]

Although the cause of the seminary fire was never definitely established, some suspected arson from the first. The Louisiana *Democrat*, for example, reported local rumors that an "incendiary" was responsi-

---

57 Address to the graduation class by D. F. Boyd, June 30, 1869, in David Boyd Papers; Alexandria (La.) *Democrat*, July 7, 1869.
58 Extra, October 15, 1869, reprinted in Alexandria (La.) *Democrat*, October 20, 1869; *Report* of the Board of Supervisors for 1869, pp. 8–9.
59 Extra, October 15, 1869, reprinted in Alexandria (La.) *Democrat*, October 20, 1869; New Orleans *Daily Picayune*, October 19, 1869; Minutes of special meeting of the Board of Supervisors, October 21, 23, 1869; *Annual Report* of the Board of Administrators and Superintendent of the Louisiana Institution for the Deaf, Dumb and Blind, in *Legislative Documents of Louisiana*, 1870.

ble. David carefully avoided speculation, listing the cause of the fire as "unknown" in his *Report* for 1869. But the *Report* was a public document, directed to a Radical state legislature, whom David was asking for money to rebuild. Privately, he was sure the fire had been set. In a diary entry made five years later he remarked, "What a scene—as grand as it was awful. And what a misfortune to our institution & to La! And how much trouble & misfortune it has given *me*! It has taken *ten* years from my life. It was burnt no doubt by the negroes in revenge for the killing of the negro Isaac Whiting by Cadet Simmons."[60]

Whatever the origin of the fire, there is no question that a seminary cadet had murdered a local black youth and that his act stirred strong resentment in the surrounding area. On September 20, 1869, David issued orders prohibiting all visits by cadets to Alexandria and Pineville without specific authorization of the superintendent. Disobedience meant dismissal. "This order," David explained, "is decreed absolutely necessary for the protection of the cadets themselves."[61]

How long the seminary would be domiciled in Baton Rouge depended upon several factors, not the least of which were money and local pride. Just days after the fire, officers of the Homer College offered to donate their building to the state if the seminary would go there. Pressure was also building in some quarters to keep the school permanently in Baton Rouge. Alarmed, the editor of the Louisiana *Democrat* recalled what stiff competition Rapides had faced in securing the seminary when it was first established. He urged the local citizenry to move swiftly to save a "major source of revenue" for the community, challenging businessmen to "SUBSCRIBE SOMETHING TOWARD REBUILDING" before other parishes did. "Colonel Boyd," the editor prodded, "is willing to head the list with his salary for two years (8000) . . . to retain the seminary in the parish. . . . Who will imitate his example?"[62]

60 Extra, October 15, 1869, reprinted in Alexandria (La.) *Democrat*, October 20, 1869; *Report* of the Board of Supervisors for 1869, p. 8; David Boyd Diary (MS in Department of Archives, Louisiana State University, Baton Rouge) October 15, 1874.
61 General Order No. 6, September 20, 1869, in Official Papers, Fleming Collection; *Report* of the Board of Supervisors for 1869, p. 15.
62 W. B. Gill to David Boyd, October 25, 1869, in David F. Boyd Family Papers, Thomas J. Boyd Papers; *Report* of the Board of Administrators of Louisiana Institution for the Deaf, Dumb and Blind, 1870, in Printed Materials, David Boyd Papers; Alexandria (La.) *Democrat*, October 27, 1869. The editor's challenge appeared in boldface type.

David's offer to spark a fund-raising campaign to rebuild the seminary in Rapides may have been sincere when he made it. But privately he had speculated with friends about more desirable locations for the school long before the fire. By the time he submitted his *Report* for 1869, it was clear that he was in no hurry to go back to the piney woods. The old location might be best "for reasons of health and auld lang syne," he told the board, even if it were not very accessible. Meanwhile, he offered a number of proposals designed to render the "temporary accommodations" at Baton Rouge larger and more comfortable.[63]

On November 1, 1869, the seminary reopened in the north wing of the state asylum for the deaf, dumb, and blind. The cadets who were sent home on October 15 with instructions to report for duty when notified, responded quickly. By the end of the year there were 138 in attendance and more expected. All of the professors except one moved to Baton Rouge, and the school seemed ready to meet whatever challenge the future had in store.[64] Since 1865 it had withstood financial crises and political assaults. It had found friends and protectors even among the Radical "enemy," and it had literally survived an ordeal by fire. There were also minor triumphs. It celebrated a reunion with its first superintendent and it sent forth its first graduating class. If all this gave David a sense of pride in past accomplishment, he can certainly be excused. Considering what lay ahead, it is fortunate that he did not have second sight.

---

63 *Report* of the Board of Supervisors for 1869, pp. 10–13; James M. Garnett to David Boyd, November 17, 1869, in Alphabetical File, Fleming Collection.
64 Alexandria (La.) *Democrat*, November 3, 1869; *Report* of the Board of Supervisors for 1869, pp. 8, 20.

Chapter V

Into the Mainstream

SEVERAL MONTHS before the seminary moved to Baton Rouge, a legislative committee visited the state asylum for the deaf, dumb and blind only to find a "magnificent" building going to ruin and a mere fifteen inmates in residence. The building ought to be restored at once, reported the committee, or else abandoned and provision made for the few inmates elsewhere. Persuaded, the lawmakers agreed to underwrite extensive repairs, and by January, 1870, under the supervision of a new superintendent and a new board of control appointed by Governor Warmoth, the number of residents had more than doubled. There would have been more, declared Superintendent J. A. McWhorter, except for the fact that most Louisianians thought the institution was an orphanage, not a school.[1]

By the time McWhorter made his comment, the asylum for the handicapped was in fact a school but not the kind the superindendent had in mind. More than 140 seminary cadets crowded the northern end of the building, and, if a local editor had his way, their stay would be permanent. Arguing that the buildings were too large for "the poor unfortunate mutes and blinds," the editor wanted the legislature to turn over the entire facility to the seminary. Other quarters in town could be found for the handicapped, he declared, and the state would

---

1 *Report* of the Committee to Investigate Charitable Institutions of the State of Louisiana, January, 1869; *Report* of the Board of Administrators of the Louisiana Institute for the Deaf, Dumb and Blind, 1870, p. 7, both in Printed Materials, David Boyd Papers.

save an estimated three quarters of the amount it would cost to rebuild the seminary in Rapides.[2]

Because the seminary needed legislative approval to occupy even a part of the asylum building legally, David had to go to New Orleans twice during the first two months of 1870. Things did not go smoothly, leading him to suspect that Superintendent McWhorter and part of the asylum board were "misrepresenting" the seminary's position before the various legislative committees, "especially the colored members." Although he thought the lawmakers would ultimately grant the seminary's request, they first insisted on sending a delegation to inspect the jointly occupied building. Some of the "august members," David believed, hoped to be bribed before issuing a favorable report. But he informed one that he "wld see . . . [the Seminary] and the State sunk so deep that plummet cld never reach," before he, David, would spend one dollar to influence a vote. Having to deal with such "scoundrels" made David feel degraded. Nevertheless, he advised Colonel Samuel H. Lockett, in charge of the school during his absence, to have the "infernal dirty kitchen and stove" cleaned up in time for the committee's visit. Meanwhile, Superintendent McWhorter continued to protest from Baton Rouge that the building was not large enough to house both asylum inmates and the cadets. David answered heatedly that the fault was McWhorter's; he and his "retainers" occupied too much space. If the asylum people really wanted to be cooperative, they should accept David's plan to combine kitchen staff and dining room facilities. That way, both schools would save money, space, and time.[3]

When the legislature finally acted, it granted temporary use of part of the building to the seminary and authorized the asylum board to rent additional space elsewhere if the need should arise. The next year, 1871, the handicapped were given permission to move out entirely thereby convincing David that the lawmakers had meant all along to give the seminary the whole building. Others were not so sure. Governor Warmoth, for example, wrote David that he was sorry asylum and seminary officials were unable to make "satisfactory" arrangements. Although willing to endorse anything the asylum board might do to ac-

2 *Report* of the Board of Supervisors for 1869, p. 8; Baton Rouge *Tri-Weekly Advocate*, December 10, 1869.
3 David F. Boyd to S. H. Lockett, January 13, 20, February 14, 1870, S. H. Lockett to David Boyd, February 20, 1870, in Boyd Letters, Fleming Collection.

commodate the seminary, Warmoth felt he had said all he could on the subject. The controversy continued for years. Ironically, when the cadets finally did leave the building, they again occupied "temporary" quarters, the United States Arsenal and Barracks at Baton Rouge.[4]

David's interest in the United States Arsenal property began in 1870 while he was in New Orleans negotiating for the deaf, dumb, and blind institute building. Still interested when he got back to Baton Rouge, he wrote General Sherman about the Federal installation. Personally, Sherman answered, he was opposed to giving up the post, even for the school. Trouble might arise in Arkansas, Texas, Mobile, or Florida which would require reinforcements from a garrison stationed at Baton Rouge. However, if Governor Warmoth pressed for the property, Sherman promised not to stand in the way. But Sherman's views prevailed. Not until 1886 would the school move into the Barracks property. By that time Federal troops had long since been withdrawn.[5]

In spite of friction with Superintendent McWhorter, cramped quarters, a debt approaching $20,000, and continued difficulty in cashing the state warrants, the seminary (renamed the Louisiana State University in 1870) enjoyed an excellent first year in Baton Rouge. Everything lost in the fire was replaced and added to; eight students were graduated in the class of 1870; the enrollment figures were the highest in the school's history, and the faculty was one of the largest in the South. In his report to the Board of Supervisors for 1870, David labeled the university "one of the best schools in the South." He saw no reason why it should not be "*the* best" soon, if the legislature would only award it the Agricultural and Mechanical college funds. If it did not prosper then, only management could be blamed.[6]

Beginning with the first graduation class in 1869, David used his commencement addresses not only to inspire the graduates, but also to discuss the condition of the school, to express his educational ideas, and to comment generally on politics and society. The anniversary addresses, delivered for the first time in January, 1870, to celebrate the

4   Fleming, *Louisiana State University*, 184–85; Governor H. C. Warmoth to David Boyd, October 7, 1872, in Scrapbook, David Boyd Papers.
5   Baton Rouge *Tri-Weekly Advocate*, February 9, 1870; William T. Sherman to David Boyd, April 24, 1870, Typescript of Sherman-Boyd Letters; Fleming, *Louisiana State University*, 434.
6   *Acts of Louisiana*, 1870, Extra Session, No. 47; *Report* to the Board of Supervisors for 1870, pp. 7–9.

university's tenth birthday, served the same purpose. Like his reports to the board, David's speeches were usually cogent, detailed, and candid enough to offend at least a part of his listeners, but considering that as many as five hundred guests attended some of the "public exercises," such results were probably inevitable. Present in the same audience might be personalities as disparate as General G. Mason Graham and Governor Henry Clay Warmoth. If David had had his way, the contrast would have been even more striking. As guest speakers for commencement and birthday exercises in 1869, 1870, and 1873, he invited William T. Sherman, Robert E. Lee, and Jefferson Davis, respectively. Sherman did visit the school in 1869 but too early to participate in commencement. Lee, occupied with his own duties as president of Washington College, had to decline, and Davis, invited to deliver the anniversary address for 1873, refused because he thought it prudent to "avoid public notice." He was glad, however, that "a faithful Confederate" headed Louisiana State University.[7]

In his commencement address for 1870, David urged the graduates to do what their parents could not: forget the past, "make a *new* La. and a new South," and participate meaningfully in Reconstruction. "Not so much *political* reconstruction," he hastened to add, "for politics, be it democratic [*sic*] or Republican is all a lie, a swindle & a cheat . . . but I mean reconstruction—moral, social, material!" To follow his advice, the young men would have to exert themselves, forget the region's ancient hatred of outsiders, and welcome enterprise, whatever its source. For too long, David charged, the South had indulged its love for politics and shown its contempt for the "mechanical arts." What it needed now was fewer "elegant planters and drones" and more hardworking farmers and laborers. Finally, the graduates ought to follow the example of Lee and Grant and Jackson and Sherman "who *knew* when to stop fighting." Only fanatics and politicians wanted to continue the strife, and whereas the first could be dismissed as fools, the latter were dangerous. Like vultures they "grow fat on corruption and like a dead carcass best." Moved by David's remarks, General G. Mason Graham rose in the audience and proposed three cheers for the superintendent. But others were more restrained. A local editor commented, "We did not hear the address of Superintendent Boyd, but learn that it

7   R. E. Lee to D. F. Boyd, copy, June 24, 1870, in David Boyd Papers; Jefferson Davis to David Boyd, July 8, 1872, in Alphabetical File, Fleming Collection.

was characterized with vigor of thought and seasonable advice to the graduates. His views on the political situation are *not*, however, receiving general commendation. The positions assumed were correct enough in principle—the illustrations inappropriate and humiliating to Southern sentiment."[8]

Another volatile subject that figured prominently in David's speeches was religion. Equally critical of "hellfire sermons" and "stylized Christianity" which operated only at 11 A.M. on Sundays, David showed no patience with what he called "pious stupidity," that brand of religion which denied man's appetites and passions. God gave these to man to enjoy and he should do so in moderation. As for the "metaphysical approach," it was just as worthless as "sheer ignorance" in the pulpit. What did matter was the "simple substance" of Christianity which David cautioned his young listeners not to renounce simply because Christ was sometimes invoked by fools and frauds. Undoubtedly David's remarks offended some of his fundamentalist listeners, as did the fact that he attended no church, professed no particular creed, and tolerated dancing at the university. But he was not irreligious; he simply objected to "narrow dogmas . . . ignorance and prejudice."[9]

Besides politics and religion, one other controversial topic received special attention in David's speeches: race. In 1873 both his anniversary address and his remarks at commencement dealt with the issue, particularly as it related to political participation and public education. "True republicanism" as established by the Founding Fathers, David told his audience, was as dead in the United States as African slavery. In its place the federal government had imposed universal suffrage, and the net effect of letting every "loafer, ignoramus and baboon," in or out of the penitentiary, vote and be voted for, was to reduce the country to a "diseased political condition." He doubted that the harm done could ever be corrected entirely, but the evil consequences might be counteracted somewhat by universal education. To that end, David advised the cadets to swallow their pride and apply for teaching positions

---

8   David Boyd, commencement address to class of 1870, June 29, 1870, in David Boyd Papers; Fleming, *Louisiana State University*, 247; Baton Rouge *Tri-Weekly Advocate*, July 1, 1870. One of the owners of the newspaper was W. J. Walter, soon to be nominated as a Democrat for a congressional seat from Louisiana. His sensitivity to David's remarks is understandable.

9   David Boyd, commencement address to class of 1871, June 28, 1871; anniversary address, January 2, 1874, in David Boyd Papers; annual address to the graduates, June 26, 1872, in Printed Pamphlets, *ibid.*; Fleming, *Louisiana State University*, 246.

in black schools. On Sundays, their mothers and sisters did similar "missionary work" in Negro churches; how could it degrade them to do the same thing during the week? David knew that "coarse and ignorant" southern whites would resist his proposal bitterly, but the cadets were educated. They must accept reality and "fling away" prejudice. "Take hold of the negro and *lift* him up," he exhorted, "educate him. He is no longer your slave but your equal before the law. You & he must dwell here together as men & citizens of a common country." Finally, to clinch his argument, David reminded the cadets that they owed their current privileged status to the labor of their former slaves. Blacks reclaimed the swamps which made their fathers rich; they had supplied the labor necessary to develop the "high and refined culture" of the antebellum South. Intellectually, David conceded, the freedman might never equal his erstwhile master, but "in all that appeals to the heart, the emotions & the imagination—as poetry, music & oratory, the cultivated negro has no superior." [10]

As racist, condescending, and paternalistic as David's remarks may seem today, they were undoubtedly considered too advanced by some of his contemporaries. Men like the Egans, and G. Mason Graham knew that David was "sound" on the race question; they came from similar family and educational backgrounds and shared David's well-developed sense of noblesse oblige. But others, perhaps less secure socially or genealogically, may have needed reassurance, and David gave it to them. He was, he told two audiences in 1873, against integrated education despite provisions in the state constitution which clearly required it. Legally, even the university was vulnerable, but no black had yet tried to enroll and he did not think any would. "Whom God hath put asunder, let no man join together," David concluded drily. It was a sound principle, although "not universally practiced outside of the schools." [11]

Two years later, in 1875, David prepared but never delivered another anniversary address dealing with race and education. On the surface, the speech, entitled "Some Ideas on Ed.; the True Solution of 'Color' in our schools, Colleges and Universities et.c.," seemed to indicate a shift in David's thinking because it no longer rejected out of

10 Anniversary address, January 2, 1873; commencement address, June 25, 1873, in David Boyd Papers.
11 Anniversary address, January 2, 1873; commencement address, June 25, 1873, *ibid.*

hand the idea of black students at the university. Actually, David was trying desperately to appease the Radicals without completely alienating white conservative Louisianians. In 1873 Governor William Pitt Kellogg's administration, considerably more equalitarian than its predecessor, cut off all support for the "whites only" university. Beneficiary cadets, whose tuition and maintenance depended entirely upon legislative appropriations, had to be sent home in midterm and, worse still, the lawmakers established a competing and integrated institution in New Orleans the following year. Because the beneficiaries constituted the overwhelming majority of the student body, the effect on the school was devastating, leading David to compose his undelivered speech. In it he still insisted that prejudice, even instinct, required racial separation in elementary and secondary schools. But at the college level, it was an "axiom to concentrate your means." Louisiana, David explained, could not support more than one university, even though "natural causes and social prejudices" seemed to demand it. How, then, could the state, short of money as always, solve her dilemma? The answer lay in reorganization. A "true university," David argued, left students free to study what they pleased, with whom they pleased. They could live and eat wherever they chose and no "social intercourse *whatever*" need occur unless individuals, formally introduced, mutually agreed to it. That was what Jefferson planned for the University of Virginia; why not apply it in Baton Rouge? How could anyone be "morally contaminated" or "socially degraded" by the mere presence of a Negro in the same class? Besides, a university which denied admittance to anyone was a contradiction in terms. Paris, Berlin, or Oxford would never refuse an "Indian or *Chinee* or African"; neither should the South. "I would no more deny access on account of race, or color from the temple of learning," David declared, "than I would exclude one, on account of race, or color, from the temple of faith."[12]

The logic was faultless, but the implementation of such a plan would have been impossible given the embattled condition of Louisiana in January, 1875. Again faced with the prospect of two legislative

---

12   D. F. Boyd, "Some Ideas on Ed., the True Solution of the Question of 'Color' in our Schools, Colleges and Universities" (Typescript in Louisiana Room, Louisiana State University Library, Baton Rouge), [?], 1875; David Boyd Diary, January 2, 1875.

bodies,[13] the state was in turmoil and, under the circumstances, David's appeal to "do away with our prejudices," and exercise a "little common sense" had little chance of being heeded. Indeed, its public expression might have made a bad situation worse.

During 1870 and 1871 David had to grapple with several problems. Some were public, directly concerned with the conduct of the university. Others were personal, involving relations with students and tax collectors. The imbroglios with students occurred at commencement time in 1870 and 1871. Both reflect, in different degree, the extreme sensitiveness, devotion to duty, pride of self, and sense of personal honor so often associated with gentlemen of the nineteenth century. The less serious incident happened in June, 1871. Just before the end of the term, David invited a graduating senior, A. A. Gunby, to a social function. Gunby declined in writing, describing himself as "equally pained and surprised" at the invitation. He was surprised because of the "little notice or regard" which David had theretofore displayed for his personal feelings. He was pained because he had to refuse the invitation. David replied to Gunby's note, calling it a "boyish whim." He asked Gunby to explain the alleged injustice, but Gunby preferred to wait until graduation when he would no longer be a cadet. On June 28 he sent a letter to David with a copy to Commandant Edward Cunningham, in which he described an incident wherein he had been insulted by a black waiter in the mess hall. Gunby refrained from "punishing the insult personally" because he did not want to hurt the school. Instead, he complained to Commandant Cunningham who insinuated that Gunby, not the waiter, was at fault. For the next three months, Gunby charged, Cunningham "abused his power" and he, Gunby, quietly endured the abuse. If the commandant derived any pleasure from his "cowardly tyranny," he was welcome to it. David's answer obviously managed to soothe Gunby's injured feelings, because a few weeks later the former student thanked him for his letter which he described as "magnanimous" and "dispassionate." For his part, Gunby was ready to forget the past and "live in the future." He was as good as his word. Thirty-three years later, when the university began con-

---

13 Following the election of 1872, Conservative candidate John McEnery and his followers claimed to be the legitimate government of Louisiana, but Federal authorities recognized the Radical Kellogg regime. In 1875 turmoil again ensued when representatives of both factions claimed victory and tried to organize the upcoming legislature.

struction of a building to honor David's memory, A. A. Gunby delivered a glowing tribute to his friend and former teacher, David F. Boyd.[14]

The second involvement with a cadet, much more serious than the Gunby incident, occurred in the summer of 1870. Following graduation, Cadet Samuel H. Lewis issued a formal challenge to David through Professor Samuel H. Lockett. According to Lewis, the superintendent had "affronted" him four years earlier; now he was "demanding satisfaction." David answered at once. He thought he remembered the incident, but "considering the relationship between them of student and sup^t," that Lewis was violating one of the well-know rules in David's presence, and under circumstances "calculated to excite" him, David did not think then, nor did he in 1870, that he had done anything "officially" to Lewis that he should not have done. But finding that Lewis was so "personally mortified," he regretted ever having disciplined him.

On June 30, just before Lewis left for New Orleans, he sent David another note, still demanding a meeting and still maintaining that David had "basely humiliated" him four years before. David answered that he was sorry, but in the interest of the school, he would have to sever his relationship with it before they could meet. He did submit his resignation, which the board promptly rejected, but Lewis continued to demand that a date be set to settle the affair. Next, David tried to reason with Lewis, suggesting that he and Colonel Lockett go to New Orleans and discuss the matter "amicably." Arguing that no good could come from a duel, that it would only wreck the school, and that "Sam" would regret it later, David declared that he still considered himself Lewis' friend, and even if they met, he (David) would never do anything to prevent the younger man from "enjoying a long and happy life." Lewis answered that he could not meet David under the circumstances. Apparently he also impugned David's courage, because the next day David dispatched a long explanatory note, regretting that Sam's letter was so "ungenerous," and declaring that he would gladly sacrifice his own life to avoid the risk of Lewis losing his. From the beginning, David insisted, he never intended to appear on the field with a loaded weapon. Lockett could verify the fact. Rather, he intended to give Lewis satisfaction by going through the form of a meeting, thereby providing him with a defense before the law. But, he pointed out,

14   A. A. Gunby to David F. Boyd, June 3, 28, July 15, 1871, in Alphabetical File, Fleming Collection; Gunby, "Life and Services of David French Boyd."

Lewis would have found out later and would never have forgiven David, Lockett, or himself.

Lewis was unmoved. A month later, on August 9, 1870, David wrote his former student once more, reproaching him for remaining so "obdurate" and reminding him that he (David) had gone much more than half way to "smooth over" the difficulty. Any further effort would have to come from Lewis; David had done all "my self-respect will allow." Then, in spite of everything, he proposed that Lewis open a preparatory school in New Orleans, promising to do whatever he could to contribute to its success.

David's last letter, or the offer in it, seems to have mollified the touchy Lewis. At any rate, he resumed correspondence with David, informing him late in August that he and a friend planned to launch a private school in the Crescent City to prepare boys for the university. Another letter was more direct. Besides asking David to send him and his partner some unused equipment from the university, Lewis asked for money to pay for advertising, circulars, and incidentals. "We would wish you to favor us with a check for seventy-five or $100, as soon as convenient," he concluded abruptly. Whether Lewis was naturally or intentionally brusque is impossible to judge, but his letter smacks of bush league blackmail. Whether David ever sent the money is also unclear, as indeed is the nature of the incident which led to the whole affair. But years later David's son, LeRoy Boyd, left no doubt regarding his opinion of Samuel Lewis. Across one of his letters LeRoy scrawled, "I never knew a man named Sam who wasn't a big bluff and a coward."[15]

The Federal revenue service also challenged David during 1870 and 1871. In June, 1870, he was notified of his failure to pay taxes on his income for 1866. As a penalty he was ordered to remit 5 percent a month on everything earned since September, 1867. If he did not comply in ten days, the collector was authorized to seize and sell his property to satisfy the debt. The following year David was in trouble with the tax collector again. A Federal law of 1870 required everyone over twenty-one whose gross income from all sources in 1870 exceeded $2,000 to file a return with the assistant assessor of the district in

15   Minutes of the Board of Supervisors, June 29, 1870; Sam Lewis to David Boyd, June 30, July 10, August 22, 30, 1870, in Alphabetical File, Fleming Collection; David Boyd to Samuel H. Lewis, June 30, July 7, 11, August 9, 1870, in Boyd Letters, *ibid.*

which he resided. The deadline was March 1, and the tax form itself stipulated that the party filing it must verify it under oath. Apparently David neither filed his return on time nor personally verified it to the assistant assessor. On April 25, 1871, "F. D. Boyde" of East Baton Rouge was ordered to appear before the assistant assessor within a week to "show cause why the penalties prescribed by law should not be assessed agst. him." What David seems to have objected to in particular was the requirement that he verify the form personally. Sometime during the controversy he scribbled across the return that his clerk's statement regarding its authenticity had always been accepted in the past. "If Mr. Van Pelt [the clerk] cannot answer for me, then this paper may go unanswered, for I will not attend to it further. D.F.B." Which party to the dispute finally won is not clear, but David's general attitude about income taxes and tax form questions certainly was. To the query "Have you included in the return the income of your wife, and . . . wages of minor children?" he answered flippantly, "Yes, if *nothing* can be counted!" [16]

David's personal difficulties with students and tax collectors were minor compared to the problems he faced as president of the university. After the school moved to Baton Rouge, it could no longer escape public notice and political pressure as it had in Rapides. Almost at once crises whose magnitude ranged all the way from grafitti on the privy walls to legislative resolutions to investigate his administration occupied David's time and attention. His first problem, which lasted throughout Superintendent McWhorter's tenure, grew immediately out of the fact that the university shared quarters with the deaf and dumb asylum. A Radical appointee, McWhorter had sufficient power in the legislature to forestall all of David's efforts to acquire the entire building. Nevertheless, David kept trying. Besides securing legislation authorizing the deaf to occupy other quarters, he used his influence with Baton Rouge politicos to get McWhorter out. But nothing succeeded. Not until 1878 did the university win control of the entire building. [17]

16 Notice of failure to pay taxes, June 21, 1870; Income tax form, 1871, in Official Papers, Fleming Collection; Summons for "F. D. Boyde" to appear before Assessor, April 25, 1871, in David Boyd Papers.
17 *Acts of Louisiana,* 1870, No. 29, p. 53; D. Boyd to J. A. Fuqua, August 29, 1873; Resolution of Baton Rouge City Council, February 23, 1871, in David Boyd Papers; David Boyd Diary, August 14, 1874; Fleming, *Louisiana State University,* 185, 263–64, 429.

Lobbying before potentially hostile legislatures provided David with additional problems as chief officer of the university. He heartily disliked the job because it was time consuming, but even more because it involved dealing with people for whom he had considerable contempt. To Colonel Samuel Lockett, professor of engineering, he described his appearances before the legislators in 1870 as personally degrading. Later in the same year, when the board's vice-president urged him to go to New Orleans in the school's behalf, he protested that he would if he had to, but he did not like "to stand around in Lobbies." He also doubted that it did the school any good. Apparently, what he really objected to was the adverse comment his trips to New Orleans seemed to stir up among the "old citizens." Their remarks "mortified" him. "God only knows," he wrote the vice-president, "my only object is to advance the Seminary [university]. I do not wish to go about the Legislature or the Radical Authorities any more than I can help." [18]

Nevertheless, David returned to the Crescent City. He spent a good part of February, 1871, lobbying for the law to authorize removal of the deaf. He also had to dispose of university warrants in order to secure enough cash to operate the school. Conditions were so bad that year that he had to sell them on the street for whatever he could get. At one point the warrants brought only 50 percent of their face value and to avoid further loss, he pledged some $81,413 worth of 1870 and 1871 warrants as collateral for a loan of $39,000. All this took a great deal of time and kept him away from Baton Rouge for long periods. Each year, David remarked in his report for 1870, his duties as superintendent seemed to increase so much that he could not be an "efficient professor." As a result, he wanted to resign. "I am convinced that no one can be superintendent here and professor too," he told the board, "and as I am only a teacher and wish to be nothing more, with no taste and less fitness for business and finance, I respectfully ask the Board to relieve me as early as practicable of the Superintendency and permit me to be simply professor of mathematics." [19]

The request was denied. David remained as superintendent and he continued to lobby despite his conviction that his forays among the

---

18   David Boyd to Samuel Lockett, January 20, 1870, David F. Boyd to William Sanford, December 20, 1870, January 30, 1871 in Boyd Letters, Fleming Collection.
19   Telegrams, D. F. Boyd to Edward Cunningham, February 16–21, 1871, in Official Papers, *ibid.*; *Report* to the Board of Supervisors for 1871, pp. 4–5; *ibid.*, 1870, p. 23.

politicians offended "old citizens." In December, 1871, he confided to Vice-President Sanford his belief that he had made several enemies in his confrontations with the Radicals. Some of them, David suspected, would try to oust him. But he was determined to let the "Radical scoundrels" know exactly where he stood; he had already informed Speaker of the House Carr that he would cane him "if he weren't such a cur." Justifying himself, David remarked, "You know, Mr. Sanford, that I have already compromised myself with the good people of La. on acc't. of my official position here, as far as a due regard for my own private character can stand."[20]

Earlier in 1871, while David was lobbying in New Orleans, an incident occurred at the university which might well have resulted in disaster for the school. Colonel Edward Cunningham, commandant and professor of natural philosophy, led a biracial legislative committee on a tour of the university. Cunningham was polite, but he refused to shake the offered hands of the black legislators as they left the building. Naturally they objected, and two board members, learning of the incident later, expected serious retaliation. Although he sympathized with the commandant, Vice-President Sanford thought Cunningham had used poor judgment, considering the university's "delicate position." Besides, Sanford reminded David, board member Harry Lott, the senator from Rapides, was black, and he had voted for Cunningham's appointment with "great cordiality and good feeling." General G. Mason Graham was even more concerned. He thought Cunningham ought to issue an official apology to the committee. He also authorized David to suspend Cunningham if he failed to "reconcile" the injured lawmakers. No one, Graham insisted, could stand in the way of the school's well-being. Meanwhile, Cunningham offered to resign but David objected, arguing that to succumb to Radical pressure would cost the school support from the "old people" of the state.[21]

The university weathered the Cunningham crisis, but in November, 1871, David himself stirred up a controversy which seriously threatened the school. On a Saturday night, November 11, an un-

20 David F. Boyd to William L. Sanford, December 23, 1871, in Alphabetical File, Fleming Collection.
21 Edward Cunningham to David Boyd, February 17, 1871, *ibid.*; G. Mason Graham to David Boyd, February 15, 1871, in G. Mason Graham Letters, *ibid.*; Fleming, *Louisiana State University*, 195.

known group of university cadets stole the bell from the belfry of the deaf and dumb asylum. Why the institution had a bell at all was a mystery, but when its theft was detected, David interrogated the cadets one by one to find the guilty parties. Twenty-four refused to answer and were promptly expelled, causing the Radical New Orleans *Republican* to demand an investigation. Professing shock that the rules allowed expulsion for such an offense, the paper sympathized with the boys "who have shown a manly spirit." "Perhaps," the editor remarked, "a legislative committee may recommend a reversal of the order of the Superintendent even though it should involve the resignation of that official." David shot back a quick reply. To preserve order and discipline, he argued, the superintendent had to exercise the power to which the *Republican* objected. "With all respect" to the editor, the legislature, and the people, he made it clear that if his right to dismiss for refusal to give information were withdrawn, he would step down. Then, to show that not everyone disapproved of his expulsion order, David enclosed a letter from the uncle of a dismissed cadet. Unimpressed, the *Republican* responded that one uncle did not offset five or six angry fathers whom the editor had heard criticize David. Pulling down the bell, the paper agreed, was serious, but a regulation that required a boy to testify against himself "violates all *usual* procedure." It smacked of the Spanish Inquisition. "If discipline can not be maintained by the superintendent without violating the rules of common sense, or compelling the . . . boys to betray their comrades, the fault is his own, and the misfortune is the State's "[22]

Friends as well as enemies thought David went too far in the bell-stealing incident. After reading about it in the newspaper, Alexandria lawyer and former superintendent William Seay advised David, "I could have told you that your tactics would not work. I have seen it [interrogation] tried twice, and in both cases it failed." Board member G. Mason Graham was also upset. He thought David's letters to the editor could have been a "little more temperate." Ironically, Graham had written David the very day of the bell-stealing incident to suggest that too many cadets had been dismissed for "demerit." "People will not send their sons to so rigid a school," Graham complained. "It seems to

22 New Orleans *Republican*, November 18, 22, 1871, in Printed Materials, David Boyd Papers.

me the idea should be to prevent demerit, and not solely [to] rely on *punishment* (and so severe) after commission."[23]

David was not oblivious to the difficulties which his expulsion order and his subsequent letters to the newspapers might cause him and the university. But tact and circumspection were not his most outstanding characteristics. If his resignation would satisfy his detractors and save the school, David wrote Vice-President William Sanford, he would be glad to submit it. Meanwhile, he meant to let his Radical critics know exactly where he stood. His determination paid off. Weeks later David's report to the board for 1871 commented on "our late *wholesale* dismissal." Of the twenty-four expelled students, all but eight returned to the university after making appropriate amends for having defied the authorities. All was "happy and *orderly*" at the school, the report continued. Those who cared to should judge conditions by the cadets, "*not* the false philanthropy" or "sickly sentimentality" of outside "ignorance and prejudice."[24]

The "bell scrape" was barely settled before David became embroiled in another controversy. This one developed in the midst of a political battle between factions of the Radicals for control of the legislature. In mid-January, 1872, David went to New Orleans to oversee university affairs, but by the end of the month he left for Baton Rouge because the lawmakers showed no "disposition to go to work." A few weeks later, the political crisis having abated, he was back in the Crescent City. "Our affairs seem promising," he wrote Commandant Cunningham optimistically. "I think there is no doubt of our getting the agricultural fund." David expected to leave the city in a few days but his plans suddenly changed. On February 17, 1872, "Mr. Worrall of Jefferson" introduced a resolution in the house to appoint a five-man committee with full power to inquire into the management of the university, "particularly with regard to the furnishing of the institution with supplies, groceries, meats, vegetables, books, apparatus, and all other necessaries . . . to the late expulsion of pupils, to the payments

---

23 G. Mason Graham to David Boyd, November 11, December 3, 1871, in G. Mason Graham Letters, Fleming Collection; W. A. Seay to David Boyd, November 12, 1871, in Alphabetical File, *ibid*.

24 David F. Boyd to W. L. Sanford, December 23, 1871, in Alphabetical File, *ibid.*; *Report* to the Board of Supervisors for 1871, p. 15. Three years after the "bell scrape" David was still convinced that he had acted correctly, despite the "big howl" caused by so many dismissals. David Boyd Diary, November 11, 1874.

demanded of the State for beneficiary cadets; to the vacancies on the academic board remaining unfilled in one case since January 1871 . . . the manner and channels of disbursing the funds, to the authority and cost of printing . . . and to *all* other matters re: the institution."[25]

The Worrall resolution indicates plainly that there were several prospective, but frustrated suppliers and a few disgruntled parents with a grudge against David and the university. But failure to fill an opening on the academic board seems to have been the immediate reason for the hostile resolution. Dr. James Burns, a New Orleans physician interested in the professorship of chemistry, composed the measure after consulting with Dr. S. O. Scruggs of Nachitoches. Scruggs was a member of the Board of Supervisors; however, by 1872 he no longer attended meetings, and David considered his position vacant. With the resolution in hand, Burns and Scruggs looked for a legislator to introduce it. A Major Blackman in the senate refused, fearing to raise the "mixed" question, but in the house another physician, Dr. Worrall of Jefferson, was willing. Immediately, friends of the school— one of whom was Harry Lott, the black member from Rapides—rushed to its defense, and the Worrall resolution failed by a vote of sixty-two to ten.

Two weeks later, on February 27, 1872, Burns published a handbill entitled "The Management of the State University." In it he explained that months before he had applied to Vice-President Sanford for the vacant professorship of chemisty. Sanford advised him to send his "testimonials" to Superintendent Boyd in time for the next board meeting in June, 1871. He also expressed doubt that anyone would be hired because the school's financial condition was so depressed. Meanwhile, Burns saw David personally and received the same advice. Next, the would-be professor submitted his letters of recommendation and solicited support from Governor Warmoth and other board members. June, 1871, passed and Burns heard nothing. Later, David told him no board meeting had taken place, but if he cared to leave his application on file, the members might consider him next year. Burns declined, asked for the return of his references, and David sent them back, unopened.

Undeterred, Burns continued to seek the professorship through

25 Jas. W. Crawford to David Boyd, telegrams, January 4–6, 10, 1872; David Boyd to Ed. Cunningham, telegrams, January 17–18, 23–25, February 16, 1872, in Official Papers, Fleming Collection; Reprint of Louisiana *House Journal*, February 17, 1872, in David Boyd Papers.

another visit to the governor and by means of a letter-writing campaign waged in his behalf by several New Orleans newspapers. When David did not respond, Governor Warmoth finally told the doctor that Boyd objected to him because of his age, his gout, and his prestige. Allegedly, the superintendent preferred a "pushing young man who had a reputation to make," not an "established scholar." Burns finally abandoned his efforts, but in February, 1872, he met Dr. Scruggs whom he had known for some time. The two agreed that the legislature should investigate the university and the resolution presented by their colleague, Dr. Worrall, was the result.

Defeat of the Worrall resolution might have ended the affair. However, on February 26, Burns received a letter from David that prompted the doctor to publish his handbill. After quoting liberally from David's letter, particularly as it applied to Dr. Scruggs, Burns declared himself unwilling to comment on the superintendent's "persistent coarseness" except to say "that I decline any direct communication with him [David], and that I should have on the instant returned his miserably ill-advised missive" except that it might constitute valuable "testimony" in case of necessity.[26]

David soon provided Burns with more "testimony." On February 29, 1872, he issued an answering broadside addressed "To Whom It May Concern." The explanatory preface took Burns to task for quoting selectively from his letter. Burns did so, David charged, in order to defeat the university appropriations bill then before the legislature. In justice to all, David intended to publish his letter to Burns in full, omitting only the name of the third party (Dr. Scruggs) as irrelevant. The complete text followed. Somewhat restrained, the first paragraph merely reproached Burns for asking the legislature to investigate the management of the university before addressing any questions to the superintendent or the board. In the second and third paragraphs, however, David warmed to his task. They are reproduced here because they illustrate so well his capacity for indignation and command of invective:

From your confrere [Scruggs], the ex-member of our Board of Supervisors, whose resignation was accepted, because I refused longer (in June, 1870) to

26   James Burns, M.D., "The Management of the State University," February 27, 1872, in David
Boyd Papers.

serve a Board, of which such a mean, slanderous creature was a member; from him, I say, I expected nothing else but a cowardly and malicious effort to mortify or injure me, *even when he knew that he was unjust to the Institution, as well as to me.*
You certainly did not know the man, or you would never form any alliance with him. Do you know that he now actually *denies* having had anything to do with the resolution, when you know that he and yourself went together to Major Blackman, of the Senate, and he [Scruggs] handed the paper to the Senator and urged him to present it?[27]

Finally, David accused Dr. Burns of hypocrisy. "The next time you want the Legislature to inquire why *you* were not appointed *professor* HERE, please say so plainly." "If I have judged you harshly in this matter," concluded David, "I shall regret it; but you can only be excused on the ground that '*a want of decency is a want of sense.*'"[28]

David returned from his personal Battle of New Orleans with less than he originally expected to win. Early in February he thought the university might secure the agricultural college fund. But "due to their best friends," he wrote William Sanford, the question had been deferred until 1873. The Burns-Scruggs affair was also dormant, although David thought it was "hardly over." He wondered if he had gone too far or not far enough. Burns was probably "ruined" in New Orleans, and Scruggs, in David's judgment, ought to be "tabooed" from all good society in the state. Referring to both as liars, he commented, "They are certainly a handsome pair to make war on the University."[29]

When "war" finally came, it was not Drs. Burns and Scruggs who were the principal aggressors. The university, like the rest of Louisiana, was about to be caught up in a long power struggle among the forces of Governor Henry C. Warmoth, the more Radical Customhouse officials, and the Democrats who played the first group off against the second. With assistance from the federal government, the Customhouse group won control of the state in 1873. The university, luckier than some state institutions, managed to survive. But for four years (1873–1877), it endured under conditions that approximated those usually associated with war.

27 David Boyd to James Burns, February 21, 1872, quoted in "To Whom It May Concern," February 29, 1872, *ibid.*
28 *Ibid.*
29 David Boyd to Wm. Sanford, undated, 1872, in Alphabetical File, Fleming Collection.

Before dealing with that melancholy period, something should be said about developments in David's family. When the seminary's destruction by fire forced them to leave Rapides in 1869, the Boyds (David, Ettie, and their six-month-old sons) moved into rooms in the asylum building. Tom Boyd, David's younger brother, was a cadet and lived in student quarters. Months later, during the summer of 1870, yellow fever visited Baton Rouge, and David sent his wife and children to Minnesota to avoid the disease. The Virginia Boyds, who still had not met their daughter-in-law, were "mortified" when they learned of Ettie's journey. But David and his father were still somewhat estranged in 1870. In one exchange David complained that his parents "had no affection for him any more," and Thomas Boyd admitted that "disparaging remarks" in some of David's letters had indeed offended him; so much, in fact, that he had stopped writing "for a season." But, Thomas Boyd insisted, he had never "lessened his affection" for his son. Ettie and the twins would have been very welcome in Virginia, and the whole family must visit Wytheville in the following summer.[30]

The family reunion occurred well before Thomas Boyd expected it. On November 19, 1870, just days after her return from Minnesota, Ettie and the twins joined David and his clerk, S. B. Robinson, on a trip to the Northeast. They traveled first to Wytheville, where one of David's sisters was about to be married. Ettie and the children stayed on, but David and Mr. Robinson left for Washington and New York to visit the "principal scientific bureaus and educational establishments" of those cities. In Washington, General Sherman conducted them through such facilities as the Smithsonian Institution. He also gave David a letter of introduction to be used at Columbia College in New York, where President Frederick Barnard acted as their guide.

The excursion convinced David that educationally the South had a long way to go. Even the University of Virginia, he thought, could not compare with the "good colleges of the North," and the reason was plain. The North believed in public education and supported it. In Louisiana, by contrast, there were practically no secondary schools in the parishes where a boy might learn simple geography, arithmetic, and English grammer. Until the public took the schools and school legisla-

---

30 Correspondence between Ettie and David Boyd [summer, 1870], T. J. Boyd to David Boyd, November 20, 1870, in David Boyd Papers.

tion out of politics, even the small amounts spent on education would be wasted. As for the university, it could not expect to compete with other states for good professors. "Teachers are used to working for very little and are not likely to expect much, still they must have enough to keep their families from want," he wrote in one annual report. "No professor can maintain his family respectably on a salary of $2,000 a year on the banks of the lower Mississippi, when the very deck hands on the steamers are paid forty to sixty dollars a month."[31]

David's concern for the low salaries the university paid its professors only rarely extended to himself. For his several duties as superintendent, treasurer, and professor he received $3,000 a year plus quarters. That figure had been raised during the summer of 1869, but following the fire, the board, at David's suggestion, reduced it to the old level. By the end of 1870 David seems to have had enough. It was then that he asked to be relieved of all duties except that of professor of mathematics.

But the board did not relieve him and it did not increase his pay. G. Mason Graham thought he appreciated David's struggles to keep the school going as much as anyone could other than David's wife. He also deplored the inadequacy of his salary. "This, I fear, will always be the case with you," Graham wrote David in June, 1871. Half seriously, he added, "I have pretty much . . . lost all sympathy with your 'Angusta domires,' to use a classical expression for the Louse in the Head, for I have realized that the biggest fool on the face of the earth is one who gives away everything that he hasn't been robbed of. . . . By the way, have you ever read the Grand Epic, title forgotten, but commencing 'Higglety pigglety snigglety Fritz, lost his money, and then his wits . . . . ' [?] If not, I would commend it to your serious perusal."[32]

David did indeed give away whatever he had. Besides supporting himself, Ettie, and the twins, he loaned money to his brother Charlie, whose inability to earn a living in Louisiana caused him to go back to Virginia in 1871. David also educated and maintained his youngest brother, Tom Boyd, at the University until the latter was graduated in

31 *Report* to the Board of Supervisors for 1870, pp. 9–10, 16; Wm. T. Sherman, letter of introduction for David Boyd, copy, November 28, 1870, Henderson French (uncle) to D. F. Boyd, June 22, 1871, in David Boyd Papers; David Boyd Diary, November 27, 1874.

32 *Report* to the Board of Supervisors for 1869, p. 14; Minutes of the Board of Supervisors, January 28, 1870; *Report* to the Board of Supervisors for 1870, p. 15; G. Mason Graham to David Boyd, June 20, 1871, in G. Mason Graham Letters, Fleming Collection.

1872. Tom left for Virginia, too, expecting to study law, but a year and a half later he was still unemployed. By that time the Kellogg regime had cut off all support for the university and several professors had been forced to resign. If Tom had "nothing better to do," David suggested, he could use him to teach some classes in mathematics. He could not promise any salary beyond room and board, but Tom would have the use of a fine library and the chance to study botany and zoology. Within a week a grateful Tom Boyd accepted David's offer. "I am under so many obligations to you," he wrote his older brother, "that I hardly know how to thank you for your kindness. . . . I can only do so by doing all in my power to help you."[33]

Perhaps the best evidence of David's willingness to assume responsibilities that others were better able to afford was his offer in December, 1870, to provide Ettie's mother, Sarah Wright, and her sister Mary with a home at the university. Technically, Mrs. Wright was not without financial resources, even in 1870. Her Greenwood Plantation, appraised in 1859 at $108,000, consisted of 1,500 acres of "bare land" in 1866 when her impatient children began to haggle seriously over it. David did not want to get involved in what he called the "family pie," but at Ettie's urging, he finally consented to act in her behalf. "God knows," Ettie wrote her husband from the family home in Cheneyville, "I want to see this division made with *justice* to all parties; if anybody is defrauded of a dollar, I would rather it be me." She had "perfect confidence" in whatever David might decide. Three and one-half years later, in August, 1869, the family property was still not divided to everyone's satisfaction, and Leroy S. Havard, married to Ettie's older sister Julia Catherine Wright, wanted David to come to Cheneyville for further discussion. David replied that he could not leave the school on such short notice. Besides, he informed Havard, his letter, plus the one Ettie was sending to her mother the same day, ought to preclude any further consultation with the Boyds concerning Mrs. Wright's affairs. "About the whole matter," he explained, "I have but *one regret*—that Ettie did not, immediately upon our marriage, do as she has done today. It would have saved me much that was annoying and unpleasant.

---

33   T. J. Boyd to David F. Boyd, August 27, 1871, C. R. Boyd to D. F. Boyd, August 29, 1872, T. D. Boyd to D. F. Boyd, August 17, 1872, August 13, 1873, T. D. Boyd to Ettie Boyd, October 23, 1872, all in David Boyd Papers; David F. Boyd to Tom Boyd, August 5, 1873, in Boyd Letters, Fleming Collection; Wilkerson, *Thomas Duckett Boyd*, 34–37.

From the first I have been anxious to have nothing to do with the ad-justment of the Estate, well knowing how easy it is for members of a family to disagree—and even to quarrel—about their share of the property—the most unfortunate and disagreeable of all squabbles, as well as the most unbecoming."[34]

Unfortunately, the remaining heirs could not reach a settlement, nor did they provide adequately for the ailing Mrs. Wright. Through her spinster daughter Mary, she finally appealed to Ettie for financial advice and assistance in December, 1870. David answered for his wife. He did not see how the Boyds could help Mrs. Wright. "I am very anx-ious not to have any business transaction with your heirs," he told his mother-in-law, "and Ettie herself could do nothing for your relief." Mrs. Wright might consider his attitude "strange," but, he reminded her, all her exertions to educate and support her children had brought her nothing but bad treatment, harassment, and persecution. Now she was a "poor old lady, sick and infirm." Under the circumstances, would it not be better for her and "Sister Mary" to "get out of the whole thing" by coming to live in Baton Rouge? "You must know that I am poor," he continued. His salary hardly supported his family in the way his posi-tion required them to live. But the Wrights would never lack the ordin-ary "care and comforts of a home" if he could possibly provide them, and Ettie and the children would be delighted to have them come. By June, 1871, Mrs. Wright and Mary had accepted David's offer. They joined the Boyds in the asylum building, remaining until 1880 when David, by that time no longer president of the university, had to find other quarters for his family.[35]

34 Ettie G. Boyd to David Boyd, undated, in David F. Boyd Family Papers, Jesse D. Wright Pa-pers. Internal evidence in Ettie's letter indicates that it was written about mid-January, 1866. David Boyd to L. S. Havard, August 11, 1869, *ibid.*
35 David Boyd to Sara R. Wright (mother-in-law), December [?], 1870, L. S. Havard to Mary C. Wright, January 27, 1877, David Boyd to Ettie G. Boyd, November 27, 1880, Account book of Sara G. Wright, January 22, June [?], 1871, *ibid.* Greenwood Planatation was not finally di-vided among the heirs until August 23, 1883. By that time Mrs. Sara Wright had been dead for two years. Mary C. Wright, the unmarried sister, willed her property to her sister Ettie Boyd, with whom she was living at the time of her death in 1888. By 1890 the Boyds no longer had any claim to Greenwood Plantation. Ettie sold her share (the amount she received in 1883 plus what she inherited from her sister Mary), in all about 700 or 800 acres, to a "Mrs. Smith." Although dead for nine years, Mrs. Sara Wright had the last word. Scrawled across an authorization to sell the last of Greenwood were these lines attributed to her: "What you leave at your death, let it be without controversy, else the lawyers will be your heirs." Final division among heirs, August 23, 1883; Will of Mary C. Wright, April 13, 1881; Kernan and Laycock, Attorneys [Baton Rouge], to Ettie G. Boyd, September 9, 1890, *ibid.*; Genealogical Scrapbook, LeRoy Boyd Papers.

On October 7, 1871, soon after the Wrights' arrival, Ettie Boyd gave birth to another son, Arthur J. Boyd, thereby increasing the Boyd household to seven members. But only a week later sorrow struck for the second time that year. In July, David's trusted clerk and good friend S. B. Robinson had died after a long illness. Now, on October 15, one of the twins, Reb, or Edward J., became seriously ill. He was so heavily dosed with paregoric on the sixteenth that "to keep him from dying from stupor," a physician administered a strong counter agent. But at three A.M. on October 18, 1871, the little boy died. Recalling the event three years later, David noted in his diary that Reb became ill on the second anniversary of the seminary fire. He was convinced that the boy died of "malpractice"; first, by whoever administered the paregoric; second, by the physician who employed a heroic antidote. The child was buried in the same cemetery as Mr. Robinson. Whenever he could, David visited both graves on the anniversary of Reb's death.[36]

For David's family, as well as for the university, conditions were desperate by the summer of 1873. Informed of his terrible financial plight, Minerva Boyd sympathized with her embattled son but could do little to help. "But for your kindness to us," she wrote David, "you would not now be in your present condition." The only way she could ever repay him was to give his family a place to live at the family hotel. From Tom Boyd, Minerva knew that rents in Louisiana were "exhorbitant" and the New Orleans people who visited Wytheville in the summertime thought the university's chances for survival were practically nonexistent. She wished fervently that David were "out of the whole mess" and so did he. Six months earlier, in December, 1872, he asked the executive committee of the board to begin looking for his successor. His health was breaking down, and he no longer felt able to stand the work and anxiety connected with the school. All of the married professors were in terrible straits, David had reported, but he and his family were in a "worse fix" than any of the others. Even if paid regularly, his salary was inadequate considering the work and extra expense connected with the superintendency. But now he had neither cash nor credit. As he explained to Vice-President Sanford, "For a month this fall my wife had to be her own nurse, as well as cook for a mess of six— all because we can't pay our servants. And all I ever expected to leave

36 Genealogical Scrapbook, LeRoy Boyd Papers; David Boyd Diary, October 15, 16, 18, 1874.

my little family in case of death—a life insurance policy—I lost the other day, because I could not continue the payment. I tell you all this in no spirit of croaking, or grumbling at an ugly state of things, for which perhaps I am more responsible than anyone, but only to let you know the desperate private straits to which I am driven."[37]

It is unlikely that David, in his anguished condition, remembered the lines sent him eighteen months earlier by G. Mason Graham, "Higglety, pigglety, snigglety Fritz, lost his money and then his wits." By the end of 1872, they seemed prophetic. In a letter to General Graham describing his and the university's condition, he wrote, "I am nearly crazy; there is a limit to everything, and I have reached mine."[38]

37 David Boyd to William Sanford, December 4, December [?], 1872, in Alphabetical File, Fleming Collection; Minerva Boyd to David Boyd, July 23, 1873, in David Boyd Papers.
38 David Boyd to G. Mason Graham, December 21, 1872, in G. Mason Graham Letters, Fleming Collection.

Chapter VI

Politics and Poverty

LOUISIANA'S chaotic political condition explained to a considerable degree the physical and mental anguish afflicting David Boyd in 1872. Personally, he regarded the current crop of politicians with contempt, but as superintendent of a public institution, he had to deal with whoever ran the state. Sometimes that was not clear. In 1872 factionalism plagued the Republican party locally and nationally, but within Louisiana the infighting was particularly severe. The trouble began two years earlier when Governor Henry Clay Warmoth announced plans to amend the state constitution in order to succeed himself. Customhouse Republicans, more Radical than the governor, were outraged, and during the state convention in 1870 Lieutenant Governor Oscar Dunn, a black, challenged Warmoth unsuccessfully for control of the party. Later, having triumphed at the polls, the governor's supporters in the senate made common cause with Democrats to strip Dunn of his power to name committees. A similar coalition in the house gave Warmoth's man the speakership but the shaky alliance fell apart when dissatisfied Democrats shifted their support to the Customhouse element.

Intraparty conflict continued in 1871 as both Republican factions fielded slates of delegates to the party's state convention and as both resorted to fraud, intimidation and the use of armed force in order to dominate that body. When the contending delegates arrived, Warmoth's people learned of plans to bar them from the meeting hall. They withdrew to another site to hold a convention of their own whereupon Cus-

tomhouse men responded by reading the governor out of the party. At
that point both factions appealed to President Grant for recognition,
but he took no immediate action to settle the dispute.

In November, 1871, Lieutenant Governor Oscar Dunn died, and
Governor Warmoth called the senate into special session to fill the vacancy. A friendly presiding officer in the upper chamber was vital,
Warmoth believed, in case the lower house, then under Customhouse
control, moved for impeachment. Meanwhile, senate Democrats held
a strategy session, deciding finally against a formal pledge to either
group of Republicans. When the senate convened on December 9,
however, the Democrats supported the Customhouse candidate. Only
a last minute switch of one vote secured the senate presidency for
Warmoth's favorite, P. B. S. Pinchback.

Republican warfare resumed in January, 1872, when legislators
assembled for the regular session. Neither faction counted enough unchallenged members to constitute a quorum in the senate while in the
house both sides fought fiercely to name the speaker. Both appealed
for Federal troops, but ultimately, the governor's men, supported by
his police force, occupied the official meeting place, Mechanics Institute. Customhouse Republicans had to make do with rented rooms
above a saloon on Royal Street. For two weeks Louisiana had two legislatures, but finally the Warmoth faction lured enough members away
from the rival body to organize for business. By that time the regular
session was almost half over.

During the spring and summer of 1872 the split in Republican
ranks at the national level between Grant Republicans and Liberal Republicans rendered Louisiana politics more bewildering than ever. At
least five distinct groups in the state ultimately held conventions and
named candidates. They have been identified as the Reformers, the
Democrats, the Customhouse Republicans, the Pinchback Republicans, and the Liberals. The Reformers, centered mainly in New Orleans, sought to break the state's power over local government by
repealing many of the laws instituted by Governor Warmoth. The
Democrats met on April 18, somewhat disconcerted by Governor Warmoth's formation the previous week of a state Liberal party, opposed to
Grant's reelection. If the Democrats and Liberal Republicans co-
alesced on the national level, they wondered, what should be the relationship between Warmoth and the Louisiana Democrats? Unable at

that time to accept cooperation with their erstwhile enemy, the Democrats adjourned to await national developments before naming a slate of candidates. Next, Customhouse Republicans met on April 30 under the leadership of United States Marshal S. B. Packard, and C. C. Antoine. They denounced Warmoth, but made efforts to win over P. B. S. Pinchback, leader of the fifth faction on the political scene. Pinchback spoke for a large contingent of black voters whom the Customhouse element hoped to woo away from Warmoth. Customhouse Republicans endorsed Grant for reelection but postponed nomination of a state ticket until later in the year. On May 28 the Pinchback group held its own convention, only to disband because it was unwilling to accept Customhouse domination of the Republican party in Louisiana. Three weeks later Customhouse and Pinchback Republicans met separately in Baton Rouge. Still unwilling to commit themselves, Pinchback's people soon withdrew to New Orleans, but the Customhouse element remained to nominate W. P. Kellogg for governor and C. C. Antoine, a Negro, as his runningmate. Ultimately, Pinchback's group endorsed the Grant-Kellogg-Antoine ticket. In return, a black, William Brown, received the Republican nomination for state superintendent of public education, and Pinchback, also a black, ran as congressman-at-large.

Meanwhile, the Democrats reassembled, agreed to consider coalitions with other groups, and named a straight Democratic slate headed by John McEnery. By July, 1872, the Reform party fell into line, endorsing McEnery for governor and promising to support the national Democratic ticket of Horace Greeley and B. Gratz Brown. That left only Warmoth and the Liberal Republicans who gathered in New Orleans on August 5, 1872, where they chose Davidson B. Penn for governor and John S. Young of Claiborne Parish for lieutenant governor.

After a series of secret meetings, Liberals, Reformers, and Democrats voted to resolve their differences. The result was a Fusion ticket composed of John McEnery for governor and Davidson Penn for lieutenant governor. Horace Greeley was endorsed for the presidency, and, according to one early historian of Louisiana Reconstruction, Warmoth won informal Fusion support in his bid to represent the state in the United States Senate.

Voters went to the polls on November 4, 1872. Both sides claimed victory, but under Louisiana law results were not official until certified by the state Returning Board. Throughout November, therefore, Governor Warmoth and the Customhouse faction waged legal warfare to win control over the board. On December 6, taking care the night before to order Federal troops to Mechanics Institute where the legislature would assemble, a Radical Federal judge acted to sustain a pro-Kellogg slate. The troops remained for the next six weeks. Meanwhile Governor Warmoth called the recently elected legislature into special session, but only those certified by the pro-Kellogg Returning Board were allowed to take their seats. Warmoth-McEnery men had to convene in Lyceum Hall. Moving swiftly, the pro-Kellogg house voted to impeach Governor Warmoth, thereby suspending him from office in favor of the acting lieutenant governor, P. B. S. Pinchback of the Kellogg faction. As they had in 1871, both legislatures proceeded to bribe each other's members, and both appealed to Washington for official recognition. The Warmoth-McEnery group even sent a delegation of citizens to petition the president personally but all to no avail. On December 12, President Grant recognized the Pinchback-Kellogg regime as the lawful government of Louisiana and promised to uphold it with all necessary force. Federal authorities did pledge, however, not to interfere with McEnery's inauguration as long as his partisans refrained from violence.

On January 6, 1873, having finally adjourned the extra session of 1872, Pinchback-Kellogg forces met in regular session at Mechanics Institute, and Warmoth-McEnery followers assembled at Odd Fellows Hall. A week later both William Pitt Kellogg and John McEnery delivered inaugural addresses, and their respective governments met regularly throughout the legislative session. But in the end only the bills adopted by the Kellogg legislature received official sanction. Finally, after disturbances between partisans of the two goverments erupted on March 5, the McEnery legislature was disbanded by armed police. To most white Louisianians, it was still the only legal government of the state.[1]

1 Lonn, *Reconstruction in Louisiana*, 72–330 *passim*; McGinty, *History of Louisiana*, 214–15; Randall and Donald, *Civil War and Reconstruction*, 691. McGinty appears to have drawn his account from Lonn. Two recent treatments of the period are Francis Wayne Binning, "Henry Clay Warmoth and Louisiana Reconstruction" (Ph.D. dissertation, University of North Carolina at Chapel Hill, 1969), and Taylor, *Louisiana Reconstructed*, 209–55. Taylor claims Warmoth had no interest in any elected post in 1872; Binning says he had "informal" support from the Fusion element. For material going beyond political developments in the period, see Roger Shugg, *Origins of the Class Struggle in Louisiana* (Baton Rouge, 1939), and William E. Highsmith, "Louisiana During Reconstruction" (Ph.D. dissertation, Louisiana State University, 1953).

While the Returning Board controversy was still before the courts in November, 1872, David wrote to General William T. Sherman about Louisiana's tangled political affairs. Apparently he urged Sherman to use his good offices with President Grant to bring peace to the state, but Sherman thought that was hardly necessary. Everyone, from the president "on down," wanted peace and harmony, he replied, but "you can't command these." He assured David that the troops in New Orleans had orders to do nothing but keep the peace. They were responsible to the Federal marshal who in turn had to answer to the Federal courts. Sherman knew the Federal judges who would decide which Louisiana state government should rule and in his opinion, they were able and learned. But David was not convinced. Late in December he wrote Sherman again, describing the "confusion and turmoil at New Orleans." Sherman answered on January 6, 1873, the same day the rival legislatures convened in regular session. Defending President Grant's recognition of the Pinchback-Kellogg regime in December on the ground that some action had to be taken until Congress or the Supreme Court could investigate Louisiana affairs, the general pointed out that McEnery's legislature had been promised freedom to meet provided it did so without disorder. "I believe," Sherman concluded, "if McHenry [sic], the Governor-elect and Legislature are the true body, they will be so declared when the case reaches Washington by appeal and in that event General Grant will surely so regard them. Keep this to yourself," he admonished David, "and don't compromise me or yourself by any disclosures."[2]

At the same time, David was corresponding with other prominent figures involved in Louisiana's disputed election of 1872. He was even trying to devise some kind of solution to the state's incredibly complicated problem. On December 17, 1872, while the two legislatures were meeting in extra session, David wrote to one of the key figures in the Returning Board dispute, state senator "Honest" John Lynch. Lynch was president of that Returning Board which declared Kellogg the victor in 1872 and whose legality was ultimately upheld in the courts. Admitting that he was "no politician," David declared that he thought the "truth" lay somewhere between the extreme claims made

2   Wm. T. Sherman to D. F. Boyd, December 4, 1872, in William T. Sherman Letters, David
    Boyd Family Papers; William Sherman to David Boyd, January 6, 1872 [sic], in William T.
    Sherman Papers, Library of Congress. The letter was obviously written in 1873.

by the two parties. David had voted the "Liberal" ticket (McEnery-Penn) against Kellogg and Antoine, but even before election day, he was sure that unfair tactics had been employed by registrars in the country parishes and that reprisals would result. If the election had been honest, he thought that Kellogg, Penn, and Robert M. Lusher, the Fusion candidate for state superintendent of public education, would have been the winners. The Liberals, David believed, would have carried two-fifths of the house and one-third of the senate. He knew it was *"too* late to compromise *now,"* but if it were possible, he would install Kellogg, Penn, Lusher, and every legislator whose election was not in dispute. To fill the doubtful legislative seats he would hold another election. Louisiana's electoral vote should go to Grant, and all of the state's congressional seats should be awarded to Radical Republicans. Finally, the acts of both legislatures adopted during the extra session of 1872 should be declared null and void. Such an outcome would be fair and honest, David declared, insisting that as a Democrat, a southerner, and a secessionist, he "would rather always *be beaten in the right than win in the wrong!*" He was glad to see Brown defeat Lusher and to see Antoine defeat Penn if the only way they could do it was by fraud. "From the days of Mr. Slidell down to *now, in all elections*, God knows we have had too much . . . [fraud] in La."[3]

Lynch admired David's fairness, but did not see how such a compromise could be brought about. "Who has the authority or the power?" he asked. Undismayed, David continued to promote his plan even though many to whom he suggested it labeled it "impractical." However, by February 20, 1873, some form of compromise seemed possible. On that day a majority of the United States Senate Committee on Privileges and Elections, to whom the Louisiana muddle had been referred, submitted a plan for settling the controversy. It called for reinstating Governor Warmoth and all those holding office under him until a new election, under Federal supervision, could take place in May. But two days of heated debate and a telling argument opposing Federal intervention in the internal politics of a state managed to kill any Senate action at all. By March 4, 1873, both houses of Congress had adjourned.

Nevertheless, David continued to work for a solution. On March 9,

3   David F. Boyd to John Lynch, December 17, 1872, copy, in David Boyd Papers; Lonn, *Reconstruction in Louisiana*, 186, 190.

1873, he wrote the Fusion candidate for lieutenant governor, Davidson B. Penn, a confidential letter, inquiring whether Penn would be willing to serve with Kellogg in a compromise administration. He doubted that John McEnery had actually won the governorship in 1872, but he did think that Penn, Robert M. Lusher, and one other had been fairly elected. Because he was "*compelled* to deal with politicians of both parties," David knew most of them "pretty well." Kellogg he did not know at all. But he had reason to believe that President Grant and Kellogg would accept a compromise administration in Louisiana composed of Kellogg as governor, Penn as lieutenant governor, and Lusher as superintendent of public education. If Penn wanted his help, David promised to do all he could to bring such a settlement about. Two months later, on May 22, 1873, David's "reason to believe" that Grant would accept a compromise finally evaporated when the president formally recognized the Kellogg regime and ordered all citizens to "retire peaceably" to their homes and submit themselves to the government and laws of Louisiana.[4]

Louisiana's turbulent political upheavals in 1872 had a disastrous effect on public institutions like the Louisiana State University. So too did the serious economic slump that plagued the entire nation during the rest of the decade. In his anniversary address in January, 1873, David discussed the school's history and its future prospects at length. The school, he told his young audience was in a "bad fix." In previous years the legislature appropriated funds for it only with the "greatest reluctance." Now, under the Kellogg regime, there would doubtless be no appropriations whatever. The crux of the problem was the state cadet law, something that David believed in and had worked hard in the past to extend. By January, 1873, 101 of the 118 cadets were beneficiaries whom the law required the state to support annually at $350 each. But the money was paid in state warrants, then selling at only forty cents on the dollar. At that rate, David estimated, it would take $1,000 annually to cover a cadet's actual cost to the university. Therefore he planned to ask for the repeal of the beneficiary law in 1873. He regretted having to part with so many "clever young men," but to keep the beneficiaries from "crushing the school with debt," they should go

4   John Lynch to David Boyd, December 26, 1872, March 15, 1873, in Alphabetical File, Fleming Collection; D. F. Boyd to D. B. Penn, March 9, 1873, in David Boyd Papers; Lonn, *Reconstruction in Louisiana*, 232–38, 240, 245; Taylor, *Louisiana Reconstructed*, 253–54.

away. In the future, the university would depend on private patronage for survival, and, if it could secure it, the agricultural and mechanical college fund.[5]

The Kellogg legislature did not repeal the law, and it did not vote the school any funds in 1873. Neither did David ask for an appropriation. In justification he explained, "The doubt and uncertainty hovering over our State government . . . and the deplorable condition of our State Treasury, together with the great poverty of our people rendered it wrong in my opinion to ask relief." At last, in March, 1873, the university issued an indefinite furlough to the state cadets. Before leaving, the young men adopted resolutions of thanks to everyone connected with the school, reserving their highest praise for the superintendent. His "heroic sacrifice," "unquenchable" zeal, and "indomitable will," they declared, had made the university "like a father's house."[6]

Professors soon joined the general exodus from Baton Rouge. On April 14, 1873, Colonel Samuel H. Lockett, David's closest and most trusted friend on the faculty, announced his intention to leave at the end of the session. Two of Lockett's friends resigned the same day. By the end of the term the number rose to six. In his letter of resignation Colonel Lockett declared that he could "not go on ignoring his first duty to his wife and children." He had seen the need to leave for two years but had put if off in order to help David in that "Herculean task . . . for which you were and still are sacrificing the best years of your life." Lockett's case was typical. Since 1871 the university had paid the professors intermittently or not at all. To avoid discount rates up to 50 percent that year, David refused to sell some $81,000 worth of warrants. Instead, he pledged them for a loan of $39,000 hoping to sell them later at more advantageous rates. Meanwhile, the salaries of professors and other employees went unpaid; they had to live on credit, thereby incurring large personal debts. David noted all this in his report to the board for 1871, warning that if the university did not pay its professors, it would soon lose them to other schools. Even if it merely deferred payment, the professors' efficiency would be impaired. Con-

5   David Boyd anniversary address, January 2, 1873, in David Boyd Papers.
6   David Boyd, quoted in Fleming, *Louisiana State University*, 220; *Report* of the Superintendent of Louisiana State University, in *Annual Report* of State Superintendent of Public Education, William G. Brown to the General Assembly for 1873 (New Orleans, 1874), 426–27; Baton Rouge *Tri-Weekly Gazette and Comet*, March 27, 1873, in Scrapbook, David Boyd Papers.

stantly "*badgered* by butcher and baker," a professor could not devote all his attention to his duties. A college professor "is a delicate organism," David explained, whose "sensitive nature revolts" at the rough treatment meted out by creditors.[7]

The six instructors who left in 1873 were somehow replaced with new men or advanced cadets who agreed to teach without pay. But by July, 1874, the staff dropped to five. A year later only two remained, David and his brother Tom. Even so, the university was probably overstaffed in relation to the small enrollment. Just before the beneficiaries were sent home in 1873, the school claimed 118 cadets and approximately 12 professors. Throughout 1874, a total of 31 cadets received instruction from a faculty of 5, and in January, 1875, there were only 8 students and 4 faculty. By mid-March the numbers shrank to 7 and 3, causing Tom Boyd to comment, "How different from our condition on arriving here in 1869, after the burning of our building. . . . The number of professors then was greater than that of professors and cadets both now." David finally agreed to open the school to day students in April, 1875, but none appeared until the following year. Of the twenty cadets enrolled as of January, 1876, fifteen resided in Baton Rouge.[8]

The annual tuition paid by each cadet, eighty dollars, plus the maintenance fees of those few who boarded at the university, provided the only income for the entire university staff after Kellogg became governor in 1873. Even the annuity from the endowment fund, invested in state bonds, yielded no support after 1874 because the legislature partially repudiated the state's debt that year, and a constitutional amendment further reduced the state's obligations by scaling down income from its bonds some 40 percent. To the university board this constituted a violation of a "sacred trust," and in protest the school refused to surrender its old bonds. Consequently, it received no annuity in 1874 and it would not cash the scaled-down annuity warrant for 1875. The embattled few at the university had to survive on credit. David revealed the level to which they were reduced when he asked Vice-

7   J. P. McAuley to David Boyd, April 14, 1873, S. H. Lockett to David Boyd, April 14, 1873, in Alphabetical File, Fleming Collection; Fleming, *Louisiana State University*, 250; *Report* to the Board of Supervisors for 1871, pp. 4–6.

8   Fleming, *Louisiana State University*, 250–52; Tom Boyd Diary, in Department of Archives, Louisiana State University, Baton Rouge, March 14, June 30, July 10, October 17, 1875, January 6, 1876; David Boyd, anniversary address, January 2, 1873, in David Boyd Papers; *Report* to the Board of Supervisors for 1874, p. 6; David Boyd Diary, January 22, February 1, 1875.

President Sanford to sign the 1875 annuity warrant. He did not intend to sell it, "But I wd like to have the warrant from you; it may help us to live on—if *I can show it to people.*"[9]

One bright note relieved David's otherwise grim existence after 1873, the excellent relations he enjoyed with the Board of Supervisors. Undoubtedly this was due to the fact that the entire board did not convene for several years after the spring of 1872, and the only active members, Vice-President William Sanford and General G. Mason Graham, lived miles away from Baton Rouge in Rapides Parish. In the absence of full board meetings the executive committee, composed of Sanford, Graham, and one other Rapides resident, had the power to approve everything David proposed; after the school moved to Baton Rouge, it usually did. William Sanford and General Graham trusted David implicitly. They had nothing but the highest praise for him as a person and as an administrator. And David, for his part, did not hesitate to exercise his administrative powers to the fullest. "You know, I am perhaps too prone to assume responsibility and act on it," he once admitted to William Sanford, "but when I see that a great good can be done the school by putting myself in a little personal danger, I assure you that I care then but little for myself."[10] Once, in 1865, General Graham felt called upon to remind David that his authority did have limits. Later, convinced that he meant nothing but good for the school, the general merely advised caution. Vice-President Sanford, more retiring still, interfered even less. In 1873 he commented to David, "I have always thought that the best service the B. S. [Board of Supervisors] could render the University would be [to] let it alone as much as possible—only aiding the Supt. to carry out whatever line of policy he might think best to adopt—for it must be patent to everybody that the Institution can only be made a success by the tact, ability, and endurance of the Supt."[11]

With two notable exceptions almost every proposal David submitted to Vice-President Sanford between 1873 and 1877 was subsequently

9   Fleming, *Louisiana State University*, 249; David Boyd to Wm. Sanford, November 3, 1874, March 4, 1875, in David Boyd Letterbooks; Minutes of the Executive Committee of the Board of Supervisors, March 30, 1875.
10   David Boyd to W. C. Black (Board member), December 28, 1874, David Boyd to W. L. Sanford, February 11, 1873, in David Boyd Letterbooks; David Boyd to W. L. Sanford, September 23, 1870, in Alphabetical File, Fleming Collection.
11   W. L. Sanford to David F. Boyd, June 22, 1873, G. Mason Graham to David F. Boyd, November 13, 1865, in Alphabetical File, Fleming Collection.

approved by the executive committee. Sanford did not press for a meeting of the entire board, and he apparently did not pass on to the executive committee or the whole board David's informal request to resign "as early as the interests of the University permit." David wanted a meeting of the entire board to approve his administration of the university, to consider its future, and to prepare a report to the legislature. He thought the board's failure to meet for over two years "looked bad" to both the Radicals and the "best people." But Sanford argued that a full board meeting in such unsettled political circumstances (1874) might do more harm than good. As for the resignation, David submitted it informally in October of the same year, at a time when the pressure from creditors was particularly intense. His letterbook and diary entries that month recorded nothing but demands for payment by butchers, bakers, servants, and loan sharks. If he did not get "absolute rest" soon, he feared for his sanity. "I am sure I have weakened my mind," he wrote the vice-president, "I am a *used up* man." [12]

During 1874 and 1875 political tensions increased in Louisiana. David was sure the Kellogg administration would soon attack the school, especially if he did anything to attract its attention. Therefore, he did not fire the usual salute to open the university session or advertise the school in any way. In January, 1875, the board authorized him to accept day students, but this, too, David considered a "dangerous experiment." He even stayed away from New Orleans for fear his presence might remind Governor Kellogg of the university and encourage him to shut it down. But if a Radical attack did come, David wanted to be prepared. Beginning in November, 1874, he begged the executive committee to approve all of his financial accounts and to endorse his entire tenure as superintendent. He was particularly anxious that it be done before General Graham left Louisiana to live in Virginia. As the "Father of the Institution," Graham knew more about it than anyone else. No one could be sure, David reminded Sanford, how soon a "*Bd.* of Carpetbaggers & *Niggers* might take over the school." In time, the executive committee complied with David's request. On March 30, 1875, and again on April 12, it adopted resolutions ratifying all the "acts performed by Col. D. F. Boyd in his capacity of Supt. during the

12   David Boyd to W. L. Sanford, October 16, 1874, David Boyd to W. C. Black, December 28, 1874, David Boyd to J. D. Kenton, undated, 1874, in David Boyd Letterbooks; David Boyd Diary, October 7, 8, 9, 13, 1874.

whole term of his service as such." Then, to show its appreciation for his self-denial and devotion to duty, it conferred upon him the honorary degree of "Dr. of laws."[13]

David's insistence that his administration be formally approved is understandable considering the potential threat posed by the hostile Kellogg regime. But he also wanted to forestall criticism from another source: the university's numerous creditors. In 1874, David reported to the governor that liabilities amounted to over $100,000 against estimated assets in movables and real property at upwards of $150,000. But the assets represented books, equipment, furniture, and land. If auctioned, they would hardly bring the value he ascribed to them. Bills from suppliers and claims for back wages accounted for most of the liabilities. One creditor alone, Swarbrick and Company of New Orleans, claimed over $16,000. In addition to this public debt, David owed a great deal personally. Some of it represented necessary expenditures for food and clothing. But much of it had been assumed in order to promote and protect the school. For example, when the university could not borrow money on its own authority, David gave his personal note for repayment. When the board announced its inability to pay professors' salaries, he employed a staff at his own expense. And when "friends of the university" reneged on pledges to purchase an expensive painting for the school, David assumed the cost himself. Before he could pay for it, the artist's agent tried to reclaim it because he had found another buyer. But David urged him to wait. If the picture left the school, the university's army of creditors would certainly misunderstand. They would not grasp the fact that the painting was secured by David's personal note. "They can't draw a line between me personally and officially," he explained, "and a few of them wd no doubt consider they had a right to take the last [?] out of the mouths of my little children to . . . secure their University claims."[14]

The truth seems to be that David could not distinguish between his public and private obligations either. He felt a deep sense of personal

13 David Boyd Diary, October 3, 1874, January 22, 28, 30, 1875; David Boyd to W. L. Sanford, November 3, 1874, February 11, March 4, 1875, David Boyd to William Van Pelt (former clerk), March 10, 20, 1875, David Boyd to Wm. A. Seay, March 20, 1875, in David Boyd Letterbooks; William Van Pelt to D. Boyd, March 12, 1875, in David Boyd Papers; Minutes of the Executive Committee of the Board of Supervisors, March 30, April 12, 1875.

14 David Boyd, *Report* to the Board of Supervisors for 1874, pp. 13–18; Fleming, *Louisiana State University*, 264; Tom Boyd Diary, January 17, 1876; David Boyd to J. H. McLean, undated, in David Boyd Letterbooks.

responsibility to the school's many creditors, pledging repeatedly in his diary and correspondence to remain "at his post" until some relief for them could be obtained. Yet, when one firm suggested taking out an insurance policy on his life to protect its investment, David was outraged. Arguing that what he did for one creditor, he felt he should "in justice" do for all, he commented, "Were my life insured for *all of them*, why, I wd *not* live six months!" Then, after reminding the creditor that the debt in question was not his but the school's, and therefore public, David somewhat inconsistently offered to assume "*personally*" $2,000 of the amount owed.[15]

More disheartening than harassment by impatient businessmen was the apparent failure of some of David's best friends—former professors at the university—to appreciate how hard he was working in their behalf. When he announced plans to leave Baton Rouge by 1877 unless conditions improved, one former colleague remarked casually that David seemed to be "giving up." Another was more direct. He sued the university demanding that its property be sold to pay his back salary. Ultimately, the court held that university property was state property and could not be seized to satisfy debt. Nevertheless, David felt personally aggrieved because the suit charged him with squandering public funds on "fine furniture and expensive paintings." Actually, he bought the items in question with his own money and gave them to the university. But the public, he was sure, would never understand. It rarely distinguished between him and the school.[16]

In January, 1875, Louisiana again had two legislatures. Included in the Kellogg body, which David called the "Rump," was J. Henri Burch, a black senator from Baton Rouge. When David learned that Burch planned to introduce a bill "for the relief of creditors of the State University," he was sure that fraud and collusion were afoot. Senator Burch had presented a similar measure in 1874. Designed to aid a specific group of Baton Rouge creditors, it was considered grossly unfair by David, and he did everything he could to defeat it. The 1874 effort, he told one creditor, "offended even *that* horrible legislature." He was

15   David Boyd Diary, December 10, 1874; David Boyd to F. V. Hopkins, September 30, 1874, David Boyd to William Van Pelt, November 28, 1875, David Boyd to George Swarbrick & Co., undated [1875–76?], all in David Boyd Letterbooks.
16   David Boyd to S. H. Lockett [1874–75], David Boyd to A. Featherman, April 14, July 15, 1875, in David Boyd Letterbooks; Fleming, *Louisiana State University*, 265; S. H. Lockett to David Boyd, November 24, 1874, in Alphabetical File, Fleming Collection.

First faculty at Louisiana State Seminary of Learning, 1860

Louisiana State Seminary of Learning at Pineville, 1860

School for the Deaf at Baton Rouge, which housed Louisiana State University, 1869–1886

Major David French Boyd, C.S.A.

Esther Gertrude Wright, who later became Mrs. David French Boyd

David French Boyd, *circa* 1866

Mrs. David French Boyd, 1903

Two views of the Pentagon Barracks, Baton Rouge, location of Louisiana State University, 1886–1932

Cadets on parade ground, Pentagon Barracks

David French Boyd, *circa* 1870

sure it kept them from locating the newly created Agricultural and Mechanical College in Baton Rouge. As for Burch's latest bill, David suspected a "put up job." A few Baton Rouge creditors, he believed, had made a deal with the black senator. He would introduce a bill for their relief, and if it passed, they would pay him a "kickback." To David this was "dastardly," amounting to simple bribery, and if his speculations proved correct, he intended to "wreck the scheme." In a bitter letter to a New Orleans friend he asked, "What must be thought of some of them [the Baton Rouge creditors], well-endowed with worldly goods . . . who wld, for a few dollars, ruin us all. Baton Rouge grew up around a *fort*—is nothing but a *sutter's* camp; and the *morals* of such trashy people, you know better than I can describe. There are a few exceptions, some fine and true men here; but the generality are . . . so small that many of them *at once* cld go thro' the eye of a needle at a gallop."[17]

What David really objected to was according any recognition at all to the Rump legislature. The law required him to send his annual report to the lawmakers, but Baton Rouge creditors had no excuse to deal with "such creatures." They should ignore the Rump and wait for the "true" legislature to convene. David could not hide his feelings from the creditors or even from Senator Burch. When the latter asked for a full statement of university accounts, David referred him to the annual report. Then he asked Burch to "consider well the advisability" of bringing up university matters when political conditions were so "fluid." The school would have plenty of friends in the General Assembly later when things "settled down." With creditors, David was more direct. To bribe was worse than to be bribed, he told one, and he would do all he could to scuttle any creditor's attempt to secure relief by offering a fee to the "infamous creatures who are . . . our legislators." How, David demanded, could Louisianians ever escape their troubles if people continued to buy laws and lawmakers? If he could help it, Louisiana's legislature would not be "prostituted."[18]

As David struggled to do his duty by the university and its creditors,

17 David Boyd to J. D. Kenton, January 9, 1875, David Boyd to R. J. McCabe, January 8, 1875, David Boyd to Jas. McVay, January 8, 1875, David Boyd to W. C. Annis, January 9, 1875, David Boyd to William Van Pelt, February 2, 1875, all in David Boyd Letterbooks.
18 David Boyd to R. M. Lusher, February 3, 1875, David Boyd to W. C. Annis, January 9, 1875, David Boyd to J. Henri Burch, January 27, 1875, David Boyd to W. E. Seebold, February 11, 1875, all *ibid*.

he often overlooked the well-being of his immediate family. A diary he began keeping during the summer of 1874 provides the best evidence of his neglect. The fairly regular entries continued until the next year when he no longer had time for his journal. But the two volumes he did fill offer abundant evidence of the impoverished circumstances endured by the Boyds during the last years of Radical Reconstruction. So do the hundreds of letters David wrote between 1874 and 1877. An extremely enthusiastic correspondent, David never used two pages if four were at hand. After 1874, when enrollment at the university dropped to a handful, he had plenty of time to indulge his eccentricity. A letter written to a former cadet and former colleague is typical:

Last week we came near starving: We had bread, beef, with a little coffee—but no sugar or anything else literally . . . and our butcher determined to stop the beef on Saturday if he could not be paid . . . When I think of the condition of my family, and how much worse they wld be in case of sickness, I feel heartily ashamed, and know that I ought to go away now. But . . . I feel it to be my duty to leave no effort untried, and to leave no personal suffering and privation unendured, to stand by the old school to the last. Consequently, I try not to think of self and family.[19]

David was not exaggerating. He literally did not know, from one day to the next, and sometimes from one meal to the next, where he might get food for his family. The weight of his responsibilities nearly drove him to distraction. As he explained to another former colleague, "To pay in part for our provisions of '72 and '73, I had to pledge our annuity of '74, which not being paid yet (and may never be) I have the weight of three years on me. . . . If my wife and children were not suffering so much, I cld stand it better; but in case of any serious illness . . . especially to my wife, I don't see how I could possibly do."[20]

Random entries from David's diary are even more illustrative of his poverty and despair. On July 25, 1874, he had the brass buttons removed from his Civil War uniform and replaced by "civil" buttons. He could not possibly buy a new coat. In August, 1874, he wondered what would become of his family if he died. To Baton Rouge creditors alone he owed $700. On September 1, he planned to go to New Orleans to borrow money with only twenty cents in his pocket because no one in

19   David Boyd to T. L. Grimes, August 11, 1874, *ibid*.
20   David Boyd to William Van Pelt, January 5, 1875, David Boyd to Pendleton King (ex-colleague), February 10, 1875, *ibid*.

Baton Rouge would advance him any funds. He did not go that day, but when he did, he had "*one* nickel . . . not another cent in the world." In the Crescent City he thought he still had some contacts; yet, on September 5, 1874, he was "mortified" when James Gresham, one of the university's principal creditors, turned down his request for twenty dollars. The worst was still to come. In a particularly hopeless entry on March 11, 1875, he noted, "Next week! What does it *not* of [trouble] promise? Where is the money to pay that $1650 note at the La Nat'l Bank, & the bill of Garig [Baton Rouge grocer] about $60, & the bread-bill, and Contreaux' bill of cloth, & Reuss' balance of tuition [remitted]? Next week!"[21]

What David feared most, serious illness in his family, did occur in the spring of 1875. It began with Mrs. Wright, Ettie's mother. Mrs. Wright was a chronic invalid but in March, 1875, she seemed so feeble that David did not think she could live much longer. A few weeks later Arthur, David's four-year-old son, developed an extremely high fever. He suffered convulsions and almost died. Fortunately, Superintendent McWhorter's wife reduced his fever by bathing him in cold water. Meanwhile, David and Tom Boyd walked all over Baton Rouge searching for a doctor. None would come to the university. Tom thought doctors did not like to go out in the rain, but David believed they were afraid they would not be paid. Ultimately Arthur recovered but he seemed so nervous that David thought his brain had been affected. Certainly David's peace of mind was shattered. Concerned over his many obligations and his child's brush with death, he could not even concentrate on reading. More than ever he realized the need to leave Baton Rouge for his family's sake.[22]

Arthur's fever had barely abated when Ettie was suddenly stricken with what Tom Boyd described as pneumonia. Her condition seemed so serious that he telegraphed David, then in New Orleans, to come home at once. A few days later she suffered a miscarriage from which she did not fully recover for months. Unlike Arthur, Ettie did have medical attention during the worst part of her illness. Dr. J. W. Dupree, the university physician, was very attentive. He refused any pay, insisting that his job required him to treat the Boyd family as well as the

---

21   David Boyd Diary, July 25, August 16, September 1, 2, 5, 1874, March 11, 1875.
22   *Ibid.*, February 15, 28, March 7, April 1–6, 1875; Tom Boyd Diary, April 1, 4, 1875; David Boyd to William Van Pelt, April 3, 1875, in David Boyd Letterbooks.

cadets. "The truth is," Tom Boyd noted in his diary, "he knows David has no money to pay him. . . . He is the only physician in the place who would come to see any of us if we were dying."[23]

Conditions in the Boyd household did not improve in 1876. If anything, they grew worse. More in debt than ever, and dependent upon his mother-in-law for enough money to clothe his children, David himself was practically in rags. Yet he had to go to New Orleans in February because the university's creditors insisted that he appeal to the legislature for relief. Tom Boyd described his departure in his diary: "D. went almost naked and carried in his valise not *one single article of clothing*, and besides, [he] had to borrow money to pay his way down."[24]

In New Orleans David did not secure relief for the creditors or an appropriation for the university. But he did succeed in winning legislative approval for the merger of the university with the Agricultural and Mechanical College. The merger bill represented the end of a ten-year struggle. It also posed an immediate problem for the Boyds. As soon as Governor Kellogg signed the bill, the merged schools would begin operations in the asylum building and David, because he was pledged to hold no office in the new institution, would have to find other quarters for his family. The Boyd apartments at the university, while not exactly luxurious, were at least rent-free. Located on the third floor, they reminded Tom Boyd of what he had read about attics and tenement houses in New York City. There were no servants; Ettie and Miss Mary Wright took care of the children and their invalid mother. They also sewed, cooked, and did the washing. Once, in 1874, Ettie proposed paying for a Negro laundress by taking in the woman's sewing, but David would not allow it. "Better do her own washing," he decided. In May, 1876, Tom Boyd wrote his father, "Our life at home [Wytheville] during the latter part of the war would compare as favorably with theirs now, as a bed of eider with an inverted harrow." Nevertheless, as June, 1876, approached, the Boyd's miserable accommodations in the asylum must have seemed almost attractive, for at the end of the term they would have to move. David still had no job and, as of June 7, not a "single dollar." To make matters worse, Ettie expected a fourth child in

23   Tom Boyd Diary, April 20, 21, 22, 24, 1875; S. H. Lockett to David Boyd, May 6, 18, 1875, in Alphabetical File, Fleming Collection.
24   Tom Boyd Diary, January 17, February 20, 1876.

September. In despair, David wrote a friend, "If this state of things is to last much longer it would be better that we were all dead."[25]

Much of the hardship endured by David and his family was unavoidable. Louisiana, the South, and to some degree, the whole country suffered from the political and economic crises which beset the last years of Reconstruction. But unquestionably David could have improved his family's circumstances somewhat if he had not been so obsessed with his mission of preserving the Louisiana State University. To a friend he frankly admitted the injustice his single-minded course imposed on his family. "I am ashamed to say it," he wrote J. D. Kenton, "but in all this struggle to keep the University alive I have not considered my wife and children once."[26]

David did have opportunities to leave the university for other jobs, and he did have several friends who were eager to help him do so. As early as 1871, a former professor at the university, Richard M. Venable of Baltimore, asked him to apply for the "superintendency" of a new school to be built in that city. The position would "pay well," Venable wrote, and the "social advantages" compared to Louisiana, "speak for themselves." Two years later the same friend and another former professor, James Garnett, tried again. They wanted David to leave Louisiana "for a place where he would be appreciated." When Venable thought of David's hard work, it reminded him of·the crumbling missions in west Texas. "How much toil they represented and yet they seem to have counted for nothing." In 1874 a school in Marshall, Texas, offered David its presidency, but he turned it down. By that time he was so overwrought with worry and responsibility that he considered leaving the education field altogether. He talked of going to Colorado or California and taking any kind of work he could find. But having been a teacher for so long, he wondered if he were fit for anything else. David knew he would never earn much in his profession.

25 Thomas D. Boyd to Thos. J. Boyd, May 14, 1876, in Letterbooks, Thomas D. Boyd Papers, Department of Archives, Louisiana State University, hereinafter cited as Tom Boyd Letterbooks; Tom Boyd Diary, March 4, 12, 1876; David Boyd Diary, October 31, 1874; David Boyd to William Van Pelt, February 14, 1876, David Boyd to J. P. McAuley, June 7, 1876, David Boyd to J. D. Kenton, July 8, 1876 in David Boyd Letterbooks. By 1876, the Boyd children included Thomas J. (surviving twin), born in 1869; Arthur, born in 1871, and LeRoy Stafford, born in 1873. The fourth living child, born September 18, 1876, was also a son. Named after his father he was always called Rex by the family. David Boyd to Richard Hancock, September 25, 1876, in *ibid*.

26 David Boyd to J. D. Kenton, June 8, 1876, in David Boyd Letterbooks.

As he put it, "One had as well try to get rich by running an alms house."[27]

Early in 1875, Dr. E. W. Hilgard of the University of Michigan wrote David about a position at the University of California. The president at California had resigned to become president of the new Johns Hopkins University, the same post David's Baltimore friends tried to interest him in two years before. Hilgard himself was leaving Michigan for California; so was Dr. Francis Hopkins, another of David's former colleagues. Professor Hilgard also informed General Sherman of the California vacancy, and Sherman, who had many influential friends in California, recommended David for the job. "If an offer comes," he urged David, "don't hesitate a moment." David was immensely flattered, but doubted his qualifications for such a high post. In any case, he thought his "duty" to the university and its creditors came first. To his friend William Van Pelt, he expressed concern that Sherman's "strong paper" might prove embarrassing. What if it induced the California board to offer him the job? For years he had vowed to keep the university "alive" and to defend its creditors. Therefore, he had to ask Dr. Hilgard to do "nothing further" in his behalf; he could not "get away" from Louisiana before 1877.[28]

Some of David's closest friends could not understand his concept of "duty." Colonel Lockett thought that he was wasting his time "trying to improve an institution which might ultimately be taken over by a Radical ring." Another one-time colleague, Powhatan Clarke, was more explicit. He understood a man who placed his country before everything else, but David's case was different. "That a man of your good judgment should so long forget his duty to his children, his wife and himself I can attribute only to a morbid habit." Clarke did not think David owed any obligation to the university's creditors. If the debt were David's personally, he might feel compelled to repay it. But "since it is owed by a defunct institution it is ridiculous." Even Sher-

27 R. M. Venable to David Boyd, May 31, 1871, September 30, 1873, in Alphabetical File, Fleming Collection; David Boyd Diary, July 25, 1874; David Boyd to T. J. Boyd, August 12, 1874, David Boyd to S. H. Lockett, October 18, 1874, in David Boyd Letterbooks.
28 David Boyd to E. W. Hilgard, undated [1875], January 20, 1875, David Boyd to William Van Pelt, February 23, 1875, in David Boyd Letterbooks; William T. Sherman to David F. Boyd, February 18, 1875, in William T. Sherman Letters, David F. Boyd Family Papers. David did ask Hilgard to submit his name in October, 1875, after another position he was seeking seemed to have become unattainable. David Boyd to E. W. Hilgard, telegram, October 21, 1875, in David Boyd Papers.

man, who admired David's "pluck" for standing by the "old 'Seminary of Learning'" so firmly, thought he carried fidelity too far. In May, 1875, he advised David to forget about his "duty" to the university and seek work elsewhere. "You have stood at your post," Sherman declared, "till necessity which knows no law compels you to seek an honorable maintenance for your family."[29]

Without presuming to psychoanalyze David one hundred years after the fact, it seems fair to conclude that he was at least neurotic as far as the university was concerned. Traits like loyalty, honor, generosity, and selfless devotion to duty are prized human qualities. But overdeveloped, as they appear to have been in him, they can distort judgment, affect one's ability to make intelligent decisions, or worse, preclude decision-making altogether. David's will and common sense were certainly impaired by his conception of his "duty" to the university. For him personally the results were bad enough, but for his family they were disastrous. The truth seems to be that an idea, what the university might someday become, and not his suffering wife and children as they actually were, came first in David's affections and his understanding of where his principal responsibilities lay.

An incident later referred to by David as his "Egypt matter" illustrates how thoroughly his obsession to serve the university interfered with his capacity to act. In the spring of 1875 William Sherman informed David that he had been authorized by the Khedive of Egypt to employ a superintendent for a military college near Cairo. With the job went a brigadier general's commission and $6,000 a year in gold. "I would prefer you in the California University," Sherman wrote, "but fear that is not a certainty. *This is.* Speak and act quick." From previous experience Sherman must have known of David's tendency to temporize and agonize whenever the question of leaving the university arose. He urged David to decide within the week and to keep his own counsel. "Consult *your wife* only, and if she consents, notify me, and when I *affirm*, then resign absolutely, and let Louisiana work out her own destiny." Sherman's advice was wasted. In the next few months, David managed to ignore all of it. After days of arguing with himself, he telegraphed Governor Kellogg asking only for a leave of absence.

29 S. H. Lockett to David Boyd, February 12, 1875, Powhatan Clarke to David Boyd, March 15, 1875, in Alphabetical File, Fleming Collection; William T. Sherman to David Boyd, April 21, May 26, 1875, in William T. Sherman Letters, David F. Boyd Family Papers.

Kellogg agreed and so did the executive committee, but because David delayed his departure so long, the leave had to be extended twice. Then, far from consulting only his wife, David proceeded to correspond with friends, former colleagues, and board members all over the country. By mid-June news of his imminent departure had appeared in several newspapers, some of it provided to the publishers by David himself.[30]

David was not the only American interested in Egypt in 1875. After the Civil War the country became a veritable colony of former Confederate and Federal officers, many of them recruited for the Khedive by General Sherman because of their training in exploration, surveying, and the construction of railroads, forts, and dams. One former officer, General Charles P. Stone, was a particular friend of Sherman's and on the latter's recommendation had become the Khedive's chief of staff. Among other things, Stone hoped to improve Egyptian military academies so that the best cadets might qualify for a staff college patterned somewhat after West Point and the Virginia Military Institute. To that end, he encouraged the Khedive to import American teachers and officers familiar with those schools. He also encouraged West Point graduates like Samuel Lockett to become officers in the Egyptian service. After Lockett left Louisiana State University in 1873, he ran a military school in Alabama, but it did not prosper. Therefore, when the chance came to go to Egypt in 1875 as a major in the corps of engineers, he did not hesitate. Just before the Locketts sailed, David informed them of his offer to head the Khedive's military school. They were delighted. Lockett pronounced David the "fittest man for the place" and urged him to let nothing stand in his way. "Now my dear Colonel," Lockett wrote, "please don't let the old Don Quixote in you get on his Rosinante and ride you to death and destruction. Let your Louisiana [Dulcinea?] try somebody else. Your duty has been done to the fullest in regard to her. A higher, greater duty now calls you. Won't it be pleasant for us to meet in the delta of the Nile after having labored together in that of the

30   William T. Sherman to David Boyd, May 26, 1875, in William T. Sherman Letters, David F. Boyd Family Papers; David Boyd, Egypt Memorandum, undated, in David Boyd Papers; David Boyd to Governor W. P. Kellogg, telegram, May 31, 1875, Donaldsonville (La.) *Chief*, June 5, 1875, Shreveport *Times*, June 10, 1875, Wytheville (Va.) *Dispatch*, July 1, 1875, (New Iberia) Louisiana *Sugar Bowl*, July 1, 1875, all in Scrapbook; Wm. Kellogg to David Boyd, telegram, undated, David Boyd to W. L. Sanford, June 1, 1875, January 26, 1876, in David Boyd Letterbooks; Minutes of the Executive Committee of the Board of Supervisors, June 18, September 11, 1875.

Mississippi? But I won't write any more. You must go by all means, and if necessary at once."[31]

But David did not go "at once." Early in June he wrote to General Stone through Sherman that although willing to go to Egypt, he preferred to delay his departure until October (when the university would reopen) or even March, 1876 (when the legislative session would be over). In a letter dated June 12, Sherman told David that he might expect a "full answer" from Stone some time in August. It usually took two months for his letters to reach Egypt and be answered, he explained, but he had advised Stone to telegraph if he wanted David to come to Egypt "at once." On July 10, 1875, Sherman notified David that he had received a dispatch from General Stone which read simply "Send Boyd—Stone." David could consider his employment "settled," wrote Sherman, adding that he ought to be in St. Louis or New York early in October. By that time the Khedive's agent would have his passage booked for Cairo. Sherman's remark in the July 10 letter, that David be in New York "early in Oct.," caused David much grief later because it failed to take into account Sherman's earlier letter of June 12 which said, in the event that Stone wanted David "at once," he should telegraph. Stone *did* telegraph and Sherman reported receipt of the telegram in the July 10 letter. Nevertheless, he still advised David to be in New York early in October instead of urging him to leave for Egypt at once.

Meanwhile, David kept busy arranging his accounts, assembling books and maps, and corresponding with friends who might later join him in the Egyptian school. In one letter, written August 5, 1875, he commented casually that it might be "best for *me* (who *can not speak French*)" to go to Egypt on a French ship. Together with his delayed departure, the linguistic inability proved disastrous. On August 26 Sherman relayed to David a letter just received from General Stone. From what he had heard of David, Stone wrote, "He will be just the man for the place." He noted that he had discussed David with the Khedive who asked if David spoke French. "As you [Sherman] had stated that Col. Boyd was formerly a professor of ancient and modern languages," Stone continued, "I answered unhesitatingly yes, adding

---

31 William Hesseletine and Hazel C. Wolf, *The Blue and the Gray on the Nile* (Chicago, 1961), 2–9, 87–88; S. H. Lockett to David Boyd, July 1, 1875, in Alphabetical File, Fleming Collection.

that he [David] had professed the modern languages. It would be a necessity in that position." Then Stone remarked that he was also telegraphing Sherman in order that David arrive in Egypt by September 1. "That would require him to leave New York by the 5th of August."[32]

Now Sherman began urging David to leave for Egypt immediately. But David was still reluctant to go before the fall term began, even if it meant losing the appointment. Furthemore, seeing Stone's comment about the "necessity" of speaking French, David felt compelled to telegraph the Egyptian authorities that he could not speak the language and that he had not planned to leave Baton Rouge until October. Not hearing anything to the contrary, he "presumed" that he was still wanted and on his terms. But on September 21, 1875, a cable arrived from General Stone which stated tersely, "Speaking French is an absolute necessity." Immediately David telegraphed General Sherman, "I presume this cancels the appointment." Sherman agreed. If David had gone to Egypt in the summer, he might have learned enough French to "pass." But under the circumstances, David had better "give up the Egypt scheme—leaving me free to select some other."[33]

For most people, Sherman's letter would have ended the Egyptian affair. But David was not like most people. Instead of giving up the "Egypt scheme," he spent the next several months brooding, speculating, and writing endless letters about it. When Sherman offered to resubmit his name to the Egyptian authorities in November, 1875, David quickly consented, pledging that by the time he could reach Cairo he would be able to speak French adequately or pay his own passage home. Weeks passed, then months, but no word came. Meanwhile, General Stone's intermittent correspondence with Sherman made no reference to David. "I begin to feel uneasy about Egypt," the well-meaning general wrote David in February, 1876. "I heard from Stone on another subject but he was absolutely silent on your case." Finally, sometime in March, David directed Sherman to withdraw his name

---

32   W. T. Sherman to D. F. Boyd, June 12, July 10, 1875, in William T. Sherman Letters, David F. Boyd Family Papers; Charles Stone to William Sherman, undated, included in W. T. Sherman to David Boyd, August 26, 1875, *ibid.*; D. F. Boyd to I. L. Lynes, August 5, 1875, in David Boyd Papers.
33   David Boyd to A. D. Bayles, September 2, 1875, David Boyd to E. W. Sutherlin, September 3, 1875, David Boyd to W. T. Sherman, telegram and letter, September 10, 1875, David Boyd to S. H. Lockett, September 17, 1875, David Boyd to W. T. Sherman, telegram, September 21, 1875, all in David Boyd Letterbooks; W. T. Sherman to David Boyd, September 22, 1875, in William T. Sherman Letters, David F. Boyd Family Papers.

from further consideration. By that time he was thoroughly convinced that the Khedive's lack of funds, not his own inability to speak French, was the "real" reason he had been "dumped" by Egypt.[34]

David's suspicions regarding the Khedive's "real" reason for rejecting him apparently grew out of a letter written by C. Woodward Hutson, in November, 1875. Hutson, a brother-in-law of Colonel Lockett, had remarked casually that, "The objection made to you not speaking French is so trivial in character . . . that I cannot help fancying it to be only a diplomatic pretense." Egyptian intrigue, a costly war with neighboring Abbysinia, or financial embarrassment were more likely causes, Hutson speculated. Besides, one could not expect frankness from a "despotic government."[35]

Hutson's conjectures took some time to register with David. During November and part of December the letters he wrote from his self-imposed exile at the university seemed to accept at face value his inability to speak French as the reason for his rejection. Most of them dwelt on the irreparable injury his professional reputation would suffer if the teaching fraternity ever discovered that he had been "dropped" for an "incompetency." At the time David was still waiting desperately for some response to his resubmitted application and the fact that most people, even those in Baton Rouge, thought he was already in Egypt only added to his "mortification." In mid-December, however, a letter arrived from Colonel Lockett which seemed to trigger David's memory regarding Hutson's speculations. Written a month earlier, the letter explained that the post for which David had been originally recruited was still unfilled. "The finance question," Lockett added, "is quite a serious one here now, and I don't think anything will be done that is likely to increase expenses."[36]

With pathetic haste David seized upon Lockett's words. If nothing else they provided support for his sagging self-confidence. "The

34 David Boyd to Wm. Sherman, September 26, 1875, David Boyd to S. H. Lockett, September 26, 27, November 17, 1875, in David Boyd Letterbooks; David Boyd to Wm. Sherman, November 6, 1875, in Boyd Letters, Fleming Collection; Wm. Sherman to David Boyd, November 2, 1875, February 26, 1876, in William T. Sherman Letters, David F. Boyd Family Papers; David Boyd to Wm. Sherman [March, 1876], in David Boyd Letterbooks. The location of this letter in David's Letterbook indicates that it was written in March.
35 C. Woodward Hutson to D. F. Boyd, November 9, 1875, in David Boyd Papers.
36 David Boyd to S. H. Lockett, November 17, 25, 1875, David Boyd to William Van Pelt, November 19, 1875, David Boyd to John P. McAuley, November 19, 1875, David Boyd to Edward Cunningham, December 3, 1875, all in David Boyd Letterbooks; S. H. Lockett to David Boyd, November 19, 1875, in Alphabetical File, Fleming Collection.

French," he wrote Lockett flatly on December 15, 1875, "was all an *excuse* to save the Egyptian Treasury a miserable sum of money—*money*! for which I have always *myself* cared so little." For the next several months correspondents received similar explanations although the letters assumed a more charitable tone after David finally withdrew his candidacy for a position in the Khedive's service. Two letters to General Stone early in June, 1876, were particularly magnanimous. In them David forgave everyone concerned for what had caused him "more pain than anything else . . . in my life." Notwithstanding, he would be happy to help Stone and the Egyptians in whatever way he could, despite the "injustice" they had done him and themselves by dispensing with his services "on a mere pretext."[37]

General Stone could not allow David's version of the "Egyptian mix-up" to go unchallenged. In July, 1876, he denied categorically that the Khedive had resorted to "pretext" in David's case. Perfect knowledge of French was essential, Stone insisted; "getting on" would not do. Furthermore, "all this occurred before anyone here believed there could be any serious financial difficulty." As Stone saw it, the trouble stemmed from Sherman's slip of the pen; he had described David as a professor of modern languages when he meant to say "ancient." Then Stone told David gently something that Lockett had written him months before: if David had started for Egypt when first engaged, stopping a month or two in Paris enroute, he might well have learned enough French to please the Khedive. "Your sense of honor and modesty made you send the fatal telegram [that he could not "speak French"] and then came all the difficulty."[38]

The Lockett letter, written on November 19, 1875, appeared rather early in the dismal Egyptian correspondence. It is quoted here at length because it states so well the real source of so many of David's problems:

Now you think you have been very badly treated in the matter and I too think it has been [a] terribly annoying and unfortunate affair. But Egypt is not altogether to blame. Your old pet the La. S. U. has been the main cause of the

37 David Boyd to S. H. Lockett, December 15, 1875, David Boyd to Wm. Van Pelt, December 19, 1875, David Boyd to S. H. Lockett, December 21, 26, 1875, May 17, 1876, David Boyd to Wm. Seay, February 16, 1876, David Boyd to W. P. Sherman, March [?], 1876, David Boyd to Mrs. S. H. Lockett, April 1, 1876, David Boyd to W. L. Sanford, May 13, 1876, David Boyd to Chas. P. Stone, June 6, 8, 1876, all in David Boyd Letterbooks.
38 Chas. P. Stone to D. F. Boyd, July 7, 1876, in Alphabetical File, Fleming Collection.

trouble, and you my dear Colonel were the immediate prime mover in bringing about the unfortunate denouement. In the first place you had a divided interest, you clung to the old LSU with desperate devotion, hoping to do something for its salvation before 'leaving it altogether.' That kept you from coming along with me last summer. Then you lost sight of your thousand and one qualifications that preeminently fit you for your duties here [Egypt], and with suicidal perversity seized upon one of the 'smallest of small matters' and made a mountain out of it by putting it into an abominable brief telegram. You must excuse me for writing such hard words. You know I have often told you, you are your own worst enemy, and it makes me right angry with *that part of you which is eternally bedeviling you*, whenever I think about any of the troubles you have gotten yourself into.[39]

What David had done for the "salvation" of Louisiana State University before "leaving it altogether" was to hire three professors, at his own expense, for the academic year 1875–1876. Then, when it appeared that he might not be going to Egypt after all, he had to find a job in order to pay their salaries. On October 21, 1875, he wired Professor Hilgard at the University of California to find out if the presidency of that institution were still open. But a few weeks later Sherman resubmitted his name to the Egyptians, and the California effort seems to have been suspended. In March, 1876, the California presidency was still vacant, and David received a letter from Professor Hilgard urging him to try seriously for the position. More in need of work than ever and clearly shattered by the Egyptian experience, David finally agreed to let his friend submit his name formally. But his first reactions to Hilgard's proposal reveal how depressed and insecure recent events had left him. If the presidency were already filled, David wrote, he was willing to try for a professorship in mathematics, Latin, English, or French. However, he wanted it clearly understood ahead of time that he was "no scholar" and did not claim to be. He also told Hilgard something that was certainly not known in Louisiana: he was "no *titled* graduate" of the University of Virginia. He had "graduated in several schools," but he did not have a formal degree from the university. Again David displayed his lack of self-confidence when he asked Hilgard to get assurances of his acceptability from professors and trustees *before* submitting his application for the presidency. Because some might object to his southern origin, Hilgard must tell "frankly"

39   S. H. Lockett to David Boyd, November 19, 1875, *ibid*.

all his bad points; then, if there were no major objections, his name could be formally considered. Neither did David intend to send any references because "anybody can get a cart-load of such paper." Instead, he would write a simple letter of application to the regents. "Picking a professor, or president, shd be done much like *choosing a wife*; and in the latter case, *potent recommendations* wd hardly do," David remarked. He added that he would never have "aspired so high" if Hilgard had not insisted. But if nothing came of his application, he would not be surprised. "One lesson has been pretty thoroughly rubbed into me of late years: *to expect nothing.*"[40]

David may have learned to expect nothing from his Egyptian experience. But he certainly did not learn to keep his own counsel. Immediately after deciding to apply at California, he fired off letters to friends and creditors in four states and on three continents telling them of his plans. He also advanced explanations as to why he probably would not get the job. His "Southern birth" and "Confederate record" would work against him, he predicted pessimistically. Dr. Hilgard did not think so, but David did not wait to find out. On July 2, 1876, he asked Hilgard to withdraw his name from consideration. He could not expect to get the appointment, he told Hilgard in explanation, and besides, his "duty" required him to stay in Louisiana until the two schools, the university and the agricultural college, finally merged.[41]

In the summer of 1876 David was still out of a job and still determined to stay in Louisiana until Governor Kellogg signed the merger bill passed earlier in the year. After that he would probably open a boarding school somewhere in Virginia, but someone else would have to "provide the property," he explained to Vice-President Sanford. When friends suggested that he run on the Democratic ticket in Louisiana for the position of state superintendent of public education, he promptly squelched the idea. *"Please say no more about it,"* he insisted. "I don't want that or any other office in *La.*, nor will

40   D. F. Boyd to E. W. Hilgard, telegram, October 21, 1875, D. F. Boyd to E. W. Hilgard, March 6, 1876, in David Boyd Papers; David Boyd to S. H. Lockett, May 17, 1876, David Boyd to E. W. Hilgard, April 10, 1876, in David Boyd Letterbooks.
41   David Boyd to A. B. Lavisse, April 11, 1876, David Boyd to Pendleton King, April 11, 1876, David Boyd to J. P. McAuley, April 12, 1876, David Boyd to Americus Featherman, April 15, 1876, David Boyd to Swarbrick's, April 15, 1876, David Boyd to C. C. Lockett, April 10, 1876, David Boyd to E. W. Hilgard, May 4, July 2, 1876, all in David Boyd Letterbooks.

I stay in the state any longer than I can find something to do *out of it.*" [42]

Late in September David set the boarding school plan in motion when he began corresponding with Richard Hancock of Albemarle County, Virginia. Hancock, who had been David's student at Homer College before the war, raised blooded stock and by 1876 was relatively well off. David asked him to investigate properties for his potential school because he was too poor to do so himself. By October, Hancock had found two suitable sites but only one, Greenwood, was available for rent. However, there was one drawback. Greenwood's owner stipulated that his aged parents had to live on the premises, and David, who did not like to be "mixed-up" with people, seems to have lost interest. He had been a schoolmaster for so long, a *"little monarch,"* that he had to "rule the roost" wherever he went. Nevertheless, by the end of the year David was thinking seriously about engaging Greenwood. [43]

David disclosed his boarding school plans to relatively few people. Besides William Sanford, the Swarbrick firm, and several former colleagues living outside Louisiana, only a handful of people knew what he intended to do or where he might go when he left the university. As he explained to Colonel Lockett, his failure to go to Egypt after announcing his plans to "all and sundry" led people to question his "good sense . . . powers of decision and even . . . my veracity." David wondered if he were not talking too much even to Colonel Lockett. If he did not go to Virginia, Lockett might "exclaim like many others, 'poor, weak vacillating fellow, he does not know what he is about: *he* can't make up his mind about anything!'" The difference between a weak man and a strong one, David declared, was that the latter thought to himself. The weak man thought out loud. Everyone heard him "weighing ifs and ands." Unwilling to make that mistake again, David promised to let Lockett know his decision "as soon as this *weak* specimen comes to anchor." But the "weak specimen" did not even weigh anchor for another five years. Not until 1881 would he leave the university to establish a boarding school in his native state. [44]

42   David Boyd to William Sanford, July 29, 1876, *ibid.*; Swarbrick's to David F. Boyd, June 9, 13, 1876, R. S. Stuart to David Boyd, July 5, 1876, in Alphabetical File, Fleming Collection; David Boyd to Swarbrick's, June 9, 1876, in David Boyd Letterbooks.
43   David Boyd to Richard Hancock, September 25, October 15, 28, December 13, 1876, in David Boyd Letterbooks; R. J. Hancock to David Boyd, October 10, 20, 1876, David Boyd to William Van Pelt, December 18, 1876, in David Boyd Papers.
44   David Boyd to Samuel H. Lockett, October 20, November 26, 1876, in David Boyd Letterbooks.

Chapter VII

More Politics, More Poverty

WHEN THE beneficiary cadets were sent home in March of 1873, fewer than twenty students remained at the university, and until 1877, enrollment rarely climbed above that number. The faculty was also sharply reduced, but even so, there were periods when the few remaining professors had little to occupy their time. Tom Boyd kept busy studying Latin, arranging papers, and copying David's correspondence. He also seems to have discovered Baton Rouge society. Numerous entries in his diary describe his frequent visits to the homes of prominent citizens in the community. Ultimately David complained. "Sociability," he told Tom, was only for rich people. But Tom thought David used their poverty as an excuse. The real reason for David's objection stemmed from his own "inborn horror" of paying and receiving social calls.[1]

Instead of "socializing," David spent most of his time trying to borrow money to keep the school and his family "alive." But he still had many hours left to read widely, write hundreds of letters, campaign for the agricultural college fund, and dabble mildly in politics. His reading was eclectic. Besides the several British quarterlies and American periodicals to which the university subscribed, he enjoyed reading history, biography, and philosophy. Emerson, Milton, John Tyndall, and

---

1 Tom Boyd Diary, January 23, October 17, 1875, March 17, May 13, 1876. In his own diary, David admitted that all forms of social activity were repugnant to him. David Boyd Diary, December 22, 1874.

Thomas Huxley were all favorites of his, and in 1874 he exchanged a number of unused text books for works by Montesquieu, Descartes, Kant, Comte, Mill, Spencer, and Darwin.[2]

In addition, David made every effort to stay abreast of new developments in the field of education and educational administration. Much of his voluminous correspondence between 1873 and 1876 was directed to other college presidents, state and city superintendents of public education, state secretaries of agriculture, and various officials in the federal government such as the United States commissioner of education. From most of them he sought copies of the reports they submitted to their respective legislative bodies. He asked the college presidents for ideas about the most efficient way to organize agricultural colleges, and from everyone he requested materials relating to "scientific" and "industrial" education.[3]

Another scheme which kept David busy was his plan to solicit Congress for federal funds to create and maintain a university in every state. Asked what he thought of the idea, Charles Eliot of Harvard, the educational giant of the era, replied that two or three "real universities" were enough for a nation with a population of forty million. But if David meant "polytechnic" schools, he agreed that there was room for one good one in each state. Even before contacting Eliot, David enlisted the aid of a congressman to pursue his plan. In 1872, General William Terry of Virginia agreed to introduce a bill that would grant one million acres of federal land, or the proceeds from the sale thereof, to each state for the purpose of supporting a college or university. At the time, another measure to increase federal land grants to the states in proportion to their size was also before the Congress. The result was a compromise that would augment each state's existing land grant for agricultural and mechanical colleges by one-half million acres. When the Senate acted affirmatively in 1873, David asked for a leave of absence so that he could help Congressman Terry move the bill through the House. If it passed, he was "almost certain" the university could claim half of Louisiana's share, perhaps $30,000 a year. The executive committee of the board granted the leave, but the Kellogg legislature's

2 Fay, *History of Education in Louisiana*, 93–95; David Boyd to Jas. A. Gresham, undated [1874–75], in David Boyd Letterbooks; David Boyd Diary, September 1, 7, 19, 1874, January 26, February 7, 13, April 1, May 22, 1875.
3 David Boyd Diary, November 1, 1874. See also numerous letters for October and November, 1874, in David Boyd Letterbooks.

refusal to appropriate any funds for the university forced David to change his plans. With no money to spend in Louisiana, the board could hardly affort to support David in Washington.[4]

Convinced that the Kellogg administration meant to "starve them out," David asked General Sherman to intercede with the governor in behalf of the university. Sherman telegraphed the statehouse and seemed satisfied that Kellogg had no plans to undermine the school, but David was not so sure. His own relations with the Radical administration were strictly formal; that is, he submitted his annual reports because the law required it. But beyond that his efforts to communicate with the governor were limited to brief notes, none of which seems to have received a reply. For example, in December, 1873, David proposed to Kellogg that the upcoming legislature merge the state university, the University of Louisiana, and the proposed agricultural and mechanical college. They should all be "one," he argued, because separately they would each be "*weak* and puny, and very apt to die." He also asked Governor Kellogg to give the entire asylum building to the merged schools for a permanent home. The law and medical "departments" (the University of Louisiana) should remain in New Orleans.[5]

In February, 1874, David tried again. The legislature was in session, and he was in New Orleans to oversee university affairs. Unsuccessful in two efforts to see Kellogg at his office, he wrote him a letter, enclosing one from Sherman that requested the governor to do whatever he could for the school. David's letter was more specific. It asked for an appropriation large enough to pay off the clamoring creditors, a permanent home in Baton Rouge, and the agricultural and mechanical fund. Instead, the legislature passed a concurrent resolution to investigate the university. J. Henri Burch, the black senator from Baton Rouge, introduced the measure early in February, and David tried to speed it through the house so that the inquiry could take place before adjournment. To the chairman of the education committee he wrote, "I hardly know its object; but you know that all such special investiga-

4   Charles Eliot to David Boyd, October 26, 1871, in Alphabetical File, Fleming Collection; David Boyd to William Terry, August 29, 1871, David Boyd to William Sanford, in Boyd Letters, *ibid.*; Minutes of the Executive Committee of the Board of Supervisors, February 3, 1873.
5   David Boyd to William P. Kellogg, August 9, December 23, 1873, in David Boyd Papers; William Sherman to David Boyd, August 12, 1873, in William T. Sherman Letters, David F. Boyd Family Papers.

tions are *reflections* on those in authority—altho' Burch protests against such an interpretation."[6]

The report of the special committee leveled a series of charges at David: mismanaging funds; expending money on pictures, statues, and artillery instead of paying off creditors and faculty; allowing the cadets to bore peep holes in the walls so that they could spy on the asylum inmates; and pocketing funds acquired by the unauthorized sale of bricks taken from the asylum building. Professor Francis V. Hopkins was outraged. In a multipaged refutation of every allegation, he declared that the entire investigation stemmed from the spiteful "machinations of a small clique in this town [Baton Rouge]." Behind the whole thing, Hopkins charged, were Superintendent McWhorter and several members of his board who wanted the university evicted from the asylum building. He urged his correspondent, a prominent Orleanian, to do all he could to correct the "slanders." The university had to acquire the agricultural fund and an appropriation to pay off its creditors, Hopkins concluded. "Otherwise, we are ruined."[7]

But the university got nothing from the lawmakers in 1874, to the complete disgust of board member William Seay who advised David to abandon the school. "Let no idea of your duty to make another effort . . . in favor of higher education in La. have any effect. . . . La. is not ready for higher education." By withholding the agricultural fund and establishing a separate institution in New Orleans, Seay continued, the legislature had dealt the university its "death blow." Even a Democratic legislature in 1875 would do no good. "Such an administration would come in on such a wave of Economy that considering the debt of the University . . . they would do nothing at all but let the school die." Colonel Samuel Lockett told David essentially the same thing: Louisiana was not ready for a first-class university. David's determined efforts to give her one and her miserable failure to support those efforts should have been enough to convince even him. But Lockett knew from experience that he "was writing to no purpose." He was right. In December, 1874, in spite of his and the school's impoverished circumstances, David could still write to one old friend, "The Radicals are disappointed, I have beaten them. They turned us out to starve—they

6   David Boyd to Michael Hahn, February 24, 1874, David Boyd to William P. Kellogg, February 20, 1874, in Boyd Letters, Fleming Collection.
7   F. V. Hopkins to A. W. Smythe, copy, March 1, 1874, in David Boyd Papers.

had not the machinery to wipe us out of existence by legislation. . . . [They] expected us to go down . . . when they refused to aid the 'rebel set' as they called us this year . . . Burch, the negro senator from here told them they cld not kill us that way."[8]

What actually saved the university in 1874 was no doubt the whole state's preoccupation with the coming legislative election. Not even David, an avowed hater of politics and politicians, could remain aloof in that supercharged political atmosphere. Besides, he had little or nothing else to do. The university's total enrollment for the year 1874 was only thirty-one students, who from July through September were not even present. Much of that time David spent in his office, worrying, writing letters, and making entries in his diary. Two themes, politics and poverty, dominated his correspondence, but by late summer the former assumed so much importance that he even forgot the "starving condition" of his family.

The events responsible for David's distraction may be sketched briefly. In the spring of 1874 it was clear that political alignment in Louisiana had polarized along racial lines. The Fusion tactic of appealing for black votes, so widely endorsed in 1872 and the short-lived Unification movement of 1873, found almost no favor in 1874. Only one conservative New Orleans paper still supported such efforts. The rest joined the country press in calling for the formation of a white man's party. By June, whites and blacks were organizing themselves into armed leagues all over the state. Military drills in the streets and rumors of stockpiled weapons further increased tension. In New Orleans some of David's friends played leading roles in the Crescent City White League. But other conservative Democrats were slow to join the new organizations, whose avowed purpose was to oust carpetbaggers and scalawags from office, whatever the cost. Like the Radicals, they considered some of the White League rank and file to be nothing but Klansmen undisguised. David shared their opinion. He thought some compromise had to be found; the two races had to live together in Louisiana. However, in late July, 1874, the prospects were not promising. In Baton Rouge the White League held nightly meetings, and the blacks, organized in what purported to be fife and drum corps, staged

8   W. A. Seay to David Boyd, May 24, 1874, S. H. Lockett to David Boyd, November 21, 1874, in Alphabetical File, Fleming Collection; David Boyd to J. C. Egan, December 10, 1874, in David Boyd Letterbooks.

nocturnal marches through the streets. To David it "looked like trouble" in November. He thought it would be "2 years more" before peace came to Louisiana.[9]

Nevertheless, he tried to avert disaster. During July, August, and September, 1874, David went to New Orleans five times for the purpose of borrowing enough to feed his family. While traveling back and forth, he discussed politics with men from all over the state, and what he learned discouraged him. Although prominent Democrats in Baton Rouge deprecated White League strength, David thought that "rash, thoughtless, extreme men" might well provoke a race war in November. Certainly the Radicals were concerned. When David arrived in New Orleans on August 3, 1874, he thought the Republicans gathering for their state convention seemed to fear for their safety, especially the "carpetbagger" class.

In the Crescent City, David saw his old commanding officer, Major General Harry Hays, who had been approached by President Grant's brother-in-law, Lewis Dent, about supporting the president for a third term in 1876. Hays informed Dent that Grant might be acceptable if he could get rid of the federal judge who upheld Kellogg in the election of 1872, and if he pursued a "peaceful and liberal" policy toward the South. David agreed and so did "Lieutenant Governor" Davidson B. Penn. A "liberal, conservative policy—no radicalism or White Leaguers" was the best policy for Louisiana, and the best way to achieve it was to work for a third term. Then David remembered why he had come to New Orleans: "Here I am talking politics and my wife and children nearly at starvation point."[10]

On August 5, 1874, the Republicans convened in the statehouse (Mechanic's Institute) to nominate candidates for the state central committee, state treasurer, six congressional posts, and the state legislature. They renominated the incumbent A. Dubuclet, a black, for the treasurer's post, whom, along with state superintendent of public education, William Brown, another black, David considered the best offi-

---

9 Charles Vincent, "Negro Legislators in Louisiana During Reconstruction" (Ph.D. dissertation, Louisiana State University, 1973), 200–202; Fanny Z. Lovell Bone, "Louisiana in the Disputed Election of 1876," *Louisiana Historical Quarterly*, XIV (July, 1931), 418–19; Oscar H. Lestage, "The White League in Louisiana and Its Participation in Reconstruction Riots," *Louisiana Historical Quarterly*, XVIII (July, 1935), 629, 635–40; Lonn, *Reconstruction in Louisiana*, 253–58; David Boyd Diary, July 24, 25, 1874; Taylor, *Louisiana Reconstructed*, 279–86. Taylor found no convincing evidence of the existence of Black Leagues.

10 David Boyd Diary, July 29, 30, August 3, 4, 1874.

cers in state government, "a credit to their race." Democrats, he thought, ought to support Dubuclet. It might help to win over the Negro race and conciliate President Grant.[11]

When David returned to Baton Rouge, he found most of the leading citizens favorably disposed to the "third term idea," providing the president would "keep out" of the coming state election. "I think the leaven is working," David noted in his diary. But a few days later he was less certain. On August 14, during the parish convention of Democrats and anti-Radicals meeting in Baton Rouge, he was disturbed to see such "grim determination" for change but no agreement on how to bring it about. "I think Louisiana's surest way out of her troubles is through Grant and the *third term*, and I happen to know almost direct that Grant wants the *3rd term* and . . . the support of the whites of La., as well as of the *whole* South," he wrote Vice-President William Sanford. If the delegates only had a definite policy and an understanding with Grant before they convened in state convention on August 24, David was sure it would be "merely a *walk over* the track" in November. But he doubted that they would be so prudent. They preferred to let prejudice be their guide, and they would probably go down to defeat. Meanwhile, he asked Swarbrick in New Orleans to find out from his friend Fred Freret if anything had been heard from Washington. "He will know what I mean," David added cryptically.[12]

The Democratic state convention met in Baton Rouge on August 24, 1874. White League sentiment predominated, and "Governor" John McEnery catered to it when he delivered what David described as an "inflamatory speech." McEnery endorsed "bloodshed" if that were necessary to rid the state of carpetbaggers. The delegates approved. They adopted a platform that began "We, the white people of Louisiana." From there they pledged themselves to remove Radicals and Negroes from power, "peacefully if possible, forcibly if necessary." Although he considered the three hundred delegates "able and dignified," David thought they went too far. To Lockett he wrote, "I think *I* could bring them out of their troubles on a more conservative line. I wd draw no white and black line and wld go for Grant for a third term. Then I wd try to pursue the policy of Gov. Kemper of Va. . . . *Individu-*

11 *Ibid.*, August 8, 1874; Lonn, *Reconstruction in Louisiana*, 261.
12 David Boyd Diary, August 11, 16, 1874; David Boyd to William Sanford, August 14, 1874, David Boyd to Swarbrick and Co., August 17, 1874, in David Boyd Letterbooks.

ally most of our leading men here think that way; but when they get together in body or convention with no one bold enough to express his real views the White League mania rises to a *white heat*." If the convention were consistent, David thought, it should have pledged itself to fight even the federal government if it continued to uphold carpetbaggers "with the bayonet." Any other course he considered "neither sensible or manly."[13]

During the next several days David recorded in his diary his fear that extremism was growing. White Leaguers were "running carpetbag office-holders off"; newspapers reported a "race war" near Shreveport, and rumors that Grant intended to send in troops circulated throughout the state. David disapproved of the violence; it was bound to bring retaliation and ultimate defeat. But if the whites meant to wage war, they should not stop after murdering a few "poor devils." That was cowardly. They should go after the real "author of Carpetbaggery (Uncle Sam)," even though failure was certain.[14]

When he returned to New Orleans on September 2, 1874, David found nothing to encourage him. Even his friends were talking of "running off" Governor Kellogg and Lieutenant Governor C. C. Antoine so that the more acceptable Tom Anderson, president of the senate, might assume the governor's office. David countered that Kellogg, Antoine, McEnery, and Penn should all resign. Then Anderson would be governor "legally." But he had little hope that his idea would be accepted. His friends were too impatient. Besides, the white man's party in New Orleans was a "miserable set." William Freret, a former board member, said even the leaders could not agree on a course of action.

To avoid bloodshed and almost certain federal intervention, David decided to approach Lieutenant Governor Davidson Penn to see if he would resign along with Kellogg, Antoine, and McEnery. Penn doubted that such an arrangement could be worked out, but he was willing to do anything possible to make the resulting government legal. Although he thought Anderson worse than Kellogg, he would accept him as governor in the interest of "peace & legality." Penn did not

13 David Boyd to S. H. Lockett, undated, [1874–75], in David Boyd Letterbooks; David Boyd Diary, August 24, 25, 1874; Lonn, *Reconstruction in Louisiana*, 262–63; Lestage, "White League in Louisiana," 645–48.
14 David Boyd Diary, August 28, 31, September 1, 2, 4, 1874. For a detailed account of White League activity throughout Louisiana during 1874, see Lestage, "White League in Louisiana," 617–95.

promise to resign in so many words, but David thought he was willing to consider it. He asked Penn to present the idea to all the other parties. If Kellogg objected, David suggested that President Grant could induce him to change his mind.[15]

For the next several days David went about New Orleans promoting his compromise scheme. He saw Tom Anderson, who thought Kellogg and Antoine would resign without difficulty. Anderson intimated that Kellogg would expect to be compensated with an appointment to the Senate. On the Democratic side, David thought McEnery was the main problem unless the "Old Democrats" could force him to withdraw. Meanwhile, the New Orleans Metropolitan Police outraged Orleanians by seizing large quantities of weapons destined for White Leaguers, and the citizenry howled at what they considered a violation of their "constitutional rights." Fearing an outbreak of hostilities, David and William Freret redoubled their efforts to get the resignation plan accepted. But if they did not succeed by Friday, September 11, David thought, it would be too late. The people would be "rushed into war" by their thoughtless leaders, and the result would be disaster.[16]

On Saturday, September 12, David had to go home, but he was back in New Orleans at 6:30 A.M. the following Monday. Before reaching the city he wrote a letter to Vice-President Sanford describing conditions in the metropolis and summarizing his own attitudes. "All is *seemingly* quiet in N.O.," David reported, "but the truth is the feeling is at a *white heat.* . . . It may be a month before the people *move*; but they are busily organizing . . . there is as yet a want of a *clear-cut* plan; nor is there a leader. . . . At present, opinion is divided whether they shd stand back for Uncle Sam if he attempts to uphold the Carpetbaggers. . . . I think half-measures in war are not wise; and once we are satisfied there can be no peaceful solution, we shd draw the sword, *and fling away the scabbard.*" Then he told Sanford of his efforts to effect a compromise which he now thought "hardly practicable." They must get ready for a fight, which would put them in a "bad box," but at least they would perish "like true men in a good cause."[17]

15 David Boyd Diary, September 4, 5, 1874.
16 *Ibid.*, September 8, 9, 10, 1874; Lonn, *Reconstruction in Louisiana,* 268–69; Taylor, *Louisiana Reconstructed,* 291–92.
17 David Boyd to William Sanford, September 14, 1874, in David Boyd Letterbooks. Actually, "Lieutenant Governor" Penn and White League leaders were hatching a plot to seize power, install McEnery in the governor's office, and transport the Radicals out of the country, all before the federal government could intervene. Taylor, *Louisiana Reconstructed,* 292.

Nevertheless, when David got to New Orleans he and Will Freret made another vain effort to see Tom Anderson in the interest of compromise. By that time it was eleven o'clock, and a huge citizens' rally, called for on the previous Saturday night, was assembling at Clay Statue. David did not attend. He was still trying to find Anderson but without success. Meanwhile, the citizenry demanded that Governor Kellogg resign, and Judge Dibble declined in his name, stating that he would not treat with a group representing an armed mob. About 3:30 P.M. David went to the steamer *Selma* on which he planned to return to Baton Rouge later that day. Enroute he saw Metropolitan Police stationed at various points along Canal Street, noting that besides muskets and sidearms they had four pieces of artillery. Then he checked the relative strength of the citizens massed in adjoining streets. At about 4 P.M. the citizen forces attacked the Metropolitans and the police fell back to the Customhouse, losing three of their guns. Governor Kellogg withdrew to the Customhouse also, as the citizens moved in to occupy the state and city public buildings. The next day Lieutenant Governor Penn replaced all the Kellogg officials with those "legally elected" in 1872. By 11 A.M. of September 15, the revolt was declared a success, and the city prepared to celebrate with a parade.[18]

David was sure that federal troops would intervene as soon as word reached the president. If Grant did not act, the Kellogg regime was certain to topple. But he doubted that Washington would let Louisiana's "poor people" off so easily. If the citizens meant to fight, David thought, their commander, F. N. Ogden, should fall back to the Atchafalaya and Red rivers. At 3 P.M. on September 15, a proclamation by President Grant appeared on the streets which ordered the citizens to disperse within five days. Faintly encouraged, David went to see Lieutenant Governor Penn the next day to urge that an explanatory wire be sent to Sherman. Penn agreed and by 3 P.M. David had borrowed enough money to send it.

In his message, David made a strong plea for understanding. "The intense disgust of the intelligence and worth of our people came naturally to a head, and like a huge boil burst," it began. But no hostility for the United States government or the president was intended. New Or-

18 David Boyd Diary, September 14, 15, 1874; Lonn, *Reconstruction in Louisiana*, 270–72; Vincent, "Negro Legislators in Louisiana," 223; Taylor, *Louisiana Reconstructed*, 292–95. Lonn, puts the number killed at 44; Vincent claims 44 Metropolitans plus 12 insurgents, and Taylor sets the total killed at 33.

leans was "quiet and orderly" and, with only a few exceptions, "perfectly satisfied" with the outcome. Only the black politicians were displeased. Representing acting governor Penn as a Liberal Republican who opposed the White League, took no part in the Baton Rouge convention, and was highly regarded by the blacks, David concluded, "If the government can only let matters remain as they *now* are, all classes of our people, except a few politicians, will be satisfied; the political status of La. will trouble the govt. and General Grant no more; and the great majority of our people (white and black) will become his fast friends."[19]

David settled back to await Sherman's answer in a city where, according to rumor General W. H. Emory, the federal commander in the area, would soon demand surrender from the Penn government. Conferences involving McEnery, Penn, Kellogg, Packard, and General Emory took place on September 17, and David hoped that some compromise would be effected. But if the rumors proved correct and Emory insisted on surrender, he thought the people should fight to "the bloody end."[20]

In the midst of the excitement in New Orleans, word reached David from Baton Rouge that blacks had attacked the nearby community of Bayou Sara on the night of the seventeenth. General Emory dispatched troops from Baton Rouge to put down the disorder while in Baton Rouge itself, a Committee of Fourteen took over the town and demanded possession of the university's guns to keep them out of the hands of the Negroes. Nevertheless, David decided to stay in the city because he wanted to help find a way out of "the scrape which our people had gotten into." But on September 19, David learned that the Kellogg government was about to be restored. Despondent, he telegraphed Sherman again before leaving for Baton Rouge. Restoration of Governor Kellogg would result in anarchy and lawlessness, he declared, insisting that "Due regard for the protection of life and property demands a military or provisional government."[21]

---

19 David Boyd Diary, September 15, 16, 1874; David Boyd to William Sherman, September 16, 1874, in David Boyd Letterbooks.
20 David Boyd Diary, September 15, 16, 17, 1874; David Boyd to William Van Pelt, September 17, 1874, in Boyd Letters, Fleming Collection.
21 David Boyd Diary, September 18, 19, 1874; William Van Pelt to David Boyd, telegram, September 18, 1874, in David Boyd Letterbooks; David Boyd to William Sherman, telegram, September 19, 1874, in Scrapbook, David Boyd Papers; David Boyd to William Van Pelt, September 18, 1874, in Boyd Letters, Fleming Collection.

A few days later David finally heard from Sherman. The general had not been at his headquarters when David's telegrams arrived. They were copied and sent to him at Columbus, Ohio. "I did not answer because it simply would have complicated matters," Sherman explained. "Matters of this nature involving the safety of a state do not belong to me as head of the army, but are properly the function of the President whose action is of course binding on me and all parts of the army." Then he expressed regret that the people of New Orleans had taken it upon themselves to change the government of Louisiana. No matter how unpopular Kellogg was, he was the legal governor, and mob action, however "respectable" the mob, could not change that fact. Sherman assured David that uprisings like the one in New Orleans did nothing but harm "the people of your section in the estimation of all people everywhere." Counseling patience and forbearance in the interest of the entire country, he also appeared to be offering David a mild reprimand and a bit of advice: "I am determined so far as I am personally concerned, to stick close to my office, which is simple and plain—*viz.* mind my own business, and if all will do likewise I think prosperity will return to all parts of the land more speedily than by any attempt to reach it by violence or unlawful measures."[22]

David answered on September 26, 1874. He was "sick over La.'s case." The people had hoped that President Grant would find "as much law to let us alone now as he did to interfere with us two years ago." David knew Sherman had not had anything "officially" to do with the federal action against Louisiana. As for the telegrams, he never expected that anyone but Sherman would see them. His only intention, David declared, was to have "poor La.'s" side known by a "thinking man" of the North in case President Grant's advisers gave him incorrect counsel intentionally to better serve their party and to "keep themselves in office." Then he closed by attacking the "gangrene" in Louisiana, universal suffrage. Unless it were removed, David predicted, it would spread over the South and the whole nation, "and then you— the General of the Army—will have your hands full indeed."[23]

The letters David wrote to his friends about the New Orleans riot were somewhat more emotional than the wires he sent Sherman. To

22 William T. Sherman to David Boyd, September 21, 1874, in William T. Sherman Letters, David F. Boyd Family Papers.
23 David Boyd to William T. Sherman, September 26, 1874, in Boyd Letters, Fleming Collection.

Colonel Lockett he castigated the "extreme Democrats" who, in the days before the uprising, refused to consider the resignation of Mc-Enery in the interest of compromise. They were "old moss-backs." To Dr. Francis Hopkins he wrote:

The La. question is now a national question. Mr. Cuffey, to secure his freedom, brought us one war—a terrible one. Will he bring on another war, in his and the Radical's silly attempt to make him, what God has said he shd not be— the equal of the *white* man? When Uncle Sam conforms to the law of nature and to the wish of nature's God, he will be safe and happy; otherwise our Uncle Sam, like all things earthly, that oppose God and nature, must perish. This must be the white man's country; It was never designed to be the Negro's or Chinaman's country. With a negro for President, John Chinaman for vice-president, an Indian for Chief Justice, a Malayan for Speaker of the House . . . and the Anglo-Saxon to *foot the bills*, this will indeed be a glorious country.[24]

When David reached Baton Rouge on September 20, 1874, the citizens' Committee of Fourteen was still in charge of the town. As in many parishes of the state, the whites had "run off" Radical office-holders during the summer and early fall. But after Kellogg was restored and federal troops began to arrive in support of his regime, the various White League committees around the state began to give up power. In Baton Rouge the Committee of Fourteen discussed the mechanics of retrocession for two days. Invited to sit in at the discussion, David advised them to do nothing until they heard from McEnery and Penn. But the committee decided to step down at once. However, before Kellogg's officials could take over, David reclaimed the university's guns. He would not give them up again unless assured they would be sent out of the parish.[25]

During the rest of 1874 David's political activity consisted almost entirely of letterwriting. He was bitter in the extreme. The East Baton Rouge Radical candidates for the legislature especially offended him. "One . . . is a poor *negro* who was actually *born* in the *Penitentiary* here—While his mother was a convict!" he informed a friend. "Is that not literally *conceived in iniquity and born in sin?*" He was not much kinder to the opposition. Louisiana not only needed less of the "Carpet-

24 David Boyd to S. H. Lockett, September 26, 1874, David Boyd to F. V. Hopkins, September 30, 1874, in David Boyd Letterbooks.
25 David Boyd Diary, September 20, 21, 1874.

bagger and the nigger," she also could stand some improvement among her "*oldest and best*." "Men of influence and high standing who *abuse* the carpet-bagger for *taking a bribe themselves* offer that bribe."[26]

On November 2, 1874, David went to the polls. Annoyed at having to wait in line with Negroes for the "august privilege" of voting, he deplored the ballot system as a "cheat and a swindle," designed solely to enable some "*cowardly sneak*" to hide the way he voted. The only honest way to vote, he thought, was *viva voce*. Radicals carried East Baton Rouge Parish easily. J. Henri Burch, the black senator, won reelection, and all three members sent to the house were Republican. But David expected Democrats to control the lower chamber. If they did, he hoped they would order a recount of the 1872 returns. A few days later, however, David was afraid that the Returning Board would count the Democrats out. General Longstreet was on the board, and "he will do anything." But David refused to believe that Tom Anderson, president of the senate, would tolerate anything so "deliberately fraudulent."[27]

By late November he had changed his mind. The Returning Board, David wrote Edward Cunningham, would surely make a "false return" unless restrained by a "wholesome fear for their lives." Most of them were "great scoundrels,—Longstreet, Gov. (Mat) Wells & a *negro* son of Duncan F. Kenner being a majority." It hurt David to see Longstreet in such company, but he was forced to conclude that the general was a very bad man. "What a fall for the associate of *Lee*." David believed the Returning Board was waiting to see what Grant's attitude toward Louisiana would be before announcing its decision. If Congress, which reconvened on December 7, 1874, and the president intended to sustain the Radicals, no doubt the Returning Board would act accordingly. In that case, everyone on it plus the Radical leaders should be "seized and hung." David was ready to help. He wrote J. C. Moncure, the Democratic candidate for state treasurer, that he was willing to fight if Moncure were counted out. When the Returning Board finally acted, it certified fifty-three Republicans and fifty-three Democrats, leaving five vancancies to be decided by the house. But the Democrats claimed a seventy-one to thirty-seven seat majority. David thought there was but one thing left: "for the people to seat their candidates by

26 David Boyd to W. L. Broun, October 21, 1874, David Boyd to E. L. Cunningham, October 24, 1874, in David Boyd Letterbooks.
27 David Boyd Diary, November 2, 5, 9, 1874.

force in the parishes." Then, on January 4, as many men as could possibly arrange it, should go to New Orleans for the opening of the legislative session. "Grant seems determined to bring on conflict," he noted in his diary, "to stir up the northern masses against us and to give him a new lease of power. And if he is 'spiling' for a fight, why let him be accommodated." [28]

The legislature convened on January 4, 1875, and a frantic struggle for control ensued. When it was over, Republicans, supported by federal troops, occupied the government buildings. Democrats met separately elsewhere. Again Louisiana had two legislatures, and again civil disorder seemed certain to erupt. Meanwhile, under special orders from President Grant, General Philip Sheridan assumed command in the area. He suggested to the president that the "ringleaders of the Armed White League" be declared "banditti," arrested and tried. The effect was immediate. Protest meetings occurred all over the country, and in the United States Senate the Louisiana situation provoked a debate that continued for weeks. But in the end, nothing was done. House action was also inconclusive although a subcommittee from the lower chamber did go to Louisiana to investigate affairs. Mainly because of the efforts of Representative William A. Wheeler of New York, a compromise plan emerged. Under its terms Democrats would control Louisiana's lower house, and Kellogg would be allowed to occupy the governor's chair until his term ended in 1877. Some Democrats, notably John McEnery and his partisans, objected, but after much pressure they too accepted the terms by a narrow margin. Finally, on April 14, the Wheeler-approved legislature met for a ten-day session. At its adjournment, many were optimistic about the future. At last the state seemed to have settled down enough so that attention could be turned to something besides politics. [29]

David's contact with the 1875 legislature was minimal. He refused

28 David Boyd to Edward Cunningham, November 29, 1874, David Boyd to J. D. Kenton, December 9, 1874, David Boyd to J. C. Moncure, undated, [1874–75], David Boyd to W. L. Sanford, December 24, 1874, all in David Boyd Letterbooks; David Boyd Diary, December 7, 1874. General Longstreet resigned from the Returning Board before it issued its final certification. Lonn, *Reconstruction in Louisiana*, 287–89; Bone, "Disputed Election of 1876," 420; Taylor, *Louisiana Reconstructed*, 303–304.

29 Bone, "Disputed Election of 1876," 421–24; Vincent, "Negro Legislators in Louisiana," 226–28; Lonn, *Reconstruction in Louisiana*, Chaps. 14–16. For a full discussion of the Wheeler compromise, see James Otten, "The Wheeler Adjustment in Louisiana: National Republicans Begin to Reappraise Their Reconstruction Policy," *Louisiana History*, XIII (Fall, 1972), 349–67.

to have anything to do with the Kellogg "Rump" as he called it. Instead, he stayed in Baton Rouge, too poor to do anything else, and wrote letters to all his friends about the withering away of the constitution. In one letter he interrupted himself long enough to marvel at a man "with nothing to feed his family for dinner . . . who sits and conjectures on constitutional questions and civil vs. military authority. . . . We cld laugh if it did not hurt so bad!" David did go to New Orleans when the adjusted legislature, organized under the Wheeler compromise, met on April 14, 1875, but he expected nothing from it. Of the ten-day session, almost half was spent "frittering away time on partisan measures." Despondent, David returned to Baton Rouge, his ailing family, and a practically deserted university. Five cadets were enrolled as of April 30, 1875, and by the end of the term there were only four.[30]

The Wheeler compromise did not last long. By mid-1875 a small but aggressive group of Democrats, always opposed to any accommodation with Kellogg, declared their intention to continue war on the governor. They appealed directly to the people, urging them to demand a statewide convention at which the Democratic party could be reorganized. The main body of Democrats opposed the convention, fearing that it would reopen the whole issue of the Wheeler compromise. But by the end of 1875, the "no-compromise" Democrats were in the ascendant, and the party scheduled a meeting at New Orleans on January 5, 1876. Besides reiterating their undying opposition to Kellogg, the delegates petitioned the president and Congress to "blot from our national history this shameful record of usurpation." They also selected delegates to the national Democratic convention.

Two days before the Democrats met in New Orleans, Louisiana's legislature assembled in regular session. Rumors that Governor Kellogg would be impeached flooded the Crescent City. But not until February 28 did the house act. The senate, dominated by Republicans, acquitted the governor at once, branding the charges against Kellogg as false, frivolous, and politically inspired. Tom Boyd agreed. In his diary for March 4, 1876, he likened the Democratic repudiation of the Wheeler compromise to an honest man attempting to win by breach of faith in a game with a professional pickpocket. By mid-March the leg-

30 David Boyd to Pendleton King, January 21, 1875, David Boyd to A. D. Bayles, January 25, 1875, David Boyd to William Van Pelt, January 20, 1875, in David Boyd Letterbooks; Tom Boyd Diary, April 21, 30, June 30, 1875.

islators moved to adjourn in order to devote themselves completely to a game with higher stakes: the presidential contest of 1876.[31]

In such a politically volatile atmosphere, David expected little attention from the legislature. Even his own correspondence dealt almost exclusively with state politics and the coming national election. He wrote General Sherman in January, 1876, describing the "deplorable" conditions in southeastern Louisiana. The violence and lawlessness, particularly against blacks, appalled him. As a southerner, David continued, he was "heartily ashamed." Wild young white men were "allowed to have their own way" because the older politicians wanted their votes. David himself had to call off some rash young men who wanted to throw out McWhorter, the superintendent of the deaf and dumb asylum. Much of the violence was the work of the "Regulators," a secret society originally organized to punish cotton thieves. But by 1876, like everything else, it was "mixed up" in politics, and in order to carry the parish for the Democrats in the next election, it was killing and intimidating as many blacks as possible. White Radical officeholders were little more secure. In late February, 1876, Tom Boyd wrote his sister that Baton Rouge had no sheriff, judge, or tax collector. All had been driven off following a mass meeting of Democrats after which a Committee of Thirty-two assumed control of the parish.[32]

Conditions had not improved much by the beginning of summer. David reported to a friend that a "reign of terror [exists] in this corner of La." The whites in East Baton Rouge Parish meant to carry it for the Democrats "by means foul if not fair." David thought it would be better for whites never to regain control if they had to resort to such methods, but he knew most people disagreed with him. To a Virginian he contrasted the morals of Louisiana with those of his home state. "In politics," he remarked, "John Slidell debauched the Democratic party be-

31   Lonn, *Reconstruction in Louisiana*, 380 *passim*; Bone, "Disputed Election of 1876," 424. 433–34; John Edmond Gonzales, "William Pitt Kellogg: Reconstruction Governor of Louisiana, 1873–77," *Louisiana Historical Quarterly*, XXIX (April, 1946), 452–55; Vincent, "Negro Legislators in Louisiana," 250; Tom Boyd Diary, March 4, 1876. Otten maintains that despite repudiation of the Wheeler adjustment by Louisiana Democrats, it was successful in the short run because it provided a brief political calm within the state, the business climate improved in New Orleans, and most important, national Republicans, split between Liberals and regulars since 1872, managed to recapture sufficient unity to present a united front in time for the election of 1876. Otten, "Wheeler Adjustment in Louisiana," 365–67.

32   David Boyd to W. T. Sherman, January 15, 1876, David Boyd to Swarbrick's and Company, January 24, 1876, David Boyd to William Van Pelt, March 21, 1876, in David Boyd Letterbooks; Tom Boyd to Mrs. W. H. Spiller (sister), February 27, 1876, in Thomas D. Boyd Letterbooks.

fore the war. . . . [W]ith his N.Y. Tammany ideas, [John Slidell] was a worse man *then* than H. C. Warmoth is today!" Then David deplored outrages against blacks, which would mean a prison sentence in Virginia, but which went unpunished and uncondemned in Louisiana. In fact, to protest against them was to almost risk one's life. "What think you," he asked Charles M. Venable, "of one negro called out of his cabin at night by masked men, *lassoed, dragged along the road till dead*, and *hung* to a tree? Another shot, but *not* killed, and then *coal oil poured over him*, and *burnt to death*! And for *what*? Nobody seems to know. *Such things have been done in this parish recently.*"[33]

David seems to have had mixed emotions about the presidential candidates in 1876. In June he predicted that Democrats would carry Louisiana "*sure*," but that Hayes would be elected. He thought Hayes was a "*good* man," but he intended to vote against him. It was too bad he was not the Democratic nominee. Two weeks later, to another friend, he remarked that "any Demo." would be better than Hayes. By July he was praising Hayes again. Hayes and Wheeler, he thought, were better men than "Tammany" Tilden and his running mate. A few months later David changed his mind again. Now he disdained the Republican nominee as "Mr. R(eturning) B(oard) Hayes."[34]

Louisiana Democrats met in convention at Baton Rouge in July, 1876. They nominated Francis T. Nicholls for governor, Louis A. Wiltz for lieutenant governor, and Robert M. Lusher for superintendent of public education. Earlier, Republicans assembled in New Orleans chose S. B. Packard for governor and C. C. Antoine, a black, as his running mate. David liked Packard personally. He had been very kind and considerate two years before when a former professor named Featherman sued the school to recover his back wages. But David thought Packard would not get a single vote "outside the Radical camp." Nicholls, a West Pointer and Confederate general, was an old acquaintance of Samuel Lockett. In August, 1876, David wrote Lockett, who

33 David Boyd to William Van Pelt, June 18, 1876, David Boyd to Pendleton King, June 27, 1876, David Boyd to Charles Venable, August 8, 1876, all in David Boyd Letterbooks; Vincent, "Negro Legislators in Louisiana," 251, 260; William I Hair, *Bourbonism and Agrarian Protest: Louisiana Politics 1877–1900* (Baton Rouge, 1969), 4–5. Hair claims that preelection activity in most of Louisiana in 1876 was relatively nonviolent except for a few parishes like Ouachita, Morehouse, East Baton Rouge, and East and West Feliciana, "where naked force remained the rule."

34 David Boyd to William Van Pelt, June 18, July 15, 1876, David Boyd to Pendleton King, June 27, 1876, David Boyd to William Sherman, July 1, 1876, David Boyd to Lewis Texada, December 27, 1876, all in David Boyd Letterbooks.

was still in Egypt, to tell him of Nicholls' nomination. Repeating a witticism then current, David declared, "With his one arm & one leg—all that is *left of him* being *right*—we hope he can successfully *stump* the state."[35]

Three days before the election, David predicted to General Sherman that Nicholls would carry Louisiana by 20,000 votes. He also thought the Returning Board would count him out. David said he would be very surprised if Louisiana, South Carolina, Florida, Alabama, or Mississippi were counted for the Democrats, but he thought all would cast Democratic majorities. "And if the Presidential election *shd* turn on the vote of any one of those states; *then what?* You can best say if there is wisdom and forbearance enough among the non-political masses of the north to prevent serious trouble and disorder."[36]

David's worst fears were realized. The election did indeed "turn" on the vote of three southern states, Florida, South Carolina, and Louisiana, each of which forwarded two sets of electoral ballots to the president of the Senate. In 1877 the Senate was Republican, and Democrats controlled the House. No mechanism existed to establish the validity of electoral returns, and the Constitution simply directed the presiding officer in the Senate to open the "certificates" in the presence of both houses. It said nothing about how they should be counted or by whom. Clearly a serious crisis loomed. But late in January, 1877, to avoid at Washington what had occurred in Louisiana since 1872 (the establishment of two governments, each claiming to be the "lawful body"), Congress created a special commission with power to evaluate the disputed returns. Composed of five members from the House, five from the Senate, and five from the Supreme Court, the commission was expected to include seven Democrats, seven Republicans, and one independent. But at the last minute the independent member, a judge, accepted appointment to the Senate and refused to serve. His judicial replacement was a Republican, and the eight-to-seven margin on the commission ultimately settled every disputed electoral ballot in favor of Hayes.

35 He forgot to mention that Nicholls had also lost his left eye. Tom Boyd Diary, July 27, 1876; David Boyd to Swarbrick's, July 12, 1876, David Boyd to S. H. Lockett, August 7, 1876, in David Boyd Letterbooks; Vincent, "Negro Legislators in Louisiana," 260–61; T. B. Tunnell, Jr., "The Negro, the Republican Party and the Election of 1876 in Louisiana," *Louisiana History*, VII (Spring, 1966), 106. Tunnell describes Packard as "without a doubt the worst candidate" the Republicans could have named.
36 David Boyd to W. T. Sherman, November 4, 1876, in David Boyd Letterbooks.

Congress accepted the commission's findings only two days before Hayes was inaugurated. On March 4, 1877, he was installed without incident, thanks to a complex deal between southern Democrats and national Republicans which managed to undercut a filibuster mounted by angry supporters of Samuel Tilden. Worked out in several behind-the-scenes meetings, the agreement promised the southerners control over federal patronage within their states; federal funds for internal improvements and construction of a southern transcontinental rail-road; and, most important, withdrawal of federal military support from the two remaining carpetbag regimes in South Carolina and Louisiana.

Although much of the Compromise of 1877 was not carried out, President Hayes did honor his commitment to recall Federal troops. In Louisiana, the hated Packard regime immediately collapsed, and Washington soon recognized Francis T. Nicholls as the state's lawful governor. Apparently, not only the "non-political" masses of the North, but their leaders, too, had enough "wisdom and forbearance" to avoid the "serious political disorder" that David had predicted.[37]

Of the several struggles David waged during the hostile Kellogg administration, the most significant was his long battle to acquire the agricultural fund for the university. Starting in 1866, every report David submitted to the legislature pleaded that the federal fund be granted to the university. The best educational theory demanded a "concentration of resources" at the college level, he argued. To create a separate agricultural and mechanical college would be a waste of money and could only produce two "weak and puny" institutions.

The agricultural fund rested on the Morrill Act of 1862, a measure which awarded to each state thirty thousand acres of public land (or its equivalent in land scrip) for each representative a state sent to Congress. The land or land scrip was to be sold and the proceeds invested in "safe" securities yielding at least 5 percent a year. Capital could not be touched, but the interest represented an annuity to be used for the

---

37   C. Vann Woodward, *Reunion and Reaction: The Compromise of 1877 and the End of Recon-struction* (New York, 1956), is still the best treatment of the Hayes-Tilden election and the events that made compromise possible. For detailed studies of Louisiana's part in the dispute, see Bone, "Disputed Election of 1876," 106–15, 234–58; Walter M. Lowrey, "The Political Career of James Madison Wells," *Louisiana Historical Quarterly*, XXXI (October, 1948), 1100–1108; Tunnell, "Negro, Republican Party and Election of 1876," 101–16; Garnie Mc-Ginty, *Louisiana Redeemed: The Overthrow of Carpetbag Rule, 1876–1880* (New Orleans, 1941). Lonn and Taylor also devote several pages to the settlement in their studies of Louisiana Reconstruction.

support and maintenance of one or more colleges wherein "The leading object shall be, without excluding other scientific and classical
studies and including military tactics, to teach such branches of learning as are related to agriculture and mechanical arts . . . in order to
promote the liberal and practical education of the industrial classes."
None of the annuity could be used to buy, build, or repair buildings,
and states had to begin educational operations no later than 1874.[38]

David's opponents insisted that it would violate congressional intent to award the fund to the university because "classical" or traditional courses dominated the curriculum. They pointed to that part of
the Morrill Act that declared its object to be the promotion of "practical
education" for the "industrial classes." But citing phrases in the same
section of the act, David replied that the measure aimed at promoting
the "liberal" education of the industrial classes, too. Furthermore,
while the law stated specifically that the leading object was to teach
such branches of learning as are related to agriculture and the mechanic arts, it was to be done without "excluding other scientific and
classical studies . . . including military tactics."[39]

In 1868 or 1869 David found a pamphlet which expressed perfectly
his ideas about what Congress had intended. Published by the Society
for the Encouragement of Arts, Manufactures, and Commerce in London, the report advocated the restructuring of existing schools and the
creation of new ones because those available were too few in number
and too restricted in course offerings. It argued that "science" should
form the backbone of the restructured schools, just as the classics
then dominated the curricula at Harrow and Rugby. Science should
be taught as a means of developing "mental discipline" and "culture";
and "science" as used in the report meant mathematics, mechanics,
chemistry, and physics. In no sense did it mean the exclusion of languages, ancient or modern, from the curriculum. What the study *did*
propose was the elevation in status of the "new studies" to the level of
the old. Care had to be taken that the new schools were as well en-
dowed as the old in buildings, staff, and financial resources. Otherwise, a "social stigma" would handicap their graduates. And finally, in
no sense should the new institutions be thought of as "trade schools."
Instead, they must provide a general education "broadly liberal" and

38 Fleming, *Louisiana State University*, 279–80.
39 *Ibid.*

theoretical in approach. Practical application could be provided for in postgraduate education.[40]

Two or three years later David acquired another valuable report which he used effectively in his battles to secure the agricultural fund. Prepared by the trustees of the University of Georgia, who like David wanted the Morrill fund awarded to the state university, the pamphlet maintained that (1) it would be more expensive to create a separate institution because of the necessary duplication of buildings, libraries, apparatus, and staff; (2) most states had awarded the agricultural fund to existing institutions; in one instance a state first created a separate institution and later consolidated it with the existing institution in the interest of efficiency; (3) graduates of strictly agricultural and mechanical colleges were considered by others to have had "inferior" training; (4) an institution that prepares students for all "walks of life" was broadening; and (5) at a university a student might transfer freely from one program to another with little or no interruption in his academic career. The Georgia pamphlet concluded with a quotation from President A. D. White of Cornell University which expressed David's views perfectly: "It is an error to suppose that agricultural education is the only kind of education that this fund is designed to provide. . . . It is designed for the 'liberal and practical education of the industrial classes'; and in order to do this, the College is required to 'teach such branches as are related to agriculture and the mechanical arts, without excluding therefrom other scientific studies.'"[41]

Even when established independently, agricultural and mechanical colleges were not immune to criticism from the more "practical" members of the public. In July, 1873, David's friend, Dr. E. W. Hilgard, addressed a letter to the editor of the *American Farmers' Advocate*. Hilgard, a professor of "agricultural chemistry," disputed those extremely "practical" persons who thought it was foolish to educate farmers. There would hardly be so much "worn out" land if farmers knew anything about soil chemistry. Denying that Congress intended to establish "simply labor schools or handicraft schools" when it passed the Morrill Act, he insisted that if such schools had been created, they

---

40   *Technical Education Report* of the Society for the Encouragement of Arts, Manufactures and Commerce, London, 1868, in Printed Materials, David Boyd Papers.
41   Board of Trustees, *Present Organization and Proposed Plan of Expansion of the University of Georgia*, 1872, *ibid.*

would have been shunned by the very people for whom they were provided. Finally, Hilgard attacked the "practical" men in state legislatures who thought "experimental farms" had to be self-supporting to justify their existence.[42]

Besides arguments about congressional intentions, plenty of controversy arose over Louisiana's agricultural fund as a result of rural-urban hostility, class antagonisms between the rich and the poor, and political partisanship. Under the circumstances, it is not surprising that the state waited until almost the last moment to qualify for Morrill grant funds. In April, 1874, the Louisiana Agricultural and Mechanical College was created by legislative act. A twelve-man Board of Control was empowered to secure a permanent site, somewhere "in the parishes," and fifty thousand dollars, appropriated over a five-year period, was to be set aside for construction of a college building. Meanwhile, the school would be housed in New Orleans in buildings belonging to the University of Louisiana. Finally, the act outlawed discrimination in every phase of the "admission, management or discipline of the institution."[43]

Louisiana's Agricultural and Mechanical College began operations in the summer of 1874. On July 14, President Thomas Nicholson informed his board that the academic community included 120 students and 4 professors. He urged the members to prepare thoroughly for the fall session in order not to lose "public sympathy" or legislative patronage. He also pointed out that the state owned 200 acres of land near New Orleans and the city owned an additional 200 nearby. Together, the property would make an excellent permanent home for the college. In conclusion, Nicholson noted that his report had been set up in type by the students as part of their "practical education."[44]

While the agricultural college was conducting its summer session in 1874, David was busily gathering data to be used against it in the next legislature. He wrote to his friend Dr. Hilgard, then at the University of Michigan in Ann Arbor, for documentation to prove that the establishment of a separate agricultural college in that state had been "a mistake." Next, he contacted A. D. White of Cornell for persuasive ar-

42 E. W. Hilgard, letter to the editor, *American Farmers' Advocate*, July [?], 1873, in Scrapbook, *ibid.*
43 Fleming, *Louisiana State University*, 278–84.
44 *Report* of the President of the Board of Control, Louisiana Agricultural and Mechanical College, July 14, 1874, in Printed Materials, David Boyd Papers.

guments to demonstrate the superiority of colleges like Cornell, "broad and liberal" in scope, over narrow institutions, restricted to little else besides "practical Agriculture and Mechanics." In addition to the testimony of experts, David thought he could count on support for his position from both whites and blacks in the country parishes. "We fear only your able *city* delegates," he confied to a New Orleans friend.[45]

In October, 1874, David thought the Louisiana Agricultural College had not resumed operations, but in November he was disabused. Instead, its Board of Control was moving swiftly to acquire a permanent campus. One of the sites under consideration belonged to Mrs. John Lynch, wife of "Honest John" Lynch of Returning Board fame in 1872. Lynch happened to be in charge of the public land sale which provided the principal for the agricultural college fund and he also served on the Agricultural College Board of Control. Not surprisingly, when Mrs. Lynch's plantation, acquired only a year before, was offered as a site for the college, David became suspicious. "Shall a *partisan* Board, composed mostly of notoriously corrupt people, thus trifle and insult the intelligence and worth of the state?" he demanded. All the appointed members of the board but three were either Negroes or Governor Kellogg's "henchmen in N.O." David wanted his friend J. D. Kenton and Mayor L. A. Wiltz of New Orleans to "wake up the public." He was sure the whole thing was a fraud, done in haste before a Democratic legislature (elected in November, 1874) could be seated.[46]

While David tried to marshal the opposition, the agricultural college board was not idle. By the end of 1874 it had paid the first installment on property at Chalmette in St. Bernard Parish. It also announced plans for an experimental farm and workshop where "practical agriculture" and typesetting could be practiced by students. Sixty students attended classes conducted by three professors and two "tutors," and the board estimated assets in excess of $400,000. For David, the only consolation lay in his hope that a "decent" legislature would be seated in 1875. If that happened, he believed, the entire agricultural college

45 David Boyd to Andrew Ten Broeck, August 14, 1874, David Boyd to E. W. Hilgard, October 24, 1874, David Boyd to A. D. White, [October], 1874, David Boyd to J. D. Kenton, November 8, 1874, all in David Boyd Letterbooks.
46 David Boyd to E. W. Hilgard, October 24, 1874, David Boyd to J. D. Kenton, November 20, 1874, *ibid.*

question would be reconsidered, and in the end the lawmakers would grant the fund to the university.[47]

All of David's well-laid plans came to nothing in 1875. There were two legislatures that year, the Kellogg "Rump," before which he refused to appear, and the Wheeler compromise body, which met for only a brief ten days. Both were too busy to concern themselves with minor questions like the fate of higher education in Louisiana. But conditions changed in 1876. Democrats were firmly in control of the lower house by then, and David had found a staunch supporter of the university in the Republican senate. J. Henri Burch, the black Radical from Baton Rouge, offered to present a bill written by David to merge the university and the agricultural college in the upper chamber, and another Republican, Judge A. B. Lavisse, agreed to introduce it in the house. One other factor contributed to its final success: the Grangers. In 1876 they claimed to control several legislative votes, and rather belligerently, they demanded a large role in determining the nature and permanent location of the existing agricultural college. To Judge Lavisse, David confided that Daniel Dennett, a leader in the state Grange, seemed to want that organization to control the college completely. If the merger bill passed, David was willing to let the Grange, and perhaps the Mechanical Association of New Orleans, have representation on the board. But he was against letting any group exercise exclusive control over an educational institution. That would make it "too narrow." Another leading Granger, Dr. Robert Ryland of West Feliciana, agreed with David that the agricultural and mechanical college should be moved out of New Orleans and located in the "country parishes," but he did not share his opinion about what it should teach. Ryland wanted the college to be "purely agricultural, conducted on a practical, not theoretical or 'scientific' basis." David thought that both opponents could be overcome. If the Grangers tried to take over the college, so much the better for his merger bill. It would cause the Radicals and many conservatives in the legislature to act together because, as David put it, "A Radical hates a *Granger* as he does the *devil*.!"[48]

47   J. L. Cross, *Report* of the President of the Louisiana State Agricultural and Mechanical College for 1874, in Thomas D. Boyd Papers, Department of Archives, Louisiana State University; David Boyd to W. M. Burwell, November 29, 1874, David Boyd to J. D. Kenton, November 20, December 12, 1874, David Boyd to G. Mason Graham, November 21, 1874, in David Boyd Letterbooks.

48   David Boyd to J. W. Dupree, January 26, February 17, 1876, David Boyd to A. B. Lavisse, February 13, 1876, in David Boyd Letterbooks.

Additional opposition to the merger of the university and the college came from New Orleans and, naturally enough, from the agricultural college itself. In its report for 1875, the Board of Control maintained that a "mere glance" at the Morrill Act proved the "absurdity" of the proposition to merge the two schools. It might be "practicable," if undesirable, to merge them but to absorb the agricultural college in the state university was out of the question. That might forfeit the national grant, "which probably is regarded by the advocates of amalgamation as the most attractive feature in the Agricultural College."[49]

New Orleans opposition to the merger bill came principally from two sources: Radical politicians and conservative newspapers. Most of it developed after David's bill passed the legislature in March, 1876. The Radicals opposed granting anything to Baton Rouge while that parish remained in defiance of the Kellogg administration and continued to terrorize its black population. They did their best to keep the governor from signing the bill for the next several months. Newspaper opposition grew out of an unwillingness to lose the college to another city. For several weeks after the merger bill passed, the city papers printed lengthy arguments against its approval by the governor. Among the principal charges made were that (1) the university was "defunct"; (2) its property and that of the agricultural college would be attached to liquidate the debt of the former; (3) the merger bill was a violation of the Morrill Act which allowed only agricultural and mechanical courses to be taught; and (4) the state university was governed by a "ring" anxious to keep itself in power. Each charge was taken up and categorically denied by "JWD" in a letter to the editor of the New Orleans *Times*. "JWD" were the initials of Dr. J. W. Dupree, but the letter that appeared over them was David's, just as everything else in defense of the merger bill, as well as the bill itself, was written by him. He complained bitterly because the very papers that attacked him and the merger bill charged him to print the letters to the editor which he wrote in rebuttal. Not only that, they usually appeared "in small type on the *last* page along with the Plow Pictures!"[50]

49 *Annual Report* of the Board of Control of the Louisiana State Agricultural and Mechanical College, 1875, in Printed Materials, David Boyd Papers.

50 "One Who Has Read the Bill," letter to the editor, New Orleans *Times*, February 23, 1876; "J.W.D.," letter to the editor, New Orleans *Times*, March 2, 1876; Editorial, "Merger of LSU and A & M," New Orleans *Times*, April 3, 1876; David Boyd to Swarbrick's & Co., April 4, 9, 1876, David Boyd to W. C. Annis, undated [1875–76], in David Boyd Letterbooks; Fleming, *Louisiana State University*, 292–95.

One attack leveled by the New Orleans *Times* against the merger bill seems to have disturbed David especially. The paper reported on April 3, 1876, that Senator J. Henri Burch, the Negro Republican from Baton Rouge, "originated" the merger bill in the upper chamber. David realized that Burch's name attached to any measure, however worthwhile, might well destroy it. When a Baton Rouge paper copied the *Times* article, David appealed to the editor. He reminded him that the merged college could mean a great deal to the town. "The college *will* come . . . if the papers don't succeed in rendering it odious to our own (Democratic) people," he explained. Pleading with the editor "not to scuttle . . . [the bill] just because of prejudice against Burch," David pointed out that a little praise now for the senator's part in getting the bill passed might win the Democrats some black votes in November.[51]

Certainly David wanted Burch to have full credit for his part in passing the measure. As he wrote candidly to Dr. Dupree:

After Stafford [his nephew and a member of the house], I rely on Burch, who seems determined to . . . [secure the governor's signature]. And to his force in the Senate we are indebted . . . for the passage of the bill. There was some trouble . . . in the House . . . but that was as nothing to the opposition we wd have had in the Senate, if Burch had even been *neutral*! Without his active advocacy, the bill could never have been passed. Also, we may be indebted to his efforts in having the Gov.'s signature. I think the people of B.R. should do Burch credit on *that* score, whatever his faults *otherwise*.[52]

To Burch himself David wrote essentially the same thing in December, 1876. "On the record of this University," he promised, "your act shall stand written." But if it ever was, it has since been expunged. That William T. Sherman was the university's (seminary's) first superintendent is still unknown to many persons not familiar with the institution's history. That David Boyd spent a lifetime in its service is slightly better known; he has been recognized to the extent that a campus building bears his name. But that a black Radical Republican played a vital part in bringing the agricultural and mechanical college to Baton Rouge, thereby aiding the university in its fight for survival, is one of Louisiana's better kept secrets.[53]

51   David Boyd to W. C. Annis, undated [1875–76], in David Boyd Letterbooks.
52   David Boyd to J. W. Dupree, March 10, 1876, *ibid*.
53   David Boyd to J. Henri Burch, December 27, 1876, *ibid*.

Chapter VIII

Winning a Battle

AS DAVID expected, Governor Kellogg continued to withhold his signature from the bill to merge the Louisiana State University with the Louisiana Agricultural and Mechanical College. "But the uniting of the two schools is only a matter of time," David assured William Sanford in April, 1876. "In all probability, the 1st Monday in Jany. next [1877] will see either a good Democrat or H. C. Warmoth, Gov. of La. *Either will sign the bill.*"[1] Only part of that prediction came to pass. By the "1st Monday in Jany. next," Louisiana again had two governors, one of whom was a "good Democrat," Francis T. Nicholls. But the other was S. B. Packard, a Customhouse Republican and a longstanding political foe of Henry Clay Warmoth. In the confusion, David's merger bill received the signature of neither. However, it was not dead. Article 66 of the Constitution of 1868 provided that acts passed by a legislature automatically became law on the first day of the succeeding legislative session if not signed or vetoed by the governor before then. From J. Henri Burch, David knew that the outgoing Kellogg had not vetoed the bill; it had become law. Nevertheless, he was concerned. Like many other laws passed by the preceding legislature, the merger act lay unpromulgated in the office of Kellogg's acting attorney general,

---

1 David Boyd to William Van Pelt, March 12, 1876, David Boyd to W. L. Sanford, April 6, 1876, in David Boyd Letterbooks.

Judge Dibble. What if it were lost, stolen, or destroyed in the struggle then going on between Nicholls and Packard?[2]

When the Packard government finally promulgated the merger act late in January, 1877, David hastened to thank Senator Burch for the "noble work" he had done in the interest of the new school. He also suggested that further steps to organize it and to appoint a Board of Supervisors for it be postponed until conditions became more stable. Then he offered to help the black senator. Burch had been forced out of Baton Rouge by "Regulators" more than a year before, and only at the risk of his life could he visit the district he represented. Tom Boyd, who did not trust Burch, regarded all of his efforts to secure the merger act as insincere, designed only to conciliate white opinion in Baton Rouge. But David was more charitable. "If you shd, possibly, have reason to fear any *personal* harm," he wrote the Radical lawmaker, "please let me know, and I shall try to protect you."[3]

Promulgation by the Packard legislature by no means ended opposition to the act of merger. If anything, it gave the strongest opponents of the law, the Grangers and the administration of the agricultural college, another chance to challenge it. When the Packard regime collapsed in April, 1877, they could claim that nothing it did had any validity. But they did not wait for Governor Nicholls to be formally recognized before launching their attacks. On January 30, 1877, a resolution in the Nicholls senate called for an investigation of the state university at Baton Rouge. David was not sure of its intent. Was it designed to help the creditors, attack his administration, or block the merger with the agricultural college? In any case, how could he legitimately defend an institution of which he no longer was a part? The university and his job ceased to exist when the merger law was promulgated. Besides, he questioned the propriety of appearing before a body which itself was not then formally recognized. What if the Packard legislature were finally sustained?[4]

Eventually David overcame his misgivings. After repeated urgings,

2   David Boyd to Swarbrick's, January 3, 1877, David Boyd to J. W. Dupree, January 13, 1877, *ibid.*; Reprint of Louisiana *Senate Journal*, January 30, 1877, in Printed Materials, David Boyd Papers.
3   Tom Boyd Diary, December 31, 1876; New Orleans *Republican*, January 31, 1877, in David Boyd Papers; David Boyd to J. Henri Burch, January 26, 1877, in David Boyd Letterbooks.
4   Reprint of *Senate Journal*, January 30, 1877, in Printed Materials, David Boyd Papers; David Boyd to J. W. Dupree, February 1, 2, 1877, in David Boyd Letterbooks.

he went to New Orleans about February 12, 1877, to testify before the appropriate committees of the Nicholls legislature. Six weeks later, when he left the city, there was no question about the legality of the Nicholls government, but the future of the merger act was still in doubt. Early in February a petition against the union of the university and agricultural college as well as a bill to repeal the merger act had been introduced in the Nicholls body. Nothing came of either, but even final adjournment did not end the opposition of the "Old Agric. & Mech. College party." Not until May 19, 1877, did the secretary of state (one of David's former students) announce promulgation of "An Act to unite the Louisiana State University . . . and the Agricultural and Mechanical College . . . into one and the same institution."[5]

Long before the act of merger received official sanction, David began thinking about men who might be appointed to the new university's board. In January, 1877, he urged Dr. Dupree, then a member of the Nicholls legislature from Baton Rouge, to work for the appointment of Dr. Robert H. Ryland, master of the state Grange and a member of the agricultural college Board of Control. If Governor Nicholls made Ryland a supervisor, David reasoned, the Grangers might cease their objections to the new school and "do it much good." Later, David boasted that he had in fact compiled the entire list from which the governor made his selections. If so, he had been very generous to New Orleans and the "old Agricultural College Party." Besides Ryland, the appointees included the secretary of the state Grange and the president of the New Orleans Mechanics Association. Furthermore, David indicated to a friend, more concessions would probably be made when the new board selected a faculty. Some of the "old profs. of both schools" would probably be named, but for himself David wanted and expected nothing. "I may have to stay here [Baton Rouge] till July, to close the session," he commented, "but I am going away sure. I shall never hold office in the new school."[6]

Before the Board of Supervisors of the new university could assem-

5 David Boyd to E. W. Hilgard, May 1, 1877, David Boyd to J. W. Dupree, February 2, 1877, D. M. Brosnan to D. F. Boyd, February 6, 1877, D. F. Boyd, Memorandum, undated [1876–77], all in David Boyd Letterbooks; Majority and Minority Reports, Committee on Charitable and Public Institutions, March 8, 1877, Louisiana *House Journal*, Extra session, 1877, pp. 23–24; New Orleans *Democrat*, June 1, 1877, in Printed Materials, David Boyd Papers.

6 David Boyd to J. W. Dupree, January 13, 14, 27, 1877, David Boyd to W. A. Seay, January [?], 1877, David Boyd to William Van Pelt, May 1, 1877, David Boyd to E. W. Hilgard, May 1, 1877, all in David Boyd Letterbooks.

ble, the agricultural college board, or a part of it, convened in the office of Robert M. Lusher, state superintendent of public education, to plan a strategy of legal delay and obstruction. Lusher was in the peculiar circumstance of being a member, by law, of both the agricultural college board and that of the new university. So was Governor Nicholls, but he stayed away from the meeting. Counting Lusher, whom the others chose to preside, a mere quorum was present. President J. L. Cross of the agricultural college opened the discussion by challenging the legality of the merger act. He wanted the group to seek an injunction against the new school's board until the statute could be tested in the courts. Essentially, what Cross disputed was the accuracy of the language in section one of the merger law which described, by location, the two schools to be united. In fact, he maintained, there was no "state University in Alexandria, in the parish of Rapides; nor does there exist an Agricultural and Mechanical College in the Parish of St. Bernard." The state university was in Baton Rouge and the agricultural college was still operating in New Orleans. Although it owned land in St. Bernard, for "want of funds" it had not moved to the new location. As Cross saw it, "all other sections of the . . . law depend upon the 1st section, and if that is defective, the whole law must be."[7]

Although Lusher wanted the agricultural college board to ask the attorney general for an opinion before applying for an injunction, the others apparently sided with Cross. But David could not have been surprised. Fifteen months before, when the merger act was first passed by the Kellogg legislature, he had anticipated delaying tactics, specifically an injunction, by the "Old Agric. College Set." What he did not expect was the passivity with which the new university board responded. When the members assembled for the first time in Baton Rouge on July 2, 1877, they did little beyond naming a committee to confer with the agricultural college board about the transfer of its property. David was offered the presidency of the new school, but he declined the "high and honorable" position for "purely personal" reasons, and with that the members adjourned to meet again in New Orleans on July 31.

David was despondent. If the board did not move to quash the injunction, he wrote his brother, litigation might result which would

7 J. L. Cross, *Report* to the Board of Control of the Louisiana State Agricultural and Mechanical College, June 5, 1877, reprinted in New Orleans *Democrat*, June 6, 1877, in David Boyd Papers.

drag on until November, 1877, or even January, 1878. Meanwhile, the new school, scheduled to open on October 5, would have no funds with which to operate other than the fees paid by the few boarding students, because the merger act made tuition free to all. But worse than the shortage of money was the danger of losing too much time. If the agricultural college failed to win its point in the district court, it would probably appeal to the supreme court. By that time, the legislature would be in session, and the university's enemies might try again to get the merger law repealed.[8]

Unable to sit in Baton Rouge doing nothing until the next board meeting took place, David went to New Orleans on July 8, 1877, to spur Governor Nicholls and the other board members into action. Nicholls was "too slow," David fumed, and no one on the board seemed willing to act against the injunction unless specifically empowered by the governor or the attorney general. Days passed and nothing changed. The injunction still went unchallenged, and Governor Nicholls still refused to convene the board before July 31. Frustrated, David grumbled to a friendly member: "If I were officially connected with the school, I might say more, do more. But as it is, I must be careful how I even suggest, lest I be told politely to 'mind my own business.'"[9]

What bothered David more than anything was the fear that the cautious university board would refuse to open the school at all if its funds were still encumbered in October. There was no reason for such timidity, he insisted. It would be easy to find five or six young professors willing to work without pay until the legal "mess" was settled. Then, if the university lost the case, the board would owe the professors nothing. But in his opinion, the school would win easily in the courts. Apparently the board did not agree. When it did meet on July 31, it spent two days in desultory discussion and adjourned without positive action. Only if the injunction were settled before October would the members reconvene to "organize" the university. Meanwhile, matters drifted, and David's alarm increased.[10]

8 *Ibid.*; David Boyd to William Van Pelt, March 12, 1876, in David Boyd Letterbooks; Minutes of the Board of Supervisors, July 2, 3, 1877; Tom Boyd to L. Bourgeois, July 14, 1877, Tom Boyd to J. L. DesLattes, July [?], 1877, in Thomas D. Boyd Letterbooks.
9 Tom Boyd to L. Bourgeois, July 14, 1877, in Thomas D. Boyd Letterbooks; David Boyd to Tom Boyd, July 21, 1877, in Thomas D. Boyd Papers; David Boyd to A. A. Gunby, July 23, 1877, in David Boyd Letterbooks.
10 David Boyd to A. A. Gunby, July 23, 1877, in David Boyd Letterbooks; David Boyd to Tom Boyd, July 31, August 1, 1877, in Thomas D. Boyd Papers.

During August, 1877, David tried several new approaches to ensure an October opening. Careful research convinced him, he told the governor, that none of the agricultural college board members bringing the injunction had a legal claim to his post. Either their appointments had expired, or they had never been confirmed by the senate as required by law. When that argument left Nicholls unmoved, David approached Dr. Williams, the board's vice-president. Insisting that the governor would not interfere, especially if Dr. Dupree instigated the Baton Rouge citizenry to "clamor" for action, David begged Williams to call a board meeting on his own authority. But Dr. Williams did not succumb either, even when David hinted that failure to open the school on time might result in its return to Rapides Parish. The vice-president was against opening the school in October under any circumstances if funds were not "in hand." On that point he felt more strongly than Governor Nicholls, who finally did agree to call a board meeting before October, if David could provide him with a list of two to four professors and a prospective president, all of whom would pledge themselves to work without pay. They must also promise to make no future claims against the state in case the injunction was not quashed. David was sure that he could secure the professors easily enough, but he was less certain about finding a president of any ability who would agree to such terms. Nevertheless, he began searching at once.[11]

By the end of August, David was more disillusioned than ever. The governor rarely visited his office, he discovered; that was the last place anyone would try to find him. But David vowed to "badger" him until he called a meeting of the board. "Our school must open Oct. 5; or I'll annoy [the] Govr., and Board of Sprs. to death," he wrote his brother in disgust. The tactic worked. Nicholls finally scheduled a board meeting for September 18, 1877, the day after a hearing on the injunction was to be held. Elated, David felt at last that the school would open as advertised as long as his own partisans on the board "stood firm" and were not swayed by Dr. Ryland's "nonsense" or some "mistaken idea of courtesy to the Gov."[12]

---

11 David Boyd, "Status of Members of Board of Control, *La. State Agric.* & Mech. College," undated [1877–78], in David Boyd Letterbooks; David Boyd to Tom Boyd, August 4, 7, 8, 13, 1877, in Thomas D. Boyd Papers; Tom Boyd to David Boyd, August 10, 16, 1877, in Thomas D. Boyd Letterbooks.
12 David Boyd to Tom Boyd, August 28, 30, September 3, 1877, in Thomas D. Boyd Papers.

When the supervisors assembled, however, David's supporters were greatly outnumbered. He was particularly hurt that the university's three alumni, provided for in the act of merger, failed to put in an appearance whereas the "Ryland" group attended en masse. Too late David realized his mistake in having Grangers named to the board after defeating them in the legislature. They repaid his generosity by voting against a resolution to open the university on October 5. After twelve years of struggle, David wrote one of the errant alumni, it would break his heart to see all his work go for nothing.[13]

Finally, David's tenacity succeeded. By the end of September the injunction against the university had been set aside, and its authors had decided not to appeal to a higher court. The governor hastened to convene the board in time for the scheduled opening, but two meetings held during the first week of October failed to produce a quorum. Undeterred, David proceeded to act on his own authority. He opened a "free school" at the university on October 5, 1877, and two weeks later enough supervisors assembled to elect a president and appoint a faculty. David's twelve-year-old dream was about to come true.[14]

Because he had vowed never to "hold a post" in the new university, David had to start looking for another job fairly soon after the merger act passed. As already described, he made serious efforts in the fall of 1876 to rent a boarding school in Virginia. But those plans were abandoned when the disputed election of 1876 and the resulting dual governments prevented promulgation of the merger law until May, 1877. Meanwhile, other possibilities developed. Friends in New Orleans tried to interest him in the city school superintendency, and two former colleagues in Maryland found a suitable boarding school property near Baltimore. Greenwood, one of the Virginia sites located by his former student Richard Hancock in 1876, was also still available. Finally, in June, 1877, he was invited to apply for the presidency of East Tennessee University at Knoxville.[15]

13 David Boyd to E. W. Sutherlin, September 19, 1877, David Boyd to T. L. Grimes, September 19, 1877, David Boyd to A. A. Gunby, September 19, 1877, in David Boyd Letterbooks; Minutes of the Board of Supervisors, September 19, 1877.
14 L. Bourgeois to Tom Boyd, October 17, 1877, David Boyd to Tom Boyd, October 7, 1877, in Thomas D. Boyd Papers; Minutes of the Board of Supervisors, October 1, 4, 17, 18, 1877.
15 David Boyd to Swarbrick's, January 14, 1877, in David Boyd Letterbooks; J. M. Garnett to David Boyd, June 4, 7, 1877, J. R. Page to David Boyd, June 5, 1877, R. J. Hancock to David Boyd, June 5, 17, 1877, R. M. Venable to David Boyd, June 25, 1877, Register of Correspondence, in David Boyd Letterbooks; T. J. Boyd to D. F. Boyd, June 20, 1877, in David Boyd Papers.

All considered, the position at Knoxville seemed like the best opportunity, but when the Tennessee Board of Trustees met in July, 1877, it failed to elect David by a margin of two votes. Later he learned that his name was the only one presented against the incumbent in what had been an effort by conservative board members to oust the university's entire staff. Because the faculty at East Tennessee was largely Republican and had been Unionist during the war, the board wanted to replace them with more "acceptable" men. David was outraged that politics was involved. He was even angrier when northern papers picked up the story and labeled it as one more example of a "concerted effort at the South" to displace Yankees and Unionists in favor of Confederates and rebels. The papers mentioned David by name as the president of the "*dying* La. State University." If he could not succeed there, they demanded, what good would he be in Tennessee?[16]

Following the East Tennessee fiasco, David authorized Richard Venable, a former colleague, to negotiate for him with the owners of the Maryland boarding school property. If all went well, he could leave Louisiana about August 15 and open the school, called St. Clement's by its former operators, on September 21, 1877. Clearly, his heart was not in the new venture. For one thing, when he wrote Venable he was still in New Orleans urging Governor Nicholls to act against the injunction; if the university's future were still uncertain in September, he would not leave the state. Furthermore, if Venable were unable to get favorable terms, the Maryland scheme might not materialize at all. Even if Venable succeeded, David wrote his brother gloomily, "It is so late now that I fear I shall have almost no boarders, and the chances are even that I shall fail in Md."[17]

David's pessimism must have increased when, only a few days after committing himself to rent St. Clement's for $1,000, he discovered that the school's charter required it to operate under a board of trustees. "I will not have any Board of Trustees, *even nominally*, over my little school," he informed the owner's agent, adding that he hoped such

---

16 David Boyd to J. P. McAuley, July 22, 1877, David Boyd to John Paulette, August 2, 7, 1877, David Boyd to John M. Fleming, August 11, 1877, in David Boyd Letterbooks; David Boyd to Editor, Springfield (Mass.) *Republican*, August 20, 1877, in David Boyd Papers. The Springfield *Republican* editorial to which David replied had been printed in the New York *Times*, August 3, 1877.

17 David Boyd to Tom Boyd, July 19, 20, 1877, in Thomas D. Boyd Papers.

"little points of difference" could be resolved. Tom Boyd was dubious. He urged his brother to abandon what looked at best like a "very risky enterprise." Unlike David, he saw no reason to honor an agreement made when one party was not in possession of "all the facts."[18]

But Tom's advice was ignored, and so was Richard Venable's, who pleaded with David to hire an assistant, "cultivate" the community and open St. Clement's to day students. "I expect to see and know but *little* of Elicott [*sic*] City [the school's location] and its people," David retorted. As for taking day students, "I would rather jump into Chesapeake Bay with a ton weight about my neck."[19] His attitude apparently exasperated Venable who accused him of seriously jeopardizing the school's chances for success. Characteristically, David fired off a brusque reply, following it a day later with a plea for understanding. "My whole soul is wrapped up in the salvation of the . . . [university]," he explained. "Never since the war has it stopped a moment; and for it now to stop (after our own people get in power) wd be an outrageous shame. . . . When you bear in mind what I have passed thro'—how much I have suffered in body, mind and soul, to save the school from destruction of the Radicals, I can't stand idly by and see it destroyed by the apathy of our own people."[20]

Finally, because he would not leave Louisiana himself, David sent Tom Boyd to Maryland to "open" his school. When as expected, no one tried to enroll, Tom arranged terms to pay the school's owners the year's rent. Then he went to visit relatives in Alexandria, Virginia, where through a New Orleans friend, he learned that the injunction had been quashed. From David he heard nothing until late in October, almost a month after the new university began operation. Excusing himself for his failure to keep his brother informed, David declared, "I have been, and am now, almost literally crazy. I am in money troubles till I can have no peace at all. Since you left, I have not had a dollar from the old school or the new . . . I am now in a worse fix than I have ever been in my life, and feel meaner this night than I ever did before.

18 David Boyd to Tom Boyd, July 21, 1877, *ibid.*; David Boyd to James MacKubin, July 28, 1877, in David Boyd Letterbooks; Tom Boyd to David Boyd, July 31, August 1, 8, 1877, in Thomas D. Boyd letterbooks.
19 Richard M. Venable to David Boyd, July 21, 24, 1877, in Alphabetical File, Fleming Collection; David Boyd to Thos. D. Boyd, August 21, 23, 1877, in David Boyd Letterbooks.
20 Richard M. Venable to David Boyd, August 24, 1877, in Alphabetical File, Fleming Collection; David Boyd to R. M. Venable, August 27, 28, 1877, in David Boyd Letterbooks.

. . . A little longer . . . and no matter what position I may hold, my own self-respect will be gone, and everybody else's respect for me too."[21]

David's despair was not surprising considering his mounting debts and his inability to provide adequately for his growing family. Nor had his failure to win the presidency of East Tennessee University done anything to restore his self-confidence. If anything, it seems to have reinforced the sense of inadequacy that had tormented him ever since the collapse of the Egyptian venture in 1875. Consequently, when the Board of Supervisors voted unanimously to make him president of the new university early in July, 1877, David's flagging spirits must have revived somewhat. But the offer presented him with another problem. Having insisted publicly and privately for months that he would "hold no post" in the merged school, he could hardly accept the position in spite of the pain it cost him to refuse.[22]

As the summer wore on, however, David seemed willing to reconsider. On August 8, 1877, he wrote his father that he did not know if he could leave for Maryland by September 1. The "pressure" on him to remain in Louisiana was very great, he explained, "but I must go, and wd only stay temporarily if I shd really find that my presence was needed." Even earlier he told a former colleague that some of his best friends were "almost abusing me for leaving La. at such a juncture." The problem was that no one was willing to accept the university presidency while the salary remained uncertain. For weeks David tried vainly to convince W. LeRoy Broun of Vanderbilt to accept the job, but Broun would not agree as long as the injunction remained alive. Besides, he considered David the "only man for the job." However, David hesitated to offer his services to Governor Nicholls for fear his motives would be "misunderstood." It would not look well, he explained to Professor Broun, for the architect of the new school to become its "beneficiary." Finally, because he thought it was the only way to get Governor Nicholls to convene the board and organize the school, David overcame his personal misgivings and offered to serve as "acting

21 Tom Boyd Diary, September 9, 1877; Tom Boyd to David Boyd, September 18, 21, 27, October 9, 23, 1877, in Alphabetical File, Fleming Collection; David Boyd to Tom Boyd, September 19, November 1, 1877, in David Boyd Letterbooks, David Boyd to Tom Boyd, October 25, 1877, in Thomas D. Boyd Papers.
22 David Boyd to Tom Boyd, November 1, 1877, in David Boyd Letterbooks; Minutes of the Board of Supervisors, July 3, 1877.

president" until the board could secure a permanent chief executive.[23]

Governor Nicholls did not accept David's offer when he made it the first time, but a month later he approached the governor through various members of the board. "Modesty" compelled him, he told Vice-President Williams, to get help in making the governor and some others on the board aware that he could be persuaded to take the university presidency. "For the good of the school and the state," he would set aside his own convictions if "responsible" men like Williams and others, in and out of the board, thought it his "duty" to serve the school. A sense of duty also compelled him to inform Dr. Ryland, his principal antagonist among the supervisors, of his "availability" for the post. "Very reasonably—since your ideas and mine wd seem to differ materially as to the proper manner of organizing and conducting our proposed new school, you wd . . . prefer another President," David commented to Ryland. He hoped the board might yet find someone else to whom it was willing to "entrust" the institution. "It wld only be with great disappointment and great violence to my personal feelings," he added, "that I cld find myself actually the President. . . . Such during the long struggle to unite the two schools, was never my intention." Ryland's reaction was not recorded, but when the board finally met on October 17, 1877, to organize the school, none of the Ryland "faction" appeared, and the others voted unanimously to name David president. Almost casually he announced the news to his wife. "Nothing of consequence was done, besides the election of a president," he informed Ettie. "I was unanimously elected again, and I have thought it best to accept the position. It is my duty to notify you of this as soon as possible. It means that we are all to stay in La.—in Baton Rouge maybe *forever!*"[24]

23 David Boyd to Thos. J. Boyd, August 8, 1877, David Boyd to J. M. Garnett, July 23, 1877, David Boyd to W. LeRoy Broun, July 23, August 25, September 5, 1877, in David Boyd Letterbooks; David Boyd to Tom Boyd, August 25, 27, 1877, in Thomas D. Boyd Papers; W. LeRoy Broun to David Boyd, July 27, 1877, in Alphabetical File, Fleming Collection.
24 David Boyd to Joseph Brent, September 20, 1877, David Boyd to J. M. Williams, September 21, 1877, David Boyd to R. H. Ryland, September 21, 1877, David Boyd to Ettie Boyd, October 17, 1877, all in David Boyd Letterbooks; Minutes of the Board of Supervisors, October 1, 4, 17, 1877. Only a handful of letters between David and his wife are included in the Boyd Papers. It may be that personal letters were removed from the collection before it was given to the Louisiana State University Department of Archives. But it is also possible that David simply did not write Ettie Boyd many letters. A letter to Tom dated July 21, 1877, remarks as an afterthought: "I hardly have time to write to Ettie. Indeed, it is not necessary. Tell her that I must go to Md. about August 15 . . . and that I fear she must stay behind." David Boyd to Tom Boyd, in Thomas D. Boyd Papers.

In addition to David, the faculty appointed by the board at its October 17, 1877, meeting consisted of J. W. Nicholson of Claiborne Parish, W. C. Wilde of the old agricultural college staff, and Dr. Joseph Jones, a New Orleans physician. Nicholson was a self-taught mathematician who in 1877 was running an academy in Claiborne Parish. Letters of recommendation, which David asked him to submit, described him as a very successful teacher of eleven years' standing, a good "moral preceptor," and a "mathematical genius" without "eccentricities" and "idiosyncrasies." He agreed to come to Baton Rouge anytime, but he hoped the university would not require his services until January, 1878, so that he could conclude his affairs in North Louisiana. Wilde, named professor of ancient and modern languages, was chosen to appease the partisans of the old agricultural college, and Dr. Jones, another Orleanian, received the chemistry professorship because of his reputation as an expert in soil analysis and cotton culture. David doubted that Jones would accept. If he did not, David hoped to get R. S. McCulloch of Washington and Lee University in his place. In fact, by September 19, 1877, he had already contacted McCulloch about the position. Admitting that he held "no formal job" in the university, David assured McCulloch that he would be acceptable to the board. "You have only to signify your willingness to come, say at a salary of $3,000 with perhaps quarters for your family."[25]

McCulloch was not the only man to whom David offered a job on his own authority. On September 23, 1877, before he was employed himself, he asked Colonel S. H. Lockett, just back from Egypt, to come back to Louisiana. Already engaged by East Tennessee University as professor of mathematics, Lockett was not interested. He found Knoxville charming and had no wish to leave it for Baton Rouge. "I do not like Louisiana," he explained. "It is a little too much like Egypt in climate and population."[26]

Only one of the professors elected at the October 17, 1877, board meeting reached Baton Rouge before November. W. C. Wilde left New Orleans with David in late October to begin his duties as professor of

25   Minutes of the Board of Supervisors, October 18, 1877; David Boyd to Tom Boyd, October 25, 1877, in Thomas D. Boyd Papers; J. W. Nicholson to David Boyd, October 14, 27, 1877, in Alphabetical File, Fleming Collection; David Boyd to R. S. McCulloch, September 19, 1877, David Boyd to Joseph Jones, October 26, 1877, in David Boyd Letterbooks.
26   David Boyd to S. H. Lockett, September 23, October 31, 1877, in David Boyd Letterbooks; S. H. Lockett to David Boyd, November 4, 1877, in Alphabetical File, Fleming Collection.

ancient and modern languages. An alumnus of the old university, Louis Bourgeois, was already there conducting classes for the students who arrived on opening day. But other than room and board, he was not being paid for his services. Sometime during November, J. W. Nicholson reached Baton Rouge, in response to David's urgent plea that he come as soon as possible so that the old "A & M College party and the Grangers" would not accuse the university of violating the merger law. He was afraid they might demand its repeal if the school were not fulfilling its comittments when the legislature met in January, 1878. Then on November 30, Tom Boyd joined David, Wilde, Bourgeois, and Nicholson. Like Bourgeois, Tom received no salary from the board. But for "reasons which he could communicate to no one," he decided to return from Virginia when David offered to send him the fare. The "reasons" were Tom's infatuation with Miss Annie Fuqua of Baton Rouge and his fear that Bourgeois might be courting her in his absence.[27]

Only the chair of "General and Agricultural Chemistry" remained unfilled at the close of 1877, but its vacancy caused David particular anxiety. Professor McCulloch, who accepted the position conditionally on November 8, 1877, after Dr. Jones refused it, wanted to delay his arrival in Baton Rouge until the fall of 1878 because he was delivering a series of lectures at Washington and Lee and did not know if he could be released before then. In addition, McCulloch planned to attend an exposition in Paris during the coming summer. But David answered that the university wanted him by January 1, 1878, "if at all possible." The main reason why the university had won the agricultural college, he explained, was because of its promise to provide a good agricultural program for Louisiana youths. It could hardly keep the farmers and planters happy if it did not have a professor of agriculture and chemistry "on the ground." The Grangers, David noted, were already "howling" at the school in their well-circulated magazine. On December 12 McCulloch acquiesced, promising to be in Baton Rouge by January 1, 1878, and reminding David again of his plans to go to Paris during the coming summer.[28]

27 David Boyd to Tom Boyd, October 25, 1877, in Thomas D. Boyd Papers; David Boyd to J. W. Nicholson, November 1, 1877, in David Boyd Letterbooks; Tom Boyd Diary, August 26, 1878.
28 David Boyd to R. S. McCulloch, November 2, December 5, 1877, in David Boyd Letterbooks; R. S. McCulloch to David Boyd, November 8, 1877, in Alphabetical File, Fleming Collection; R. S. McCulloch to David Boyd, December 12, 1877, in David Boyd Papers.

The hostility of the Grangers and the "Old Agric. College Party" which David reported in his urgent letters to Professors Nicholson and McCulloch was also present in the Board of Supervisors. As early as November 1, 1877, David, then in New Orleans sorting and receiving the agricultural college property, remarked to his brother Tom:

There is a hard and bitter feeling in our Bd. of Supervisors; and the upshot of it may be that we must put Ryland and Co. out—Even if we must defeat their nomination before the Senate. And I look for the fight to begin in the State Grange, which meets here [New Orleans] in Dec. . . . . Nicholson, our Math professor is a Granger; and I expect we shall make things lively for Ettie's Babtist friend Ryland . . . Ryland and Harris [also on the old agricultural college board] both stayed away from our last [board] meeting here to prevent a quorum.[29]

David's allusion to "Ettie's Babtist friend Ryland" probably referred to Ryland's visit in the Boyd household three years before. In 1874 the Grangers met in Baton Rouge, and David invited Dr. Ryland to stay at the asylum building while the convention was in session. Ettie Boyd was an ardent Baptist and apparently found Dr. Ryland a very compatible houseguest. But whatever cordiality David may have felt for Ryland in 1874 had certainly vanished by November, 1877. In one of his rare letters to Ettie from New Orleans he declared bitterly, "I am now fighting a desperate game—one in which we have very little to gain, much to lose! Your good Baptist *brother Ryland* is giving me all the trouble he can. He is a mean man—a hypocrite and a coward too, I think—his religion is all on the *surface*; under the skin is much of human nature of the worst type! And he—the *sneaking dog* he is—is poisoning others toward me—including perhaps the Govr."[30]

The Board of Supervisors of the Louisiana State University and Agricultural and Mechanical College submitted its first formal report to the legislature in February, 1878. It consisted of several parts. The first section, written by the board's secretary, W. H. Goodale of Baton Rouge, included a broad statement of the board's educational philosophy and an explanation of the letter and spirit of the merger law. David's report to the board came next, and a series of appendices rela-

29 David Boyd to Tom Boyd, November 1, 1877, in David Boyd Letterbooks. The meeting referred to is the one at which David was elected president.
30 David Boyd Diary, December 3, 5, 6, 1874; David Boyd to Ettie Boyd, Novmeber 15, 1877, in David Boyd Letterbooks.

tive to "Industrial" and "Technical" education in Europe and America completed the document. Noting how recently the merger had taken place, David declared that he would report not on what had been done, but on what was planned. He reminded the members that students were present and classes in session before the board met to appoint a president and staff. "In a word, the Institution opened itself—began of itself! And those of us *afterwards* entrusted with its care, have been trying hard ever since to catch up with our work."[31]

Then David offered a series of comments and recommendations. First, the beneficiary law ought to be enforced or repealed. Personally, he favored it, but the rest of the board apparently did not. Next, he noted that General Sherman was doing everything possible to secure an army officer for the university. In the meanwhile, Tom Boyd taught infantry tactics and conducted a daily drill although the board paid him nothing for his services. In the field of agricultural education, David reported that the university was in contact with the Louisiana Sugar Planters' Association through Professor McCulloch and that the Grange had shown its goodwill by adopting a resolution of good wishes for the university at its recent convention. He responded by offering the organization office space on campus. As for the school itself, David anticipated an increase in enrollment and thought the board should hire more professors. To pay for them, all legal "obstacles" to the use of the seminary (old university) fund would have to be removed. In addition, the board should ask the legislature to restore the 40 percent loss suffered by the agricultural fund when it surrendered its old bonds for new securities in accordance with the Funding Act of 1874. It should also petition the lawmakers to relieve the creditors of the old university. Another proposal urged that steps be taken to remove the deaf-mutes from the asylum building, and still others asked for creation of Catholic, Jewish, and Protestant chaplaincies and the purchase of new volumes for the library. "The library of any institution of learning," David declared, "is its main arm—more important even than its faculty; and too much expense can hardly be bestowed on it." Finally, David suggested a little empire-building. The "wisest citizens," he claimed, had thought for a long time that it would be good policy to "unite under *one* charter" the University of Louisiana at New Orleans and the re-

31   *Report* of the Board of Supervisors for 1877, p. 37.

cently merged institution at Baton Rouge. The New Orleans institution was in reality composed of only a law and medical school while
Baton Rouge had only an academic department. Each, without the
other, was "but a *fragment* of a University." Why not amend the constitution to "rid Louisiana of her present anomalous condition as to
higher education—with *two* universities, yet with none!"[32]

Of the several proposals David made to the Board of Supervisors in
1877, approximately half received positive action during the next two
years. The suggestion to incorporate the law and medical departments
of the University of Louisiana will be discussed later. Others, particularly those involving increased expenditures, generally failed to be enacted. For example, the board did increase the faculty from four to
thirteen between 1877 and 1879. But it did so by cutting salaries drastically or employing "assistant" professors, "instructors," or even advanced cadets at minimal figures. Even so, David had to persuade the
board by offering to cut his own income and, in one instance at least,
by agreeing to pay part of the new man's salary.[33] The library and other
facilities were not improved to any degree before 1880, nor did the
board employ chaplains. The beneficiary law remained a dead letter
and the board did not ask the legislature to relieve the creditors of the
old university. Instead, it resolved formally that it was not the legal
successor of the old board; hence, it could not be held accountable for
its debts. David heartily disagreed, but as a member of the new university board, he thought it improper to differ publicly with his colleagues.
When the resolution was presented, he simply abstained from voting
after expressing his dissent to the assembled members.[34]

Other proposals made by David in his report for 1877 fared better.
The board did appeal for the restoration of the 40 percent loss the university sustained when the agricultural and mechanical college bonds
were funded under the law of 1874. It also took action to free the old
university or seminary endowment fund from a legal snarl resulting
from the old board's refusal to present its bonds for scaling down in

32 *Ibid.*, 37–54.
33 Minutes of the Board of Supervisors, July 15, 1878, October 18, 1879, February 13, 1880;
    Baton Rouge *Capitolian*, October 18, 1878; Fleming, *Louisiana State University*, 309–11;
    David Boyd to Tom Boyd, March 2, 1880, in Thomas D. Boyd Papers.
34 Minutes of the Board of Supervisors, May 9, 1879; Fleming, *Louisiana State University*,
    312–13; 318–20, 428–29.

1874. Because of that refusal, no annuity had been paid on the seminary fund for over three years.[35]

Finally, the board did endorse David's suggestion to ask the legislature for control of the entire asylum building. After drafting a resolution to that effect, David found a friend to present it to the legislature
in 1878. But because the resolution made no provision to cover moving
expenses, a serious breach developed between David and Jonathan
Preston, superintendent of the evicted inmates. In a written challenge
Preston accused David of bad faith and authorized the bearer of his
note to "act for me" when he delivered it. Characteristically, David answered with a tortuous, underlined, and detailed explanation which
seems to have satisfied the sensitive Preston. At least he withdrew his
challenge and sent David another note to celebrate "the complete restoration of our formal relations."[36]

The Preston imbroglio was not the only affair of honor to engage
David's attention in the spring of 1878. At a board meeting in January,
1878, E. H. Farrar of Orleans, a Ryland partisan, introduced a resolution, endorsed by the board, requiring the president of the faculty to
prepare a report of the name, residence, age, and coursework of each
student plus the textbooks "actually used" in each course. Compelled by
a sense of duty to comply, David duly prepared the report for submis-
sion at the board's next meeting on April 1, 1878, as stipulated in Farrar's resolution. But personally he regarded the request for a list of
textbooks as both "improper" and "extraordinary." To Professor Nicholson he stormed, "A professor shd be treated with at least as much consideration as a common mechanic: he shd be allowed to pick his own
tools!"[37]

Two days before the scheduled board meeting David sent a sealed
envelope to W. H. Goodale, the board's secretary. A covering note explained that the sealed letter was dated April 1, 1878, and sent to the
secretary before he (David) could possibly know which members
would appear for the meeting. He did not care who came or stayed

---

35 *Report* of the Board of Supervisors for 1877, p. 7–8; Minutes of the Board of Supervisors,
    May 9, 1879.
36 John Preston to David Boyd, March 16, 17, 1878, David Boyd to John Preston, March 16,
    1878, in David Boyd Paperes. David's letter was sent only after he put it through several
    drafts, the last of which was considerably more conciliatory than some of the earlier ones.
37 Minutes of the Board of Supervisors, January 18, 1878; David Boyd to J. W. Nicholson,
    March 28, 1878, in David Boyd Letterbooks.

away, but he did not want anyone to say later that the contents of the sealed letter were influenced in any way by the "kind of quorum" which assembled. Then David asked Goodale not to open the sealed letter until after his official reply (the report) to the Farrar resolution had been received by the board. If no quorum appeared, Goodale was directed to send the letter, unread, to Governor Nicholls. What the secretary could not know was that the sealed envelope contained David's resignation and an explanation for it. The Farrar resolution, David told the governor, was "improper." Nevertheless, he had complied with it despite feelings of "humiliation and shame." "It wd seem," David concluded, "if the order was meant in *good* part—for the *public* good—and I can presume nothing else—that the professors are *incapable* of selecting their textbooks! In short, the resolution means a want of confidence. My duty, then is plain; and my resignation is in your hands."[38]

During the next two days David wrote more letters. One, addressed to E. H. Farrar, regretted that no quorum had assembled for the April 1 board meeting. David had done his "official duty" by turning in the required report, but, he continued, "I must now do my duty to *myself*; and I hereby charge you as the author of the resolution, to have acted with no proper or worthy motives, but with the deliberate intent to injure this institution and to cast reflections upon my colleagues and myself professionally." Then he accused Farrar of conduct "unbecoming" a supervisor and a gentleman, adding that his letter would be presented by his nephew, George Stafford, who "is fully authorized to act for me."[39] Next, David wrote a covering letter to George Stafford. After explaining the circumstances of the Farrar resolution, he gave Stafford his interpretation of its intent and noted that he had resigned. "I take it for granted," he concluded, "that this [David's challenge] will lead to serious consequences with Mr. Farrar. I am ready for it." The next day, April 2, 1878, David wrote still another letter to his friend W. A. Freret asking him to go with Stafford when he called on Farrar. "I wish to be a man of peace," he told Freret, "as any poor man with a wife and four children ought to be; but I cannot permit Mr. Farrar . . . to willfully and meanly try to injure me personally."[40]

38 David Boyd to W. H. Goodale, March 30, 1878, David Boyd to the President and Members of the Board of Supervisors, April 1, 1878, in David Boyd Letterbooks.
39 David Boyd to E. H. Farrar, April 1, 1878, *ibid.*
40 David Boyd to George Stafford, April 1, 1878, David Boyd to W. A. Freret, April 2, 1878, *ibid.*

Two weeks passed before David heard from Stafford. Urging his uncle to reconsider, Stafford announced that he had not yet delivered the note to Farrar and if David insisted on pursuing the matter, he ought to come to New Orleans so that the letter could be "re-worded." But Stafford thought David should drop the whole matter. Farrar's act was official, he pointed out. In no way must David appear to be avoiding an "official" investigation into his "official" career. David must have been convinced. Ultimately he did go to New Orleans, but no challenge went to Farrar. The two did not meet again until August, when the board convened in special session.[41]

Meanwhile, David's resignation was in the hands of Governor Nicholls, but at the regular board meeting on July 4, 1878, it was presented and then referred to a three-man committee. After a recess during which the committee met with the president and the faculty, another letter from David was submitted to the supervisors. In it David claimed that he "never intended" to question the board's right to make any inquiry concerning the university which it thought proper. Nor did he think that the board intended to reflect on him personally in the Farrar resolution. What did concern him was what the public and professors might conclude. But convinced by the committee that he "labored under a misapprehension," he agreed to its request that he withdraw his resignation. Ironically, a resolution introduced the same day played a large part in forcing David out of the presidency almost exactly two years later. On July 5, 1878, Dr. J. A. Taylor moved that the secretary of war be requested to assign Lieutenant M. F. Jamar to the university as professor of military tactics. David's campaign to block the appointment and later to have Jamar removed contributed to his own removal by the board on July 2, 1880.[42]

Besides late organization, factionalism in the board, lack of funds, and two narrowly averted duels, David had to deal with a yellow fever epidemic in the merged university's first year of operation. By August, 1878, yellow fever had reached Baton Rouge from New Orleans although local physicians and the Board of Health did not want to admit its presence. In his diary entry for August 29, 1878, Tom Boyd noted the existence of over 80 cases in the town and "only 5 deaths so far."

41 George W. Stafford to D. F. Boyd, undated, in David Boyd Papers; David Boyd to George W. Stafford, telegram, April 12, 1878, in David Boyd Letterbooks.
42 Minutes of the Board of Supervisors, April 1, July 4, 5, 1878, July 2, 1880.

The fever, he thought, came to Baton Rouge earlier that month when New Orleans delegates arrived to attend the state Democratic convention. To combat the disease, the town ordered a general "disinfection" but 12 persons were dead by September 4, and the number of stricken had climbed to somewhere between 150 and 300. In 1878 the cause and manner of transmission of yellow fever were still subjects of debate in medical circles. Tom Boyd's diary reflects one commonly accepted theory: that the disease generated in filth. As he described it:

The disease began near the Oil Mills in the extreme northern part of town. The Board of Health *overlooked* that part of town when disinfecting. It is said 2 bbls of water had been standing for 6 mos. They were thrown into a ditch one day last wk and the 5 workmen who emptied them *all* took ill at once. Stench unbearable. Whole factory was filthy as was yard of Dr. Curry which adjoined it. Thence fever spread to the blind asylum nearby, thence *south* along river. As yet *four* cases *south* of Boulevard. . . . Few precautions taken to prevent spread of disease. People meet as usual in market place, on corners. Go to funerals of Y. F. victims. Inmates of blind asylum where fever is raging walk the streets in groups of 2 or three.[43]

On September 4 a former professor visiting the Boyds developed a fever which Dr. Dupree labeled "suspicious." He was treated with calomel and quinine, and after three days the fever disappeared, which makes the diagnosis seem questionable. But there was no doubt about yellow fever's presence in the asylum building later that month. On September 16, 1878, Mrs. Jonathan Preston, the wife of the asylum superintendent, developed chills and fever, and the next day she was dead. Dr. Dupree also became ill but he survived. And David's death was reported, but like Mark Twain's proved to be grossly exaggerated. Other citizens were not so fortunate. Even the city fathers, concerned with preserving the town's "image," admitted to 139 deaths and 2,274 cases of fever by mid-October, 1878. Flight seemed to be the only effective way to avoid the disease, but that became more difficult as news of the dead and dying reached potential refugee centers. On October 25, 1878, Superintendent Preston decided to leave Baton Rouge to protect his four small children. With Tom Boyd and two other adults, the Prestons went by covered wagon from Baton Rouge to Amite City, where they boarded a train for Louisville, Kentucky. Througout the

43   Tom Boyd Diary, August 29, September 4, 1878.

journey, Tom noted, it was necessary to "*hide* the fact that they came from Baton Rouge." [44]

Because of the epidemic the Board of Supervisors did not meet in October, 1878, and classes did not resume until December. Nevertheless, enrollment for the year 1878–1879 increased over that of the previous session. By late February, 1879, conditions were certainly normal when General Sherman, two of his daughters, and a military aide paid a visit to the university. Although he was a "bitter enemy in war," General Sherman had been a "good friend in peace," one of the local papers remarked. It was, therefore, a pleasure to welcome him. Sherman reviewed the cadet corps, made a public address, and visited with several of the local dignitaries David invited to the university to meet the renowned soldier. One guest described him as "plain and unostentatious . . . jovial and frank." The general, he noted incidentally, favored turning over to the university the United States barracks property at Baton Rouge. [45]

By 1879 the idea of acquiring the United States barracks as a home for the university was at least nine years old. David corresponded with General Sherman about it soon after the fire that forced the school to move to Baton Rouge from Rapides. But at the time Sherman opposed giving up the barracks on the ground that troops had to be accessible if "necessity" required them in Texas, Arkansas, Alabama, or Florida. By 1879, he had changed his mind and offered to endorse David's request for the property, pointing out that the school must promise to keep it in good repair and surrender it on demand if the federal government ever needed it again. Apparently the qualification caused David to lose interest because by the end of April, 1879, he wrote Sherman that the asylum building was "better suited" to the university's purpose. Not until 1886 did the school finally move to the federal property, but even then the limiting restriction remained in effect. [46]

44 *Ibid.*, September 4, 16, 22, October 3, 5, 21, 25, 1878, September 14, 1879. A detailed description of the epidemic of 1878 and all of Louisiana's bouts with yellow fever can be found in Joan Carrigan, "Yellow Fever in Louisiana" (Ph.D. dissertation, Louisiana State University, 1961).

45 Fleming, *Louisiana State University*, 312; Baton Rouge *Capitolian*, February 15, March 1, 1879.

46 W. T. Sherman to David Boyd, April 24, 1870, in Typescript of Sherman-Boyd Correspondence; Baton Rouge *Capitolian*, March 15, 1879; W. T. Sherman to David Boyd, April 5, 2 , 1879, in William T. Sherman Letters, David F. Boyd Family Papers, Fleming, *Louisiana State University*, 442.

The new university seemed to be functioning well under its two-year-old charter as the session ended in 1879. Hundreds of people attended commencement exercises and listened attentively to the closing remarks of the university's "learned and gifted President." His "indomitable will," reported a local journalist, had enabled the school to survive reverses that would have overwhelmed any man of less ability and energy.[47]

47   Baton Rouge *Capitolian*, July 12, 1879.

Chapter IX

Losing a War

THE MAN who praised David so extravagantly after the July, 1879, graduation was Leon Jastremski, Confederate captain, newspaper editor, mayor of Baton Rouge, and a growing influence in the state Democratic party. His support for David's administration, so firm in 1879, turned to active opposition by the following year when, as vice-president of a reorganized Board of Supervisors, he led the drive to oust David from the university presidency. Before discussing Jastremski's motives, however, the political developments that put him in a position to act against David must be briefly sketched.

Louisiana was "redeemed" in April, 1877, when Francis T. Nicholls and Louis A. Wiltz took over the statehouse following the federal government's decision to withdraw support from their Republican opponents. Nicholls was a typical Redeemer. A graduate of West Point and a lawyer, he served as a general in the Confederate Army, receiving wounds that left him severely maimed. Following the war he returned to his home in LaFourche Parish where he engaged in planting and politics until his election as governor in 1876. Wiltz came from New Orleans. A banker by profession, he became mayor of the Crescent City in 1872. A third figure who contributed to the Nicholls-Wiltz success in 1877 was Major E. A. Burke. Burke's history before 1870 was obscure, but by 1876 he was powerful enough in Louisiana Democratic councils to act as a liason man between the Nicholls government and Hayes Republicans during negotiations leading to the Compromise of

1877. The next year the party rewarded him with its nomination for state treasurer. By that time, however, Burke and Wiltz were already working together against Governor Nicholls in a struggle to control the Democratic party. They had an ally in the Louisiana State Lottery Company and its president, Charles T. Howard. Chartered by Radicals in 1868, the lottery company was astute enough to switch its allegiance in 1876. Allegedly it bribed away enough Packard legislators in 1877 to provide the Nicholls body with a quorum. The lottery company also played a prominent role at the Democratic convention of 1878, at which Burke won nomination for state treasurer. Tom Boyd remarked on Major Burke's "most wonderful shrewdness" among the delegates; he also noted the obvious lobbying engaged in by lottery company agents who, according to rumor, sought to protect the company's monopoly charter by offering liberal bribes. But the agents' efforts did not succeed. In 1879 the legislature passed and Governor Nicholls signed an act to repeal the lottery's charter. Only a rapidly secured injunction saved the company from going out of business.

While the case was still before the courts, delegates assembled at Baton Rouge in May, 1879, to construct a new state constitution. This time the lottery agents proved more effective. As finally adopted, the new organic law incorporated the company charter, thus protecting it from reformers and ingrates who might control Louisiana's government in the future. Another provision in the new constitution disciplined Governor Nicholls by shortening his term by more than one full year. The supreme court was also "reorganized" and the way opened for its personnel to be entirely replaced. In the end, only one elected officer escaped this "clean sweep"—E. A. Burke. His term was increased to six years. According to one scholar, this was Burke's "payoff" for having led the fight in the constitutional convention against repudiation of the state debt. Contracted during Reconstruction, much of the debt was fraudulent, and poorer Democrats, from the country and New Orleans, demanded that it be written off. But by 1879 wealthy Louisianians of both parties held the state's bonds. In the name of saving Louisiana's "honor," they opposed scaling down the interest as well as the principal owed by the state. Finally, after much haggling and amid charges of large-scale bribery, a compromise emerged: the principal owed by the state remained intact, but the interest rate owed the bondholders was reduced from 7 to 4 percent.

E. A. Burke continued to be a power in Louisiana when Louis Wiltz and S. D. McEnery of Monroe ran for governor and lieutenant governor in December, 1879. Wiltz had tuberculosis and died in October, 1881, but long before then Burke's influence in the governor's office was well established. If anything, it increased when McEnery took over. Described as a "weak, affable man," McEnery let Burke, Charles Howard of the Lottery Company, and a few others run the state. In time, various individuals complained of fraud and corruption, and some newspapers demanded reform. But they fell silent when the governor's friends equated any attack on the McEnery regime with disloyalty to the South and collaboration with Republicans.

Among those McEnery supporters who let loyalty to party and patron overcome their better judgment was editor Leon Jastremski, mayor of Baton Rouge and, by 1880, potential antagonist of David Boyd. Jastremski was a close personal friend of McEnery's, which probably explained why he was made vice-president of the university Board of Supervisors in May, 1880, and why his brother, John Jastremski, was appointed superintendent of the asylum for the deaf and dumb after the death of Jonathan Preston. Early in McEnery's tenure Leon Jastremski's newspaper urged the Democratic party to purge itself of corruption. But by 1882 it was defending the administration against any and all charges. To do otherwise, it argued, would merely lend comfort to the Republican enemy. Also, in 1882 Baton Rouge became the state capital, and Jastremski's paper became the state's official journal.

Leon Jastremski was a typical Bourbon. He even liked the term although he thought Stuart would be more appropriate. Louisiana in the 1880s, he explained, was like England in the 1660s: sick of the "pseudo-Liberalism" of Cromwell and ready for a restoration of safe conservative rule. Like many of his more famous contemporaries, Jastremski was an ardent Confederate veteran who loved to invoke memories of the past, but who also did all he could to promote the expansion of business and industry in the South. Efforts by rural interests to regulate business annoyed him. The South should admire and emulate northern millionaires, not denounce them, Jastremski argued. Unlike some Louisianians, he was not disturbed when Jay Gould moved to increase the size of his already immense holdings in Louisiana. It merely represented the working out of a natural law: survival of the fittest. The "grumbling" of the poor against the law was "futile, infantile and impudent."[1]

The accession to power of Nicholls, Wiltz, and McEnery may have represented "Redemption" for most Louisianians. For David Boyd it spelled disaster. Under the Nicholls administration David encountered increasing antagonism in the University Board of Supervisors, a board which Nicholls chose from a list made up by David himself, but which included several partisans of the Grangers and the old agricultural college. After Wiltz became governor, the Nicholls board was replaced with another even less sympathetic to David's conduct of the university. Finally, under the leadership of Lieutenant Governor McEnery, presiding in the absence of the ailing Wiltz, the hostile board fired David in the summer of 1880. Their reasons will be examined in detail later. But first, a series of events which laid the groundwork for David's removal requires explanation.

By 1879 the university seemed to have met and conquered its most serious challenges and settled down to its primary task: the education of Louisiana youth. Leon Jastremski announced to his readers that under David's "able supervision," the merged schools had become a "great success." The university had an accomplished faculty, the experimental farm and "mechanical appurtenances" were being rapidly developed, and there was no longer a "shadow of a doubt" that the university would soon join the "first rank among similar ones in this country." Even observers as familiar with the school's past as former Vice-President William Sanford thought the future looked encouraging. In the spring of 1878 he trusted that David was getting along "smoothly now." If so, he wondered how David managed to live without trouble: "You have been in it so long that you can hardly be content to sail in smooth water now."[2]

In fact, David was not "getting along smoothly." Neither was he happy in adversity. To a Virginia friend he regretted ever having left his home state. "I am very free to say that were I back again to 1857, no

1   C. Vann Woodward, *Origins of the New South, 1877–1913* (Baton Rouge, 1951), 11–13, 44, 70–71, 75; William I. Hair, "The Agrarian Protest in Louisiana, 1877–1900" (Ph.D. dissertation, Louisiana State University, 1962), 23–27, 148–53, 157–64. Woodward proposes that the term *Bourbon* be abandoned as a source of confusion, but Hair finds it useful to describe one faction of the Louisiana Democracy. Hair, *Bourbonism and Agrarian Protest*, 21–24.
2   William Sanford to David Boyd, April 28, 1878, in Alphabetical File, Fleming Collection; Baton Rouge *Capitolian*, February 22, 1879.

earthly consideration cld . . . induce *me* to *leave Va*. It was a *great mistake* for *me*. I have really never been satisfied. *Am not now*."[3] Basic to David's dissatisfaction was the growing opposition his administration encountered after 1877. His difficulties with Dr. Ryland and other board members who championed "practical education" have already been described. So has his disagreement with board member E. H. Farrar, whose demand for a list of textbooks employed by each professor led David to submit his resignation in April, 1878. Both disputes represented something new in David's experience: division within the board and the board's determination to participate actively in running the university. Boards before 1877, led by William Sanford and G. Mason Graham, imposed few restraints on David. They delegated much of their authority to him, and they usually endorsed his actions after the fact. After 1877 the boards were never as passive and rarely of one mood. Considering David's distaste for sharing power and his reputed zest for combat, clashes between him and the men he served were practically inevitable.[4]

Besides antagonists in the Board of Supervisors, David acquired some powerful enemies among state and local politicians. One, W. B. Leake of West Feliciana, was a delegate to the constitutional convention in 1879 and a member of the Louisiana state senate in 1880. In the convention, Leake fought David's efforts to consolidate the professional departments of the University of Louisiana with the state university at Baton Rouge, and the following year he introduced a bill in the legislature to completely reorganize the Baton Rouge school. In 1879 high maintenance costs and inferior food were the principle reasons for Leake's opposition. Sometime earlier his son attended the university, but the food was so poor and limited in quantity that he had been forced to send the boy several dollars worth of "extra provisions." David replied sarcastically in a letter to the editor of the New Orleans *Times*. Leake paid only ten dollars a month for his son's food, he retorted. The other ten dollars of monthly maintenance costs covered

---

3 David Boyd to Chas. M. Venable, March 25, 1878, in David Boyd Letterbooks.
4 In 1876 David admitted that he had been a "little monarch" for so long that he would find a partnership impossible. As for his combative tendencies, G. Mason Graham and Samuel Lockett, the two men who knew him best, noted his "delight in troubles" and his tendency to "upturn things." David Boyd to R. J. Hancock, December 13, 1876, in David Boyd Letterbooks; G. Mason Graham to David Boyd, September 1, 1879, in G. Mason Graham Letters, Fleming Collection; S. H. Lockett to David Boyd, August 26, 1879, in Alphabetical File, Fleming Collection.

rent, laundry, medical, and fuel bills. Besides, there was no need to send a "particle" of extra food; if the father did so, it was simply a "sign of parental affection." However, if the elder Leake insisted that the box was necessary, David could only explain it on the ground "that Father knew [his son] to be of Leaky stock . . . [the boy] cld not hold his provisions well." Pointing out that Leake could board his son anywhere he chose under university regulations, David concluded acidly: "To expect St. Charles hotel fare on $10 to $15 a month shows conclusively, I respectfully submit, that the delegate from West Feliciana is Leaky in more ways than one; in brains as well as in belly!"[5]

David's intemperate letter was particularly unfortunate considering the fact that Leake's complaints were not without foundation. Only a month later one of David's best friends on the Board of Supervisors, General Joseph L. Brent, urged him to improve the quality of the food at the university. In the interest of keeping costs low, Brent thought, David was charging too little for board and consequently providing inferior fare. Brent had heard several complaints which convinced him that improvements were essential.[6]

The issue that sparked the clash with delegate Leake won David additional enemies in the constitutional convention of 1879. Sometime during late June, David induced a Mr. George of Webster Parish to introduce an ordinance which would have united the law and medical departments of the University of Louisiana in New Orleans with the state university at Baton Rouge. David did not propose to move the professional departments out of New Orleans or make any essential change in their organization. He merely wished to join them with the state university at Baton Rouge under a single charter. This was by no means a new idea in 1879, having been suggested by a superintendent of public education as early as 1858. David himself promoted the plan in various reports, but nothing positive was done until 1878 when a proposed amendment to the Constitution of 1868 authorized the "academic department" of the University of Louisiana to locate outside New Orleans. At the time there was no operating "academic department." But the very suggestion that one be set up somewhere outside the Crescent City caused one to be created in November, 1878. In a memorial presented to the convention on July 7, 1879, David ex-

5   David Boyd to Editor, New Orleans *Times*, July 9, 1879.
6   Jos. L. Brent to David Boyd, August 20, 1879, in Alphabetical File, Fleming Collection.

plained the reasons behind Mr. George's resolution. He wanted the state to support "*one good* school, complete in every way." If it provided for a separate University of Louisiana with its own "Academical Department," it would again be "scattering . . . money in all directions." Let the city take over the newly created "Academical Department" and run it as a city college or high school; the law and medical schools should be added to the state university.[7]

Both George's proposal and David's memorial caused a furor in the convention and the New Orleans press. Apparently, the New Orleans *Democrat* charged, Baton Rouge would not be satisfied until it "stole" every "State facility" from the Crescent City. It already had the university, the schools for the blind and deaf, the penitentiary, and the state capitol. Now, the editor declared, Baton Rouge was after the city's law and medical schools too. The George proposal did not succeed. Neither did David's attempt to keep the state from "scattering its resources." As finally approved, the Constitution of 1879 authorized the legislature to appropriate up to $10,000 annually for each of the two universities. About the only thing David gained from his efforts in the convention of 1879 was the enmity of the New Orleans delegation.[8]

Finally, for the first time in his experience David faced serious opposition from his own faculty. Several professors ultimately manifested some dissatisfaction with his administrative policies, but R. S. McCulloch, professor of "agriculture and general Chemistry," and Lieutenant M. F. Jamar, military instructor, spearheaded the drive which led to his dismissal. McCulloch came to the university in January, 1878, at age sixty after a long teaching career at Princeton, Columbia, and Washington and Lee. His reputation, based on a textbook and some field research in sugar manufacture, both done before the Civil War, seems to have impressed the Board of Supervisors. They hired him to inaugurate the university's program in "scientific agriculture" at $3,000 "and quarters," more than any professor had ever received.[9]

7   David Boyd, Notes for Arguments favoring unification of L.S.U. and U. of La., in David Boyd Papers; David F. Boyd to Constitutional convention of 1879, June 25, 1879, in Official Papers, Fleming Collection; David F. Boyd, *Memorial* to the Constitutional Convention, July 7, 1879, in Printed Materials, David Boyd Papers.
8   Baton Rouge *Capitolian*, July 12, 1879; *Official Journal* of the Proceedings of the Constitutional Convention of the State of Louisiana (New Orleans, 1879), 242–43; Fleming, *Louisiana State University*, 324–31.
9   R. S. McCulloch to David Boyd, October 17, 1877, in Alphabetical File, Fleming Collection; Fleming, *Louisiana State University*, 308–309, 332–33.

Besides teaching, the board hoped Professor McCulloch would conduct experiments in sugar culture for the benefit of Louisiana planters. Member Joseph L. Brent, himself a sugar planter, asked David and McCulloch what it would cost to provide an appropriate laboratory at the university, expecting to ask the legislature for the necessary funds. But Brent did not count on the extreme thrift practiced by the Redeemers, particularly in areas like education. Not only did the lawmakers fail to fund a laboratory in 1878; in 1879 the new constitution reduced the interest owed by the state on seminary and agricultural funds, thereby significantly lowering the university's guaranteed annual income.[10]

The constitution did not take effect until January, 1880. But even before then, inadequate appropriations by the legislature and the state's failure to pay university annuities when due contributed to the breach between David and Professor McCulloch. In order to expand the faculty and the curriculum to comply with the merger act, David urged the board to cut some existing salaries and to eliminate all quarters allowances. During the summer of 1878, his own pay was dropped from $3,500 to $3,000, McCulloch's and Nicholson's remained at $3,000 and $2,000 respectively, and Professor Wilde was dismissed. Two men replaced him, each of whom received $1,200. Finally, the board provided for a professor of mechanics at $2,000, a commandant and instructor of "drawing" at $1,000 each, and a clerk-librarian at $800. No one, including David, would receive any allowance for quarters after October 1.[11]

Professor McCulloch was in Virginia when he learned about the board's action. A letter from David in August, 1878, outlined the details and suggested that in the future McCulloch, too, might be asked to accept less pay. Considering the "general poverty" of the state, David thought the request would not be "unreasonable." What McCulloch thought is not recorded, but the following year he must have been disturbed. During the summer of 1879, in an effort to "equalize salaries,"

10   Jos. L. Brent to D. F. Boyd and R. S. McCulloch, undated, David Boyd and R. S. McCulloch to Sugar Planters' Association, February 5, 1878, Memorandum, February 7, 1878; Jos. L. Brent, Speech to Sugar Planters' Association, January 3, 1878, all in Summary of Correspondence between Louisiana State University and Sugar Planters' Association, in Printed Materials, David Boyd Papers; Fleming, *Louisiana State University*, 318–24. Fleming provides a detailed discussion of university finances for the years 1877-1880.
11   Minutes of the Board of Supervisors, July 4, 15, 1878.

the board decreased David's pay from $3,000 to $2,500; reduced the mathematics and mechanics professors' salaries from $2,000 to $1,500; left the three lowest paid men at the same level ($1,000 to $1,200), and cut the highest paid, Professor McCulloch, from $3,000 to $1,500. As David saw it, the pay cut and his (David's) "agency" in bringing it about explained McCulloch's subsequent hostility.[12]

Another factor that strained relations between the two men was Professor McCulloch's disinterest in the more "practical" aspects of the university's agriculture program. Willing to advise the "Sugar Industry" and prepared to teach "Mechanics, Pure and Applied" if the school would provide a shop, McCulloch wanted no part of the "Agricultural Department," particularly as it related to a proposed experimental farm. In August, 1878, he wrote David from Virginia, "I have not regarded it [the agricultural department] as under my charge, except in so far as 'Agricultural Chemistry' is concerned; nor do I desire further responsibility for it. Indeed, the farm seems likely to be an 'Elephant,' which the Supervisors will arrange *as they please*, whatever others may think desirable."[13]

Very disturbed, David answered that the university had to "do something" immediately in the agriculture and mechanical departments or the legislature would "break us up." He scoffed at McCulloch's argument that they could not act without specific approval from the board and a special appropriation by the legislature. If they waited for those bodies to act, nothing would happen for "years to come." But if McCulloch agreed, David would press the board for $500 to activate the department of "Agric. Chemistry" at once. "Only tell me what," he pleaded. "Let us stop this stagnation—this *do nothing* if possible."[14]

McCulloch's department was still not functioning in 1880. He had the space, "five rooms, clean, neat and fit," by that time, but he still lacked the "necessary appliances." David did not know when, if ever, he would get them. But of one thing he was certain: they were not

12   David Boyd to R. S. McCulloch, August 17, 1878, David Boyd, note, March 6, 1880, Excerpt of correspondence between D. F. Boyd and R. S. McCulloch, in Boyd Letters, Fleming Collection; Minutes of the Board of Supervisors, May 9, 1879; Tom Boyd Diary, September 29, 1880; Fleming, *Louisiana State University*, 333.
13   R. S. McCulloch to David Boyd, August 1, 1878, in David Boyd Papers.
14   David Boyd to R. S. McCulloch, October 22, 1878, in Boyd Letters, Fleming Collection; R. S. McCulloch to David Boyd, August 1, October 27, 1878, in David Boyd Papers.

complying with state and federal law and the sooner they admitted it the better. In a letter to Professor McCulloch dated January 5, 1880, David declared: "For any and every omission here . . . I hold myself responsible. That we are no school of applied sciences, *tho' professing to be*, let the fault be *mine*. I am tired making excuses. I shall admit that as an Agric and Mechl College, we are doing *nothing*—that in that regard we are a failure." Then, in the bluntest terms, David told McCulloch that if "they" did not "turn over a new leaf," he would ask the board to abolish the "scientific chairs" altogether.[15]

There is no record that David ever carried out his threat. In March, 1880, he remarked to his brother that the January 5 letter, like others written to McCulloch earlier, was meant as "a *spur*—to try and get *him* to do something" about the agricultural department. "But the truth is," David concluded, "Mr. McC. never wished or intended, if he could help it, to have to do with the farm. . . . I hold that all he wanted was his salary as big as possible, and his work as little as possible! And everybody knows *that*: that is *notorious!*"[16]

The difficulties with Professor McCulloch in 1878 and 1879 were serious enough, but they seem almost trivial compared to the problems caused by the appointment of Lieutenant M. F. Jamar to the faculty. Trouble began long before Jamar arrived. In November, 1877, David asked General Sherman to have Lieutenant Mumford of the Thirteenth Infantry assigned to the university as professor of military science. Sherman answered that if David wanted a particular individual, he would have to apply for him through the governor to the secretary of war. But, he added, the number of men available for such duty was limited, and the school might have to wait some months before securing an officer. Meanwhile, the Board of Supervisors had a candidate of its own, Lieutenant M. F. Jamar, also of the Thirteenth Infantry. Jamar had been stationed at the Baton Rouge garrison and counted several local politicians among his friends. When the board moved to have him assigned by the War Department, David refused to endorse the request. Instead, he asked General Sherman to block the appointment. But Sherman explained that "these College details" were purely

15   David Boyd to R. S. McCulloch, January 5, 1880, excerpt of the original, in Boyd Letters, Fleming Collection.
16   David Boyd to Tom Boyd, March 14, 1880, in Thomas D. Boyd Papers.

political and the board's preference for Jamar would probably decide the issue.[17]

General Sherman's prediction proved accurate. In April, 1879, Leon Jastremski announced to his readers that M. F. Jamar, recently promoted to first lieutenant, would soon be at the university as professor of "Tactics and Military Science." Jastremski did not think a better choice could have been made. "We take the greatest pleasure," he remarked, "in welcoming back in our midst this really clever gentleman." Tom Boyd's evaluation was a little less flattering. Commenting on Jamar, whose appointment relieved him of a distasteful duty, Tom remarked, "He is a rollicking, drinking, smart, smutty anecdote telling fellow of about 27 and an admirable drill master." Even more critical, David labeled Jamar "no gentleman, and an unfit associate for the cadets." Worse still, he was convinced that Jamar secured the post by circulating false rumors about Lieutenant Mumford, the brother officer whose appointment David originally requested.[18]

The conflict between David and Jamar became more serious in October 1879, when Tom Boyd resigned his post as commandant and professor of drawing. Tom never enjoyed being commandant, especially after a disciplinary crisis arose in the spring of 1879. By October, however, because the job required him to work closely with both David and Lieutenant Jamar, and because Jamar wanted the board to draw a "line of demarcation" between their departments, Tom decided to resign. David encouraged him, if only to avoid charges that he opposed Jamar in order to favor his younger brother.[19]

Now David's fight with Jamar commenced in earnest. After accepting Tom Boyd's resignation "with regret," the board offered the post of commandant to Jamar, whereupon David protested to Governor Nicholls that a man who lacked a "refined sense of honor" and "delicacy of feeling" was not a "proper person" to place in immediate control of the cadets. Nicholls responded that David's allegations, if meant as a formal charge, would have to be "sustained by evidence" and presented to

17 William Sherman to David Boyd, November 23, 1877, January 15, April 29, June 25, August 4, 1878, all in William T. Sherman Letters, David F. Boyd Family Papers; David Boyd to W. T. Sherman, April 25, 1878, in David Boyd Letterbooks; Minutes of the Board of Supervisors, July 5, 15, 1878; Fleming, *Louisiana State University*, 333.

18 Baton Rouge *Capitolian*, April 12, 1879; Tom Boyd Diary, September 14, 1879, September 12, 1880; G. Mason Graham to David Boyd, November 19, 1879, in G. Mason Graham Letters, Fleming Collection.

19 Tom Boyd Diary, September 14, 1879, August 27, September 12, 1880.

Jamar so that he could prepare to defend himself when the board met in December.[20]

Meanwhile, David's campaign against the lieutenant continued. One board member, G. Mason Graham, thought he was wasting his time. If Jamar was "congenial to the tastes and sentiments of the majority of the Board . . . why! let them have him." General Sherman, too, thought David should wage a more limited war. To Graham, who solicited his advice, Sherman wrote that "he [David] should *keep* the matter *inside the family*—and should simply question the adaptability of Jamar to the office he holds and *not attack his personal character.* Every army officer *must resent that.*" Instead, David should submit his objections to the board and abide by its decision. "He shd *not* resign or make captious opposition," advised the general, "but crave time to vindicate his opinion—or satisfy him of honest error."[21]

In February, 1880, part of the difficulty was resolved when Jamar decided to refuse the post of commandant. Planning to marry, he considered the quarters David assigned him, previously occupied by bachelor Tom Boyd, unsuitable for his prospective bride. Tension was further reduced when the Board of Supervisors authorized David to ask for Lieutenant Jamar's recall by the War Department at any time if there was a "want of harmony" between himself and the lieutenant.[22]

Ostensibly, David had won the battle to keep Jamar from becoming commandant, which probably pleased him a great deal. Among his friends David had a well-deserved reputation for enjoying hard-fought conflicts. Former vice-president Sanford's remark that David would be unhappy without "troubles" and G. Mason Graham's comment on David's "delight in troubles" have already been noted. But Colonel Lockett said it best. Asked to apply for the presidency of the University of Alabama, Lockett sought David's advice. David warned him of the hardships he could expect if he accepted such a job, but Lockett replied, "If I go there, I am not going to upturn things. I shall not stir up trouble if I can avoid it, just to see if I am not strong enough to come

20   David Boyd to Francis T. Nicholls, October 27, 1879, copy, in Boyd Letters, Fleming Collection; Francis T. Nicholls to David Boyd, November 6, 1879, in Alphabetical File, *ibid.*
21   G. Mason Graham to David Boyd, November 19, 1879, in G. Mason Graham Letters, *ibid.*; W. T. Sherman to G. Mason Graham, November 24, 1879, in William T. Sherman Letters, David F. Boyd Family Papers.
22   Minutes of the Board of Supervisors, February 11, 12, 14, 1880; Tom Boyd Diary, August 27, 1880.

out first—best—in the struggle, which you know I have often told you, was a failing of yours. I shall consider my duty done if I . . . carry out the orders of . . . the Board of Trustees. I am going to let them do all the fighting."[23]

Far from letting others do all the fighting, David was making new enemies inside and outside the university family. One of them was a prominent Baton Rouge grocer and businessman, William Garig. The university purchased most of its provisions from Garig's firm until October, 1879, when David decided to take his business elsewhere. The reason is not clear, but the effect on his relations with Garig was. Asked for an explanation by the firm, David replied through a third party, "In my present way of considering Mr. Garig, I do not wish to have any further communication with him." A few months later Garig returned the compliment. He and his partner *"mutually agreed"* that they wanted nothing to do with David.[24]

Indirectly, David's fight with Garig was bound to have repercussions. Like Lieutenant Jamar, Garig was a personal friend of Dr. Williams, vice-president of the university board. He was also related to the Kleinpeters, a prominent family in East Baton Rouge Parish. In 1880 one of the men Baton Rouge sent to the legislature was a Representative Kleinpeter. When several of David's enemies tried to enact a bill to reorganize the university, Kleinpeter helped to direct their efforts in the house.[25]

On January 10, 1880, Leon Jastremski's newspaper, the *Capitolian*, dropped what Tom Boyd described as a "bombshell in our midst." Jastremski printed a blistering article which attacked David's administration of the university as "the most absolute autocracy now in existence." All authority was vested in a single individual. "Professors . . . have no more authority in shaping the educational tone and spirit of the institution than Gov. Nicholls has in regulating the affairs of France." The author thought the professors were unhappy. But the president ignored their discontent. No matter how "able and well-meaning" President Boyd might be, he should realize that "twelve

23 G. Mason Graham to David Boyd, September 1, 1879, in G. Mason Graham Letters, Fleming Collection; S. H. Lockett to David Boyd, August 26, 1879, in Alphabetical File, *ibid.*
24 David Boyd to [?], December 11, 1879, David and Garig (grocers) to David Boyd, April 30, [1880], in David Boyd Papers.
25 David Boyd to Tom Boyd, January 25, 1880, in Thomas D. Boyd Papers; Louisiana *House Journal*, March 2, 1880, p. 227.

heads are better than one." In any case, when the community in which a school was located could not "point to it with pride," there must be some serious fault in its management. Mismanagement, the author declared, "may not arise from any criminal purpose." It could result from bad judgment. Then the writer proposed a series of changes which the "intelligence of Baton Rouge" ought to insist upon before the entire state "is disaffected:" (1) The military feature of the school should be limited to a study of military science and enough drill to provide physical training for the cadets. "It is surely a mistake to try to set up a West Point in Louisiana." (2) Some means should be found to bring the students into closer contact with the "better class" of Baton Rouge society. (3) The president must share policy-making with the whole faculty. (4) Regulations and disciplinary procedure should be spelled out and all "discretionary powers" whatever should be withdrawn. (5) The boarding department should be run by a hotelkeeper, not the university authorities. (6) A preparatory department of specific entrance requirements ought to be established. Otherwise the school would never "advance." If the citizens of Baton Rouge could not convince the university administration to make the suggested changes, they should at least "speak out." It was their duty to "compel, by thorough public ventilation a change not only of policy but also of [the school's] organic structure."[26]

The article in the *Capitolian* was signed simply "Louisiana," but David could think of several persons who might have been its author. In late January he wrote his brother, then in New Orleans: "Jamar is a mean character, Garig a dog, Williams friend to both, & McCulloch afraid of losing his place. . . . Please say to Capt. Jastremski that I do consider the article in the *Capitolian* as personal[ly], as well as officially, reflecting on me. Hence I wish the names of *all* parties responsible therefor."[27]

R. D. Haislip, a young assistant professor at the university, proved to be the author. A Louisiana native, Haislip held a master's degree from Professor McCulloch's old school, Washington and Lee. In 1879 he applied at the university for a position in ancient languages, but someone else got the job. However, David was so anxious to hire him

---

26   Baton Rouge *Capitolian*, January 10, 1880; Tom Boyd Diary, September 29, 1880.
27   David Boyd to Tom Boyd, January 25, 1880 in Thomas D. Boyd Papers.

that he persuaded the board to pay him $600 as assistant professor of modern languages and instructor in English, supplementing that amount with $400 from his own pocket. According to Tom Boyd there was much surprise among the faculty when Haislip's authorship became known. Professor McCulloch had seen the article in manuscript, and Lieutenant Jamar took it to Leon Jastremski. But everyone else claimed no knowledge of it prior to publication. Tom Boyd was not so sure. The mathematics professor, J. W. Nicholson, had been "sleeping with" Haislip, yet he professed to be "horrified"when the article appeared. He also declared that he would break with Haislip, "but didn't," Tom noted in his diary.[28]

The Haislip "bombshell" was carefully timed to burst just before the legislature convened in New Orleans with the result that David, who normally went to the city to lobby for the school, did not dare leave Baton Rouge and his several enemies in January, 1880. Instead, he sent Tom, whose resignation from the faculty had left him unemployed since the previous November. Besides overseeing the university appropriations bill in the legislature, Tom, David hoped, could influence Governor Wiltz to make favorable appointments to the vacancies on the board. He also wanted him to interview the officers of the Thirteenth Infantry, particularly Lieutenant Mumford. The Thirteenth was Jamar's old outfit and David needed ammunition to use against Jamar in February, 1880, when the board would meet to consider his appointment as commandant. David wanted Tom to see a Mr. Johnson in the United States Customhouse too. Mr. Johnson was in a position to let General Sherman and the secretary of war know how David had jeopardized himself and the school because he had tried to prevent "my Democratic people" [the board] from doing an injustice to a "Republican army officer [Mumford]." Jamar had to be recalled. "There will never be peace here, with *Jamar* here! *He must go.* And let our friends all unite in that purpose. Only how and when to get rid of him, must be the question."[29]

Despite his obsession with the Jamar struggle, David sensed more trouble brewing. "I can feel it in the air, as well as in my bones," he wrote Tom on January 27, 1880. He thought the state superintendent

28 Minutes of the Board of Supervisors, October 18, 1879; Tom Boyd Diary, September 29, 1880.
29 Tom Boyd to David Boyd, January 24, 1880, in Alphabetical File, Fleming Collection; David Boyd to Tom Boyd, January 25, 27, 28, 30, 1880, in Thomas D. Boyd Papers.

of public education, E. H. Fay, had become "prejudiced against us." Because the university charter gave the superintendent ex-officio membership on the Board of Supervisors, Fay's attitude could be important. David already had enough enemies in that body. Vice-President Williams, for example, was frankly hostile. David knew he conferred regularly with Lieutenant Jamar and other Boyd enemies. Another antagonist, E. H. Farrar, was also busily attacking David and the school. David asked Tom to visit Farrar. "Talk calmly and kindly with . . . [him]; tell him politely that it is impossible for him to know the real situation else his views would materially change." But if Farrar talked "violently and rudely" of David, he hoped Tom would "shut him up, *if you have to slap his face!*" It did not surprise David that people were beginning to complain about the school: "If I went out on the street, & hollered fire, I wd expect people to gather around my house, and holler fire too. And if Mr. Farrar and Mr. Williams etc. of the Board, and Mr. Haislip, McCulloch and Jamar of the Faculty, will go *outside*, and holler fire— cry down the University,—why the people must, (or will, at any rate) take them *at their word*, and abuse the school too! That is, the public clamor against our school comes from *within!*"[30]

What David "felt in his bones" in late January surfaced in the Louisiana senate a few days later. On February 5, 1880, a bill to "reorganize the L. State University & A & M" appeared in the upper chamber. Its sponsor was Senator W. B. Leake, chairman of the senate committee on public education, and the same man with whom David had waged a public battle the year before during the constitutional convention. After its introduction Tom Boyd spent all his time trying to block, or at least stall, the passage of Senator Leake's measure. He sent David a summary of it as soon as he had a chance to read it. The bill that finally passed the senate on March 11, 1880, was a substitute, but it included the main elements of Leake's original measure. It also incorporated most of the changes suggested in Haislip's "bombshell" article of January 10. Essentially, the Leake bill would (1) change the school's name; (2) change the composition of the board by requiring three of the fifteen members to be residents of Baton Rouge, but dropping the provision which required three alumni members; (3) repose the entire management and control of the university in the faculty; (4) give the

30   David Boyd to Tom Boyd, January 25, 27, 30, February 1, 1880, in Thomas D. Boyd Papers.

faculty the power to nominate a president whom the board would appoint; (5) require the president to be one of the department heads; (6) stipulate that a new president be nominated and appointed every four years; (7) establish "military discipline" but require it to be subordinate to the "literary" departments; (8) organize three departments: a preparatory department and two others which Tom could not remember, but one of which "struck me as ridiculous"; (9) repeal David's merger act of 1877; and finally (10) make the new law effective October 1, 1880.[31]

David's first reaction was characteristic; he would seek total war, not compromise or reconciliation. "I shall insist," he answered his brother, "now that these people up here have begun the fight—on everything being sifted to the bottom. Let the question of *Union* of the two schools be gone over again. Then, if it is thought best to separate the two, let the A. & M. College go to Chalmette . . . and ours back to Rapides. If Baton Rouge is so short-sighted as to make war on us, then let B. R. take the consequences—lose both schools."[32] But the war had to be postponed briefly so that David and the cadet corps could participate in Fete Day, or Mardi Gras, which occurred on February 10, 1880. The cadets returned to Baton Rouge next day. David, however, remained to attend the special session of the board, which lasted for the rest of the week. As already described, Lieutenant Jamar refused the post of commandant at the February session, and the board authorized David to ask the War Department for his recall if the two could not work in harmony. Other topics dealt with by the board included the Leake bill introduced only a few days ealier. G. Mason Graham presented his colleagues with a detailed argument against it, praising David's energy, perseverence, and zeal and declaring that the school owed its very existence to the "self-sacrificing devotion of *Col. Boyd.*" If the university were left alone, he continued, it might survive and prosper, but no consideration of "party," either personal or political, should be allowed to disturb its growth. Change of any kind was disturbing; political interference would spell disaster. Graham proceeded to summarize the institution's history. In twenty years, he pointed out, its name changed three times. From a "seminary" it had become a uni-

31 Tom Boyd to David Boyd, February 6, 1880, in Alphabetical File, Fleming Collection; Tom Boyd Diary, September 29, 1880; Louisiana *Senate Journal*, Regular session, 1880, p. 72, 203.
32 David Boyd to Tom Boyd, February 6, 1880, in Thomas D. Boyd Papers.

versity, "of which it does not possess one single attribute proper and will be most fortunate if, in this vast country, it shall have earned the title in a hundred years to come." Finally, General Graham delivered a strong argument in favor of retaining the school's military character and its strong executive control. A "diffusion of power" among the faculty would be fatal to the institution. Therefore he urged his colleagues to "deprecate" that part of the Leake bill which, he felt, was not only unnecessary, but if enacted, would have a "baleful" effect on the university's future. The board minutes do not record how each man voted, but a majority of those present supported a resolution opposing passage of the Leake bill as "unwise," and in favor of the sentiments expressed by Graham.[33]

Whether a majority of the legislature felt the same way remained to be seen. Tom Boyd, who had been in New Orleans almost a month by mid-February, thought David ought to return to the city if only to answer some of the lawmakers' questions and to protect the appropriations bill which still reposed in committee. Besides, he had heard that a Mr. Atkins had introduced a resolution in the house to examine the university books. Atkins wanted to determine if the agricultural fund had been "misapplied," that is, employed by the "literary" departments. David intended to go to New Orleans on February 23, but he had to change his plans. Affairs in Baton Rouge, he wrote Tom, were "a mess"; McCulloch, Haislip, and Jamar were "in an ugly mood," and the cadets, too, appeared to be demoralized. "I know the *risk*—possibly the loss of our appropriations, and more headway to Leake's bill; but if an outbreak shd occur here—while I might be away—that would effectually stop our progress before the Legislature."[34]

Part of the "mess" to which David referred was a memorial which Professor McCulloch was preparing to present to the legislature. McCulloch was so "embittered" against him and the board that David expected a very "severe" and "disrespectful" document. The memorial certainly was severe. It charged that the university's existing charter was so "imperfectly" framed that it could not possibly carry out the purpose of the federal government as intended in its laws establishing

---

33 David Boyd to Tom Boyd, February 14, 1880, *ibid.*, Minutes of the Board of Supervisors, February 11, 12, 13, 14, 1880.
34 Tom Boyd to David Boyd, February 19, 21, 1880, in Alphabetical File, Fleming Collection; David Boyd to Tom Boyd, February 20, 22, 1880, in Thomas D. Boyd Papers.

the seminary and agricultural funds. Specifically, McCulloch charged, the charter deprived the professors of all authority. Instead, the president exercised "indefinite and unlimited" control over all the financial, educational, and disciplinary affairs of the school. No man, "however great may be his ability," could discharge successfully such "mixed and incongruous duties." The result, according to Professor McCulloch, was (1) a "financially encumbered, if not hopelessly insolvent" institution; (2) a haphazard system of instruction wherein classes were taught in a "most irregular" manner and graduation was "rendered simply impracticable"; (3) an unjust disciplinary system, administered by one man, from whose decision there was no appeal; and (4) an absence of clearly defined rules and regulations for the government of cadets. McCulloch declared that the "facts" he presented in his memorial were well known and that most of his colleagues supported his views. Therefore he urged the legislators to reorganize the university as proposed in the bill sponsored by Senator Leake's Committee on Public Education.[35]

A few days after his memorial appeared, Professor McCulloch resigned from the university to spend the rest of the legislative session in New Orleans where he labored diligently for the passage of the Leake reorganization bill. David wrote Tom that McCulloch's resignation caused "scarcely a ripple in the school." However, it was noted by Leon Jastremski in his newspaper, who claimed that he did not want to become involved in the "disagreements and complaints" existing among the university faculty. But if the charter were responsible for the discord and "faulty organization" of the school, he hoped the legislature would amend and correct it "to the extent . . . that the services of such talented gentlemen as Prof. McCulloch . . . may be permanently secured to the college."[36]

McCulloch's memorial to the legislature was supplemented by a petition which grocer William Garig circulated among the leading citizens of Baton Rouge. Ultimately, it secured fifty-four signatures, among which were those of the parish priest, the Episcopal rector, the editor of the town's other newspaper, the principal of the local private

35 David Boyd to Tom Boyd, February 22, 1880, in Thomas D. Boyd Papers; Richard S. McCulloch, Petition, February 28, 1880, in Printed Materials, David Boyd Papers.
36 Tom Boyd Diary, December 29, 1880; David Boyd to Tom Boyd, March 2, 1880, in Thomas D. Boyd Papers; Baton Rouge *Capitolian*, March 6, 1880.

school, a leading physician, and a district judge. Later David learned that many persons signed the petition without reading it first. They were "tricked," he declared, "on the ruse" that he (David) favored the Leake bill. When they learned otherwise, they wrote the Baton Rouge senator Dr. T. D. Buffington to have their names removed from the document. *"Garig is truly one big dog,"* David wrote his brother on February 29. And Haislip, McCulloch, Jamar, and Dr. Williams were just as bad. None of them was honestly interested in reorganizing the school; they simply wanted to get rid of him. To "test their sincerity," David instructed Tom to get Senator R. H. Luckett of Rapides and "all our friends" to support a change in section one of Leake's bill, striking out Baton Rouge in favor of Alexandria as the school's permanent location. "Then see if Dr. Buffington and Co. have the same zeal in changing [the university's] organization."[37]

David's rebuttal to the Haislip article, the Leake bill, the McCulloch memorial, and the Garig petition appeard in several forms. In the senate R. H. Luckett led the debate against reorganization with ammunition fed to him by Tom Boyd and David himself. Leake's bill would change the nature of the school by altering its "military character," David wrote Senator Luckett. That would not do "in the city." It would also end the president's exclusive power over discipline, and he knew from experience that a division of disciplinary authority between the professors and the president would not work either. Some persons were trying to drive a wedge between him and Professor J. W. Nicholson by "harping" upon Nicholson's expressed opinion that the faculty's power should be increased and the president's reduced. But David denied any discord. He and Nicholson "pull[ed] perfectly together," even when they disagreed. Besides, David informed Luckett, Nicholson himself admitted that "when he ran his large academy, he took no advice from any, ran it himself, did all the discipline and his word was law."[38]

Another section of Leake's bill would revise the membership of the Board of Supervisors by requiring that three board members be appointed from Baton Rouge. David objected because it would make the

---

37 William Garig, Petition to the legislature from the citizens of Baton Rouge, February 26, 1880, in Official Papers, Fleming Collection; David Boyd to Tom Boyd, February 25, 29, March 4, 1880, in Thomas D. Boyd Papers.
38 David Boyd to Dr. R. L. Luckett, edited copy, February 25, March 6, 1880, in Boyd Letters, Fleming Collection.

university nothing more than "a tool of the locality, not a State school at all." Baton Rouge was the state capital. It already had plenty of representation on the board in the persons of the governor, the state superintendent of public education, the president of the faculty, and the vice-president of the Board of Supervisors. If any more evidence were needed, David suggested that Luckett cite another bill then pending before the legislature which sought to reduce, not augment, the hold of Baton Rouge over the asylum for the blind.[39]

As received by Dr. Luckett, David's letters were fairly moderate in tone largely because Tom Boyd carefully deleted the more offensive remarks before forwarding them to the lawmaker. For example, in his original draft David objected to having three men appointed to the board from Baton Rouge because "I assert without fear of contradiction, that there are not 3 men to be found in all this town of 8000 souls who are *eminently qualified*, by virtue and intelligence, to be supervisors of this state University!" For five years Vice-President Williams rode by the school every day, yet never paid it a visit. "And if Dr. Buffington, the present *senator*, or Kleinpeter, [the] Representative, have either of them put foot in the grounds in the last seven years," David was not aware of it. Even David realized his remarks were "very bitter." He authorized Tom to edit his letters if he thought them too "imprudent," but in David's opinion, the time for "mincing words" was past; "My best policy now is to fight with all my power."[40]

To counter the efforts of Garig and McCulloch, David deluged the legislature with petitions of his own. One favored the existing disciplinary system because it trained the cadets in "manly conduct." Another, signed by New Orleans alumni, opposed the Leake bill because too much change was bad, and still another, from a number of the university's principle creditors in Baton Rouge, testified to continuing faith in the institution and its management. Even the faculty and students were drawn in, the former disclaiming any desire to influence pending legislation and the latter dismissing as nonsense all rumors to

---

39   David Boyd to R. L. Luckett, February 25, 1880, *ibid.*
40   *Ibid.*; David Boyd to Tom Boyd, February 25, 1880, in Thomas D. Boyd Papers. David was not above scandalmongering if it would save the university. He asked Tom to tell Senator Luckett "fully about Garig—his animus, his character etc. . . . Mention his coming to the Cath.[olic] Ladies Fair in B.R. in '73 with a *negro* strumpet on his arm, insisting that white ladies shd wait on him & her, was put out by Father Delacroix, and fined next day $25.00 by Mayor Schorten!" David Boyd to Tom Boyd, March 7, 1880, in Thomas D. Boyd Papers.

the effect that many cadets would resign if the president's power were not reduced. When all else failed, David appealed personally to Lieutenant Governor McEnery for a postponement of final action on the Leake bill until a joint committee could investigate the university. But the senators were adamant. On March 11, 1880, they voted twenty-one to ten to reorganize the school.[41]

With only minor variations in tactics, David moved to block the Leake bill in the house. But this time Tom Boyd had help from Dr. Pendleton King, professor of natural history at the university, and several former cadets who lived in New Orleans. David sent them orders on March 14, 1880, to appear before the house education committee and to do everything possible to delay action. Considering the "unscrupulous opposition," he thought such efforts "perfectly permissible." In no case should Tom make any concessions. The reorganization bill, David reminded his brother, was directed against him personally by:

Garig—because I quit dealing with him in October last. He then said he wld do all he cld to keep cadets from coming here . . . *McCulloch* because his salary was cut down. *Haislip* because after trying to break McCulloch down in my estimation—saying he was an *impractical* man, and asking me for McCulloch's classes, and being refused—then he tries another way, to get a full Professorship, by breaking down this organization and me. Jamar—because he has been disappointed in his hopes and aspirations—of getting the Commandant's place. . . . I do not wish nor can I afford any compromise or concession.[42]

Meanwhile, the senate responded to David's suggestion that a joint committee of the legislature be chosen to investigate the university. Now the plan was to prevent the house committee on public education from reporting the Leake bill favorably until the joint investigating committee could visit the school. If possible, Tom and King were to try to delay the investigating committee's visit to Baton Rouge until the weekend of Friday, April 2, 1880. The cadets had a hop scheduled that

41 Citizens of Baton Rouge, Petition Against Reorganizing University, February 28, March 4, 1880; Ex-cadets from New Orleans, Petition, March 1, 1880; Creditors of University, Petition, March 6, 1880; Resolution of University Faculty, March 5, 1880; Cadets of the University, Petition, March [?], 1880, in Official Papers, Fleming Collection; David Boyd to S. D. McEnery, March 10, 1880, in Boyd Letters, *ibid.*; David Boyd to Tom Boyd, telegram, March 6, 1880, in Thomas D. Boyd Papers; Louisiana *Senate Journal*, Regular session, March 1, 1880, p. 203.
42 David Boyd to Tom Boyd, March 14, 1880, in Boyd Letters, Fleming Collection.

night, and the Board of Supervisors would convene the following Monday. If the committee came then, David thought, the school would appear in its best light, their enemies in Baton Rouge would not be as effective, and above all, they would gain valuable time. However, Tom must not let it appear that they were trying in any way to discourage an investigation. After all, David had asked for it.[43]

Tom and Professor King did their best, but by the end of March the house education committee seemed determined to recommend passage of the senate bill. If it did, David's friends in the house would charge bad faith, arguing that there had been no investigation of the university, and a "fair one" could not possibly take place before the session closed. A filibuster could also prevent the house from taking action. But just in case, David urged Tom to "secure the Republican vote . . . [it] may turn the scales." In the end, the Louisiana lottery, not the Republicans, gave David his victory. A measure affecting lottery interests came before the house during the last few days of the session. It generated so much debate that the Leake bill, recommended for passage on March 29, failed to be called up before adjournment on April 10.[44]

Pendleton King urged David to "be moderate" in his jubilation, but the latter had very little reason to celebrate. Even before the legislature adjourned, David learned from his friend General Brent that Governor Wiltz planned "wholesale" changes in the board. "This," Tom Boyd noted in his diary, "was a new danger from a rather unexpected quarter." David could hardly have been completely surprised. He knew the governor and Lieutenant Jamar were friends. "I think he is a good officer," Wiltz wrote David in February, 1880, "and would like to have him remain in our state."[45] Thus, board members like Brent, Graham, Egan, McCollum, and the alumni who supported David in his battles against Jamar were likely candidates for removal. David argued that only members whose terms had expired could "legally" be replaced.

---

43 Tom Boyd to David Boyd, March 13, 1880, Alphabetical File, *ibid.*; David Boyd to Tom Boyd, March 14, 1880, in Thomas D. Boyd Papers. The cadets advertised their hop as an "Autocracy Ball." It was a huge success.
44 Pendleton King to David Boyd, March 25, 1880, in David Boyd Papers; David Boyd to Tom Boyd, March [25], 26, 30, April 4, 1880, in Thomas D. Boyd Papers; Louisiana *House Journal*, Regular session, March 29, 1880, pp. 359–60.
45 Pendleton King to David Boyd, April 8, 1880, in David Boyd Papers; Tom Boyd Diary, September 29, 1880; Louis A. Wiltz to David Boyd, February 20, 1880, in Alphabetical File, Fleming Collection.

But Governor Wiltz held that all terms ended when the new constitution took effect in January, 1880. Therefore he could name a completely new board. In May, 1880, his selections were announced to the press. Besides himself, Superintendent of Public Education E. H. Fay, and David Boyd, ex-officio members, the new slate included Leon Jastremski of East Baton Rouge as vice-president, Dr. W. A. Robertson of St. Landry, T. L. Bayne, and John Dolhonde of Orleans, George S. Walton of Concordia, W. H. Pipes of East Feliciana, A. A. Gunby of Ouachita, F. W. Price of Jackson, R. T. Beauregard of Plaquemines, W. A. Strong of Winn, Dr. J. C. Egan of Caddo, and G. Mason Graham of Rapides. Of the old board, only Graham managed to keep his seat.[46]

A few days after Governor Wiltz made his appointments, David exercised a power granted to him by the old board. He asked the War Department to recall Lieutenant Jamar and replace him with another officer. He also asked General Sherman to do what he could to "effect the change." Sherman agreed, but the order instructing Lieutenant Jamar to rejoin his regiment in New Mexico did not reach Baton Rouge until June 27, 1880. Unfortunately for David, the first meeting of the Wiltz board occurred the next day. In Tom Boyd's opinion, Jamar's recall had more to do with its subsequent decision to fire David "than any of the reasons afterwards alleged."[47]

When Vice-President Leon Jastremski called the new board to order at twelve o'clock, Monday, June 28, 1880, only Messrs. Fay, Walton, Dolhonde, Graham, Gunby, and Boyd answered the roll. By Wednesday W. H. Pipes and R. T. Beauregard had taken their seats, giving the majority faction six, and the arrival of Will Strong increased David's strength to four. Other than the appointment of committees to investigate the "state of the college" and its current financial condition, the only substantive action taken during the first three days was the board's request to General Sherman that he "revoke the order requiring Jamar to rejoin his regiment." David and his partisans voted "nay."[48]

David still had four votes and his opponents six when the board convened at 1 P.M. on Thursday, July 1. But a change had clearly

46 David Boyd to Tom Boyd, undated, in Thomas D. Boyd Papers; Baton Rouge *Tri-Weekly Capitolian*, May 18, 1880; Fleming, *Louisiana State University*, 341.
47 Tom Boyd Diary, September 29, 1880; William T. Sherman to David Boyd, May 27, 1880, in William T. Sherman Letters, David F. Boyd Family Papers.
48 Minutes of the Board of Supervisors, June 28, 29, 30, 1880.

taken place. The official minutes, succinct as they are, reflect a quick-
ened pace in the board's deliberations and a more hostile attitude toward David on the part of the majority. The members began by in-
specting the university building, voting later to expend $1,200 to set
up a department of "practical" mechanics and another $1,200 for an
experimental farm. Adoption of a financial report that labeled the existing system of making disbursements "very bad" and "not businesslike"
came next, followed by receipt of a telegram from the adjutant general
of the United States. Addressed to acting governor S. D. McEnery, the
message stated, "The Secretary of War directs me to inform you that
Lieut. Jamar was relieved from duty at Louisiana University on application of the President, acting for Board of Supervisors, on recommendation of General Sherman, who desired Lieut. Jamar to accompany
his regiment to the field." [49] Finally, Colonel George Walton of Concordia presented a resolution which must have stunned David and his
supporters. After accusing the president of gross mismanagement, it
called for a complete reorganization of the university, vacated every
existing position, and urged the immediate election of a new president,
secretary and treasurer. Professorships could be filled later when the
board met in August. An attempt by David's friends to refer the motion
to a subcommittee went down to defeat, and shortly thereafter the
board recessed until eight o'clock in the evening. [50]

When it reconvened, it invited two professors, the acting commandant, three cadets, and one former cadet to testify. According to undated notes made later, David requested their testimony in "order to
ascertain the cause of the great falling off in cadets," which Walton's
resolution attributed to his mismanagement. Assuming that he, too,
would have an opportunity of being heard, David was upset when "no
such privilege was granted." In fact, he charged, a member told him
later that the majority would have preferred him to be absent. Exactly
what the witnesses said was not recorded, but it must have been absorbing. The session did not adjourn until one o'clock Friday morning. [51]

49 *Ibid.*, July 1, 1880; R. C. Drum to S. D. McEnery, telegram, June 29, 1880, in Baton Rouge
    Tri-Weekly Capitolian, July 6, 1880.
50 Minutes of the Board of Supervisors, July 1, 1880.
51 *Ibid.*, night session, July 1, 1880; [David Boyd] notes, undated, in Official Papers, Fleming
    Collection. Written in Tom Boyd's hand but obviously dictated by David, the notes appear to
    be a reply to an editorial by Leon Jastremski in the *Tri-Weekly Capitolian*, July 13, 1880.
    They may have been drafted as a letter to the editor, but Jastremski's paper did not carry any
    communication based on them during July or August of 1880.

When the board convened for its fifth and final session on July 2, 1880, everyone was present except David and G. Mason Graham. Graham was ill, and David, who had to prepare for commencement ceremonies, was excused "on account of business." Colonel Walton began by calling up his resolution to reorganize the university, whereupon Gunby and Strong again tried to have it referred to a committee, and again the majority voted them down. Then Gunby tried another tack. He moved that the resolution be tabled until August, when a "full meeting" could consider the proposal. That too was defeated by a strictly partisan vote. Meanwhile, a note arrived from G. Mason Graham, explaining his absence and protesting the Walton resolution. The majority acknowledged the note's receipt, but refused Graham's request that its contents be "spread upon the minutes." At that point Gunby and Strong rose. The "character" of Walton's resolution and the circumstances under which it was being considered were "*so* extraordinary," they charged, that they "could *not* sanction same" by their presence. They withdrew, reserving the right to file a protest later with the secretary.

Unhampered by any opposition, the six remaining members proceeded to adopt Walton's reorganization resolution, whereupon he proposed two more. First, he urged the governor to apply at once to the "proper authorities" for a cancellation of Lieutenant Jamar's orders. Next, he moved to condemn the action of Graham, Gunby, and Strong. By refusing to act with the board, Walton declared, they were "setting a dangerous precedent, one calcualted to bring about discord and cause irreparable injury to this Institution." Finally, Dolhonde moved to elect a president, secretary, and treasurer. W. H. Goodale kept his post as secretary, Harney Skolfield, described by Tom Boyd as a "ring Demo. politician," replaced "old Col. Markham" as treasurer, and Samuel H. Lockett, one of David's closest friends, won unanimous election to the presidency. Only one thing could save David now, the university charter. Under its terms, as few as five board members could transact university business, but such transactions had to be reviewed by at least eight members before they became binding. Therefore, by withdrawing from the final session on Friday, July 2, Graham, Gunby, and Strong guaranteed David more time and a chance to be heard by the entire board when it met again on August 4.[52]

For the next four weeks the board members and the partisans of each faction filled the public prints with protests and petitions. Almost every issue of Leon Jastremski's paper, whose name changed to the *Tri-Weekly Capitolian* sometime in May, 1880, contained editorials and letters relative to the reorganization of the university and the removal of David Boyd. On July 13 Jastremski printed the letters of protest and explanation submitted by Gunby, Graham, and Strong when they withdrew from the July 2 session of the board. In general, they concurred on three points: (1) that a newly appointed board, meeting for the first time, could hardly know enough about the university to act wisely; (2) that to vacate all offices without notice and without hearings was unprecedented and unfair; and (3) to have done so with only a bare quorum in attendance was an affront to board members who could not be present. "I am satisfied," Will Strong concluded, "that they [the absent members], like myself never dreamed of this change until the introduction of the resolution by Mr. Walton." [53]

Jastremski leaped to the majority's defense. On July 13, but more forcefully on July 20, 1880, he argued that four days of listening to minority arguments, explanations by Colonel Boyd, and testimony from faculty and cadets was more than enough to convince the board of the university's "completely unsuccessful management" which only a "thorough reorganization" could correct. But since David's partisans on the board and a group of New Orleans alumni publicly demanded a detailed explanation for the "gross injustice" done to "the man who signed our diplomas," Jastremski was willing to provide a bill of particulars. As evidence of poor financial management, he cited David's failure to provide a full financial statement at the July meeting when he must have known that unpaid faculty salaries, an $8,000 debt in the maintenance fund, and more than $5,000 expended for books and furniture without authorization would be subjects of interest to the newly named board.

Nor were the six supervisors who voted for David's removal the only critics of his administration. Cadets who testified at the July board

---

52 Minutes of the Board of Supervisors, July 2, 1880; Baton Rouge *Tri-Weekly Capitolian*, July 6, 1880; *Acts of Louisiana*, 1877, pp. 18–19; Tom Boyd Diary, September 29, 1880.

53 Baton Rouge *Tri-Weekly Capitolian*, July 13, 1880.

meeting complained about the food, thought the president imposed the rules arbitrarily, and protested the departure of Professors Mc-Culloch and Haislip and the recall of Lieutenant Jamar. "In a word," Jastremski concluded, "it was clearly shown to the Supervisors that he [David] was the ruler of everything."

The editor did not question David's integrity or his dedication; he had certainly worked to "keep up" the university. But how had he done it? Jastremski answered his own question. President Boyd had salvaged "the wreck" of the bankrupt institution in Baton Rouge by "breaking up" the agricultural and mechanical college in New Orleans. And what had been accomplished to justify the merger? The new school still offered nothing of consequence in the "agricultural and mechanical branches;" it was still "riddled with liabilities" and losing enrollment besides. Under the circumstances, Jastremski declared, "six practical men, having the interest of the State at heart," could come to only one conclusion: David Boyd, the "unfortunate General," had to be replaced.[54]

The same issue of the *Tri-Weekly Capitolian* that carried the alumni protest and Jastremski's rebuttal also contained a defense of David by his friend Willian Seay, editor of the Shreveport *Standard*. Seay noted that the majority, after vacating all professorships, filled only one: David's. "It is difficult to discover," Seay sneered, "which is the most prominent feature of this small piece of business, its malignity or its stupidity." Because only six men acted, their work was "a nullity." Besides, no one but a group who had "bitten themselves mad" would replace David with his best friend. Lockett would "suffer his right hand to be palsied" before he would become a party to "such nefarious work."[55]

While the newspaper war raged, David and his partisans were not idle. G. Mason Graham learned of a supreme court decision involving New Orleans flour inspectors which he thought might apply to the university board. In that case the court held that appointments to vacancies that occurred prior to legislative adjournments had to be confirmed by the senate in order to become effective. Therefore, if adoption of the new constitution gave Governor Wiltz the right to appoint a

---

54 *Ibid.*, July 13, 20, 1880; An article by Colonel George Walton, making essentially the same points as Jastremski's, appeared in the *Tri-Weekly Capitolian* for July 24, 1880.
55 William Seay, editorial in Shreveport *Standard*, quoted *ibid.*, July 20, 1880.

completely new university board, he should have named it and had it
confirmed before the senate adjourned in April, 1880. But he did not
act until the middle of May. The new board was not confirmed, and, if
the flour-inspector case were applicable, its acts could not be considered legal.

Lieutenant Governor McEnery was acting for Governor Wiltz in
July, 1880, when Graham heard about the supreme court's decision.
Graham wrote to him about it, asking him to invite the ten "ousted"
members of the old board to attend the Wiltz board's meeting scheduled for August 4. Then he sent David a copy of his letter to the governor. If McEnery did not act, Graham told David, some of the old members ought to go to court. Meanwhile, they must do everything in their
power to make sure all of their friends on the new board attended the
August meeting. Their six opponents would certainly be there and
they would not let David vote.[56]

Governor McEnery did not act, and all of David's friends did not attend the August meeting. However, several members of the old board
did institute a suit. Ironically, one of them, W. B. Egan, was attorney
general in the Wiltz administration and his brother, Dr. J. C. Egan,
was a member of the new board against which the suit was brought.
Even more interesting, Attorney General Egan served as one of the attorneys for the old board when the case went to court. And W. H.
Goodale, appointed secretary by the new board at its meeting in July,
joined several others as counsel for the defense. One can only speculate as to what constituted a conflict of interest in the legal ethics of
that day.[57]

The board met as scheduled on August 4, 1880. As Graham expected, the six who voted to remove David in July, Jastremski, Fay,
Walton, Beauregard, Pipes, and Dolhonde, attended *en masse*. David's
partisans did not. Graham, Gunby, Strong, and Price participated but
Dr. J. C. Egan and David himself did not appear. The new men, named
since the July meeting to replace two who had resigned, also took their
seats. H. L. Edwards, an alumnus, joined David's faction, giving it a
total of five votes, and E. C. Payne joined the opposition, increasing its

56 G. Mason Graham to S. D. McEnery, copy, July 15, 1880, G. Mason Graham to David Boyd,
     July 22, 1880, in G. Mason Graham Letters, Fleming Collection; Tom Boyd Diary, September
     29, 1880.
57 J. C. Egan to David Boyd, July 24, 1880, in Alphabetical File, Fleming Collection; Tom Boyd
     Diary, September 29, 1880; Fleming, *Louisiana State University*, 343.

strength to seven. Lieutenant Governor S. D. McEnery presided in the absence of Governor Wiltz, who was ill in Colorado.

McEnery showed the board a letter from Attorney General W. B. Egan announcing his intention to seek an injunction against those members of the new board whose appointments had not been confirmed by the senate. Hoping to keep the new board from acting in any way until the old board could test its legality in the courts, Egan directed his assistant, Andrew Herron of Baton Rouge, to secure the injunction from Judge H. Newton Sherburne of the Seventeenth District Court, but Herron was too late. By the time he reached Sherburne, then twenty-five miles away from Baton Rouge, the Jastremski faction had already contacted him through A. C. Calhoun, a mathematics instructor at the university. Sherburne refused to grant the injunction, but before hearing of his decision, the board, on motions by Jastremski and Walton, moved to employ counsel for defense against the old board's pending suit and to bond itself in case Herron did return with the injunction. Thus the new board could act while the question of its legality was still before the courts. To no one's surprise, both motions passed on strictly partisan votes.[58]

Other actions of the board during its August meeting were equally predictable. After a few efforts to distinguish between the words *approve* and *ratify*, the board voted, again along party lines, to ratify the Walton resolution to reorganize the university. Additional business included the appointment of several professors and the adoption of new regulations concerned with the boarding and lodging of cadets. The university presidency, which David would hold until October 1, 1880, also came before the board. Colonel Samuel Lockett, chosen to fill it by unanimous vote in July, declined the honor "for personal and private considerations," whereupon the board opened communications with William Preston Johnston, the son of General Albert Sydney Johnston. A graduate of Yale University, William Preston Johnston served on Jefferson Davis's personal staff during the war. Later he taught English literature for several years at Washington College in Lexington, Virginia. In 1878 he published a biography of his famous father, which, together with Louisiana family connections, brought him to the uni-

---

58 Minutes of the Board of Supervisors, August 4, 1880; Tom Boyd Diary, September 29, 1880; Fleming, *Louisiana State University*, 343.

versity board's attention in 1880. Meanwhile, Vice-President Jastremski moved that J. W. Nicholson, the mathematics professor, be notified to come at once to Baton Rouge. There he was to perform whatever duties David found "too onerous" to perform himself.

Jastremski was clearly annoyed with David. For one thing, the ousted treasurer, William Markham, refused to surrender the university books and papers to his replacement, Harney Skolfield. For another, David failed to furnish the Permanent Committee of Finance, of which Jastremski was chairman, the information it had been asking for since the previous July. On August 6, therefore, Jastremski presented a resolution which would have made J. W. Nicholson temporary president of the faculty. David had abandoned his responsibilities, Jastremski charged, by boycotting board meetings, by failing to submit reports to the finance committee, and by questioning the board's validity in court. Friends managed to block Jastremski's efforts to replace him as president, but another proposal sponsored by the vice-president severely curtailed David's powers by awarding control over the university boarding department to a committee of the Board of Suprevisors. After some additional haggling, which followed partisan lines, the board adjourned until October, 1880.[59]

A few days after adjournment Jastremski commented on the board session in his newspaper. Despite the "bitter denunciations" leveled against him and his colleagues in July, Jastremski declared, the course they charted then had been "duly sustained" by a vote of seven to five in August. He praised the majority for its "conscientious attention" to the school's interests, recounted what steps had been taken to reform the organization, fees, and faculty of the institution, and announced that henceforth all fees would be payable in advance. All that remained, Jastremski concluded, was for the citizens to give the new administration a "fair trial."[60]

In the most literal sense the new administration was already on trial. G. Mason Graham, W. B. Egan, T. L. Grimes, J. G. Deslattes, M. A. Strickland, J. L. Brent, R. A. Ryland, and David Boyd, all mem-

---

59 Minutes of the Board of Supervisors, August 4, 5, 6, 1880; Baton Rouge *Tri-Weekly Capitolian*, August 5, 10, 1880; Fleming, *Louisiana State University*, 381–82; Arthur Marvin Shaw, *William Preston Johnston: A Transitional Figure of the Confederacy* (Baton Rouge, 1943), 157, 161–62.
60 Baton Rouge *Tri-Weekly Capitolian*, August 12, 1880.

bers of the old board, brought suit against Jastremski and his colleagues on the new board sometime during July, 1880. Their action, designed to test the new board's legality, was still pending in the Seventeenth District Court when attorney General W. B. Egan sought his injunction in August. As already described, Judge H. Newton Sherburne refused to grant the injunction. Sometime later he also upheld the legality of the new board, whereupon Graham and the other members of the old board appealed to the Louisiana Supreme Court.[61]

Meanwhile, David still thought of himself as president of the university. Others disagreed. When the board convened on October 4, 1880, for its regular fall session, George Walton moved that the board invite "Mr. D. F. Boyd" to appear before it in order that he might state his grievances, "with the view of having same removed if possible." The board assured "Mr. Boyd" that his appearance would not constitute any recognition by him of the board's legality. David accepted the invitation, but no meeting of minds seems to have occurred. A resolution adopted the following day declared: "Whereas Col. D. F. Boyd, the late Pres. of this institution is now *functus officio* [out of office] by resolution of this Bd . . . and neglects to turn over to said board the property belonging to said institution, therefore be it resolved that the Vice Pres., Leon Jastremski is fully authorized to make an amicable demand upon Boyd for the rendition of his accounts as president and to demand the turn over of all property of the Institution and to further demand that Boyd cease & desist from obstructing the Bd. . . . And in the event of refusal by Boyd to accede in whole or in part, then Leon Jastremski is authorized to take *any legal action* necessary."[62]

Next the board moved to elect a president. On the first two ballots three votes went to William Preston Johnston, two to Dabney H. Maury, and one to David Boyd. On the third, however, David's only champion, H. L. Edwards, cast a blank ballot, and Johnston defeated Maury four to one. Notified by telegram, Johnston accepted the position at once. Tom Boyd and S. M. Robertson, whom David had nominated as "acting professors" in September, were also appointed to the faculty by the board. A. A. Gunby registered shock when he learned they intended to

61 Tom Boyd Diary, September 29, 1880; Brief of Appeal to the Supreme Court of Louisiana by G. Mason Graham *et al versus* Leon Jastremski *et als*, undated, in Printed Materials, David Boyd Papers.
62 Minutes of the Board of Supervisors, October 5, 1880.

serve the new administration. "I was much surprised," he wrote David, "at the course pursued by [S. M.] Robertson & T. D. Boyd in accepting positions from your destroyers. There is something in my constitution or environment that precludes me from shaking hands 'across a bloody chasm.'"[63]

David, however, was not a "vengeful" man. He advised Robertson and Tom to ask the new board for jobs, and although he declared his intention to act as president until prevented by "legal process," he did not balk when Vice-President Jastremski obtained a court order to accomplish that very end. On October 7, 1880, Judge H. N. Sherburne enjoined David from interfering in any way with the Board of Supervisors and its management of the university. David acquiesced. Pending the outcome of the old board's appeal to the supreme court, David did everything in his power to encourage good order among the cadets and to organize the university's accounts in case the appeal proved unsuccessful. If he had not, Tom Boyd commented, few cadets would have been present to greet President Johnston when he arrived in November.[64]

The Louisiana Supreme Court heard the old board's appeal sometime during the winter of 1880–1881. Instead of rendering a verdict, it dismissed the case on a technicality. Because the suit involved a contest for public office to which "no salary or pecuniary perquisite" was attached, the court refused to exercise jurisdiction. For David and his family, a "pecuniary interest" certainly was involved. They were so poor in late 1880 that David could not afford fare to New Orleans to hear the case argued. Then, as if his cup were not bitter enough, he learned from General Sherman that Lieutenant M. F. Jamar had been reassigned to the university at the request of Governor Wiltz and the Board of Supervisors. In January, 1881, Jamar arrived to resume his duties as instructor of military tactics. This time, however, he also became commandant, the post David fought so hard to deny him over a year before. In what amounted to a letter of condolence, Sherman exhorted David to leave Louisiana. He had hoped, when the war ended,

63   *Ibid.*, October 4, 5, 1880; David Boyd to Thomas Boyd, September 30, 1880, in Thomas D. Boyd Papers; A. A. Gunby to D. F. Boyd, October 17, 1880, in David Boyd Papers.
64   Tom Boyd Diary, November 22, 1885; G. Mason Graham to David Boyd, October 4, [?]; H. N. Sherburne, Injunction against David Boyd, October 7, 1880, in Official Papers, Fleming Collection.

that Louisiana would "shake off the shackles of party" and rise to the dignity of a "modern state." But it had not happened. Would David "still cling to the wreck and go down with it?" Sherman hoped not. "Look over the new census tables," he urged David, "and see where flows the strongest part of new life. Get into it [the current] and keep in it, and it may [yet] land you and yours in a better place. You can hardly get into a worse."[65]

The long and bitter struggle waged in the spring and summer of 1880 was by no means the first battle David had fought. But it was the most intense and it ended in his defeat. It also revealed in stark outlines some of the more striking aspects of his personality. First and foremost, David was a man incapable of guile, dissimulation, circumspection, and even tact. If any quality in his character stood out above all others, it was his almost obsessive need to express what he regarded as the truth. This trait, coupled with his capacity for invective and sarcasm, managed to attract many enemies during his long career. But if he detected anything corrupt, dishonest, or self-serving in the action of anyone, particularly if it might bring harm to the university, nothing could stop him from pointing it out. As Professor Nicholson put it years later, David was not an "artful planner." When he thought he was right, he forged ahead, "little thinking of or caring for the exposure of his plan to the enemy, and little calculating how much might be gained . . . by 'going around a mountain rather than through it.'"[66]

Under the circumstances it is just as well that David did not shrink from combat or controversy. He did issue and receive several challenges during the course of his career, although none ever went beyond the letter-writing stage. As for controversy, his friends thought he could not exist happily without it. Colonel Lockett once accused him of getting into battles just to see if he could win, and David himself thought he did his best work when under attack. But even when his fights were deadly serious, David did not bear a grudge. McCulloch

---

65 Mary Bell Huff, "A Legal History of Louisiana State University and Agricultural and Mechanical College" (M.A. thesis, Louisiana State University, 1935), 68; Tom Boyd Diary, November 22, 1885; Fleming, *Louisiana State University*, 344; David Boyd to J. D. Kenton, November 27, 1880, W. T. Sherman to David Boyd, telegram, November 23, 1880, in David Boyd Papers; W. T. Sherman to D. F. Boyd, December 2, 1880, in William T. Sherman Letters, David F. Boyd Family Papers.
66 J. W. Nicholson, Remarks on the first anniversary of David Boyd's death, May 27, 1900, in David Boyd Papers.

and Jamar, for example, later became his friends, and at least one board member who voted to fire him in 1880 later admitted his regret.[67]

Just as prominent in David's character as his devotion to the truth and his need to tell it was his highly developed sense of duty. Duty, David taught his students, was the most noble word in the language. It was the most valuable quality they could develop. If they learned nothing else in four years at the university, their education would be worth the cost. The boys did not always agree while they were still undergraduates. But years later they appreciated David's training, and they loved and admired him for practicing what he preached. The fact is that David set higher standards for himself than anyone else. His friends thought they were impossible. They remonstrated with him to leave the university when its survival seemed unlikely. But he would not "leave his post" until forced out as he was in 1880.

Other aspects of David's character that should be mentioned were his broadness of view, his inability to count costs, and his impatience with those who would not or could not share his vision of what a university ought to be. As the merger law he composed indicates, David believed in educating the whole man: his mind, his body, and his spirit. To that end he spent sizable amounts on paintings, books, exhibits, and experimental programs. David thought it was well worth the cost, but critics accused him of extravagance and bad judgment. None, however, could fault his honesty, whatever they thought of his administrative skills or his educational priorities.

David's inability to share power with his colleagues and to defer to his superiors is also worth noting. He was a strong personality who believed in strong executive leadership in university organization. As a result, he made sure that his merger law incorporated provisions that limited the professors to classroom teaching and allowed the president a free hand in shaping policy. No doubt General Sherman's ideas and David's own experience under an inactive board convinced him that such a system worked best. No doubt, too, the limited enrollment and faculty of the university before 1900 contributed to such concentration of authority in the person of the president. But it is also true that David liked power for itself. He bragged about his willingness to assume the board's responsibility when the institution's needs seemed to require

67   R. T. Beauregard to David Boyd, May 25, 1897, in Thomas Boyd Papers.

it, and he once refused to run a boarding school unless he could control it absolutely. By 1880, however, the board was no longer inactive, and many of David's colleagues had grown restive under one-man rule. Not only his enemies, but some of his friends, too, thought he should relinquish some of his powers to the rest of the faculty.

Finally, the very traits in David's character that enabled him to save the university after 1865 seemed to interfere with his ability to run it successfully in 1880. For fifteen years he battled doggedly and alone against every threat to the institution's existence. Nothing could distract him from his self-imposed mission. But by 1877 the major battles had been won. Native whites controlled the legislature; the agricultural fund guaranteed the school a small but regular income; and David's proudest achievement, the act of merger, provided a legal foundation for the future development of a truly comprehensive university. What the school needed in 1880, therefore, was a competent manager, not a dedicated gladiator; someone who could operate within the meager budget and in harmony with an activist board. Unfortunately, David could not accommodate to the changed conditions. He had run the university alone for so long that he could not accept a subordinate role gracefully. Worse, he mistrusted the motives of his critics, and he equated their efforts to check his authority with assaults on the institution itself. In sum, David identified so completely with the university that he could not distinguish between its existence and his own. Indeed, he had no existence separate from the university, and therein lies the tragedy. By 1880 the school could stand alone, but David could not. The rest of his life was mute testimony to that fact.

Chapter X

Exile

ON FEBRUARY 5, 1881, David formally surrendered most of the university property in his possession to Vice-President Jastremski. The rest, including his claims against the school, was turned over in time for a special board meeting in New Orleans on February 25. By that time Treasurer Harney Skolfield had examined David's accounts, but some members were unwilling to act on his report until the finance committee or a hired "expert" certified its accuracy. In the end the board voted to postpone action until its regular session in April.

Meanwhile, David hired his own "experts," S. L. Guyol of St. James Parish and George Henderson of Baton Rouge. Guyol had been David's clerk before 1877 and was familiar with his record-keeping technique. Every cent received and disbursed was properly accounted for, Guyol reported to G. Mason Graham, and the only discrepancy could easily be repaired if Graham would submit an outstanding travel voucher. David wanted Guyol to attend the April board meeting to present his findings, but the former clerk could not leave his business. However, he did advise David to remove his private correspondence from university files. "Bundle up your things and leave that bldg. as soon as your acct's are turned over," Guyol urged. "Never sacrifice *yourself* and your *family* and your *friends* for another public institution. You'll never get any thanks for it, you'll lose your friends and most people will call you a fool. You have done more for the University than any man will ever do . . . and where are you today? Kicked out like a dog!"[1]

When the board met in April, Harney Skolfield verified Guyol's findings in every respect. He also reported that the university's endowment and cadet maintenance funds owed David more than $5,000, money he had advanced from his own pocket to pay employees' salaries, freight and travel expenses, equipment purchased for laboratory and library, and the claims of some creditors. Nevertheless, the finance committee disallowed more than $1,500 of David's claim, charging that some of the expenditures were unauthorized and others exceeded the amounts budgeted. The committee did recommend the return of several pieces of furniture belonging to David, and it did agree to pay him $1,000 in back salary. But it refused to assume responsibility for a $1,300 personal note which David negotiated to pay for an expensive painting of Robert E. Lee and Thomas (Stonewall) Jackson. Known as the Julio painting (after the artist), it had been commissioned some years before on the understanding that it would be paid for by "friends" of the university. But the friends subscribed less than a third of its cost and to "save it for the University" David gave the artist's agent his personal note for the balance ($1,300). In a letter to the finance committee he explained, "I would gladly pay the notes and let the picture remain in the University, but that seems impossible. So my last chance to save the picture for the school is a faint hope that your honorable body can in some way satisfy the executor's claim." Instead, the committee advised the board to return the painting whenever its owners appeared to claim it. Somehow, David managed to retire the note and make the university a gift of the controversial art work. This time the board was more receptive. On July 4, 1881, they accepted the Julio painting for the school "with thanks."[2] The painting, now regarded as one of the university's most valued, hangs in the foyer of the Thomas Boyd Administration Building.

To David the board's refusal to pay him the full amount claimed was like adding insult to injury. On May 14, 1881, in a bitter letter to alumni and former cadets he reviewed the main points in what he

1   Minutes of the Board of Supervisors, February 25, 26, 1881; S. L. Guyol to G. Mason Graham, April 2, 1881, in Alphabetical File, Fleming Collection; S. L. Guyol to David Boyd, April 2, 1881, in David Boyd Papers.
2   David Boyd to Board of Supervisors, copy, April 4, 1881, in Thomas D. Boyd Papers; Minutes of the Board of Supervisors, April 4, 5, July 4, 1881; Baton Rouge *Tri-Weekly Capitolian*, April 5, 1881.

scorned as the "so-called reorganization of the University." Its sole object, David declared, had been to get rid of him, not to alter the institution in any significant respect. The instigators were Lieutenant Jamar and his friends; some disgruntled professors whose salaries had been cut, and the "little clique or ring" that wanted to run Baton Rouge for its own political and pecuniary aggrandizement. Unable to admit the "real" reason for his removal, they had to resort to a series of "pretexts," indicting him for a decline in enrollment, failure to keep his accounts up to date and violating board policy by extending credit. "But if I was a failure with 70 cadets on my roll," David demanded, "what are they, this new Board who have today but [56]?" As for the charge that his books were in arrears, David answered that he used to do the work of "three or four . . . with the pay of only one." The new president, on the other hand, "keeps not a Book, nor makes a figure of account." Finally, if the extension of credit constituted a "crime," the new board was guilty of it too. In spite of its own rule requiring payment in advance, it had been granting credit to cadets from the beginning of its tenure.[3]

Even more indicative of David's dissatisfaction with the board's disposition of his case was a letter he sent to the editor of the New Orleans *Democrat* on April 27, 1881. Because the board had not published Harney Skolfield's report on the condition of his accounts, David thought the *Democrat* should have a copy, together with the letters and reports of the two other "experts," George Henderson and S. L. Guyol, on the same topic. All three, he pointed out, found his records to be correct. David also sent the *Democrat* summaries of the assets and liabilities of the endowment and cadet maintenance funds. Both, he noted, showed credit balances. This, too, was not clear in the board's published account of its April meeting. David had not attended that meeting, but "unofficially," he learned that several objections had been raised to repaying him all the money he had spent from his own pocket in behalf of the university. If the board ever informed him "officially" of the reasons for its objections, he might "deem it worthwhile to show the public, if not the new Board," that its objections were "not well-founded." Meanwhile, what the Board *had* printed about his claims, he considered purposely misleading. "A singular fatality has attended the published proceedings of this new Board of Supervisors in

<hr>

3   David Boyd to Alumni and Ex-Cadets of the University, May 14, 1881, in Official Papers, Fleming Collection.

nearly everything relating to me," he complained. "If anything, it would seem, could be omitted, or committed to the disadvantage, detriment or injury of me, such disparagement or misrepresentation was almost sure to be."[4]

David's struggle to have his presidency of the university fairly evaluated continued for months after his letter to the New Orleans *Democrat*. But in the summer of 1881 he had more compelling challenges to confront. Ettie was expecting their seventh child, and how long he would be able to pay the twenty-five dollars a month for their rented house was a serious question. G. Mason Graham, custodian of the old seminary property in Rapides, offered to let the Boyds live in one of the unoccupied professor's cottages on the seminary grounds. But the board's decision in April, 1881, to pay part of David's claim against the university, and a sheriff's sale of a house from a bankrupt estate the following June kept the family in Baton Rouge. David, however, had to go elsewhere to find a job.[5]

For awhile he considered taking some kind of work not related to education. A Louisiana congressman offered him a position as clerk of a congressional committee concerned with levees and other improvements planned for the Mississippi River. Colonel Lockett thought he should apply for an engineering job on the same project, but General Sherman advised him to avoid government service altogether. "Everyone," he told David, came to Washington looking for a job and then barely managed to "eke out" a living. Besides, even those who found good positions often lost them four years later.[6]

Sherman's advice must have convinced David. By June, 1881, he was again looking for employment in the only area he knew: education. The presidency of the University of West Virginia was vacant, and David, who learned of it rather late, made a serious effort to get the job. He asked several prominent people for letters of recommendation,

4   David Boyd to Editor, New Orleans *Democrat*, May 15, 1881, in Scrapbook, David Boyd Papers.
5   G. Mason Graham to David F. Boyd, March 11, 1881, in G. Mason Graham Letters, Fleming Collection; Baton Rouge *Tri-Weekly Capitolian*, June 25, 1881; David Boyd, Account Book entry, June 25, 1881; Ettie Boyd to Mamie [Mary C.] Wright, August 6, 1881, in David Boyd Papers.
6   E. W. Robertson to D. F. Boyd, telegram, December 16, 1880, in David Boyd Papers; S. H. Lockett to David Boyd, May 9, 1881, in Alphabetical File, Fleming Collection; W. T. Sherman to David Boyd, May 13, 1881, in William T. Sherman Letters, David F. Boyd Family Papers.

including Governor Wiltz of Louisiana, General Sherman, and John Eaton of the United States Bureau of Education. But the Board of Trustees of West Virginia chose to retain the acting president, and David decided not to seek a vacant professorship there although Sherman and Colonel Lockett both thought he should.[7]

Instead, David carried out plans first drafted in 1876. He returned to Virginia to run a boarding school for boys preparing to enter the University of Virginia. On May 22, 1881, F. H. Smith of the Virginia Military Institute informed him of facilities available in Madison County, Virginia. Known as Locust Dale Academy, the property was owned by a Mrs. Gordon whose husband operated it until his death a few months earlier. Gordon, a Yankee, had run Locust Dale successfully for thirty years according to R. J. Hancock, David's former pupil who lived in Albemarle County. Hancock was sure David could succeed there too. He knew the school through a friend and offered to visit it for David in an effort to get the best possible terms.

By July, 1881, David had made up his mind. Hancock was delighted. He urged him to hire the two men then teaching at the school; both had "good reputations" and would no doubt be able to convince most of the Virginia boys to stay on. They accepted David's offer and he hired two others. One, J. T. Bringier of Louisiana, had formerly attended the university when David was president. He replaced Tom Boyd as commandant after Lieutenant Jamar refused the post in 1880.[8]

Lieutenant Jamar, incidentally, whose recall to active duty David had obtained in June, 1880, and whose return to Baton Rouge the board managed to arrange six months later, received orders to leave the university again in July, 1881. Only the day before those orders arrived, President William Preston Johnston had praised Jamar in the most extravagant terms as practically indispensable to the university's good order. Noting that Jamar's recall caused "weeping and wailing and gnashing of teeth," Tom Boyd insisted that "this time, Col. Boyd

---

7   R. G. Ferguson to D. F. Boyd, May 31, 1881, Louis A. Wiltz to Governor H. M. Matthews of West Virginia, June 2, 1881, John Eaton to David Boyd, June 4, 1881, S. H. Lockett, to D. F. Boyd, June 2, 1881, all in David Boyd Papers; W. T. Sherman to D. F. Boyd, June 2, 1881, in William T. Sherman Letters, David F. Boyd Family Papers.

8   F. H. Smith to D. F. Boyd, May 22, 1881, R. J. Hancock to D. F. Boyd, June 8, 30, July 7, 1881, Larkin Willis to D. F. Boyd, July 12, 1881, all in David Boyd Papers; *Prospectus* of Locust Dale Academy, 1881–82, in Printed Materials, *ibid.*

had nothing whatever to do with the matter, though of course, it was attributed solely to him."[9]

David left Baton Rouge for Locust Dale in August, 1881. Thirteen months later he moved again, this time to Greenwood, only a few miles away from the University of Virginia at Charlottesville. Neither location proved very successful, partly because David could not break a bad habit. Only a week after he left Louisiana, G. Mason Graham had written: "I have but one piece of advice to volunteer. . . . Let it be a Mede and Persian law to you that *you credit noone, no matter who,* or where from. If you once deviate from this rule, yr. balance will always be on the wrong side of the sheet."[10] But Graham's advice had little effect. Even before his departure for Virginia, David advertised in several Louisiana papers that he would educate a number of Louisiana boys "*free* on their *promise* to pay." It was precisely this sort of "indulgence" which the university board charged against David when it fired him in 1880 and which his successor, William Preston Johnston, claimed to have stopped within a year of his accession to the presidency.[11]

Operating his boarding school on a credit basis was one reason for David's lack of success; another was his failure to stay on the job. A survey of his correspondence during the two years spent in Virginia indicates that he was absent some 248 days out of 737. Even generous allowances for Christmas holidays and summer vacations could not account for such a poor record, and in time, strangers, relatives, and close friends made reproving comments about his frequent trips away from the state. Charlie Boyd heard rumors far away in Wytheville about David's prolonged absences, and R. J. Hancock, who often loaned him money to meet his commitments, criticized him for seeking new pupils from "Charleston to Galveston." Instead, Hancock thought, David ought to cultivate Virginians. Outside the state he might better rely on newspaper advertising. "A short card in all these papers will not cost half as much as your traveling expenses . . . and would meet the eyes of *100,000* people—*Don't you see?*" implored Hancock.[12]

9   Minutes of the Board of Supervisors, July 1, 2, 1881; Tom Boyd Diary, November 22, 1885.
10   G. Mason Graham to David F. Boyd, August 16, 1881, in G. Mason Graham Letters, Fleming Collection.
11   Ernest Wyche to David Boyd, August 17, 1881, in David Boyd Papers; Minutes of the Board of Supervisors, July 1, 1881.
12   C. R. Boyd to David F. Boyd, January 29, 1883, R. J. Hancock to D. F. Boyd, November 3, 1882, in David Boyd Papers.

Hancock's entreaties did little good. Convinced that he "wd *starve* depending on Va.," David continued his frequent recruiting trips to Louisiana with results that hardly justified the cost. On September 21, 1881, he opened Locust Dale with thirty-five students, only eleven of whom came from Louisiana. Fifty were enrolled just before Christmas, but when the term ended in June, only thirty-five remained. How many were Louisianians is not clear, but at least twelve were day students from the immediate vicinity.

Conditions did not improve the next year. Tom Boyd conducted a summer school at Locust Dale in 1882 while David went to Louisiana in search of credit and new students. When he returned, the entire operation was transferred some thirty miles away to Greenwood in Albemarle County. Expenses at Greenwood were considerably lower than they had been at Locust Dale, and, because the new building lay only twenty feet from a railroad track, the school was certainly less isolated. But neither feature contributed anything to David's coffers. On October 2, 1882, Greenwood opened with only twenty boarders and two day students. Two months later nothing had changed, and David was planning another recruiting trip. Just before he left he wrote his brother, "My situation here is very critical—indeed desperate. And that with the horrible condition of my family in La. makes *me* nearly desperate. . . . I must—*ought*—to go to La. this month to try and get me more boys; yet I don't see how I am to go, or if I get there, how I am to get back shd I fail to get some boys down there. And every dollar I spend traveling is but so much food and clothes taken from my family." [13]

Little came of the December journey to Louisiana and one more made in April, 1883. In fact, the only "stray boys" David managed to recruit on the second trip were his own sons, Jack, Arthur, and Leigh. Ettie, her sister Mary, and the four youngest children remained at the "Baptist Church," David's nickname for his strictly run household in Baton Rouge. How long they could stay there depended on the patience of the man who held David's note. The second of three installments,

13 David Boyd to Tom Boyd, September 22, October 12, December 9, 1881, August 12, October 8, November 16, December 2, 1882, all in Thomas D. Boyd Papers; J. T. Bringier to D. F. Boyd, January 9, April 7, 1882, R. J. Hancock to D. F. Boyd, May 31, 1882, T. D. Boyd to D. F. Boyd, September 5, 8, 1882, all in David Boyd Papers; Locust Dale Academy Roll Book, 1881–82, in MS volumes, David Boyd Papers; *Catalog*, Locust Dale Academy, August, 1881, *Prospectus* for Greenwood, 1882–83, in Printed Materials, David Boyd Papers.

over $1,800, fell due in July, 1882, but David's creditor allowed him to defer payment, except for interest, for several months. When he finally pressed for the principle, David asked Tom Boyd to find a buyer for the property. In June, 1883, Tom succeeded, and David agreed to sell at whatever price "3 *dis*interested parties" might agree it was worth. If possible, David would be in Baton Rouge by July 1 and could handle the sale himself. But he expected to be so poor by the end of the session, "without a dollar and with bills to pay," that he was not sure he could even "get away" from Greenwood. Even if he did, his children would have to stay at the school with his assistant, J. T. Bringier, or go to their grandparents' home in Wytheville. In any case, too few boys would remain at Greenwood during July and August to justify a summer session, and many from Louisiana would probably not be back the next fall. Even David's friends in nearby Charlottesville could not cheer him up. They invited him to attend the university's gala commencement celebration in 1883, but under the circumstances, he confided to Tom, he had no heart to go.[14]

In addition to frequent absences from Virginia and an apparent incapacity to operate on a cash basis, David was guilty of something else that practically guaranteed his failure at Locust Dale and Greenwood. He simply did not care as much about Virginia and his preparatory schools as he did about Louisiana and the state university. Common sense dictated that he commit himself totally to the affairs of the former and leave the conduct of the latter to his successor, William Preston Johnson. But David never really left Louisiana in spirit. Even when he was physically present at Locust Dale or Greenwood, his primary interest was a thousand miles away in Baton Rouge.

In Louisiana, David's principal contact was Tom Boyd, then teaching in the preparatory department of the university. Comprehensive as Tom's letters were, they still could not satisfy David's thirst for information from home. Within weeks of his arrival in Virginia, David was begging his brother to "write me soon all you know of La. and the University." A postscript was more specific: "What did the Bd. do? Did you have a full meeting? I see Gov. Wiltz is dying. Do you know where

14   David Boyd to Tom Boyd, October 8, 1882, February 10, 15, March 1, 22, June 7, 1883, all in Thomas D. Boyd Papers; Morning Report, May 3, 1883, Greenwood Academy, in MS Volumes, David Boyd Papers.

General Graham is? Is the railroad finished from Cheneyville to Alex?
. . . Where is Mr. McCulloch? and how is he?"[15]

One of the first letters Tom sent David from Baton Rouge contained a newspaper article of particular interest. Clipped from Leon Jastremski's *Tri-Weekly Capitolian*, it speculated that Governor Mc-Enery planned to call a special legislative session late in 1881. If so, David intended to be present when it met. "I want my whole stewardship at the University reviewed and passed on," he informed his brother. As for the school's current operations, he did not see how it could meet its obligations unless the extra session of the legislature voted a special appropriation. Otherwise, the new management would have to continue diverting money from the endowment fund to the maintenance fund, which David considered illegal. "The new Board's record," he declared, "is . . . $5000 of endowment spent for *bread and meat*, and scarcely a dollar for the library or apparatus! *Belly versus brains* is their motto!" Under the circumstances, David thought any investigation of the university ought to "embrace the *new* regime as well as the *old*."[16]

When Governor McEnery finally set the date for the special session, Tom Boyd urged David to come south as soon as possible to oversee his case. But David demurred, having concluded that it would "look better" if he did not appear until a prospective committee of inquiry called him to testify. That way, no one could accuse him of "beginning the war" against his opponents. Meanwhile, Representative William Seay of Caddo Parish, who planned to guide David's affairs through the lower house, counseled additional delay. Seay thought David ought to postpone his request for an investigation until the regular session convened in May, 1882. If they were to do a thorough job of "unmasking" the opposition, Seay argued, they would need the extra time to gather material and plan strategy.[17]

In amassing data and making it available to Seay, David expected to rely heavily on his brother. Tom was still a professor at the university in 1881, but how long his job would last was uncertain. President

15 David Boyd to Tom Boyd, September 22, October 12, 1881, in Thomas D. Boyd Papers.
16 *Ibid.*, October 14, 1881.
17 Tom Boyd to David Boyd, November 6, 1881, in David Boyd Papers; David Boyd to Tom Boyd, November 10, 24, 1881, in Thomas D. Boyd Papers; Baton Rouge *Tri-Weekly Capitolian*, December 1, 1881; [William Seay] to David Boyd, November 22, [1881], in Boyd Letters, Fleming Collection.

William Preston Johnston suspected him of disloyalty, and Tom hoped to leave the university when school ended in June. David thought he ought to get away sooner and in January, 1882, offered him a position at Locust Dale. Weeks passed but Tom did not reply. Finally, with apologies for his "no accountness," he declined the Locust Dale offer, primarily because he planned to marry Miss Annie Fuqua of Baton Rouge on March 15. As for the future, he would stay at the university until he found a better job unless the board fired him when it met in July.[18]

Tom's decision to stay in Baton Rouge obviously wounded David. He conceded that it was probably best from Tom's standpoint. But it was already causing comment to the disadvantage of them both. "The public generally consider you as either indifferent or against me, in my affairs with that Board," David complained, "and the 'Ring' at Baton Rouge consider it *secretly* as a *patronizing* act towards you & me; and *outwardly*, in public, they will no doubt claim that their conduct to me cannot be so bad, if my own brother is willing to serve them!" Besides, David continued, if he became a candidate for the post of superintendent of public education in Louisiana, which some of his friends were urging him to do, he hoped to give Tom, rather than someone else, whatever advantage his labors at Locust Dale had produced. As for Tom's approaching marriage, David thought it was a bad idea. Not because there was anything wrong with Miss Fuqua; he thought she was a "fine girl." But unless Tom were an exception to the family rule, he would probably be a *"mighty poor* husband." All the Boyd men were. "Show me a single one of *all* our family . . . who have not made *their* wives anything else but content & happy!"[19]

Long before he learned of Tom's impending marriage, David planned to visit Louisiana in the spring of 1882. The trip, scheduled to coincide with Ettie's expected confinement in late March, had been announced months earlier to several friends in Baton Rouge and New Orleans. Therefore, although he would miss the wedding, and although Ettie's baby arrived late in February, David did not cancel his

18 Tom Boyd to David Boyd, October 29, 1881, February 27, 188[2], in David Boyd Papers; David Boyd to Tom Boyd, December 4, 9, 1881, February 4, 1882, in Thomas D. Boyd Papers. As an afterthought, Tom, in his letter of February 27, 1882, reported the birth of David's seventh child.
19 David Boyd to Tom Boyd, March 6, 1882, in Thomas D. Boyd Papers.

journey. If nothing else, it allowed him an opportunity to gather additional information to be used later by Representative Seay. For example, a treasurer's report, not yet available to the public, indicated that the university had a current debt of $12,000 which the management disguised by diverting money from the endowment fund to the cadet maintenance fund. As David suspected, no new books or equipment had been purchased, and many on the board were disgusted with President Johnston, who, besides his $2,500 salary, received free rent, free board, free servants, and free feed for his horses. When the board met in April, 1882, everything but his salary was cut off and Johnston was "*unhappy.*" These and other "points" David wanted Seay to present to the legislature when it met in May, but Seay must be careful not to do anything to injure the school's interest. David expected to visit Baton Rouge again in June, but he would go earlier if summoned by the legislature. Meanwhile, Seay could get all the material he would need for David's case from Tom Boyd or Sam Robertson, the university commandant and the representative to the legislature from Baton Rouge.[20]

On the same day that David offered Tom Boyd's services to Seay (April 27, 1882), Tom made it clear that he did not intend to wage a "Jamar-Haislip type of conspiracy" against President Johnston in spite of great provocation. At a recent faculty meeting Johnston had been so hostile that Tom had considered resigning on the spot. But Sam Robertson and C. C. Bird, a powerful local politician, dissuaded him. The trouble stemmed from Johnston's conviction that Tom was "making war" on him in David's behalf. Tom denied it. As far as he was concerned, the "Boyd Fight" was a dead issue, and as much as he loved David, he would rather see him "clerking in a store than being president of LSU." Two weeks later Tom made his position even plainer. He had seen Seay, who wanted his help in preparing David's request for a legislative inquiry. But Tom refused to discuss "*Univ. matters*" with him. "I am determined," he wrote David, "to do nothing that would savor of disloyalty to the Board while I am one of its employees."[21]

Then Tom lectured his older brother on the possible harm his demand for an investigation might do the university and David himself.

20 *Ibid.*; David Boyd to Wm. A. Seay, April 27, 1882, in David Boyd Papers. David's letter to Seay was written after his visit to Baton Rouge and after his return to Virginia.
21 Tom Boyd to David Boyd, April 27, 1882, in Alphabetical File, Fleming Collection; Tom Boyd to David Boyd, May 10, 1882, in David Boyd Papers.

Because David had decided to limit the proposed inquiry to his own tenure, letting Johnston's "weak points" speak for themselves when the treasurer's report was published, Tom doubted that whatever vindication David might finally secure would be worth the trouble. But of one thing he was sure. David would certainly get all the blame if the legislature used the investigation as an excuse to attack the school. "All your professions of friendship . . . for [it] will be disbelieved," he warned, "and all your efforts to help it misunderstood."[22]

What David thought of Tom's remarks about the proposed investigation is not recorded. But he did concede that it was "perhaps best" for Tom to remain aloof from his "troubles with the Board" as long as he was employed by the university. Later, when Tom failed to write for several weeks while the legislature was in session, David urged him not to "carry *that* [his aloofness] too far!"[23]

On May 19, 1882, Representative Seay presented David's petition asking for an investigation of the "management and affairs of the La. St. Univ. and Ag. & Mech College" by a joint committee of the legislature. Nine days later he wrote David that a resolution to that effect had passed the house and a "stacked committee of course" had been named by the speaker. David's friend, Dr. R. L. Luckett of Rapides, was "managing" in the senate and would, "of course," be one of two senators named to the committee. Seay also reported that the men most anxious to include President Johnston's administration in the investigation were the very men who "put him in," specifically C. C. Bird. But the resolution that finally passed covered only the years of David's tenure, 1865–1880. On July 6, 1882, the last day of the legislative session, the joint committee submitted its reports. Three members, William Seay of the house, R. L. Luckett of the senate, and one other, signed the majority report which David composed in every particular; the other two, Representatives A. L. Atkin and W. Vincent, presented a statement for the minority. In less than ten paragraphs they found David to be a "good and efficient professor, but . . . a poor financier." One newspaper labeled the investigation "thorough and searching" and "fair and impartial." But under the circumstances, Tom Boyd's remark to David, made before the inquiry began, seemed more accurate.

22   Tom Boyd to David Boyd, May 10, 1882, in David Boyd Papers.
23   David Boyd to Tom Boyd, May 15, June 8, 1882, in Thomas D. Boyd Papers.

Only David could decide whether the "vindication" received was worth the "trouble necessary to secure it."[24]

Just before the joint legislative committee issued its findings, the Board of Supervisors decided to reappoint the entire university faculty for the coming year. Tom Boyd, already at Locust Dale to conduct a summer school for his brother who was in Louisiana, heard the news with mixed emotions. For one thing, his salary would be lower than what he received the first year he taught. Furthermore, considering President Johnston's bitter feeling for him, Tom had serious doubts about the kind of future he might expect if he accepted the appointment. By late summer, 1882, Tom was still undecided. David had already asked him to teach in Virginia, and Johnston, disclaiming any effort to force him out, had informed him of an opening in a Texas "normal" school. But Tom's friends urged him to stay in Baton Rouge. Milton Strickland, an alumnus then serving on the board, declared, "The Johnson [sic] party tried to supplant you altogether, but having failed in that, they will now in all probability vote to increase your salary." Then, rather dramatically, Strickland remarked, "However disagreeable it may be, our friends must take the parts assigned them in the game we are playing to regain control of the University and her destinies."[25] Another friend, Sam Robertson, agreed with Strickland. Tom should return to Baton Rouge and "leave the matter with your friends." Robertson had talked with board members Leon Jastremski and Allan Thomas. Both thought the board would grant Tom a raise and appoint him to a "more dignified Position" when it met in October. Jastremski had told him that President Johnston now realized he "could not afford to continue the fight" against Tom for reasons Johnston appreciated better than anyone else. "Nobody knows where Johnston is," Robertson told Tom. "He takes no interest whatever in the future of the University; Jastremski . . . is much disgusted with W. P. J.'s lack of interest in the welfare of the institution."[26]

24 Louisiana *House Journal*, Regular Session, 1882, pp. 84, 566–74; William Seay to David Boyd, May 22, 1882, in Alphabetical File, Fleming Collection; Tom Boyd to David Boyd, May 10, 1882, David Boyd, MS of Majority Report, undated, in David Boyd Papers; Claiborne *Guardian* (Homer, La.), July 26, 1882.

25 Milton Strickland to Tom Boyd, July 10, 1882, William Preston Johnston to Tom Boyd, September 4, 1882, in Thomas D. Boyd Papers; Tom Boyd to David Boyd, September 5, 1882, in David Boyd Papers.

26 S. M. Robertson to Tom Boyd, August 21, 1882, in Thomas D. Boyd Papers.

Ultimately, Tom was convinced. On September 5, 1882, he declined David's offer to teach at Greenwood, the new location to which David's school was moving, explaining that if he stayed at the university, a "chance" existed for him to apply for the professorship of English. Obviously Tom knew something in September which many would not learn for months: that President William Preston Johnston, then holder of the English chair, was planning to resign. Board member G. Mason Graham was certainly unaware until he heard about it from Tom. Events were occurring with "Buonapartian rapidity," Graham answered, and he did not even have his "knapsack packed."[27]

What was rumor in September, 1882, was announced officially the following January, when Johnston submitted his resignation to become head of the newly organized Tulane University in New Orleans. By that time Tom Boyd had replaced Johnston as professor of English at a substantial raise, and David, after spending Christmas in Louisiana, was back in Virginia struggling to keep Greenwood afloat. Meanwhile, as senior professor at the university, J. W. Nicholson would serve as acting president until the board could choose a permanent replacement for the departed Johnston.[28]

When David learned of President Johnston's resignation, he again allowed himself to put first things second. At once he became so involved in the political machinations surrounding the selection of Johnston's successor that Greenwood, already in serious difficulty, was practically doomed to failure. Even he realized it. On February 10, 1883, he told Tom that Louisiana parents who owed him money for their sons' fees at Greenwood were using the possibility of his [David's] appointment to succeed President Johnston as a pretext not to pay him. The same thing hurt him in Virginia. Speculation that he would soon return to Louisiana was discouraging prospective patronage from that state. For a while, the situation became so critical that he even considered making a public statement denying any interest in the presidency of the university. "I cannot be positively ruined *now* for some possible future benefit!" But a month later David was still very

27 Tom Boyd to David Boyd, September 5, 1882, in David Boyd Papers; G. Mason Graham to
    Tom Boyd, September 15, 1882, in G. Mason Graham Letters, Fleming Collection.
28 Baton Rouge *Weekly Truth*, January 13, 26, 1883; Minutes of the Board of Supervisors, October 2, 1882; Morning Report, Greenwood Academy, in MS Volumes, David Boyd Papers;
    David Boyd to Tom Boyd, January 27, 1883, in Thomas D. Boyd Papers.

absorbed with developments in Louisiana and still hoping to be recalled. "I am playing my usual foolish game," he admitted to Tom,
"risking the *wrecking* of my *little business here* for a mere matter of
sentiment—to run a possible chance of having a place *offered* me,
which I might decline if offered!"[29]

That the Board of Supervisors would actually reappoint David to
the presidency in 1883 was just what he called it, "a possible chance."
There were far too many political obstacles to make his selection likely.
Tom Boyd outlined the hazards and speculated shrewdly on the probable outcome in a series of revealing letters he wrote David between
January 20, 1883, when Johnston resigned, and April 1, when the
board finally chose his successor. From the very beginning Tom
doubted that his brother would be elected, and a ten-page letter he
wrote David on January 22 explained why. Because it describes so
fully the various presidential candidates, board members, and political
powers in Baton Rouge, as well as their relationships with David and
the price he would be asked to pay to be considered seriously for the
presidency, that letter is summarized here.

On the day President Johnston announced his intention to resign,
J. W. Nicholson, professor of mathematics, invited Tom Boyd to his
home. As senior professor and acting president of the university,
Nicholson was the most likely candidate to succeed Johnston permanently. But he insisted to Tom that he did not want the job and intended
to do all he could to secure it for David. He even wrote David a letter to
that effect which he showed to Tom during the interview. Tom was
skeptical. He thought Nicholson went a "little too far" when he denied
ever wanting the presidency for himself, protesting that his trip to
Baton Rouge in the summer of 1880, when David was fired, was made
totally in David's "interest," not his own.

A day or two later Nicholson informed Tom that he had written a
board member of his disinterest in the presidency. He also claimed to
be rather "thick" with Jastremski and responsible for the appointment
of two members then serving on the board. In addition he thought he
could induce one other member, Superintendent of Public Education
E. H. Fay, to cast his vote for David. "All this looked so like work for
Nicholson himself," Tom remarked, "that I asked him . . . [again]

29   David Boyd to Tom Boyd, February 10, March 15, 1883, in Thomas D. Boyd Papers.

whether he would accept the presidency if elected." Again he denied any ambition, but one "significant" remark disturbed Tom: Nicholson said he thought David could "beat him" in a contest for the job. That made Tom suspect that Nicholson found out that David was going to be president and wanted a large part of the credit for bringing it about. "Can he be after posing in the role of Warwick, the Kingmaker?" Tom wondered.

Next, Tom speculated on the motives of several local politicians and the possible votes of various key board members. "Everything seems to indicate that Jastremski will vote for you," Tom reported, but that would give David only six votes against seven for someone else. However, if General Allan Thomas, a member of the board, also sought the job, Tom thought Jastremski and his friends, too, would vote for David. The problem was Dr. J. W. Dupree and David's friendship with him. Dr. Dupree was the university physician and a bitter enemy of Leon Jastremski. The latter had tried to have Dupree removed in favor of Dr. L. F. Reynaud soon after David was fired, but Dupree had enough defenders on the board to prevent it. More important, Dr. Dupree had defied Jastremski and several other local politicians more than a year earlier by supporting someone they opposed in a congressional contest. On Saturday night, January 20, 1883, Tom met Major Thompson Bird, his lawyer son Charlie Bird, Leon Jastremski's brother John, and several other Baton Rouge politicians in a local tobacco shop. "Major Bird," Tom reported, "rather intimated that he would do all he could for you if it wasn't [sic] for Dupree." Later, Sam Robertson, the representative from East Baton Rouge and commandant at the University, indicated that Major Bird would support David anyhow, but that he merely wanted to get Tom to commit David to a "line of policy adverse to Dr. Dupree."

The next night Tom, who must have smoked a great deal, was back in the tobacco shop. In its "back room" he met the two Jastremskis, Andrew Jackson, a local merchant whom David had considered his enemy since 1879, and various others. In a loud voice Jackson declared, "There is one man that I think ought to be the next President of the University and that is Col. Boyd." He promised Tom he would do everything in his power to get David elected. Tom thanked Jackson, but questioned his sincerity. "Whether all this means that these men are really working for you and merely want to influence you beforehand against Dupree; or that they are nominally working for you in order to secure your good will, while in reality determined to beat you with some one who will aid them in venting their spleen upon Dupree," was something Tom left to David's judgment. Then, because he knew his brother's prodigious letter-writing ability and his incapacity for circumspection, particularly with his enemies, Tom begged David to "let all your communications with parties here until April [when the Board would act] be of the Yea and nay kind." David would have to thank Nicholson for his letter of support, but he should choose his words with great care. "And above *all*," Tom begged, "*don't write a line to Dupree!* It would be better if all means of communication between you and B. R. were shut off."[30]

David agreed in most respects with Tom's appraisal of his chances for the presidency and the political scene in Baton Rouge. "I do not expect the place to be offered to me," he wrote on January 29, 1883. As for Nicholson's motives, "Knowing him as well as I do, I think he is playing for the presidency." By David's reckoning, Jastremski, Fay, and one other would support Nicholson on the first ballot; President Johnston's friends on the board, five men, would vote for General Thomas, and the remaining five members would cast votes for him. On succeeding ballots Nicholson would pick up almost all of the Thomas vote while David could not expect to pull more than a total of six. Only Major Bird could defeat Nicholson by influencing Jastremski and the other Nicholson votes to go for David on the first ballot. But David simply could not believe that the "alleged support" for him in the board actually existed. It would have to consist, after all, of essentially the same men who forced him out in 1880. He was sure, therefore, that "This Board as now organized will never have me back. Nicholson or some unknown man will be elected."[31] As for the possibility of Major Bird or his son, Charlie, using their influence with Jastremski to support him instead of Nicholson, David was sure that Nicholson, as acting president, had already promised Jastremski his vote on the board to oust Dr. Dupree. That would be enough for the Birds whose main object was "beating Dupree." "It is not reasonable from any stand-point—," David declared to his brother, "*those* people *support-*

30   Tom Boyd to David Boyd, January 22, 1883, in David Boyd Papers.
31   David Boyd to Tom Boyd, January 27, 29, 1883, in Thomas D. Boyd Papers.

244   DAVID FRENCH BOYD

ing me; and I don't believe they will." In any event, he intended to stand by Dr. Dupree "to the last."[32]

The Birds made one more effort. They asked Tom to induce David's friends on the board to join Jastremski in his fight against the doctor. If he agreed, David's election to the presidency would be assured. Tom refused, probably giving the "death blow to your chances," he wrote his brother on February 10, 1883. David replied that his brother had done the right thing. "The B[irds]'s do not and cannot rise to a proper sense of dignity & duty in the matter," David commented. "The idea of suggesting that one cannot become Presdt. of a school, unless he and his friends consent to throw out, (by way of bargain) some poor devil of a medical doctor, is on a par with what they did with me in 1880, because I wd not then turn against poor old Mr. Markham [the board's treasurer]."[33]

As for Nicholson, David's contempt for him was growing. On February 15, he labeled him "simply unfit to be presdt. of anything. . . . He has simply sold himself, turned against poor Dupree, to get the presidency." Ten days later: "I feel certain that he is playing a double part. . . . I think we ought to tell him so. . . . The fellow played me false in 1880; I don't think I ought to let him do so in 1883."[34]

Tom thought it would be a serious mistake for David to write Nicholson that "we see thro' his game." He argued that it did no good to tell a man you had caught him in a lie. It merely made him your enemy, a commodity David already possessed in abundance. Besides, anything David said to Nicholson of a disparaging character would be interpreted as jealousy. Then Tom urged David not to make another trip to Louisiana before the board met on April 2, 1883, despite his pressing need for money. His visit would certainly be misunderstood by everyone. David could borrow as much through the mail or through Tom as he could in person. "Then why ruin your chance of election to the Presidency by such a step?" he asked his brother.[35]

By March 29, 1883, Tom had clearly decided that David could not be elected. "With Jastremski and McEnery dead against you," he wrote David, "it would require the very ablest political engineering to elect

32 *Ibid.*, January 31, 1883.
33 Tom Boyd to David Boyd, February 10, 1883, in David Boyd Papers; David Boyd to Tom Boyd, February 15, 1883, in Thomas D. Boyd Papers.
34 David Boyd to Tom Boyd, February 15, 25, 1883, in Thomas D. Boyd Papers.
35 Tom Boyd to David Boyd, March 3, 1883, in David Boyd Papers.

you, and no one on your side possesses the skill to manage it." And later, in the same letter, "I have little doubt that he [Nicholson] will be the next President." Tom promised not to let David's name be "presented" unless his election were certain, but the whole issue was moot two days later. In a postscript to his still unmailed letter of the twenty-ninth Tom noted, "Nicholson has come out and consented (?) to accept the presidency if tendered . . . and everybody has come to the conclusion that he will get it."[36]

After a brief executive session on April 3, 1883, the Board of Supervisors accepted Leon Jastremski's resolution that J. W. Nicholson be elected president by acclamation. David reached Baton Rouge a few days later. If he had occasion to congratulate the university's new president, he left no record of it in his papers, nor is there any evidence of a meeting with Dr. Dupree. But in July, 1883, Leon Jastremski's newspaper revealed the "little Doctor's" fate. With only two members dissenting, the board elected the editor's friend, Dr. L. F. Reynaud, as university surgeon in Dupree's place. President J. W. Nicholson voted with the majority.[37]

David's April visit to Baton Rouge lasted a month. As already described, he returned to Greenwood in May, 1883, with no new students, hopelessly in debt, and seriously in doubt as to whether he would be able to finish the session. He did not have enough students to operate a summer school, and he was afraid many of his "La. cadets" would not return in the fall. Only two developments seemed to offer any way out of his difficulties. Tom Boyd found a buyer for the house that David could not afford to keep in Baton Rouge, and an old friend in Alabama informed him that the Alabama Agricultural and Mechanical College at Auburn was looking for a new president. The friend, Professor W. LeRoy Broun, Sr., was leaving the job for a new position in Texas. If David were interested, Broun wanted him to send the names of several persons with whom the Board of Trustees might correspond before it met to name his replacement in late June. Then Broun told David something about the school and the town. Auburn was a "small village" of about a thousand people, "very quiet." The Board of Trustees and the people wanted to make the college a *"genuine"* science

36   *Ibid.*, March 29, 31, 1883.
37   Minutes of the Board of Supervisors, April 3, 1883; Baton Rouge *Capitolian-Advocate*, undated, in Printed Materials, David Boyd Papers.

center which it had not been up to that time. "I had proposed many chgs," Broun wrote, "all of which I leave to my successor."[38]

Early in June, David sent Broun a few names to whom the Auburn trustees might write for references, adding that he was not a "candidate" for the job but if appointed to it he would accept. Clearly the trustees did not restrict their inquiry to the names on David's list. Informed by Tom Boyd of a glowing tribute written by President Nicholson, David reasoned that if the Auburn trustees asked Nicholson about him, they would also contact Governor McEnery, Superintendent of Public Education E. H. Fay, and Leon Jastremski. He hoped they would. The Alabama trustees ought to know "all they can" before they took any action. David thought Nicholson might very well write a second letter to Alabama which would "neutralize" the first. But on second thought, he speculated, "If that crowd [Nicholson, McEnery, Jastremski, and Fay] thought by praising me they wd. send me off to Ala. and forever be rid of me, they might write *favorably*."[39]

David did not really believe he had a chance to win the Auburn post. In view of all the people in Louisiana who felt "unkindly" toward him and considering the "Ala. *Dragnet* system of inquiry," he had to expect that some severely critical letters would be sent to the trustees. "No, I do not expect the appointment," he wrote his brother in mid-June, "and am working away here [Greenwood] getting ready for next year."[40] David was too pessimistic. On June 28, 1883, after considerable debate, the Board of Trustees of the Alabama Agricultural and Mechanical College elected him to its presidency for a term of one year. All appointments were for one year only because the board also adopted a sweeping reorganization plan designed to change the school from its "semi-literary character to a more decided course of scientific and industrial training." Very probably, therefore, some of the "literary" staff would not be rehired when the next session ended.[41]

38 David Boyd to Tom Boyd, June 7, 1883, in Thomas D. Boyd Papers; W. LeRoy Broun to David F. Boyd, May 25, 1883, in Alphabetical File, Fleming Collection; W. LeRoy Broun to David Boyd, May 30, 1883, in David Boyd Papers.
39 David Boyd to Tom Boyd, June 8, 1883, in Thomas D. Boyd Papers; D. T. Merrick to J. W. Dupree, June 4, 1883, J. W. Dupree to David Boyd, undated, in David Boyd Papers.
40 David Boyd to Tom Boyd, June 13, 1883, in Thomas D. Boyd Papers.
41 Record of the Proceedings of the Board of Trustees of the Agricultural and Mechanical College of Alabama, June 25, 27, 28, 1883, Department of Archives, Auburn University. On June 30 and August 7, 1883, the Montgomery *Daily Advertiser* applauded the reorganization of the curriculum because as a "polytechnic" school, the A & M College would not compete with the University of Tuscaloosa.

David was in Baton Rouge when the Alabama Board of Trustees made its decision. After selling his house, he left for Auburn where he spent ten days and then continued to Virginia. Affairs there were in horrible shape. There was no chance to sublet Greenwood for the coming year or to sell the furniture without suffering a great loss, and to make matters worse, he would get no pay at Auburn until January 1, 1884. "I fear when I take hld *down there*," he confided to Tom, "I may be so annoyed and bedeviled, with my affairs here and in La. that I can do no good in Ala." [42] Unable to settle anything in Virginia, David returned to Auburn briefly in mid-August and then went to Baton Rouge for the rest of the month. He had to be back in Alabama by September 1, although he did not think he would move his family there that fall. Later he changed his mind, but exactly when Ettie Boyd, her sister, and the seven children arrived in Auburn is not clear. They were certainly there by October 8, 1883, however, when a letter David sent to Tom Boyd closed, "We are all well and send best love to you and yours." [43]

Six weeks later, Arthur Boyd, David and Ettie's twelve-year-old son, was shot and killed accidentally by his younger brother David French Boyd, Jr. (Rex). Seven-year-old Rex and his ten-year-old brother Leigh had been playing with a shotgun used earlier in the day by their eldest brother Jack. When the gun discharged, the shot hit Arthur in the face and head, killing him instantly. For days David was so distraught that he could not bring himself to describe the "particulars" to Tom, sending a newspaper clipping to him instead. Ettie was heartbroken, David told his brother: "The shock upon her was dreadful. She happened to look out her window just as it was done, and saw it with her own eyes! And then she ran screaming down the street—*for me!* We are all in terrible fix—awful condition. . . . My business alone is nearly driving me crazy; and what I am to do—off here among strangers—under such circumstances—at such a time, without means, God only knows." [44]

The reference to God was ironic. Many devout Alabamans thought

---

42 W. LeRoy Broun to David Boyd, telegram, June 30, 1883, in Official Correspondence of President D. F. Boyd, Department of Archives, Auburn University; Baton Rouge *Weekly Truth*, July 6, 20, 1883; David Boyd to Tom Boyd, August 8, 1883, in Thomas D. Boyd Papers.
43 David Boyd to Tom Boyd, August 8, 11, 1883, in Thomas D. Boyd Papers.
44 Baton Rouge *Daily Capitolian-Advocate*, November 27, 1883; Montgomery *Daily Advertiser*, November 27, 1883; Baton Rouge *Weekly Truth*, November 30, 1883; David Boyd to Tom Boyd, November 29, 1883, in Thomas D. Boyd Papers.

David was an atheist, and some, basing their efforts on information received from W. H. Goodale, a Baton Rouge lawyer, secretary to the
Board of Supervisors, and a prominent Methodist layman, had done all
they could to deny him the presidency of the Alabama Agricultural and
Mechanical College. "That was the cause of the Board's hesitation
from Monday [June 25] to Thursday [June 28] to elect me," David explained to his brother in mid-August, 1883.[45] Even before then a brief
visit to Auburn in July convinced him that he could expect trouble
from "church people." A note to Tom declared, "Our Ala. school is en-
crusted all over thick with Methodism, and all its concommitants—
ignorance, prejudice, narrowness & bigotry; and with Goodale's *send
off*, God only knows how I will get along there. I went to the *Methodist*
church there on Sunday; and, some of the '*Bretheren*—and *sistren*'
seemed to look at me as if I were a wild beast!"[46]

David was not exaggerating. In late August the whispering campaign against him had grown to such proportions that a local newspaper tried to defend him. To the charge that David was not a "be-
liever" the editor replied, "This we believe is false." Colonel Boyd might
not be a church member, but neither was Jesus; and no one, the editor
commented, would complain seriously about His religion. But some of
the paper's readers were not convinced. By October local Methodists
had stepped up their attacks, and David was becoming a notorious
character. Describing the "venomous" charges against him to Tom,
David reported, "One of them said at *Opelika* the other day: 'The college first had for its president a *Methodist* minister; then a Baptist
preacher, next an Episcopalian, and now it has the devil!' And *today*, at
a farmer's club held here I was told that at the *Methodist Conference*
held in North Alabama, some time since, I was openly attacked on the
score of irreligion on the floor of the body! . . . But I have not opened
my mouth and don't propose to do so."[47]

45 David Boyd to Tom Boyd, August 11, 1883, in Thomas D. Boyd Papers. Tom Boyd was not im-
    pressed with Methodist Elder Goodale either, whom he once found engaged in a contest to
    relate the most off-color anecdote. Tom Boyd Diary, January 15, 1876.
46 David Boyd to Tom Boyd, August 8, 1883, in Thomas D. Boyd Papers. The Alabama Agricul-
    tural and Mechanical College, located in buildings donated by Methodists in 1856, continued
    to be influenced by that denomination well into the twentieth century. LeRoy Boyd, "Recol-
    lections of the Early History of Nu Chapter of Kappa Delta Fraternity at the Alabama Poly-
    technic Institute" (Typescript in LeRoy Stafford Boyd MS Collection, Department of Ar-
    chives, Auburn University), hereinafter cited as LeRoy Boyd, "Recollections."
47 David Boyd to Tom Boyd, October 6, 1883, in Thomas D. Boyd Papers; Opelika (Ala.) *Times*,
    August 24, 1883.

Newspapers kept the war alive for months. "Is he an Atheist?" asked the Monroe *Journal* on November 6, 1883. It decided he probably was since he offered no defense against the allegation. Various Louisiana friends tried to answer for him by sending letters to prominent Alabama ministers and laymen attesting to his moral character but although David appreciated their efforts, he doubted that anything they said would do him any good. Even if the "religious crusade" against him did not succeed, David was sure that "trouble" within the "badly organized" college would force him out soon. Under the circumstances, he decided to resign and go back to Greenwood. With all the "hue and cry" against him in Alabama, he told Tom in October, 1883, he could never hope to get another college job anywhere.[48]

Actually David had already resigned when he informed his brother of his intentions. Besides the "religious crusade," restrictions limiting his authority seem to have prompted the action. Early in September he asked F. M. Reese, secretary of the Board of Trustees, precisely when his tenure began and what his powers and responsibilities entailed. Reese replied that he took it for granted David's term began when Broun's ended, on June 28, 1883. "As to the duties of your office," he continued, "I can only refer you to the Rules and Regulations adopted by the Board . . . at their regular session in June."[49] The response did not satisfy David. He thought he had a mandate to proceed with the reorganization plan suggested by President Broun and endorsed by the Board of Trustees at the time of his election in June, 1883. That would require a significant reduction in the number of "semi-literary" courses offered by the college and a concentration on "Science and its applications." It would also mean that only the Bachelor of Science degree would be granted in the future. But the rules and regulations, David found out, required him to share certain decision-making powers with the faculty. The "semi-literary" professors naturally opposed any plans he had to "administer" them out of employment, and they formed what David later called a "*junta*," partly inside and partly outside the college, to force him out of the presidency. "It is the old story," he wrote

48   Monroe (Monroeville, Ala.) *Journal*, November 6, 1883; Robert L. Stuart to David Boyd, October 4, 1883, in David Boyd, Personal Correspondence, Department of Archives, Auburn University; David Boyd to Tom Boyd, October 11, 1883, in Thomas D. Boyd Papers.
49   David Boyd to Board of Trustees, September 23, 1883, F. M. Reece to D. F. Boyd, September 13, 1883, Official Correspondence of the President, Auburn University.

his brother, "those who have controlled the school here for years, do not like any questions asked or criticism made."[50]

The fact that his resignation was on file did not keep David from making suggestions to the executive committee of the Board of Trustees. In October, 1883, he asked the committee to "define" his duties because other officers, particularly the college treasurer, seemed to be carrying out functions normally reserved to a college president. The disciplinary system also needed reorganization. "Under existing rules and regulations," David advised, "[the discipline] is in a very dangerous and precarious condition. I find a military institute under a faculty government which is a contradiction in terms and almost a nullity in practical effect. . . . You have military requirements enough to harrass [sic] your boys and raise a row but not enough military honor in the hands of your president to put down a row. You hold him responsible for the discipline . . . yet you give him very little authority. . . . The whole thing needs overhauling . . . and it cannot be done too soon."[51]

David's warning that a breakdown in discipline was inevitable unless the regulations were revised at once proved to be prophetic. Early in December, 1883, a group of boys met without authorization in the college chapel to protest some disciplinary action of the authorities. David responded by restricting their privileges on Saturday and Sunday nights whereupon a few appealed to the faculty who petitioned David to rescind the restriction. Ultimately the trustees investigated the crisis but David was not satisfied with their findings. On December 20, 1883, he notified them that "all the facts" had not been elicited and that his duty to himself required him to identify the two members of the staff who gave the cadets "improper advice of an insubordinate nature" when the crisis occurred. Their aim was to keep him, the president, "in ignorance of the mutinous attitude of the cadets." One was the treasurer, whose office David thought encroached on his own, and the other was the professor of mathematics. Both, David charged, tried

---

50   David Boyd to Tom Boyd, November 8, 1883, in Thomas D. Boyd Papers; Wm. LeRoy Broun, Report to the Board of Trustees, June 27, 1883, in Proceedings of the Board of Trustees, Auburn University; David Boyd, General Orders No. 1, Alabama Agricultural and Mechanical College, September 26, 1883; David F. Boyd, Card to advertise the Alabama Agricultural College, November 10, 1883, in Official Correspondence of the President, Auburn University; LeRoy Boyd, "Recollections."
51   David Boyd, Report to the Executive Committee of the Board of Trustees, typescript, October 15, 1883, Department of Archives, Auburn University.

to keep the commandant from informing him about the cadets' rebellious conduct.[52]

What action (if any) the Board of Trustees finally took is not clear, but it was not enough to mollify David. His resignation, on file since the previous September, was explained verbally to the board in December and again in writing just before he left Alabama in June, 1884. He regretted having to withdraw from the institution, but it was impossible for him to do "proper or successful work" under the existing system. "There is a bright future here," he concluded, "for some one with a proper charter in his hands, and with proper authority to carry it out."[53]

When he wrote those words, David himself was looking forward to a brighter future. On March 1, 1884, less than a year after taking office, J. W. Nicholson announced his intention to resign the presidency of Louisiana State University in order to resume teaching and the writing of mathematics text books. Immediately David's friends throughout the state mounted a campaign to bring him back to Baton Rouge. Some, like board members G. Mason Graham and Milton Strickland, a state senator and prominent alumnus of the university, had never ceased their efforts in his behalf. Usually outvoted or outmaneuvered by Jastremski and his friends, they enjoyed little success before 1884. But Nicholson's resignation was enough to tip the scales. On April 7, 1884, the Board of Supervisors voted unaminously to recall David from Alabama.[54]

Several developments, inside and outside the university, contributed to the decision. For one thing, resignations, realignments, and new appointments to the board after 1880 served to strengthen support for David in that body. For another, Nicholson's conduct of the university, like that of his predecessor, William Preston Johnston, had not pleased everyone. Tom Boyd, for example, thought most of the faculty shared one professor's opinion that "the bottom has dropped out of the Shebang." Finally, and perhaps most important, Leon Jastremski's

---

52 David Boyd to Board of Trustees, December 20, 1883, Faculty Petition to David Boyd, December 12, 1883, in Official Correspondence of the President, Auburn University.

53 David F. Boyd, Report to the Board of Trustees, Typescript [June 23, 1884], Auburn University.

54 Minutes of the Board of Supervisors, April 7, 1884; Baton Rouge *Weekly Truth*, April 11, 1884; Milton Strickland to Tom Boyd, July 10, 1882, G. Mason Graham to Tom Boyd, March 23, 1884, Max Feazel to Tom Boyd, March 23, 1884, David Boyd to Tom Boyd, April 2, 1884, in Thomas D. Boyd Papers.

principal objections to David as president no longer existed in 1884. Dr. Dupree had been ousted as university surgeon in 1883 to make room for the editor's favorite, and the year before that, the board restricted the powers of the university president by awarding exclusive control over fiscal affairs to its executive committee. Leon Jastremski was chairman of that committee.[55]

Late in the afternoon of April 7, 1884, the Board of Supervisors notified David officially of his reelection to the presidency. Nicholson's resignation would not take effect until the following October, but David's telegram of acceptance ignored that detail. Making no effort to conceal his eagerness to return, he replied immediately: "Presidency of the University accepted with thanks for the honor. Will do my best for La. again. Post me thoroughly on . . . policy of the Board before the Legislature, and the plans for next year. No time to lose now, we must push things vigorously. D. Boyd."[56]

As Tom Boyd once remarked about his brother, David was not a "vengeful" man. He proved that when he urged the cadets not to leave the university after his removal in 1880. He proved it again in the spring of 1884 when he tried to save Professor McCulloch's job after the Board of Supervisors and President Nicholson acted to force the elderly chemist to resign.[57] Nevertheless, David was human. It must have afforded him particular satisfaction to be recalled to the university in 1884 with the votes of men like Vice-President Leon Jastremski and Governor McEnery, both of whom supported the move to fire him four years before. His friend G. Mason Graham was certainly pleased.

---

55   Fleming, *Louisiana State University*, 383–84, 390–94; Thomas D. Boyd to David F. Boyd, February 2, 1884, in David Boyd Papers; Baton Rouge *Capitolian-Advocate*, July 6, 1882, and undated clipping in Printed Materials, *ibid.*

56   Minutes of the Board of Supervisors, April 7, 1884.

57   As explained in Chapter 9, Professor McCulloch, one of David's principal antagonists in 1880, resigned that year to lobby for the Leake reorganization bill. But William Preston Johnston, a personal friend, rehired him. President Nicholson, however, was no friend of McCulloch's, and, as a Granger and an astute politician, Nicholson supported "practical education," whereas McCulloch was a "theoretician." Repeatedly Nicholson urged the board to pressure McCulloch, and finally, just before David's return, the too-theoretical professor's chair of chemistry was merged with that of agriculture. McCulloch planned to leave in June, 1884, but meanwhile he and David had resumed their friendship. David wanted McCulloch to remain as professor of "natural philosophy," but Tom advised against it. No one, including Tom himself, wanted him retained in any capacity. Minutes of the Board of Supervisors, October 1, 1883, January 4, April 7, 1884; J. W. Nicholson to David Boyd, February 27, March 13, April 1, 1884, in Alphabetical File, Fleming Collection; Baton Rouge *Daily Capitolian-Advocate*, October 10, 1883, January 22, 1884; M. A.Strickland to David Boyd, April 28, 1884, Thomas Boyd to David Boyd, April 9, 14, 1884, in David Boyd Papers.

The original draft of an exultant telegram he asked Tom to send David read: "unanimously elected President eight members present. Nominated by Favrot [an antagonist in 1883 when Nicholson was elected], seconded by Jastremski and the Governor. . . . Wish you could have witnessed the torrent of recantation. G. Mason Graham."[58]

Other friends also considered David's reappointment a victory over his "political enemies" and an apology for the "past mistake." One staunch partisan hoped Louisiana had learned a lesson after having experienced the presidencies of William Preston Johnston and J. W. Nicholson. "I hope," wrote J. W. Bringier, "that our only university may yet be turned from a political machine and a nursery for children, into a place of *learning* of which this state . . . [can] be proud." Whether any man could have achieved those goals in the forseeable future was a question. But David was willing to try. In a note to Tom, which unwittingly paralleled Abraham Lincoln's words when he assumed his presidency for a second term, David pledged, "I go back with no resentments for the past, but with good will towards all, and with hope for the future. Let us bury the hatchet and . . . go to work. . . . We have plenty to do."[59]

58 G. Mason Graham to David Boyd, telegram draft, April 9, 1884, Tom Boyd to David Boyd, April 9, 14, 1884, in David Boyd Papers.
59 J. T. Bringier to David Boyd, April 10, 1884, P. Lane to David Boyd, April 8, 1884, in David Boyd Papers; David Boyd to Tom Boyd, April 9, 1884, in Thomas D. Boyd Papers.

Chapter XI

Bitter Homecoming

DAVID BOYD was approaching his fiftieth birthday when the Board of Supervisors recalled him to the Louisiana State University presidency in 1884. Bruised in spirit, mentally and physically fatigued, and materially far poorer than when he first arrived in Louisiana twenty-six years before, David was, nevertheless, still in love with the Pelican State. "I don't believe," he wrote Tom Boyd from Auburn, "I wd have changed my plans . . . [of going back to Virginia] for the presidency of any other *State* college." Then, with an enthusiasm he could never muster for projects not related to the university, David outlined ambitious plans for the coming summer. In late June, after ending his official connection with the Alabama Agricultural and Mechanical College, he would visit Baton Rouge for commencement and the regular meeting of the Board of Supervisors. From there he would go to Virginia to sell or "get rid of" the furnishings left at Greenwood in 1883, and finally, he would return to Louisiana to "canvass" the state for the coming session of the university. Ettie, her sister Miss Mary Wright, and the six children would have to stay in Auburn until the first frost, after which he would pack them all up and transport them to Baton Rouge.[1]

Circumstances forced David to change his plans. After a brief visit to Baton Rouge to attend commencement, he returned to Auburn. But

1 David Boyd to Thomas Boyd, April 9, 1884, in Thomas D. Boyd Papers.

his affairs there were too tangled to settle quickly, and the serious illness of his mother, Minerva French Boyd, required him to visit Wytheville sometime during July. By the time he reached Louisiana to begin
his "canvass" it was already August 10, and the transfer of his family
from Auburn to Baton Rouge had to be delayed. Ettie Boyd did not
seem particularly dismayed. On August 4, 1884, she told Tom Boyd,
"We talk a good deal about leaving here in Dec., but I will not feel sure
of it, until we can secure a house in Baton Rouge." Because the place
they occupied in Auburn could not be rented by the month, she
thought it might be advisable to keep it another year, "with the hope of
sub-renting . . . if we do get off to B.R." The children were healthier in
Auburn than they had ever been in Louisiana, and she enjoyed her
garden. Besides, it was cheaper to live in Alabama, and the prospect of
occupying temporary quarters in the university building, not to mention the expense of moving, did not attract her at all. In closing, Ettie
noted that her letter sounded as if they expected to stay in Alabama.
Ultimately, that is what David's chaotic financial and professional
problems forced them to do. With the last of the Wright family inheri-
tance, Ettie and her sister Mary bought a house in Auburn, and by
1888 Ettie was giving music lessons and renting rooms to support and
educate her children. David sent her money whenever he could, but
his circumstances in Louisiana were so uncertain by that time that
Ettie had no plans to leave Alabama.[2]

When he finally got to Louisiana in August, 1884, David went at
once to Minden, where the Louisiana Educational Association was
holding its first state convention. Speaking on the subject of "industrial and technical education," he told his audience that education had
to catch the "spirit of the age" to be of any value. Mankind was absorbed with material things, he continued, and only a "material education" could fit modern youth for life. Consequently, literary education
had become a luxury and scientific education a necessity. The situation pained him somewhat because he began his career teaching the
ancient languages. But the world was "crying out" for knowledge
about the material forces of nature, and educators who did not respond
failed to do their duty. Besides, the study of science was not without a

2 Ettie Boyd to Tom Boyd, August 4, 1884, January 9, 1888, *ibid.*; William C. Stubbs to D. F.
   Boyd, August 11, 1887, Rex Boyd (son) to David F. Boyd, March 4, 1888, in David Boyd
   Papers.

certain beauty. To those who doubted, he suggested the contemplation of a snowflake's perfect symmetry, the majesty of the heavens, and the forces, directed by God, which imposed order on the universe. The response was gratifying. A Shreveport journalist pronounced it the "speech of the occasion," and David himself wrote his brother that he could not "complain of the Newspaper reports from Minden."[3]

From Minden, David went to Shreveport. He stayed there longer than planned, but thought his efforts would provide several new cadets for the university in October. After Shreveport his itinerary called for a tour through Bossier and Claiborne parishes where he would join Professor Nicholson. Both would go to Monroe; then David would return to Shreveport, travel down the Red River to Alexandria, and head for Opelousas and southwestern Louisiana. Nicholson would cover the eastern half of the state. Finally, David expected to go through New Orleans enroute to Auburn where he planned to spend a few days with his family before returning to Baton Rouge in late September. In general David kept to the route and schedule he outlined to Tom on August 20, 1884. But as time passed, his earlier enthusiasm gave way to a deepening concern for the university's prospects and his own in the coming session. As usual, his personal finances were in chaos, and the unlikelihood that he could borrow enough to pay his traveling expenses made him think seriously of abandoning his recruiting efforts and returning to Alabama. On August 28 he wrote Tom that he had "no business *now* in *public* position." He could not devote his whole attention to it, and he was so poor that people had lost respect for him. "A man in debt; and getting old, with a large, young family, and with pay barely sufficient for his & their support, with no chance to lay by anything, is a pitiable, & worthless object indeed."[4]

By September, David was "much tempted to *quit* B.R. (& L.S.U.) for good," and go back to Virginia or some other "quiet place." Harney Skolfield, the board's treasurer, sent him some money on September 7, which cheered him, but the very next day he learned that a check written before he left Alabama had not been honored in New Orleans. Such things were crushing his spirit and killing his self-respect. He

3   Baton Rouge *Daily Capitolian-Advocate*, August 15, 1884; Baton Rouge *Weekly Truth*, August 22, 29, 1884; David F. Boyd, speech to Louisiana Educational Association, [August 13, 1884,] in David Boyd Papers; David Boyd to Tom Boyd, August 20, 1884, in Thomas D. Boyd Papers.
4   David Boyd to Tom Boyd, August 20, 28, 1884, in Thomas D. Boyd Papers.

wanted to go away, anywhere, to escape the shame of not meeting his obligations. "I feel today that I wd prefer never to see Baton Rouge or N.O. again," he told his brother. He did not know what he would do, some "humbler business" perhaps, but the university had gotten him into his difficulties; if he stayed with it any longer things would only get worse.[5]

A two-day visit in Alexandria with old friends seemed to revive David's spirits, and for the rest of the trip he said nothing more in his letters to Tom about quitting. However, he doubted if they would get many students from Rapides that year. People there accused the university of lax discipline and neglect of the sick, David reported. Meals had to be improved, too, or they should give up the "Boarding Dept." By the time David reached Washington, Louisiana, another serious complaint had been lodged against the school. Critics in that community thought the university was "mixed up with . . . state (ring) politics," which was not surprising considering that the commandant, Sam Robertson, had presided over the recent Democratic convention. Sam must "quit playing politician" or he would ruin the school. "Professors and employees running a political machine," he fumed to Tom. "It is no place for me."[6]

After visiting Auburn late in September, 1884, David returned to Baton Rouge in time to report to the Board of Supervisors at their regular fall meeting. His trip convinced him that "loose discipline" was the main complaint most people had against the university. He thought the charge arose out of the fact that cadets did not always behave properly while wearing the uniform off campus. To correct the situation he wanted students living in town to wear civilian dress when not on duty. But the board took no action on his suggestion, so David attacked the problem from another angle. He instituted a very strict military regimen which restricted cadets living and boarding on campus to the university grounds except for one hour a week. Even so the effect was limited because increasing numbers of students chose to live, or at least board, off campus to avoid the relatively expensive and inferior meals provided by the university.[7]

5   *Ibid.*, September 1, 2, 7, 8, 1884.
6   *Ibid.*, September 10, 13, 14, 15, 1884.
7   Minutes of the Board of Supervisors, September 29, 1884; Baton Rouge *Daily Capitolian-Advocate*, October 7, 1884; Baton Rouge *Weekly Truth*, November 14, 1884; Fleming, *Louisiana State University*, 412–14.

Well before completing his canvassing tour in 1884, David knew the "table fare" at the university would have to be improved. If the "quartermaster," Mr. L. Jadot, did not do better, David had written Tom Boyd, they would have to "abandon" the "Boarding Dept." But David decided to abandon Jadot instead. Late in October, Leon Jastremski's paper, the *Daily Capitolian-Advocate*, reported Jadot's resignation, and another local paper noted that "A misunderstanding with Col. Boyd is the rumored cause." Jadot's connection with the university began when Jastremski and the Wiltz-appointed board reorganized the school in the summer of 1880. Like Jastremski, Commandant Sam Robertson, and board Treasurer Harney Skolfield, Jadot was a power in "regular" Democratic political circles in Baton Rouge. If a dispute with David really did bring about his resignation, David's relationship with the influential editor and Governor McEnery was probably not improved as a result.[8]

Besides "loose discipline" and a poor boarding department, two other problems confronted David when he returned to the university in 1884. One concerned the school's curriculum and the other the quality of its students. In April, 1885, David made recommendations on both subjects in his report to the Board of Supervisors. The bulk of the students, he pointed out, were very young and ill-prepared to do college work. As long as the entrance requirements remained so undemanding, the school could not claim to be a college. The board should decide, David thought, whether it was running a university or merely a preparatory school. A second, more serious criticism, concerned the fact that although they styled themselves an "Agricultural College," they did not teach agriculture, "at least nothing like practical agriculture." David urged the board to establish a chair of agriculture and fill it with what "our people" would call a "live" man. Other southern universities had done so and were very popular with "agricultural" people as a result.[9]

Three months later David was more specific. With the concurrence of his staff he recommended to the board that it raise the entrance requirements and abolish the preparatory department. He also repeated

8 David Boyd to Tom Boyd, September 13, 14, 1884, in Thomas D. Boyd Papers; Baton Rouge *Daily Capitolian-Advocate*, October 22, 1884; Baton Rouge *Weekly Truth*, October 24, 1884.
9 Minutes of the Board of Supervisors, April 6, 1884.

his request for a professorship of agriculture: "This is . . . necessary, even if other (comparatively unimportant) professorships have to be abolished. It places an *agricultural* college badly on the defensive to have no professor of agriculture, and an active, able man in this chair would do much good for the school and the people."[10] This time the board acted. It raised the entrance age to fifteen, abolished the preparatory department, and set up a "sub-freshman" class to provide remedial work for those students whose precollege training proved inadequate. The board also named a committee to confer with the Sugar Planters' Association about cooperative action to operate and support a sugar experiment station and a professorship of agriculture at the university. David and two board members were authorized to act with the sugar planters to hire someone for the joint position, but in the end David selected the candidate and the others approved his choice. On August 5, 1885, the *Capitolian-Advocate* was "pleased" to announce that Professor William C. Stubbs, state chemist of Alabama and a professor at the Alabama Agricultural and Mechanical College, had accepted the "joint proposition of the Bd. of Supervisors and the La. Sugar Planters' Association." Stubbs would become professor of agriculture at the university and director of the sugar experiment station set up independently by the planters in 1884.[11]

Not everyone was satisfied with David's efforts to make the Louisiana State University and Agricultural and Mechanical College live up to its name. The state Grange, for example, proposed the separation of the agricultural and mechanical college from the university at its convention in December, 1884. In December, 1885, it repeated the suggestion, charging that "the agricultural department of said institution is a most lamentable failure." Six months later its president, Daniel Morgan, felt the same way, but by that time Professor Stubbs was teaching agriculture at the university and conducting two experiment stations: one for sugar culture at Kenner, Louisiana, and the other for "general agriculture" in Baton Rouge. In addition the school boasted a well-appointed chemistry department under W. LeRoy Broun, Jr., and a shop for "practical" instruction in mechanics. "This is no longer an

10   *Ibid.*, June 29, 30, 1885; Baton Rouge *Daily Capitolian-Advocate*, July 1, 1885.
11   Minutes of the Board of Supervisors, June 30, 1885; Baton Rouge *Daily Capitolian-Advocate*, August 5, 1885.

Agricultural College with agriculture left out," David could report to the Board of Supervisors in 1886.[12]

Sometime during the summer of 1885 Governor S. D. McEnery appointed David Boyd commissioner of the North, Central and South American Exposition scheduled to open in New Orleans on November 10, 1885. The "American Exposition," as it was usually called, had grown out of the World Industrial and Cotton Centennial Exposition held the previous year in the Crescent City. Opened on December 16, 1884, the World Exposition was a financial failure almost immediately. In spite of repeated efforts by editors like Leon Jastremski to herd his readers through the turnstiles, the public stayed away in such numbers that the promoters had to appeal to Congress "for another half million" to keep their enterprise afloat. Congress responded in March by granting some $330,000, and the World Exposition managed to operate until June, 1885. Nevertheless, many observers thought it had been good for Louisiana. For one thing, it brought capitalists to New Orleans from all over the country. Surely, one paper commented, their visits must have convinced them what a rich field the "backward South" offered for investment. As for Louisiana, it needed "new blood" in its sagging industries. "The South needs monied men," concluded the editor, "and the Exposition served to attract them."[13]

Such sentiments probably explain why Bourbon politicians like Governor S. D. McEnery and Leon Jastremski were willing to encourage the directors of the World Exposition to continue operations for a second year. Under the new title, North, Central, and South American Exposition, it opened on the old site on the appointed date in November. The American Exposition quickly proved to be a bigger financial fiasco than its predecessor. For David it was a personal disaster. As state commissioner, it was his job to provide Louisiana with an exhibit worthy of the state. Several faculty members from the university could provide him with assistance, and the directors of the exposition promised him $2,000 for necessary expenses. But in David's opinion $10,000 would not be enough to do Louisiana justice. Therefore, in a printed

12   Baton Rouge *Daily Capitolian-Advocate*, December 11, 1884, December 21, 1885, January 27, February 1, 2, 1886; Baton Rouge *Weekly Truth*, July 16, 1886; Minutes of the Board of Supervisors, April 6, 1886.
13   David Boyd to Wm. C. Stubbs, August 5, 1885, in David Boyd Papers; Pamphlet announcing the North, Central and South American Exposition for 1885–86, September 1, 1885, in Printed Materials, *ibid.*; Baton Rouge *Daily Capitolian-Advocate*, December 17, 1884, January 2, 6, 10, May 16, 1885; Baton Rouge *Weekly Truth*, June 5, 1885.

folder he appealed to every parish for contributions to supplement the $2,000. He also urged every craft and industry in the state to cooperate with the university in preparing Louisiana's exhibit. "There will be no separate colored department," David's brochure announced. "All are citizens of Louisiana alike; and all are welcome within the Louisiana space."[14]

David spent most of the summer of 1885 in New Orleans working feverishly with Professors Broun and Stubbs to prepare Louisiana's exhibit. In October he visited Baton Rouge briefly for a board meeting, indicating that he would "necessarily" be away from the university for much of the coming session as well. But with Professor Nicholson in charge, he did not think his duties at the exposition would interfere with the school's operation. Still, he reported, there were some things for which the board ought to be prepared. Because admission standards had been raised and the preparatory department abolished, they must not expect more than one hundred students in the coming year. And if only fifty boarded at the school, they could not hope to meet expenses in the "Boarding Dept." David regretted having to raise such "disagreeable" matters, but duty compelled him to warn the members of danger ahead.[15]

In his newspaper Leon Jastremski gave no indication that he shared David's concern for the university's financial future. But unpublished minutes of the board's October proceedings do show that the members wanted to minimize unnecessary expenditures. When David asked the financial committee to approve, after the fact, his purchase of a "valuable herbarium" for the university museum, committee chairman Jastremski maintained that the whole board, not merely his committee, would have to sustain David's action. With only one dissent the members did so, but then they resolved that thereafter only the executive committee could make such expenditures. Leon Jastremski, it should be noted, chaired that committee too.[16]

14 David Boyd, Pamphlet Announcing the North, Central and South Amercian Exposition for 1885–86, September 1, 1885, in Printed Materials, David Boyd Papers; Minutes of the Board of Supervisors, October 5, 1885; Baton Rouge *Daily Capitolian-Advocate*, October 28, November 23, 1885; Baton Rouge *Weekly Truth*, March 19, 1886.

15 D. F. Boyd to W. C. Stubbs, August 9, 1885, in David Boyd Papers; Baton Rouge *Weekly Truth*, October 2, 9, 1885; Baton Rouge *Daily Capitolian-Advocate*, August 19, 1885; Minutes of the Board of Supervisors, October 6, 1885.

16 Minutes of the Board of Supervisors, October 5, 6, 1885; Baton Rouge *Daily Capitolian-Advocate*, October 7, 1885.

That relations between David and Jastremski were deteriorating late in 1885 is clear from the minutes of the December board meeting. Since October 5, David told the members, his duties as state commissioner of the exposition rendered his presence in New Orleans "absolutely necessary." Consequently, he could not present a formal report. Neither could Leon Jastremski's finance committee. Because of the "continued absence of the President of the Faculty," the editor noted tartly, that committee had not even met. Later, when alumni member Milton Strickland moved that David be granted three months salary in advance to defray the heavy expense of living in New Orleans, Jastremski objected. His newspaper provided some amplification. The Strickland motion carried, Jastremski reported, but only after a lengthy argument during which it became clear that "some [board] members" favored withholding salary from professors who had "recently been absent from duty." The result was board approval for a proposal offered by Jastremski: "Resolved, that it is the sense of this Board that whenever a member of the faculty shall absent himself on his private business he shall not be allowed pay during such absences."[17]

Apparently Jastremski did not accept Milton Strickland's statement that David was "at present employed in a dual capacity" as president of the university and state commissioner of the exposition. He was being paid to perform the duties of the former, insisted the editor, which he clearly could not do when absent from Baton Rouge. Neither could the several younger professors whom David had called out of the classroom to help him in New Orleans. At least two of them, W. LeRoy Broun, Jr., and Leonard Sewell, realized it. On November 11, 1885, Broun wrote David from Baton Rouge after the two left New Orleans without David's knowledge. "I would have told you of our going," Broun explained, "but honestly I was afraid you would keep [us]." For days Broun had had little to do in the Crescent City. He was anxious to work, and he knew his classes at the university were not being taught. If David wanted anything analyzed, he could mail it to Baton Rouge, and Broun would do it gladly. But he begged not to be summoned to New Orleans any more. Or, if David would return to the university, Broun would gladly "take charge" in New Orleans. At least it would

17 Minutes of the Board of Supervisors, December 7, 8, 1885; Baton Rouge *Daily Capitolian-Advocate*, December 10, 1885.

give David a rest. "But to come down there and do a negroes [*sic*] work, while my classes are suffering here, and I doing no good, excuse me." Then, pleadingly, he begged David to come to Baton Rouge for his own good. "Come please if it is only for a day, once a week. . . . Come up please and let yourself be seen by the students and people of the town."[18]

David was certainly not enjoying himself in New Orleans, and Strickland's efforts to secure his salary in advance, while appreciated, did little to make his life more pleasant. On January 20, 1886, he wrote Tom Boyd that he had tried to "get away to Baton Rouge, but with no luck." If possible, he would leave New Orleans the next day to spend the weekend at the university. But whatever he did or wherever he went no longer seemed important. "I am doing no good," he told Tom, "making no progress—altho' I have never worked so hard—nor suffered so much in all my life as recently. My life is now a *hell on earth.* Death wd be a great relief."[19] Two days later he was still in New Orleans, still despondent, and still planning to go to Baton Rouge the "next day." But now he had reached a decision:

It is my intention to resign on *Feb. 1st,* to take effect immediately. Somehow, I hope to get the money to refund the *Feb.* pay already paid me. My return to La. was an error. The Exposition has probably only hastened the *denouement* [,] the end! I feel grateful to you, and to my friends generally, for yr. interest in me, and in my welfare. I only wish now to get away from La.—where to God only knows. I shall try and stay here in N.O. . . . till the close of the Exposition. But that looks like . . . an impossibility—for I have not a dollar in the world. But the future must take care of itself.[20]

David did not write his letter of resignation until April 5, 1886, and it was not presented to the board until the following June. His "private affairs," he explained to Governor McEnery, were in such bad condition as to make him "unfit" to discharge his duties properly. Therefore he begged to be relieved as early as possible. The reason offered was sound enough, but it was probably not the only one for David's resignation. By the late fall and winter of 1885–1886, he was under fire from several quarters for his prolonged absence. Since the previous

18 Baton Rouge *Daily Capitolian-Advocate,* December 10, 1885; W. LeRoy Broun, Jr. to David Boyd, November 11, 1885, in David Boyd Papers.
19 David Boyd to Tom Boyd, January 20, 1886, in Thomas D. Boyd Papers.
20 *Ibid.,* January 22, 1886.

August he had not spent more than a few days in Baton Rouge, and many of the local citizens clearly resented it. Leon Jastremski's paper pointedly reported in late February, 1886, the "pleasure of meeting Col. Boyd this morning, who came up last night and returned to New Orleans this morning." But the most telling criticism may have been that of O. P. Skolfield, an irate parent who complained directly to Governor McEnery. Following the intermediate examinations in February, 1886, Skolfield's son and eleven other cadets had been asked to "withdraw" from the university for academic reasons. Out of a possible one hundred points, young Skolfield scored only forty-four; his professors, the father learned, labeled him a "drag" on his class. But, demanded Skolfield, were not the professors also at fault for "so much *absence*" which was "*so* well known?" "Those who sit in judgement," he declared, "should first pluck the mote from their own eyes before they seek to find it elsewhere."[21]

Besides extreme poverty and criticism for his long absence from Baton Rouge, a feeling that the state and the university did not appreciate his drudgery at the exposition may have caused David to resign in June, 1886. It undoubtedly hurt when a Baton Rouge paper described the entire exposition as "rather dull," but singled out David's contribution, the Louisiana exhibit, for special criticism. From New Orleans, the paper's correspondent reported: "I guess you think I wasted my time here, but after I had seen Louisiana's exhibit, which seemed to be principally alligators, I felt as if I needed a little rest to recover from the effects of such a representation of our State. There were big alligators, middle-sized alligators, and little alligators. Also a figure of a negro man ploughing up the ground with alligators attached to his plow."[22]

The Board of Supervisors considered David's resignation on June 28, 1886, but for some reason, perhaps the lack of a quorum, did not act on it until several days later. Meanwhile, his friends on the board and among his former students had enough time to organize a modest campaign begging him not to leave. It proved effective. On July 9 the

21   O. P. Skolfield to Governor S. D. McEnery, undated, incorporated in Minutes of the Board of Supervisors, April 6, 1886; David Boyd to S. D. McEnery, April 5, 1886, *ibid.*, June 28, 1886; Baton Rouge *Daily Capitolian-Advocate*, February 25, 1886; Leon Jastremski to David Boyd, March 1, 1886, in Thomas D. Boyd Papers.
22   Baton Rouge *Weekly Truth*, March 19, 1886.

board reconvened and approved a motion that "Col. Boyd be requested to reconsider and withdraw his resignation." Governor McEnery appointed a committee to confer with David, and shortly thereafter he agreed to remain as president "at the Bd's. request."[23]

Whether David intended his June, 1886, resignation seriously or merely as a test of his strength in the board is not clear from the records that remain. He certainly had plenty of sound reasons to resign, but he also had a history of subjecting his administration to votes of confidence, somewhat like a British prime minister. If that is what he was doing in this instance, the results must have pleased him. If not, his decision to stay on merely prolonged his agony. In any case, the next time he resigned no committee of the board would visit him in an effort to change his mind.

On July 29, 1886, Governor McEnery summoned the board into special session for its third meeting of the summer. Two pressing issues required immediate attention. One concerned a drastic economy program, and the other involved acquisition of the United States Barracks property in Baton Rouge as a permanent domicile for the university. After two days of spirited discussion the members voted to cut all salaries drastically and to reduce the staff by abolishing some positions and combining others. David, whose pay as president dropped from $2,500 to $1,900, was assigned to teach civil engineering, presumably on the basis of his mathematical training and practical experience during the Civil War. Additional economy measures included the adoption of a resolution presented by Joseph Spearing that no expenditures be made in the future except for absolutely necessary repairs and that no expense of any sort be incurred without first receiving approval from the executive committee.[24]

Also on July 29, 1886, the board voted to accept the federal bar-

23   Minutes of the Board of Supervisors, June 28, 29, July 9, 1886; Henry Favrot to David Boyd, June 30, 1886, in David Boyd Papers.
24   W. H. Goodale to David Boyd, July 29, 1886, in David Boyd Papers; Minutes of the Board of Supervisors, July 29, 30, 1886. The practice of shifting faculty members from one "chair" or discipline to another regardless of qualifications was not uncommon throughout much of the nineteenth century. One educational historian commented critically in 1890: "It is not the South alone that has not yet awakened to the belief that there should be special training for special work." Fay, *History of Education in Louisiana*, 96. Contrasting American educators in the nineteenth century with their European counterparts, another historian labeled the former primarily pedagogues and guardians of youth, not scholars or patrons of learning. Theodore Crane (ed.), *The Colleges and the Public, 1787–1862* (New York: Bureau of Publications Teachers' College, Columbia University, 1963), 6.

racks as the university's new home and authorized David to take possession as soon as the deed of transfer became effective. Acquisition of the property had not been easy. David first tried to secure it after fire destroyed the seminary building in 1869. But at that time the federal government felt compelled to maintain troops in the southern states. Later, when troops were finally withdrawn, local interests began arguing over disposition of the property. Some, like David, wanted it for the university, while others suggested it as a state asylum for the blind. Still others, notably Mayor Leon Jastremski and the Baton Rouge City Council, wanted it sold to the highest bidder. As the state capital, Baton Rouge needed room to expand, they argued, and to block its residential and commercial development northward along the river by locating any state institution on the federal site would be foolish and unjust.

Meanwhile, Louisiana's legislature endorsed the efforts of various congressmen to obtain the barracks for the school, and in 1886 a bill presented by A. B. Irion of Avoyelles Parish finally secured congressional approval. Besides transferring the property to Louisiana for use by the university, it required the state to insure, maintain, and return it to the federal government if it ever ceased to be used for educational purposes. Not everyone was pleased. Editor Leon Jastremski found the conditions objectionable, and Governor McEnery advised the legislature to reject the "Trojan gift." After allowing Louisiana to use and maintain the property, he predicted, the federal government would prove to be an "Indian giver." But the lawmakers ignored the governor's warnings, the Board of Supervisors formally accepted the property, and by the first week in September, 1886, David was living in one of the buildings. His eagerness to move the rest of the school into its new home accounted for his final resignation as president of the university.[25]

Because the Board of Supervisors had no funds to pay moving costs, it appealed to the people of Baton Rouge for whatever assistance they could provide. The response was gratifying. At a citizens' meeting,

25 Minutes of the Board of Supervisors, September 29, 1884, June 29, July 29, September 5, 1886; E. W. Robertson to David Boyd, December 14, 1881, in Alphabetical File, Fleming Collection; Baton Rouge *Daily Capitolian-Advocate*, February 4, 9, 18, June 30, 1882; Baton Rouge *Weekly Truth*, December 18, 1885, April 30, May 11, September 3, 1886; Fleming, *Louisiana State University*, 429–32.

leading business men offered to furnish wagons, free of charge, to transport university property from the asylum building to the barracks. In addition, a means was devised to provide the university with a grant of $1,000 for expenses. But two weeks passed and nothing happened. Finally, when the executive committee reminded the city of its promise, the mayor replied that the expected "cooperation" had not materialized and he could not take any further action on his own authority. Under the circumstances, the executive committee decided it could do nothing until the next legislature met. At that time it would apply for a special appropriation to move the university.[26]

David was a member of the executive committee, along with H. M. Favrot, Superintendent of Public Education Warren Easton, and vice-president of the board Leon Jastremski. David signed the executive committee report that declared the school had to stay in its old quarters. But on his own authority he somehow arranged to have the barracks buildings cleaned and the most essential repair work done during the month of September. He also managed to have everything except the chemistry laboratory, the library, the museum, and the "mechanical" workshop moved to the new location. Every class except the "chemical class" could be conducted at the barracks, he told the board when it met on October 4. And, "unless ordered *not* to, *and* in accordance with orders given Sept. 7, 1886," he expected to open the 1886–1887 session at the "U. S. Military Garrison" on October 5.[27]

Apparently no one ordered David not to open the session at the barracks in October. But obviously his unilateral decision to move the university in defiance of the executive committee's September 18, 1886, injunction, offended certain members of the board. To make matters worse, he bragged about it at a special board meeting held on November 8, 1886. The university had moved, he declared in his report, "in *spite* of a Resolution *not* to." Then he presented the board with a financial statement. He had "already" spent $1,800 to clean up and move the school. But that figure was not "necessarily a debt agst. the University." It was incurred for the "best interest" of the school; and, if the board could pay it somehow, he thought it would be "altogether best to

---

26 Minutes of the Board of Supervisors, July 29, October 4, 1886; Baton Rouge *Weekly Truth*, September 10, 1886.
27 Minutes of the Board of Supervisors, October 4, 1886.

do so." The board adopted a motion to that effect, but then an unidentified member secured passage of another motion to have Joseph Spearing's resolution against any unauthorized expenditure, adopted in July, 1886, published in Leon Jastremski's newspaper. It was that action which caused David to resign the presidency for the last time on November 11, 1886.[28]

Convinced that the board meant to "reprove . . . [him] publicly," he dashed off a letter of resignation to Governor McEnery who endorsed it and referred it to the executive committee. Exactly what the letter said is not clear, but David later claimed he wrote it while "under a sense of wrong done me." On December 6, 1886, the committee accepted his resignation and at McEnery's suggestion, chose a president *pro tempore* to replace him. The man selected was David's brother, Thomas D. Boyd. McEnery was delighted. "I hope," he wrote Tom in an undated note, "your temporary appointment may result in your receiving the position permanently."[29]

How David reacted when he learned the identity of his successor is not recorded. But many agreed with the governor that Tom would make an excellent president. His "fine executive ability, broad views and discreet judgement," remarked the Baton Rouge *Weekly Truth*, convinced his "many warm friends" that Tom would administer the school with honor to himself and great advantage to the institution. Then, as an afterthought, the paper added: "It is probable that Col. D. F. Boyd will be tendered a professorship at the University." The editor was right. Minutes of the executive committee for January 4, 1887, indicate that David, "having reconsidered . . . his resignation" insofar as his professorship was concerned, would be retained by the university in the chair of civil engineering. His salary, fixed at $1,425 per year, would be paid from December 4, 1886, the day his resignation as president took effect.[30]

By April, 1887, when the Board of Supervisors met for its regular spring session, Tom Boyd had served as president for four months, and David had "reconsidered" his letter of resignation once again. In fact,

---

28 *Ibid.*, November 8, 1886, April 4, 1887.
29 *Ibid.*, April 4, 1887; Samuel D. McEnery to Thomas Boyd, undated, Harney Skolfield to S. D. McEnery, December 7, 1886, in Thomas D. Boyd Papers.
30 Baton Rouge *Weekly Truth*, December 10, 1886; Minutes of the Board of Supervisors, April 4, 1887.

he must have done little else from the time he stepped down as president. By his own admission David was never comfortable when forced to share power with others. His administrative career in Alabama, as well as in Louisiana, reveals numerous instances of his unwillingness or inability to compromise or cooperate effectively with those who challenged his authority. For him to adjust gracefully to a subordinate position in the institution he had once governed absolutely must have been extremely difficult. For him to do so under the presidency of Tom Boyd, who was twenty years his junior, whom he had literally reared, and whom he thought of more as a son than a brother, was probably impossible. A letter to Governor McEnery, dated April 4, 1887, and delivered just before the board convened, provides some indication of David's conflicting emotions. "With your approval, and only with the consent and withdrawal of my brother from candidacy for the permanent presidency of the University," David began, "I wd ask the permission of the Board of Supervisors to retract my resignation. . . . I think such a course wd be best for all parties concerned." "But," he wrote, "I will do nothing without your knowledge and consent; nor without the hearty approval of Prof. Thos. D. Boyd, who also now has interests and feeling to be considered. Besides, he has made you an admirable president, and is well worthy of the honor of the permanent appointment." David had not discussed "this matter" with his brother. Therefore he asked Governor McEnery to refer "this *private* letter" to Tom for his information and whatever action he might choose to take after consultation with the governor. David also told McEnery that he did not think he should remain at the university if the only post he could expect to hold were that of professor of civil engineering. *"There is*—as the classes have been arranged, *little or nothing for me to do,"* he explained, and he did not want to be a burden to the institution. "This, together with a wish to save wounded pride, and to give the Board an opportunity to relieve its sting [?], causes me to ask with the approval and assistance of your excellency and my brother . . . to have the past undone." [31]

McEnery honored David's request immediately. With a covering note he sent David's confidential letter to Tom Boyd, remarking that Tom already had his (McEnery's) endorsement for permanent appoint-

31 David Boyd to S. D. McEnery, April 4, 1887, in Thomas D. Boyd Papers.

ment to the presidency. However, if Tom saw "fit and proper" to withdraw in favor of his brother, the governor would not oppose David's application to the board to retract his resignation. It must have been a painful decision for Tom to make. He certainly wanted the job, and the board wanted him to have it. But David's latest attempt "to have the past undone" and his own sense of obligation to his older brother made him step aside. In a letter to E. L. Stephens, written in 1896, when he finally did become president of the university, Tom declared, "Strange irony of fate that ten years ago when it was my highest ambition to hold the presidency of the State University, the glittering prize slipped through my fingers, and that now, when I do not want it, it should be offered to me." [32]

When the board convened on April 4, 1887, it moved at once to appoint Tom permanent president. Parliamentary maneuvering prevented an immediate vote, but the following day Tom was elected unanimously. He thanked the members but had to decline the honor. An effort to keep him as president *pro tempore* until the end of the session was also declined. Under no circumstances, Tom explained, would he serve in a position that his brother wanted. At that point the board's deliberations were interrupted by the sudden illness of H. M. Favrot, and Leon Jastremski moved that selection of a president be postponed until July, 1887. Then, after authorizing the executive committee to appoint a president *pro tempore* in Tom's place, the board adjourned without acting on David's request to withdraw his resignation. [33]

There were at least half a dozen applicants for the vacant presi-

32 S. D. McEnery to Thomas Boyd, April 4, 1887, unsigned note in Tom Boyd's handwriting, July 2, 1888, *ibid.*; Tom Boyd to E. L. Stephens, July 13, 1896, in Thomas D. Boyd Letterbooks. One line in Tom's letter to Stephens remarks that when he was a student he used to "wonder" that "with such equipment and such a faculty," the school had failed to accomplish "grand" results. "The reason assigned on all sides," Tom recalled, "was that it lacked a head, a president to harmonize and unify and concentrate all the forces that work in and around the school." Twenty-five years later, when Tom was president of the Louisiana State Normal School at Nachitoches, the university still needed a president who could harmonize and unify all those forces. J. W. Nicholson held the university presidency between 1887 and 1896, but apparently his administration too, failed to provide the necessary harmony. In the letter to Stephens Tom explained that he finally agreed to leave Nachitoches for Baton Rouge "to bring order out of chaos." Then he added, "What I have said about the president of the University in this paragraph is, of course, confidential." For a full discussion of Tom Boyd's success at Nachitoches, see Wilkerson, *Thomas Duckett Boyd*, Chaps. 6 and 7.
33 Minutes of the Board of Supervisors, April 4, 5, 1887; Wilkerson, *Thomas Duckett Boyd*, 88–89. Under existing rules, the senior professor, J. W. Nicholson, would serve in the presidency until a permanent replacement was named by the board. Leon Jastremski to Tom Boyd, April 8, 188[7], in Thomas D. Boyd Papers.

dency by the time the board convened in July. But again the members put off a decision, and again they failed to act on David's application to "have the past undone." The same thing occurred at the October meeting, but in December, 1887, a provisional quorum of seven members agreed tentatively to make no appointment until the following July. State politics clearly influenced their decision. Under a reform banner, former governor Francis T. Nicholls was preparing to challenge McEnery's bid for renomination at the Democratic party's state convention scheduled for January, 1888, and the winner of that battle would have to face Henry Clay Warmoth in the general election. Under the circumstances, reasoned the Board of Supervisors, any university president selected by a group of McEnery appointees, could expect a brief career if either Nicholls or Warmoth finally won.[34] Nicholls defeated McEnery in the intraparty contest and then proceeded to overwhelm Warmoth in the general election. But even before the new administration took over, it was apparent that the lame duck university board, its personnel considerably altered by death, resignation, and new appointees, could not agree upon anything of substance. On April 2, 1888, Joseph Spearing presented a two-pronged motion to ratify the December provisional decision against naming a president until July, 1888, and to take no action on David's year-old request to withdraw his resignation. Both efforts failed in a tie vote. Indeed, every motion presented resulted in deadlock. Governor McEnery might have resolved the impasse, but he chose to stay away from the April board meeting entirely.[35]

Meanwhile Governor Nicholls took office and, with the advice of his attorney general, made several new appointments to the university board. One major change put Baton Rouge businessman William Garig in Leon Jastremski's place as vice-president, and another declared two other members (who usually supported David) ineligible because one had won an elective office and the other failed to have his oath of office recorded. By July, 1888, David could hardly have entertained any hopes of regaining the presidency. Even if he had, the following motion offered by a Nicholls appointee would have laid them to rest: "Whereas Col. D. F. Boyd's letter . . . requesting withdrawal of his res-

34 Minutes of the Board of Supervisors, July 4, 5, October 3, December 5, 1887; Hair, *Bourbonism and Agrarian Protest*, 136–40.
35 Minutes of the Board of Supervisors, April 2, 1888.

ignation . . . could not be acted on in April, 1887, (due to the sudden illness of H. M. Favrot); and since then . . . by *unavoidable* circumstances [the board has] had to *postpone* an answer . . . therefore be it resolved: That since more than a year has elapsed since Boyd's resignation was tendered *and* accepted, during which time the school has been *ably* conducted by 2 *other* men, we do not deem it expedient to assent to the withdrawal of Boyd's resignation."[36]

In other action taken the same day Tom Boyd resigned to become president of the Louisiana State Normal School at Natchitoches, and the board named a three-man committee to find a person "suitable for Pres." By July 28, 1888, the committee was ready to report, and, following an executive session, the members elected J. W. Nicholson permanent president of the university. They also adopted Vice-President Garig's motion to vacate all existing professorships. But the reorganization did not affect David personally. He had already submitted his resignation as professor of civil engineering on July 27, 1888, the day before the board convened for its special session. "Pecuniary obligations" made it necessary for him to find a better paying position, he explained in a letter to the governor. For twenty-nine years he had served the school at "virtually no pay," and if it still needed him, he would do so again. But in 1888 even David had to admit that "no such necessity" existed. Of all the burdens he took with him as he left the university, knowledge of that fact was probably the hardest to bear.[37]

36 *Ibid.*, July 2, 3, 1888. Leon Jastremski left Baton Rouge for New Orleans in 1888, where he remained until Grover Cleveland appointed him consul to Peru in 1893. He returned to Louisiana in 1898, made an unsuccessful bid for the governor's office, and died in 1907. New Orleans *Daily Picayune*, November 29, 1907.
37 Minutes of the Board of Supervisors, July 3, 28, 1888; Draft of a letter from David Boyd to Francis T. Nicholls, July 27, 1888, in Boyd Letters, Fleming Collection.

Chapter XII

Hell on Earth

WEEKS BEFORE he resigned his professorship at Louisiana State University, David began making plans to assume the superintendency of a military academy at Farmdale, Kentucky. In March, 1888, he opened negotiations to lease the Kentucky Military Institute for "a term of years," and by mid-July his association with the school was announced in a printed circular and a Kentucky newspaper. Founded in 1845 and chartered by the state two years later, the Kentucky Military Institute was located six miles south of the state capital, Frankfort, on the turnpike to Harrodsburg. Like so many schools of its type, it closed during the Civil War when professors and students resigned en masse to enter military service. After the war it resumed operations, continuing with diminishing success until 1887 when it closed for one session. Apparently David learned of its availability from General Simon Buckner, who was governor of Kentucky in 1888.[1]

Almost nothing of David's personal circumstances during the time he lived in Kentucky is revealed by his papers. Even the many letters he must have received from Baton Rouge and Auburn are missing from the collection. It may be that LeRoy Boyd, who later became the family genealogist and archivist, chose to suppress what must have

---

1 Crutcher and Starks, Men's and Boys' Outfitters, to David Boyd, March 18, 1888, in David Boyd Papers; Circular, July 21, 1888, in Printed Materials, *ibid.*; *Western Argus* (Frankfort, Kentucky), July 12, September 2, 1888; Barksdale Hamlett, "History of Education in Kentucky," Department of Education *Bulletin*, VII (July, 1914), 304.

been painful testimony to a bitter period in his father's life. Whatever the explanation, only a few business letters, canceled checks, printed circulars, and scattered entries in a school register remain to document David's unhappy tenure at Farmdale.

As for the school itself, its faculty, curriculum, and discipline are reasonably well described in a prospectus David published in 1889. Besides the superintendent (who taught "natural philosophy" and civil engineering), the teaching staff consisted of six instructors. Two positions were "temporarily" vacant, but David expected to fill the one in military tactics shortly with a United States officer. Operated under a state charter and a Board of Supervisors named by the governor, the Kentucky Military Institute was, nevertheless, privately owned. Only the superintendent could assume responsibility for the "*management of its affairs*," cadets had to enroll for an entire year, and fees would be assessed accordingly. Furthermore, parents would have no control over their sons "while at the Institite," nor must they attempt in any way to interfere with the school's regulations. "Parents or guardians who do not *assent* to the above conditions," David warned, "are requested *not* to enroll their sons or wards as cadets."[2]

Undeterred, forty-six cadets attended the institute in 1889–1890; over forty enrolled in a summer session in 1891, and by the following October the school's morning report listed a student body of fifty-six. On the surface, the Kentucky Military Institute seemed to be doing well, and old friends like General Sherman and Professor Schele de Vere of the University of Virginia were glad to hear it. They congratulated David, wishing him good luck and "continued success." Other signs, however, indicated that David was heading for financial trouble. In January, 1891, he agreed to buy two shares of stock in the "KMI Corp.," apparently to show his faith in the institute's future. But he could not raise the necessary cash so he left the stock with the seller as collateral, along with his note to be retired in six months. Later that year a printer and a brewer in nearby Frankfort sent him dunning letters, and he transferred the school's business from one druggist to another when the first made repeated demands that he settle his bill. Telegrams, notes, and canceled checks drawn on Tom Boyd's bank account offer additional evidence of David's financial instability between

2 *Prospectus* for Kentucky Military Institute, 1889–90, in Printed Materials, David Boyd Papers.

1888 and 1893. The telegrams, which Tom seems to have answered positively in every instance, usually requested loans ranging in size from fifty to seventy-five dollars. Quite urgent in tone, they frequently asked Tom to deposit money in a Frankfort bank in time to cover checks David had already written to some of his numerous creditors.[3]

By 1893, his last year as superintendent of the Kentucky Military Institute, David was certainly in desperate straits. His father, Thomas Jefferson Boyd, died on February 16 and David probably went to Wytheville for the funeral, although nothing in his papers confirms the trip. What is clear, however, is the fact that he borrowed over five hundred dollars from someone in New Orleans to retire a debt owed by the Boyd family in Virginia. To secure the loan, he ordered some four hundred books in his personal library (then stored in Baton Rouge) shipped to his creditor. If the money were not repaid within a year, the creditor was authorized to sell the books and apply whatever they brought against David's debt. Ultimately that is what happened, not only to his library, but also to the only other valuable possession David still owned in 1893. Years earlier he purchased some furniture which once belonged to Bernardo de Gálvez, Spanish governor of Louisiana between 1777 and 1785. Left behind when the university moved to the barracks in 1886, the furniture was still in the asylum building in 1892 when Samuel McEnery advised David to remove it before someone on the asylum board claimed it as the property of that institution. But he did nothing until the next year when a group of ladies in charge of the Louisiana exhibit at the Columbian Exposition asked permission to ship the furniture to Chicago at their expense. According to LeRoy Boyd, they did not pay the freight charges and David had to assume the debt. Even worse, the furniture had to be put in storage when the exposition closed, and it was still there in 1907 as security for a two-hundred-dollar debt David never managed to repay.[4]

3   Morning Report, Kentucky Military Institute, 1891, in MS volumes, *ibid.*; L. B. McBrayer to David Boyd, January 6, 1891, David Boyd to W. S. Favrieur, undated; Numerous overdue bills to David Boyd, July 1, 1889, to January 1, 1892, *ibid.*; Wm. T. Sherman to David Boyd, September 15, 1890, in William T. Sherman Letters, David F. Boyd Family Papers; Schele de Vere to David Boyd, December 4, 1890, in Alphabetical File, Fleming Collection; Telegrams, cancelled checks, requests for loans to Tom Boyd, 1888–93, in Thomas D. Boyd Papers.
4   Obituary of Thomas Jefferson Boyd from Wytheville (Va.) *Dispatch*, February 24, 1893, in Thomas D. Boyd Papers; David Boyd to H. L. Favrot, February 20, 1893, David Boyd to John Jastremski, February 20, 1893, S. D. McEnery to David Boyd, June 3, 1892, T. A. Faries to David Boyd, April 20, 1893, in David Boyd Papers. A note by LeRoy Boyd on the back of the Faries letter records the history of the Gálvez furniture through 1907. What became of it after that is unknown.

More telling than unpaid bills and appeals for loans as an indication of David's plight in 1893 were the entries he made in the morning reports during his last semester at the Kentucky Military Institute. On February 1, 1893, only David and one other instructor appeared on the faculty roster. A matron and a chaplain completed the staff which, considering the number of cadets enrolled (ten), must have been more than adequate. On May 20 a boy was expelled for insubordination, and two more were dropped the next day for "continued absence w/o leave." The last formal entry appeared a month later: "On June 15, 1893, 7:30 o'clock A.M. session closed. By publication of Gen. Orders # 1 Superintendent's office." Then, in a penciled scrawl, David added, "Closed forever."[5]

Still on the grounds at Farmdale in August, David thought about opening a "select private school" in Frankfort, Lexington, or Louisville, Kentucky. But lack of funds made him abandon that plan. Instead, he went to Germantown, Ohio, a small town about thirty miles north of Cincinnati, where he spent a year on the staff of a military academy. Exactly what he did there is not clear. Even Tom Boyd did not learn of the Germantown association until a year after David's death, when Ettie sent him a corrected newspaper summary of her husband's career.[6]

David's whereabouts after he left Germantown are somewhat easier to establish. Early in September, 1894, Colonel J. Sumner Rogers, superintendent of the Michigan Military Academy, contacted him in Frankfort, Kentucky. David had just joined the academy staff as instructor of Latin and English, but his principal duty as the school's "Southern representative" was to recruit new cadets. To that end Rogers sent him a number of circulars advertising the academy, and a letter of introduction which he could use in his search for potential students. Rogers himself planned to "canvass" Chicago during September while David concentrated on the territory encompassed by Cincinnati, Louisville, St. Louis, and Indianapolis. Any sons of Con-

5 Morning Reports of the Kentucky Military Institute, February 1 to June 15, 1893, in MS Volumes, David Boyd Papers. Actually, the Kentucky Military Institute was reopened under new management ten miles east of Louisville in 1896. It was still operating in 1914. Hamlett, "History of Education in Kentucky," 304.
6 David Boyd to LeRoy Stafford Boyd, August 8, 1893, A. W. Hyatt to E. B. Kruttschnitt, August [?], 1896, Ettie Boyd to Tom Boyd, May 4, 1900, all in David Boyd Papers.

federate colleagues David could secure would be welcomed cordially, Rogers promised. "Their sons will receive the same treatment . . . at this Academy as the sons of Union soldiers."[7]

Besides Superintendent Rogers and David, the Michigan Military Academy staff included "four well-trained military men" and ten instructors in the "academic" department described in a brochure as graduates of Harvard, Yale, the University of Virginia, and other leading institutions. The physical plant was equally impressive. Located twenty-six miles northwest of Detroit on Orchard Lake, and consisting of "all new brick buildings" with the "finest plumbing that money can buy," the Michigan Military Academy occupied an ideal site. Furthermore, its "broad, liberal . . . spirit" and its isolation would keep its students free of any "demoralizing influences."[8]

However inviting the academic and physical environment was at Orchard Lake, Tom Boyd found his brother's financial arrangements with Colonel Rogers decidedly unattractive. David accepted the job on a commission basis, expecting to receive 25 percent of the $450 fee of each student he recruited. But he did not join the school until September, 1894, too late to secure many cadets that session, and his various trips through Indiana, Ohio, and Missouri the following winter proved equally unproductive. As a result, he had to borrow heavily from his more solvent brother. At first he did so without asking Tom's permission, merely issuing "sight drafts" on Tom's bank and notifying him of it later. Not surprisingly, Tom objected: "I have never failed to honor your drafts, and shall honor this one . . . but it does seem to me not unreasonable that your friends should ask you to use some less disagreeable method of calling upon them for loans. . . . I shall cash no more sight drafts, unless they have been drawn with my full knowledge and consent." Tom hoped David's connection with the Michigan Military Academy would be profitable but advised him nevertheless to seek a

---

7 J. Sumner Rogers to David Boyd, September 3, 1894, *ibid.* David may have learned about the Michigan Military Academy originally from General Sherman who delivered a commencement address there in 1879. Wm. Sherman to David Boyd, June 15, 1879, in William T. Sherman Letters, David F. Boyd Family Papers.

8 *Prospectus* of the Michigan Military Academy, October 1, 1894, in Printed Materials, David Boyd Papers. The intellectual atmosphere may have been pure at Orchard Lake, but in June, 1896, one of David's friends at the academy informed him of "eleven cases of vereal [sic] disease in the school this year . . . the matter concealed from parents for fear the boys would be called home." H. E. Cook to David Boyd, June 27, 1896, *ibid.*

salaried position through a "Teacher's agency." Meanwhile, he would help his brother to the best of his ability.[9]

Later Tom seems to have lost patience. When David telegraphed for more cash, Tom sent it "against my better judgement." If he thought David were using the money on himself, he would give him his "last cent." But he was certain David was spending it to "advance" the school. The Michigan Military Academy meant nothing to Tom; neither should it to David unless it paid him "a living" for his work. He urged his brother to quit "bldg up someone else's business," and to think of his own interests, even if he had to "get out of education."[10]

By the end of the school year David was looking for another job. But it was still in education, and, as matters developed, on terms even less satisfactory than those at Orchard Lake. On May 28, 1895, Colonel A. F. Fleet of the Missouri Military Academy responded to David's letter of application for employment. Fleet made no secret of the fact that he wanted David's services at the lowest possible figure, inquiring how many children David had and how much salary he thought he needed to "exist." The Missouri Military Academy had not done well in recent years, Fleet explained, and he had to be careful not to overstaff the institution. On June 30 he offered David the entire $350-fees of the first two boys he might recruit, and 20 percent, or $70, of the fees of additional cadets secured from states other than Missouri, Illinois, Texas, Kansas, or Iowa. David could teach if he wanted to, but during the first year he could expect nothing extra for his work.

David accepted Fleet's offer by telegram. Then he borrowed enough money from Tom to make a brief visit to his family in Alabama. In late July he visited Fleet's academy at Mexico, Missouri, and by August he was back in Kentucky looking for students around Louisville and Frankfort. However, few people there had ever heard of the Missouri institution, and Colonel Fleet made it clear that he did not intend to spend any money on advertising. Neither would he advance David any funds for expenses. Their agreement had been made on the grounds that David was well known in Kentucky. As for expense money, wrote

---

9 Tom Boyd to David Boyd, September 5, 1894, in Thomas D. Boyd Letterbooks; David Boyd to Harney Skolfield, May 29, 1895, in Thomas D. Boyd Papers. In his letter to Skolfield, David credited his "old army overcoat" with keeping him free from cold and illness during the winter of 1894–95.

10 Tom Boyd to David Boyd, undated, in Thomas D. Boyd Letterbooks.

Colonel Fleet, "If I had understood at the start there was any uncertainty about your having money to carry on a vigorous campaign, I can say frankly that this would have ended the matter. . . . I have not the money to spare for it."[11]

By mid-September, after trips to Chicago and Louisville, David had to report to Colonel Fleet that he had not secured a single cadet for the Missouri Military Academy. Their agreement called for him to serve the school for a year, but if Fleet thought he could be relieved without "injustice," David wanted to be notified to that effect at once. Colonel Fleet agreed, and a week later David resumed his association with the Michigan Military Academy at Orchard Lake. Until October he stayed around Louisville when, on the advice of Colonel Rogers, he shifted his base of operations to Cincinnati. From there he could recruit boys in neighboring towns and cities like Hamilton and Dayton which the Michigan superintendent thought much more promising than Louisville.[12]

In spite of his poverty David seems to have enjoyed his stay in Cincinnati during the fall and winter of 1895–1896. He did not enroll more than six or seven cadets in the academy, but in the course of his recruiting efforts he did form a number of warm friendships with congenial people in the community. In addition, he began contributing articles to at least two Cincinnati newspapers. Based largely on his reminiscences of Generals Sherman, Joseph E. Johnston, and other heroic figures in the Civil War, they were well received by readers of the Sunday supplements, and, to a limited extent, they augmented his meager income. One reader, president of the Venetian Marble and Mosaic Art Company of Detroit, was so pleased with David's stories in the Cincinnati *Inquirer* that he offered to publish them in book form. The volume never materialized, but he and David did become good friends. Speaking generally of his Michigan and Ohio acquaintances in one of his letters to his wife, David remarked, "The more I see of northern people, the better I like them. Morally, they are as good as we are South; and in taking care of their families, they are far our superiors. Their

11 A. F. Fleet to David Boyd, May 28, June 30, July 2, 4, August 26, 1895, J. A. Fleet (son) to David Boyd, August 8, 1895, all in David Boyd Papers; Tom Boyd to David Boyd, August 12, 1895, in Thomas D. Boyd Letterbooks.
12 David Boyd to A. F. Fleet, September 14, 1895, A. F. Fleet to David Boyd, September 16, 1895, H. E. Cook to David Boyd, September 21, October 7, 1895, J. Sumner Rogers to David Boyd, September 21, 1895, all in David Boyd Papers.

industry and economy in all classes, is something marvellous to a Southerner."[13]

Late in January, 1896, Colonel Rogers reminded David that a note for three hundred dollars that he negotiated the previous November would be due in February. Rogers (who was David's cosigner) did not think the bank would extend the loan unless the interest and at least a part of the principal were paid. "Can not you arrange to take care of this?" he asked. Disturbed, David left Cincinnati for Orchard Lake early in February, but what he found there made him forget about his personal problems. One of his "recruits," he discovered, was dangerously ill, and another, the son of his best friend in Cincinnati, was so desperately unhappy that his father was thinking seriously of removing him from school. David reported his misgivings to the father, Thomas T. Heath, who was not surprised. The letter confirmed what the elder Heath already knew by "spiritual instinct and intuition": that the Michigan Military Academy, "a nest of drunken, lying, thieving, fagging, hazing, brutes," was no place for an "inexperienced boy." If he could talk with David for twenty minutes, he could decide immediately what to do about his son. Heath did not expect David to stay at Orchard Lake either. "I wish I could hope for peace to you," he wrote, "but I cannot . . . feel that you will be very happy there for evidently your ways are not their ways."[14]

Heath was right. David was not happy at Orchard Lake, and by late February, 1896, he was back in Cincinnati looking for a job. At one point he even considered selling insurance. The Bay State Beneficiary Association, to whom he applied during the spring, informed him it would be "glad to sign him on" at 50 percent of whatever he sold. But he did not pursue the offer. Meanwhile, Ettie Boyd was trying to find her husband a position. She asked Tom Boyd to use his political influence in David's behalf, but he was reluctant for several reasons. "As he has always been a non-partizan [sic] in politics," Tom replied, "it would be no easy matter to get him a good position at Washington and I am pretty sure he would not accept a minor clerkship." Tom did not want to discourage Ettie, but he did not want to get his brother any job

---

13   H. E. Cook to David Boyd, November 29, December 28, 1895, A. L. Bresler to David Boyd, January 8, 1896, *ibid.*; David Boyd to Ettie Boyd, January 4, 1896, in Scrapbook, *ibid.*
14   J. Sumner Rogers to David Boyd, January 23, 1896, A. L. Bresler to David Boyd, February 3, 1896, Thomas T. Heath to David Boyd, February 8, 15, 1896, all *ibid.*

unless he was sure David would take it and that he could hold it. "In this matter," he explained, "I had sad experience . . . in connection with his going to Auburn and his return to the University in 1884." Besides, only a year earlier David had refused a school principalship Tom secured for him at Greensburg, Louisiana. The salary was not large, Tom admitted, but, "success in a small position gives better leverage by which to rise to higher things than the reputation of year after year of failure."[15]

By the late spring and early summer of 1896, David's circumstances were more desperate than ever before. He wrote Colonel A. F. Fleet of the Missouri Military Academy asking for any kind of work, but Fleet replied that he could not help him. A letter to an old friend in Knoxville, Tennessee, about a position at the university elicited a similar answer. However, the friend, John Paulett, thought David could earn something if he compiled a book of reminiscences entitled something like "*Recollections of Three Men: Sherman, Johnston and Stuart.*" Paulett might even join David in publishing it. But he warned, "You would have to be careful not to say too much in praise of *Sherman*! He may have been misunderstood by the Southern people, but it is certain that he has not been forgiven by many."[16]

Even before Paulett's suggestion, David had been preparing numerous articles drawn from his wartime experiences and personal recollections. His most ambitious literary effort in 1896, however, was a manuscript based on the boyhood of J. E. B. Stuart. Designed for the edification of youth and dedicated to the children of his old friends and schoolmates in Virginia, David's narrative traced Stuart's life from the time he and Stuart first met in Wytheville in 1845. They attended the same school for several years, and later, when Stuart went off to college, the two exchanged numerous letters. As depicted by David, Stuart was a carefree, frolicsome boy who loved to dance and sing "negro songs" and Methodist hymns with equal abandon. But Stuart's widow did not care for David's portrait of her husband. When he sent her the manuscript in April, 1896, she returned it with several suggestions for

---

15 J. W. Simcock to David Boyd, February 26, 1896, D. B. Barnes to David Boyd, April 16, 1896, *ibid.*; Tom Boyd to Ettie Boyd, March 26, 1896, Tom Boyd to LeRoy Stafford Boyd, March 26, 1896, in Thomas D. Boyd Letterbooks.
16 A. L. Bresler to David Boyd, April 30, 1896, J. Sumner Rogers to David Boyd, May 7, 1896, David Boyd to J. Sumner Rogers, May 8, 1896, A. F. Fleet to David Boyd, June 3, 1896, John W. Paulett to David F. Boyd, June 3, 1896, all in David Boyd Papers.

its revision. For one thing, she considered it too "sophisticated" and too full of digression for its intended audience. For another, several expressions and anecdotes in it "grated" upon her ear. Aware of the general's shortcomings, Mrs. Stuart was unwilling to have them included in a book, and certain passages, she complained, could "*never* [be] read to her grandchildren" without serious injury to the memory she hoped to preserve. To call him "Jim," for example, was "undignified." As for references to Stuart's dancing and singing "negro songs and Methodist hymns," David must be mistaken. Not only had she never known him to dance, but he was not even a Methodist. Finally, Mrs. Stuart offered to send David a biography of Robert E. Lee which she considered more appropriate than David's treatment of her husband. David wrote a gracious reply, but the widow's determination that only her husband's "finer, higher traits" should be dealt with by any biographer appears to have discouraged him from trying to publish his manuscript.[17]

Only one event in 1896 seems to have offered David any encouragement whatever. For a fleeting moment during the spring and summer, he apparently entertained a faint hope that he would be recalled to the presidency of the Louisiana State University. A serious student uprising occurred there in April following the allegedly undeserved promotion of two cadets to officer rank by President J. W. Nicholson and his commandant. When seventy cadets threatened to resign their commissions or refuse future appointments unless Nicholson rescinded the "unearned" promotions, he refused on the ground that to honor such a demand would be destructive of discipline. The students resigned; Nicholson gave them time to reconsider; but thirty-seven remained adamant, whereupon he promptly suspended them for the rest of the session. The results were a public controversy, a legislative investigation, and Nicholson's decision to resign the presidency. Tom Boyd was unanimously chosen by the board to succeed him, but he refused; so did Athur T. Prescott, the president of Louisiana Polytechnical Institute at Ruston. At that point the board adjourned, and letters of application for the job began to pour in.[18]

17 David Boyd, "Reviving the Rank of Lieutenant General," undated, David Boyd, "General W. T. Sherman: His Life in the South Before the War and His Relations with Prominent Southern Men," undated, David Boyd, "Boyhood of J. E. B. Stuart," undated (MSS in David Boyd Papers, Department of Archives, Louisiana State University); Mrs. J. E. B. Stuart to David Boyd, April 23, May 23, 1896, *ibid.*

18 Baton Rouge *Weekly Truth*, April 11, 1896; J. W. Pearce to David Boyd, June 24, 1896, in David Boyd Papers.

David did not personally apply for the presidency, but some of his friends tried to influence the board to consider him after Tom Boyd's initial refusal. Others, like Harney Skolfield and Dr. J. W. Dupree, thought that David was the only one who could "bring order out of chaos," but they did nothing in his behalf because they were not sure what Tom Boyd would do. Ultimately, Tom did take the job when it was offered a second time, and Dr. Dupree explained to David later, "Had he not have [sic] accepted, we were ready to move in the matter and I believe [we] would have succeeded."[19]

Tom Boyd disagreed. In a letter to his brother on August 2, 1896, he explained at length why he had changed his mind. Friends convinced him, Tom wrote, that it was his duty to accept the post, because he was the only one who could bring back to the school the confidence and affection it once inspired. Before deciding, Tom spent two weeks in Baton Rouge. But, he told David, "[I] did not hear your name mentioned for the presidency . . . by anyone but myself. I had mentioned you in that connection both in letters and conversation before and after the position was offered to me; but, while everyone spoke of you in the kindest terms, the opinion seemed to be general that an effort to elect you would re-open the old wounds . . . and would not succeed. If I had thought there was any chance of securing the place for you, I would not for a moment have entertained the idea of accepting it."[20] There is no reason to doubt the accuracy of Tom Boyd's explanation. Neither is there any evidence to support Dr. Dupree's speculation that David could have won the post if Tom had remained adamant. What is more likely is that the doctor was trying to cheer up his longtime friend, then serving a miserable exile far away from friends, family, and his greatest love, the Louisiana State University.

A month after Tom Boyd became president of the university, friends contacted David again about a position they thought he could secure in Louisiana. J. V. Calhoun had just become state superintendent of public education, leaving a vacancy in the principalship of Boys' High School in New Orleans. Harney Skolfield, treasurer of the university Board of Supervisors, was the prime mover in the effort to get the job for David, together with John Jastremski, formerly superintendent of

19   J. W. Pearce to David Boyd, July 11, 1896, J. W. Dupree to David Boyd, July 18, 1896, in David Boyd Papers.
20   Tom Boyd to David Boyd, August 2, 1896, in Thomas D. Boyd Letterbooks.

the deaf and dumb asylum at Baton Rouge. Both men contacted former governor S. D. McEnery and the current governor, Murphy Foster,
in David's behalf. They also asked a prominent citizen of Orleans Parish, Colonel Arthur W. Hyatt, to use his influence with the New Orleans school board. No "politics" were involved, Skolfield assured
Hyatt; the "Board of Control" wanted a "scholar and a teacher" for the
principalship, and David was both. In Skolfield's words, "The dear old
man needs help [,] Arthur [,] and will give his best service to your high
school. He could have been President of this school today had he not
thought he was rebuked by the [university] Board when they *requested* him to *endeavor* to be more economical in his management. . . . He resigned simply because, in my opinion, he was over-
sensitive." [21]

For the next two months, August and September, 1896, E. B.
Kruttschnitt, president of the New Orleans school board, was inun-
dated with letters from David's friends. David himself took an active
part in soliciting those letters, asking friends all over the country
to write the New Orleans authorities in his behalf. Kruttschnitt,
David remarked to his son, was probably growing weary of the number of "testimonials" he had received, not to mention the flood of
personal calls friends of David's had paid him at his office. Tom
Boyd agreed. On August 30, 1896, he wrote his brother that the job
was probably "safely" his unless "too many cooks" were spoiling the
soup. [22]

School board president Kruttschnitt himself favored David's appointment to the vacant principalship. But in his opinion David could
not be elected without the support of F. D. Chrètien of Orleans Parish.
Chrètien was chairman of the committee on high schools, a subcommittee of the school board. Normal procedure called for Chrètien's
subcommittee to present its candidate for the principalship to a second
subcommittee, the committee on teachers, for concurrence. Then the
entire board would make the formal appointment. If Chrètien's committee acted decisively, there would be no contest, but if the members

21   Harney Skolfield to A. W. Hyatt, August 7, 1896, in David Boyd Papers.
22   Thos. T. Heath to E. B. Kruttschnitt, August 10, 1896, J. Stoddard Johnston to E. B. Krutt-
     schnitt, August 11, 1896, J. H. Lane to E. B. Kruttschnitt, August 12, 1896, W. H. Butts to
     E. B. Kruttschnitt, August 14, 1896, S. D. McEnery to E. B. Kruttschnitt, September 9, 1896,
     all *ibid.*; David Boyd to LeRoy Stafford Boyd, August 25, 1896, in Selected Letters, LeRoy
     Boyd Papers; Thomas Boyd to David Boyd, August 30, 1896, in Thomas D. Boyd Papers.

could not agree, the full board would have to settle the issue. The situation was especially complicated in 1896 because of local politics. As Tom Boyd explained to his brother, many of David's partisans in New Orleans had supported the Citizens' League movement against the "machine"; they would have little or no power with influential members of the school board. Besides, David's strongest opponent was the current vice-principal of the high school, Frank W. Gregory. Many people believed that the incentive of "in service" teachers would be killed if persons not connected with the system were appointed to supervisory posts.[23]

David thought one other factor might cost him the job. On September 4, 1896, he wrote Harney Skolfield that the "Catholic influence" in New Orleans was being used against him. Vice-principal Gregory was a Catholic; so was the state superintendent of public education, J. V. Calhoun, the former principal. Calhoun, David learned from a New Orleans friend, was "helping his brother Catholic." "It is but natural, and proper, for Calhoun to stand by his old colleague and friend," David confided, "but I don't like to be beaten by Catholics! If I am, my wife will have a good laugh. It has been her fear for years that if I joined any church it wd. be the Catholic."[24]

In spite of his letter to Skolfield, David must have thought his campaign for the principalship would ultimately prove successful. At least he prepared a speech some time during August or September designed for delivery at his inaugural. Addressed to the faculty and students of Boys' High School, it consisted of some thirty-five pages and sought to reconcile any who might have resented his appointment rather than Gregory's to the "much sought after" position. However, when the school board finally acted, it chose Gregory, not David. Chairman Chrètien's committee on high schools had not been able to agree on a single name to present to the committee on teachers. A majority favored David, and a minority, including Chrètien himself, supported vice-principal Gregory. The two subcommittees conferred, but when no decision could be reached, David's name was withdrawn, leaving only Gregory and a contestant from Waco, Texas, in the field. A few

23   E. B. Kruttschnitt to Murphy Foster, August 28, 1896; clipping from New Orleans *Times-Democrat*, September 30, 1896, in David Boyd Papers; Tom Boyd to David Boyd, August 30, 1896, in Thomas D. Boyd Papers.
24   David Boyd to Harney Skolfield, September 4, 1896, in Thomas D. Boyd Papers.

days later the entire board elected Gregory by a vote of nineteen to four.[25]

David was crushed. Failure to secure the New Orleans job forced him to borrow more money from Tom Boyd. "You can't imagine," he wrote his brother in mid-October, "how it mortifies me to be a *beggar* in this way." If possible, David wanted Tom to get a statement from board president Kruttschnitt explaining that his failure to win the principalship was due to the board's unwillingness to break its rule about promoting classroom teachers. Otherwise people in Ohio and Kentucky would misunderstand. "People away from there [Louisiana]," David wrote, "can't understand why so ordinary a position shd be refused me; nor can I blame them; for it does seem to me that Louisiana has but one more kick to give me—refuse me a nigger school in Cat Fish Town [a black slum in] B.R. and, maybe, fate has this disgrace in reserve for me." Then, in a final burst of despair, he asked his brother to omit his name from anything he planned to publish about the university: "Don't speak of me. Nicholson was pleased to 'drop' me out of the history [he wrote] of the school. Let me stay 'dropped.' I don't regret my work for the school. I wish it well and I dearly prize the affection the old cadets have for me; but I don't want my name publicly or officially used in connection with the Univ. I wish the public would forget that I was ever there and I wish I cld forget it too."[26]

The last three months of 1896 may well have been the most miserable David ever spent. After failing to get the New Orleans job, he considered opening a private school in Cincinnati or Louisville, but poverty forced him to abandon the idea. Nor did anything come of a friend's suggestion that they collaborate in the establishment of a "classical" school in the Crescent City. Instead, David eked out a bare existence by delivering lectures on Civil War themes to any audience willing to engage him. A handbill he had printed in November, 1896, announced his availability as a speaker on "Lyceum circuits" and at posts and encampments of the Grand Army of the Republic. Interested parties were invited to contact "D. F. Boyd, a soldier under Jackson, at 112 Malvern Place, Cincinnati, Ohio." The address listed was a rooming

25 David Boyd, speech planned for delivery to faculty and students of Boys' High School, undated; clipping from New Orleans *Picayune*, September 26, 1896; clipping from New Orleans *Times-Democrat*, September 30, 1896, in David Boyd Papers.
26 David Boyd to Tom Boyd, October 11, 1896, in Thomas D. Boyd Papers.

house which David first made his headquarters while still connected
with the Michigan Military Academy in 1895. Late in 1896, however, he
was so poor that he had to ask the landlady to wait for the rent. "I have
been trying to arrange my affairs," he explained, "so that I could leave
Cincinnati; if I should find not occupation in the city. I find it difficult
to find work here. I think I must leave your city."[27]

By mid-December, 1896, David was bitter as well as poor. His son,
LeRoy Boyd, wrote to announce that he was leaving Auburn where he
had been a librarian at the college for approximately three years. Le-
Roy wanted to "read" law and had made arrangements to do so in the
office of a judge in Clinton, Louisiana. David did not want him to go to
Louisiana, but "since the living is not easy anywhere," he did not order
him not to go. However, for David's sake, LeRoy was to avoid the university at all costs. He should visit his Uncle Tom and the family, of
course, but only in the town. "I love the old school," David explained to
his son, "but the Board . . . did not treat me right, and I wish nothing to
do with them. . . . I do not wish to visit the school, and I wd like my
children not to go there."[28]

Ironically, David himself was on the university campus only a
month later. On January 4, 1897, Tom Boyd wrote to his brother's Cincinnati rooming house, not even sure that David would still be there.
Mr. W. H. Goodale, professor of "moral philosophy" and civics at the
university, had suffered a fatal accident during the Christmas holidays. While riding his bicycle in downtown Baton Rouge, Tom explained, Goodale caught the front wheel in a wagon rut, was thrown
head first into the street and broke his leg. He also sustained internal
injuries that caused his death a few days later. Tom wanted David to
replace Professor Goodale. In fact, Harney Skolfield had already spoken
to Governor Foster about recalling David and Vice-President Garig approved whole-heartedly. David could take over all or part of Goodale's
teaching duties and serve as secretary to the president and the board

27 David Boyd to [?] (landlady), November 6, 1896; David Boyd, Lecture Notes, [October
through December, 1896,] in David Boyd Papers; Newspaper reports of lectures by David
Boyd in unidentified Cincinnati newspapers in Scrapbook, *ibid.*; David Boyd to LeRoy S.
Boyd, November 15, 1896, in Selected Papers, LeRoy Boyd Papers; Handbill announcing lecture series by David F. Boyd, 1896, reprinted in Baton Rouge *Morning Advocate*, January 25,
1942.
28 LeRoy Boyd to David Boyd, December 11, 1896, in David Boyd Papers; David Boyd to LeRoy
Boyd, December 14, 1896, in Selected Papers, LeRoy Boyd Papers.

as well. If convenient he could start at once. Or, if he preferred, he could defer his return until the fall session.[29]

David accepted. He would settle his affairs in Ohio, "run by" Auburn, Alabama, to visit his family, and arrive in Baton Rouge in plenty of time to help Tom prepare for an agricultural conference scheduled to take place on the campus sometime in late January. But a telegram changed his plans. On Saturday, January 16, 1897, a message from his daughter Mary arrived at his Cincinnati address announcing, "Leigh [LeRoy Stafford Boyd] was accidentally shot, is dying, come immediately." With money Tom provided a few days earlier, David left for the South at once. He went through Auburn, but did not stop until he reached Clinton, Louisiana, where Ettie Boyd, already on the scene, was busily caring for their gravely wounded son. Convinced after a few days' vigil that LeRoy would probably survive, David left him in Ettie's care and proceeded to Baton Rouge where Tom Boyd, about to undergo a frequently postponed operation, put him in charge of arrangements for the agricultural convention.[30]

In a letter written to Ettie from Baton Rouge on Sunday, January 24, 1897, David apologized for not visiting Clinton that weekend. But in addition to preparing for the convention, he had to take over his ailing brother's official correspondence and conduct the weekly inspection for him as well. This restricted him almost exclusively to the university campus. However, David informed his wife, "I attended services today at *your* (Baptist) Church." Ettie was pleased. On the envelope of David's letter she scrawled a comment to one of her children, "How lovely in your Papa to go the first Sunday he spent on his return to my church. It was unfashionable, perhaps unattractive outwardly, but he had a reason for going. E.G.B."[31]

Tom Boyd did not return to the university until February 6, 1897. By that time the spring term had already begun. Operations were not disrupted, because David and Professor J. W. Nicholson made all the

29 Tom Boyd to David Boyd, January 4, 1897, in David Boyd Papers; Wilkerson, *Thomas Duckett Boyd*, 85–86.
30 Tom Boyd to David Boyd, January 13, 1897, Mary Boyd to David Boyd, telegram, undated, David Boyd to Ettie Boyd, January 24, 1897, all in David Boyd Papers; David Boyd to Ettie Boyd, undated, in Scrapbook, *ibid.*; David Boyd to Mary Boyd, January 21, 1897, in Selected Letters, LeRoy Boyd Papers. David was in Baton Rouge when he wrote his daughter. He explained that Leigh was "on the mend" and that Tom needed him "so much that I came here subject to your mother's call."
31 David Boyd to Ettie Boyd, January 24, 1897, in David Boyd Papers.

necessary arrangements based on Tom's written instructions. Besides doing clerical work, David taught ten hours a week, a teaching load that soon increased when illness forced a staff member to resign. Nevertheless, David threw himself totally into all sorts of additional work. For example, in a long memorandum prepared for his brother, David listed what he considered serious shortcomings in the university operations. Faculty record keeping was "too casual" and so was discipline. Smoking in class should not be tolerated, and chapel attendance should be required of professors as well as cadets. Other serious criticisms concerned the dining room, the food, and the unkempt appearance of the student body. Finally, David commented on the scholarly attainments of the corps of cadets. "In passing casually among them, and talking with them, their standard of general information appears *low*," he complained. What must the school have been like five months earlier before Tom replaced Nicholson? "You know," David concluded, "I shd be excused at feeling sad and depressed at such a deplorable state of things. I believe you can rectify matters here; and I believe too you will. But I don't believe you can do it without a sweeping reorganization." [32]

Tom did not record what he thought of his brother's "impressions." However, he must have considered the remarks about cadet discipline and unsanitary facilities worthwhile, because David spent much of the spring of 1897 seeing that conditions were improved. In April the school newspaper, the *Reveille*, commented on David's progress: "Persons in Baton Rouge and vicinity in need of 'scrubouts' can apply to Col. D. F. Boyd. The 'old colonel' is having his 'Ku Klux Klan' scrub off their demerits. His classroom floor is beginning to glisten like a ship's deck. Down on his knees 'holy stoning' a floor, is about as near to heaven as a 'Ku Klux' will ever get." [33] The "Ku Klux Klan" was a recently formed organization of the "less serious" cadets who insisted that they should not be confused with an older group of the same name that terrorized carpetbaggers and "political niggers." Describing themselves as "innocent fellows, if a little wild," the Ku Klux considered themselves the special pets of David, whom they affectionately

---

32 Tom Boyd to David Boyd, February 3, 1897, *ibid.*; David Boyd, Memorandum book for Thos. Boyd, Pres., February 18, 1897, in MS volumes, *ibid.*; David Boyd to Tom Boyd, February 4, 1897, in Thomas D. Boyd Papers.
33 The *Reveille*, April 24, 1897.

labeled the "old colonel." They groaned about the demerits he assigned
during Sunday morning inspections, but they invited him to their social functions, at least those that took place on the university campus.
In May, 1897, they reproved him mildly in the columns of the *Reveille*
for failure to attend an entertainment at the pavilion. "If it had been a
'stag' German or something where the boys didn't want him," the Ku
Klux correspondent remarked, "he would have been on hand for sure.
He is never on hand at the right time. The boys missed him because he
was not there to chase them around." [34]

In spite of his excellent relations with the cadets and a few old
friends like Dr. Dupree and Harney Skolfield, David was heartily sorry
he had returned to the university. By March, 1897, he had applied for
the vacant presidency at the University of Alabama, and nine months
later he sought the same position at the Texas Agricultural and Mechanical College. In neither case did he expect serious consideration,
but his life at the university was so miserable, he wrote his son, that he
had to get away, perhaps to Kentucky or Ohio. "To stay in La. even if
the situation were not a sort of *hell on earth* would not be wise or prudent," David told LeRoy. "[To] work at my age [sixty-three] about 10 to
18 hours every day 7 days a week in this climate, with no recreation or
change, always in this office or classroom, is simply death and that
very soon. . . . But about all this, please say nothing." [35]

Sympathetic but unconvinced, LeRoy reminded his father that the
job at Baton Rouge provided a "good living" and that the family certainly needed all the help it could get. How Ettie Boyd and the three
children still living at home managed to subsist, LeRoy remarked, was
a "mystery." He could not send them anything just then, and he would
not be able to when he left Clinton for Tulane law school unless he secured a government job. Meanwhile, LeRoy hoped that his comments
did not offend David. But considering the family's "present condition,"
he felt it was necessary to speak out.

What David thought of his son's lecture is not recorded, but he, too,
must have worried about Ettie's precarious financial circumstances.
In 1897 the three oldest Boyd children, Jack, David Jr. (Rex), and Le-

34 *Ibid.*; May 1, June 12, 1897.
35 Ettie Boyd to LeRoy S. Boyd, March 27, 1897, David Boyd to LeRoy S. Boyd, April 20, 1897,
    in Selected Letters, LeRoy Boyd Papers; C. W. Hutson to David Boyd, January 8, 1898, in
    David Boyd Papers.

Roy were at least self-supporting, if not contributing, to the Alabama Boyds. But Mary and the two youngest sons, Guy and Jesse, were still in school. To keep them there, Ettie gave piano lessons and took in boarders while David sent whatever he could spare after paying something to all his creditors scattered around the country.[36]

David did not resign his professorship in 1897, but he did go to Ohio that summer to lecture at the Miami Valley Chautauqua on "General W. T. Sherman: His life in the South Before the War." Then he visited his family in late August, returning to the university on September 1, just as a yellow fever epidemic was beginning. Ettie Boyd thought David "seemed tired" when he was in Alabama. They discussed the family's situation fully, she told LeRoy, agreeing that it was best for her and the children to stay in Auburn. David, however, had spent such a "wretched" year at Baton Rouge that he still intended to leave the university if conditions did not improve.[37]

Because of the epidemic, the university's 1897–1898 session did not begin until December 1. But David was not idle. He spent the enforced holiday having the buildings renovated and the grounds thoroughly cleaned. Later, when the army recalled the commandant to active duty because of the impending war with Spain, David inherited many of his duties. Tom announced David's added responsibilities in a general order issued in the spring of 1898. Besides supervising buildings and grounds, David would conduct "special" inspections of the mess hall and the meals, the hospital and the sick, and oversee the "sanitary" conditions of the university. He would also make regular daily and weekly inspections and report the results to the president. But more work did not cure David's depression. "It was the great blunder of my life that I ever came down here," he wrote his son in January, 1898. "The climate makes against hard mental work; and then we are a *mongrel* set—no unity—of race, religion or anything—except in *doing nothing*." Even an invitation to deliver a lecture in New Orleans did nothing to lift David's spirits: "I don't wish ever to see the place

---

36   LeRoy S. Boyd to David Boyd, July 13, 1897, J. Sumner Rogers to D. F. Boyd, September 9, 1897, November 30, 1897, in David Boyd Papers; Ettie Boyd to LeRoy S. Boyd, September 2, 1897, in Selected Letters, LeRoy Boyd Papers; Tom Boyd to Thomas Jackson Boyd (nephew) June 4, 1896, in Thomas D. Boyd Letterbooks. Between 1895 and 1899 David's oldest son Jack was living in Texas. Employed only intermittently, he sometimes appealed to his uncle, Tom Boyd, for funds. The Alabama Boyds rarely heard from him. LeRoy S. Boyd to D. F. Boyd, May 18, 1896, in David Boyd Papers.
37   Ettie Boyd to LeRoy S. Boyd, September 2, 1897, in Selected Letters, LeRoy Boyd Papers.

again," he declared of the Crescent City. "And I would not like Rex, or you, or any of my people to visit here—B.R. No; all of you keep away; and I want to get away—and stay away, as soon as I can. *I have had enough of La.!*" [38]

The Spanish-American War diverted David's attention somewhat in the spring and summer of 1898, not only because Rex had been an ensign aboard the *Maine*, but also because he thought the "splendid little war" might be exactly what the nation needed to dispel any discord left over from the Civil War. When he learned that Alabama's Congressman Joseph Wheeler, once a Confederate general, planned to form a volunteer brigade, David immediately offered his services. Later he proposed to Wheeler that the government encourage the enlistment of black troops. The congressman responded graciously to David's "patriotic offer" of service. But his other suggestion, Wheeler thought, would create more bad feeling than goodwill between the sections and the races. David must have persisted, however, because Wheeler was still corresponding with him on the subject in May, 1898. By that time David had also presented his idea to Congressman S. M. Robertson of Baton Rouge. Robertson discussed the matter with General Wheeler in Washington, and they agreed, he wrote to David, "that the glory of the defense of our country should be committed to the hands of the Caucasian race." In his opinion, David would be well advised not to "agitate" such an unpopular question. [39]

By the time school opened in the fall of 1898, the war was over, and David, after a brief visit to Auburn during September, was busily supervising buildings and grounds, making inventories of plant and equipment, and seeing to it that every cadet observed his high standards of neatness all over the campus. He took his duties very seriously as the following excerpt from a January, 1899, issue of the student newspaper indicates: "Professor—'What parasite is it that takes possession of and destroys your books when they are left lying around?' Student—'The Old Colonel!'" [40]

38 David Boyd to LeRoy S. Boyd, January 17, 1898, *ibid.*; Thomas D. Boyd, *Bulletin* to Louisianians, November 1, 1897; Thomas D. Boyd, *Circular*, November 24, 1897, in Printed Materials, David Boyd Papers; Draft of General Orders to Cadets, undated, in Scrapbook, *ibid.*

39 Joseph Wheeler to David Boyd, March 14, April 26, 30, May 3, 1898, S. M. Robertson to David Boyd, April 30, 1898, in David Boyd Papers.

40 The *Reveille*, January 4, 1899; Inventory of property, Louisiana State University [1898]; List of Cadets at University, 1889–97, February 25, 1898, in David Boyd Papers.

Clearly, much of David's work was self-imposed, and while the cadets may have considered his constant harassment an amusing idiosyncrasy or a quirk of old age, employees of the university probably wished he were a little less conscientious. It may be that David was trying to drown his sense of personal failure and frustration in hard work as some men do in drink. Days filled with exhausting labor and mindless routine would leave little time to contemplate the past or brood about the future. But if that was his intention, the effort failed. By early May, 1899, even David realized he could not keep up the pace. In his last letter to LeRoy, he apologized for not writing earlier. But his usual work week included twenty-four hours inside the classroom and an additional thirty hours outside in "extra" work for the university. "Indeed, I have no rest here," he complained, "and some of this extra work is so monotonous & wearing—such as [being] present during every cadet meal and surgeon's call, with looking to the care and cleaning of the buildings. I will *not* be *here next* year. Nor have I other work *elsewhere*. But I hope I can find something *somewhere*."[41]

As the term drew to a close, David was practically exhausted. On Friday morning, May 26, he wrote his wife, "I fear I am breaking down. I am not sick, but so weak, and at times faint, with some dizziness. I have simply worked too hard—especially exposed too much to the sun since I came back to La. . . . Yes, I am glad my time is so short in La. I could not possibly go through another year *here*."[42] David mailed his letter, then lay down in his office about one o'clock to take a nap. No one disturbed him until five when Dr. J. W. Dupree, a frequent visitor, found him in a comatose state and ordered him moved to Tom Boyd's residence. Immediately Tom telegraphed Ettie Boyd in Auburn, LeRoy in New Orleans, and Jack, then in Cheneyville, Louisiana. But only LeRoy managed to reach Baton Rouge before his father died on Saturday night. Jack arrived early Sunday morning, and Ettie, with Rex (then home on leave), did not get there until Sunday night. Their train had broken down in Alabama causing them to miss connections in New Orleans where Rex learned of David's death from a local paper.

Dr. Dupree attributed his friend's death to apoplexy. For days David had been working very hard to prepare the cadets for a dress parade and drill at the Louisiana Fair in New Orleans. Almost the entire college community, as well as many Baton Rouge citizens, accompanied the corps to the Crescent City on a special train. But David stayed behind "to look after what was left." In addition to his regular chores, that included the preparation of a special edition of the *Reveille*. Apparently the several trips back and forth to the printer, under a hot sun, proved too much for him. On Thursday, May 25, he was so exhausted that he had had to lie down most of the day. The next afternoon he was stricken and never regained consciousness.[43]

After one of the longest funeral processions ever witnessed in Baton Rouge, David was buried in Magnolia Cemetery with "impressive civilian and military honors" on Monday, May 29, 1899. Those who could not attend sent letters or telegrams of condolence from all over the country. One, from L. L. Hooe of Alexandria, was typical; it assigned David sole credit for the university's "present success" and indeed, "its very existence." Another, from A. A. Gunby of Monroe, was more extravagant, predicting that someday Louisianians would honor their "noblest son" by erecting his statue in front of the statehouse. But the most fitting and balanced tribute to David Boyd came from the man who knew him best. In a brief statement to the Board of Supervisors on June 26, 1899, Tom Boyd declared, "It is not for me . . . to extol his virtues; but whether he was great and good, and wise, or the reverse, all that he was and all that he had he gave to his fellow men. His career is a large part of the history of this institution, which he served so long and with such unselfish devotion; and his best memorial is the monument of love in the hearts of the many men he taught."[44]

---

43 *Ibid.* Description of David's illness and death, undated, *ibid.* Although unsigned, the description was probably composed by LeRoy Boyd who by 1903 was gathering data for a family history. Ettie Boyd to LeRoy Boyd, October 12, 1903, in Selected Letters, LeRoy Boyd Papers.
44 Levin L. Hooe to Thomas D. Boyd, May 29, 1899, in David Boyd Papers; Monroe (La.) *Bulletin*, June 1, 1899, in Scrapbook, *ibid.*; Minutes of the Board of Supervisors, June 26, 1899. In a letter to the author, Mrs. Annie Boyd Grayson, daughter of Thomas Duckett Boyd, wrote of her uncle, "Father used to say that he [David] was a very brilliant man—that he could go in any classroom and take over the subject and finish the lecture better than the prof. Father always said that Uncle David was the 'father of the university.'"

Bibliography

Manuscripts[*]

C. R. Boyd Papers
David F. Boyd Papers
    Diary
    Letterbooks
    Manuscript Volumes
    Printed Materials
    Scrapbook
    William T. Sherman Letters as College President
David F. Boyd Family Papers
    William T. Sherman Letters
David F. Boyd, Report to the Board of Trustees, June 23, 1884, Department of Archives, Auburn University.
David F. Boyd, Report to the Executive Committee of the Board of Trustees, October 15, 1883, Typescript, Department of Archives, Auburn University.
LeRoy Stafford Boyd, "Recollections of the Early History of Nu Chapter of Kappa Delta Fraternity at the Alabama Polytechnic Institute," Typescript, Department of Archives, Auburn University.
LeRoy Boyd Papers
    Selected Letters
    Genealogical Scrapbook
Thomas D. Boyd Papers
    Diary
    Letterbooks

[*]Except when otherwise indicated, the manuscripts are located in the Department of Archives, Louisiana State University.

Thomas J. Boyd Papers
Walter L. Fleming Collection
    David F. Boyd Letters and Papers
    Alphabetical File
    Louisiana State University Official Papers
    G. Mason Graham Letters
Kentucky Military Institute Volumes
Samuel H. Lockett Papers
Samuel H. Lockett, "Louisiana as It Is," 1873, Tulane University Archives, Tulane University.
Louisiana State University Collection
    Board of Supervisors Letterbooks
    Faculty Minutes Book
Robert M. Lusher Papers
    Diary
Minutes of the Board of Supervisors of the Louisiana State Seminary of Learning and Military Academy, 1860–1869, Office of the President, Louisiana State University.
Minutes of the Board of Supervisors of the Louisiana State University, 1870–1900, Office of the President, Louisiana State University.
Official Correspondence of the President, Department of Archives, Auburn University.
Personal Correspondence of the President, Department of Archives, Auburn University.
Record of the Proceedings of the Board of Trustees of the Agricultural and Mechanical College of Alabama, Department of Archives, Auburn University.
William T. Sherman Papers, Library of Congress.
Sherman-Boyd Correspondence, typescript, in possession of Annie Boyd Grayson, Baton Rouge, Louisiana.
Jesse D. Wright Papers
    David F. Boyd Family Papers

Government Documents

1. FEDERAL

United States Senate. *Report on the Transfer of the U.S. Barracks at Baton Rouge to Louisiana State University for Educational Purposes, 1886.* Report No. 1137, 49th Cong., 1st Sess., 1885–86.
The War of the Rebellion: A Compilation of the Official Records of the Union and Confederate Armies. 127 vols. Washington: Government Printing Office, 1880–1901.

2. STATE

Louisiana *Acts,* 1877.

Louisiana *House Debates*, 1870.
Louisiana *House Journal*.
    Extra Session, 1877.
    Regular Session, 1880.
    1st Extra Session, 1881.
    2nd Extra Session, 1881.
    Regular Session, 1882.
Louisiana *Legislative Documents*, 1860–82.
    Annual Reports of the Board of Supervisors of the Louisiana State Seminary of Learning and Military Academy, 1859–60, 1865–69.
    Annual Reports of the Louisiana State University, 1870–71, 1873 (partial), 1874, 1880–82.
Louisiana *Proceedings* of the Constitutional Convention, 1879.
    Official Journal
Louisiana *Senate Debates*, 1864, 1870.
Louisiana *Senate Journal*.
    Extra Session, 1877.
    Regular Session, 1880.
    1st Extra Session, 1881.
    2nd Extra Session, 1881.
    Regular Session, 1882.

Newspapers

Alexandria (La.) *Democrat*
Alexandria (La.) *Caucasian*
Baton Rouge *Bulletin*
Baton Rouge *Grand Era*
Baton Rouge *Morning Advocate*
Baton Rouge *State-Times*
Baton Rouge *Tri-Weekly Advocate*
Baton Rouge *Weekly Press*
Baton Rouge *Capitolian*
Baton Rouge *Daily Capitolian-Advocate*
Baton Rouge *Tri-Weekly Capitolian*
Frankfort (Ky.) *Western Argus*
Louisiana State University *Reveille*
Monroeville (Ala.) *Journal*
Montgomery (Ala.) *Daily Advertiser*
Montgomery (Ala.) *Semi-Weekly Advertiser*
New Orleans *Daily Picayune*
New Orleans *Democrat*
New Orleans *Republican*
New Orleans *Times-Democrat*
Opelika (Ala.) *Post*

Opelika (Ala.) *Times*
Selma (Ala.) *Morning Times*

Unpublished Theses and Dissertations

Aillet, Joseph. "The History of Education in Claiborne Parish." Master's thesis, Louisiana State University, 1937.

Beasley, Leon Odum. "A History of Education in Louisiana During the Reconstruction Period, 1862–1877." Ph.D. dissertation, Louisiana State University, 1957.

Becnel, Joseph R. "A History of the Military Establishment at Louisiana State University." Master's thesis, Louisiana State University, 1953.

Binning, Francis Wayne. "Henry Clay Warmoth and Louisiana Reconstruction." Ph.D. dissertation, University of North Carolina, 1969.

Carrigan, Joan. "Yellow Fever in Louisiana." Ph.D. dissertation, Louisiana State University, 1961.

Hair, William I. "The Agrarian Protest in Louisiana, 1877–1900." Ph.D. dissertation, Louisiana State University, 1962.

Hall, Douglas Miller. "Public Education in Louisiana During the War Between the States, with Special Reference to New Orleans." Master's thesis, Louisiana State University, 1940.

Highsmith, William E. "Louisiana During Reconstruction." Ph.D. dissertation, Louisiana State University, 1953.

Huff, George Adams. "Public Education in Louisiana During the Reconstruction Period, 1866–1876." Master's thesis, Louisiana State University, 1939.

Huff, Mary Bell. "A Legal History of Louisiana State University and Agricultural and Mechanical College." Master's thesis, Louisiana State University, 1935.

McKay, William David. "A History of Education in Rapides Parish, 1805–1915." Master's thesis, Louisiana State University, 1936.

Marsala, Vincent J. G. "The Louisiana Unification Movement of 1873." Master's thesis, Louisiana State University, 1962.

Memelo, Germaine. "The Development of State Laws Concerning the Negro in Louisiana." Master's thesis, Louisiana State University, 1956.

Rey, Myrtle. "Robert M. Lusher and Education in Louisiana." Master's thesis, Louisiana State University, 1933.

Singletary, Otis A. "The Restoration of White Supremacy in Louisiana." Master's thesis, Louisiana State University, 1949.

Turner, Howard. "Robert M. Lusher." Master's thesis, Louisiana State University, 1944.

Varnado, Otto Singleterry. "A History of the Early Institutions of Higher Learning in Louisiana." Master's thesis, Louisiana State University, 1927.

Vincent, Charles. "Negro Legislators in Louisiana During Reconstruction."
    Ph.D. dissertation, Louisiana State University, 1973.
Williams, Richard Hobson. "General Banks's Red River Campaign." Master's
    thesis, Louisiana State University, 1934.
Willis, Curley Daniel. "The Grange Movement in Louisiana." Master's thesis,
    Louisiana State University, 1935.
Windham, Allie Bayne. "Methods and Mechanisms Used to Restore White
    Supremacy in Louisiana, 1872–1876." Master's thesis, Louisiana State
    University, 1948.

Pamphlets

Boyd, David French. *Address of Col. D. F. Boyd on the Anniversary of the
    Delta Rifles, 4th La. Regiment, Confederate States Army, at Port Allen,
    W. Baton Rouge, Louisiana.* Baton Rouge: Capitolian Advocate Book
    and Job Printing Co., 1887.
————. *Address of D. F. Boyd to the Graduating Class, Delivered June 30,
    1869.* New Orleans: Jas. A. Gresham, 1869.
————. *Annual Address to the Graduates of 1872 of the L.S.U. by David F.
    Boyd, Supt., June 26, 1872.* New Orleans: A. W. Hyatt, 1872.
————. *General History of the Louisiana State University and Agricultural
    and Mechanical College, 1806–1888.* Baton Rouge: Bauer Print Co.,
    1899.
————. *Letter Addressed to the Citizens of New Orleans by D. F. Boyd, Sept.
    17, 1873,* Baton Rouge: (n.p.), 1873.
————. *Memorial* to the Honorable Members of the State Constitutional Con-
    vention, Concerning a State University. New Orleans: A. W. Hyatt,
    [1879].
————. *Scheme to Raise an Endowment Fund: Patronage to be Increased; Tu-
    ition Fees to be Reduced. A Benefit to the Patron, as well as to the Uni-
    versity.* New Orleans: T. H. Thomason, [1872].
Burwell, W. M. *Address Delivered Before the Faculty and Students of Louisi-
    ana State University, June 25, 1871.* [New Orleans]: Price-Current
    Printing Co., [1871].
Conway, Thos. W. *Compilation of the Laws of Louisiana Now in Force, for the
    Organization and Support of a System of Public Education.* New Or-
    leans: *Republican,* 1870.
Dalrymple, Wm. H. *A Brief Sketch, Illustrated, of the Louisiana State Univer-
    sity and Agricultural and Mechanical College.* Baton Rouge: The Uni-
    versity, [1922].
DeVere, Schele M., comp. *Students of the University of Virginia: A Semi-
    Centennial Catalog With Brief Biographical Sketches.* Baltimore: Charles
    Harvey and Co., [1875].
Edwards, Charles Wesley. *Auburn Starts a Second Century.* Auburn: [Univer-
    sity], 1958.

Egan, B. *Address Delivered at the Commencement Exercises, June 29, 1866.* (Louisiana State University *Quarterly*, Vol. I, No. 1) Baton Rouge: [Louisiana State University], 1901–1902. (First published in 1866: Alexandria, La., n.d.

Fletcher, Joel. *Louisiana Education Since Colonial Days.* Lafayette: Southwestern Louisiana Institute, 1948.

Gunby, Andrew Augustus. *National Aid to Education: Commencement Address, July 4, 1884.* Baton Rouge: Capitolian-Advocate Steam Job Printing Co., 1884.

Louisiana State Agricultural and Mechanical College. *Petition on Behalf of the Agricultural and Mechanical College of the State of Louisiana, Praying Against its Removal from its Present Location, Chalmette.* New Orleans: German Gazette Job Printing Office, 1877.

Louisiana State Seminary of Learning and Military Academy. *Regulations for the Government of the Louisiana State Seminary of Learning and Military Academy, Near Alexandria.* Cincinnati: Moor, Wilstach, Keys and Co., 1860.

Louisiana State University. *Prospectus* for Session 1873–74. [Baton Rouge: University, 1873.]

Louisiana State University and Agricultural and Mechanical College. *Cadet Regulations of the Louisiana State University and Agricultural and Mechanical College at Baton Rouge, Louisiana.* Baton Rouge: Capitolian Book and Job Printing Co., 1881.

———. *Industrial Education and Military Education.* New Orleans: A. W. Hyatt, 1878.

———. *Memorial of the Board of Supervisors [to the General Assembly of Louisiana]. 1880.* New Orleans: Democrat Printing Office, 1880.

———. *Military Education, Baton Rouge, Louisiana, February 22, 1878.* New Orleans: A. W. Hyatt, 1878.

———. *Official Register of the Officers and Cadets of Louisiana State University and Agricultural and Mechanical College, 1877–78.* New Orleans: A. W. Hyatt, 1878.

———. *Prospectus* for Session 1880–81. [Baton Rouge: University, 1880.]

[Nicholson, J. W.] *Report of the President* [of Louisiana State University and Agricultural and Mechanical College] *for the Year Ending June 30, 1893 to the Secretary of the Interior and the Secretary of Agriculture.* Baton Rouge: Truth Book and Job Office, 1893.

Prescott, Arthur Taylor. *Semi-Centennial of Louisiana State University, January 2, 3, 4, 1910.* Baton Rouge: Independent Printing Co., 1910.

Vallas, Anthony. *History of Louisiana State Seminary, 1864.* Baton Rouge: Pike Burden, 1935.

Books

Ambler, Charles H. *Sectionalism in Virginia from 1776 to 1861.* New York: Russell and Russell, 1964.

Bedsole, Vergil L., and Oscar Richard, eds. *Louisiana State University: A Pictorial Record of the First Hundred Years*. Baton Rouge: Louisiana State University Press, 1959.

Biographical and Historical Memoirs of Louisiana. 2 vols. Chicago: Goodspeed Publishing Co., 1892.

Biographical and Historical Memoirs of Northwest Louisiana. Nashville: Southern Publishing Co., 1890.

Blassingame, John W. *Black New Orleans, 1860–1880*. Chicago: n.p., 1973.

Booth, Andrew B., comp. *Records of Louisiana Confederate Soldiers and Louisiana Confederate Commands*. 3 vols. New Orleans: n.p., 1920.

Brasher, Mabel. *Louisiana: A Study of the State*. Atlanta: Johnson Publishing Co., 1929.

Chambers, Henry E. *A History of Louisiana: Wilderness-Colony-Province-Territory-State-People*. 3 vols. Chicago: American Historical Society, Inc., 1925.

Coulter, E. Merton. *The Confederate States of America, 1861–1865*. Vol. VII of *A History of the South*. Edited by Wendell Holmes Stephenson and E. Merton Coulter. Baton Rouge: Louisiana State University Press, 1950.

———. *The South During Reconstruction, 1865–1877*. Vol. VIII of *A History of the South*. Edited by Wendell Holmes Stephenson and E. Merton Coulter. Baton Rouge: Louisiana State University Press, 1947.

Crabitès, Pierre. *Americans in the Egyptian Army*. London: George Routledge and Sons, Ltd., 1938.

Crane, Theodore, ed. *The Colleges and the Public, 1787–1862*. New York: Bureau of Publications, Columbia University, 1963.

Davis, Edwin A. *Louisiana: The Pelican State*. Baton Rouge: Louisiana State University Press, 1959.

Fay, Edwin Whitfield. *The History of Education in Louisiana*. Vol. XX of *Contributions to American Educational History*. Edited by Herbert Baxter Adams. Washington: Government Printing Office, 1898.

Ficklen, John Rose. *The History of Reconstruction in Louisiana Through 1868*. John Hopkins University *Studies in Historical and Political Science*, Series XXVII, No. 1. Baltimore: Johns Hopkins University Press, 1910.

Fischer, Roger A. *The Segregation Struggle in Louisiana 1862–77*. Urbana: University of Illinois Press, 1974.

Fleming, Walter Lynwood. *Louisiana State University, 1860–1896*. Baton Rouge: Louisiana State University Press, 1936.

Fortier, Alcee, ed. *Louisiana: Comprising Sketches of Parishes, Towns, Events, Institutions, and Persons, Arranged in Cyclopedic Form*. 2 vols. Atlanta: Southern Historical Association, 1909.

Hair, William I. *Bourbonism and Agrarian Protest: Louisiana Politics, 1877–1900*. Baton Rouge: Louisiana State University Press, 1969.

Hammond's Complete World Atlas. New York: C. S. Hammond and Co., 1950.

Harris, Thomas H. *The Story of Public Education in Louisiana.* [Baton Rouge: Louisiana State University], 1924.

Hesseltine, William B. *Confederate Leaders in the New South.* Baton Rouge: Louisiana State University Press, 1950.

Hesseltine, William B., and Hazel C. Wolf. *The Blue and the Grey on the Nile.* Chicago: University of Chicago Press, 1961.

Howard, Perry H. *Political Tendencies in Louisiana, 1812–1952.* Louisiana State University *Studies, Social Science Series,* No. 5. Baton Rouge: Louisiana State University Press, 1957.

Howe, M. A. DeWolfe, ed. *Home Letters of General Sherman.* New York: Charles Scribner's Sons, 1909.

Johnson, E. Polk. *A History of Kentucky and Kentuckians.* 3 vols. Chicago: Lewis Publishing Co., 1912.

Johnson, Robert U., and Clarence O. Buell, eds. *Battles and Leaders of the Civil War.* 4 vols. New York: n.p., 1887–88.

Kendall, John S. *History of New Orleans.* 3 vols. Chicago, 1922.

Lonn, Ella. *Reconstruction in Louisiana after 1868.* New York: G. P. Putnam's Sons, 1918.

McGinty, Garnie William. *A History of Louisiana.* 3rd ed. New York: Exposition Press, 1951.

———. *Louisiana Redeemed: The Overthrow of Carpetbag Rule, 1876–1880.* New Orleans: Pelican Publishing Company, 1951.

McKitrick, Eric L. *Andrew Johnson and Reconstruction.* Chicago: University of Chicago Press, 1960.

McVey, Frank L. *The Gates Open Slowly: A History of Education in Kentucky.* Lexington: University of Kentucky Press, 1949.

Napier, Bartless, comp. *Military Records of Louisiana, Including Biographical and Historical Papers Relating to the Military Organizations of the State.* New Orleans: L. Graham and Co., 1875.

Nicholson, James W. *Stories of Dixie.* New York: American Book Co., 1915.

Owen, Thomas McAdory, ed. *History of Alabama and Dictionary of Alabama Biography.* 4 vols. Chicago: S. J. Clarke Publishing Co., 1921.

Padover, Saul K. *Jefferson.* Mentor Abridged edition. [New York]: New American Library, 1952.

Phelps, Albert. *Louisiana: A Record of Expansion.* New York: Houghton-Mifflin and Co., 1905.

Randall, J. G., and David Donald. *The Civil War and Reconstruction.* Boston: D. C. Heath and Co., 1961.

Roussève, Charles B. *The Negro in Louisiana: Aspects of His History and His Literature.* New Orleans, 1937.

Shaw, Arthur Marvin. *William Preston Johnston: A Transitional Figure of the Confederacy.* Baton Rouge: Louisiana State Univesity Press, 1943.

Sherman, William T. *Memoirs of General Wm. T. Sherman.* Civil War Centennial Series. Bloomington: Indiana University Press, 1957.

Shugg, Roger W. *Origins of the Class Struggle in Louisiana: A Social History of White Farmers and Laborers During Slavery and After, 1840–1875.* Baton Rouge: Louisiana State University Press, 1939.

Southwest Virginia and the Valley: Historical and Biographical Illustrations. Roanoke, Va.: A. D. Smith and Co., 1892.

Stafford, G. M. G. *General Leroy Augustus Stafford: His Forbears and Descendants.* New Orleans: Pelican Publishing Co., 1943.

Stampp, Kenneth M. *The Era of Reconstruction 1865–1877.* New York: Random House, 1965.

Taylor, Joe Gray. *Louisiana Reconstructed.* Baton Rouge: Louisiana State University Press, 1974.

Taylor, Richard. *Destruction and Reconstruction.* London: Wm. Blackwood and Sons, 1879.

Thorndike, Rachel Sherman. *The Sherman Letters.* New York: Chas. Scribner's Sons, 1894.

Vandiver, Frank E. *Mighty Stonewall.* New York: McGraw-Hill Book Co., 1957.

———. *Rebel Brass: The Confederate Command System.* Baton Rouge: Louisiana State University Press, 1956.

Vaughan, William Preston. *Schools For All: The Blacks and Public Education in the South, 1865–1877.* Lexington: University of Kentucky Press, 1974.

Vesey, Lawrence R. *The Emergence of the American University.* Chicago: University of Chicago Press, 1965.

Warmoth, Henry Clay. *War, Politics and Reconstruction: Stormy Days in Louisiana.* New York: Macmillan Co., 1930.

Wilkerson, Marcus. *Thomas Duckett Boyd: The Story of a Southern Educator.* Baton Rouge: Louisiana State University Press, 1935.

Williams, T. Harry. *Romance and Realism in Southern Politics.* Baton Rouge: Louisiana State University Press, 1966.

Winters, John D. *The Civil War in Louisiana.* Baton Rouge: Louisiana State University Press, 1963.

Woodward, C. Vann. *Origins of the New South, 1877–1913.* Vol. IX of *A History of the South.* Edited by Wendell Holmes Stephenson and E. Merton Coulter. Baton Rouge: Louisiana State University Press, 1951.

———. *Reunion and Reaction: The Compromise of 1877 and the End of Reconstruction.* 2nd ed. revised. Garden City, N.Y.: Doubleday Anchor Books, 1956.

Articles

Bone, Fanny Z. Lovell, "Louisiana in the Disputed Election of 1876." *Louisiana Historical Quarterly*, XIV (July, 1931), 408–40 (October, 1931), 549–66; XV (January, 1932), 93–116 (April, 1932), 234–265.

Boyd, David French. "General W. T. Sherman as a College President," Louisiana State *University Bulletin*, I (October, 1910), 1–8.

———. "Major Bob Wheat, Commander of the 'Louisiana Tigers' Killed at the Battle of Gaines Mill, Virginia," *Rifle Shots and Bugle Notes: The National Military Album* (1884), 141–44.

———. "William Tecumseh Sherman, First Superintendent of Louisiana State Seminary, Now the Louisiana State University," Louisiana State University *Alumnus*, V (1909–10).

Boyd, Thomas Ducket. "The Louisiana State University: A Historical Sketch," *Louisiana*, I (March, 1929), 7–8.

Bringhurst, William L. "Recollections of the Old Seminary," Louisiana State University *Alumnus*, V (1909–10), 15–18.

Cox, Lawanda, and John H. Cox. "Negro Suffrage and Republican Politics: The Problem of Motivation in Reconstruction Historiography." *Journal of Southern History*, XXXIII (August, 1967), 303–30.

Fleming, Walter Lynwood. "A Historical Sketch of the Louisiana State University," Louisiana State University *Alumnus*, IV (October, 1908), 5–14.

———. "General W. T. Sherman as a College President," Louisiana State *University Bulletin*, III (March, 1912), 3–24.

———. "Life at the Seminary Before the War," Louisiana State University *Alumnus*, V (1909–10), 126–131.

———. "The Louisiana State Seminary, 1865–1869," Louisiana State University *Alumnus*, V (1909–10), 167–86.

———. "Louisiana State Seminary During the War," Louisiana State University *Alumnus*, IV (January, 1909), 61–73.

———. "Records of the Old Seminary Selected by Walter L. Fleming," Louisiana State University *Alumnus*, IV (July, 1909), 127–55.

———. "Some Early Professors of the University," Louisiana State University *Quarterly*, VI, (November, 1911), 148–58.

———. "The Seminary During the War," Louisiana State University *Alumnus*, V (1909–10), 132–39.

———. "W. T. Sherman as a History Teacher," Louisiana State *University Bulletin*, II (October, 1911).

Garnett, James Mercer. "Reminiscences of the Louisiana State Seminary in 1867," Louisiana State University *Alumnus*, V (1909–10), 19–22.

Gayle, Edwin A. "The State University as a Factor in the Economy of Louisiana: An Address," Louisiana State University *Alumnus*, III (August, 1907), 56–65.

Gonzales, John Edmond. "William Pitt Kellogg: Reconstruction Governor of Louisiana, 1873–1877." *Louisiana Historical Quarterly*, XXIX (April, 1946), 394–495.

Grosz, Agnes Smith. "The Political Career of Pinckney Benton Stewart Pinchback." *Louisiana Historical Quarterly*, XXVII (April, 1944), 527–612.

Gunby, Andrew Augustus. "Life and Services of David French Boyd," Louisiana State *University Bulletin* (June, 1904), 2–35.

Hamlett, Barksdale. "The History of Education in Kentucky," Kentucky Department of Education *Bulletin*, VII (July, 1914), 304.

Hardin, James Fair. "The Early History of the Louisiana State University, and Subsequent History of Its Site 'Camp Stafford' in Rapides Parish," *Louisiana Historical Quarterly*, II (January, 1928).

Harlan, Louis R. "Desegregation in New Orleans Public Schools During Reconstruction." *American Historical Review*, LXVII (April, 1962), 663–75.

Hutson, Charles W. "Reminiscences of the Louisiana State University in the Early Seventies," Louisiana State University *Alumnus*, IV (July, 1909), 167.

Leach, Marguerite. "The Aftermath of Reconstruction in Louisiana," *Louisiana Historical Quarterly*, XXXII (July, 1949), 631–717.

Lestage, Oscar H. "The White League in Louisiana and Its Participation in Reconstruction Riots." *Louisiana Historical Quarterly*, XVIII (July, 1935), 617–95.

Ligon, Moses E. "A History of Public Education in Kentucky," University of Kentucky *Bureau of School Service Bulletin*, XIV (June, 1942).

Lowrey, Walter M. "The Political Career of James Madison Wells." *Louisiana Historical Quarterly*, XXXI (October, 1948), 995–1123.

Mobley, J. W. "The Academy Movement in Louisiana," *Louisiana Historical Quarterly*, XXX (July, 1947).

Moore, John Hammond, ed. "The Old Dominion Through Student Eyes, 1852–1855: The Reminiscences of Thomas Hill Malone," *Virginia Magazine of History and Biography*, LXXI (July, 1963), 294–326.

Otten, James T. "The Wheeler Adjustment in Louisiana: National Republicans Begin to Reappraise Their Reconstruction Policy," *Louisiana History*, XII (Fall, 1972), 349–67.

Perkins, A. E. "James Henri Burch and Oscar James Dunn in Louisiana." *Journal of Negro History*, XXII (July, 1937), 321–34.

Porter, Betty. "The History of Negro Education in Louisiana," *Louisiana Historical Quarterly*, XXV (July, 1942), 728–821.

Postell, William Dosite. "David French Boyd, A Louisiana Educator," *New Orleans Medical and Surgical Journal*, XCIII (April, 1941), 491–95.

Prichard, Walter, ed. "A Tourist's Description of Louisiana in 1860," *Louisiana Historical Quarterly*, XXI (October, 1938), 1110–1214.

Reed, Germaine M., ed. "Journey Through Southwest Arkansas, 1858, *Arkansas Historical Quarterly*, XXX (Summer, 1971), 161–69.

Singeltary, Otis A. "The Election of 1878 in Louisiana," *Louisiana Historical Quarterly*, XL (January, 1957), 46–53.

"Sketch of the First Graduating Class," Louisiana State University *Alumnus*, I (May, 1905), 21–23.

Stafford, G. M. "Autobiography of Geo. Mason Graham," *Louisiana Historical Quarterly*, XX (January, 1937), 2–17.

Stephens, Edwin Lewis. "Education in Louisiana in the Closing Decades of
    the Nineteenth Century, *Louisiana Historical Quarterly*, XVI (January,
    1933), 38–56.
Tunnell, T. B., Jr. "The Negro, the Republican Party and the Election of 1876
    in Louisiana." *Louisiana History*, VII (Spring, 1966), 101–16.
Whittington, George Purnell. "A History of Rapides Parish Schools and School
    Teachers, 1800–1860," *Louisiana Historical Quarterly*, XVII (January,
    1934), 112–23.
Williams, T. Harry. "The Louisiana Unification Movement of 1873." *Journal
    of Southern History*, XI (August, 1945), 349–69.

Index